# THE HIDDEN HAND

# BY THE SAME AUTHOR

*Slave Soldiers and Islam: The Genesis of a Military System* (1981)
*In the Path of God: Islam and Political Power (1983)*
*An Arabist's Guide to Egyptian Colloquial (1983)*
*The Long Shadow: Culture and Politics in the Middle East (1989)*
*Greater Syria: The History of an Ambition (1990)*
*The Rushdie Affair: The Novel, the Ayatollah, and the West (1990)*
*Friendly Tyrants: An American Dilemma (coeditor; 1991)*
*Damascus Courts the West: Syrian Politics, 1989-91 (1991)*
*Sandstorm: Middle East Conflicts and America (editor; 1993)*
*Syria Beyond the Peace Process (1996)*

# THE HIDDEN HAND

*Middle East Fears of Conspiracy*

Daniel Pipes

**St. Martin's Press**
New York

ISBN 0-312-16254-5

**Library of Congress Cataloging-in-Publication Data**

Pipes, Daniel, 1949-
    The hidden hand : Middle East fears of conspiracy / by Daniel
Pipes.
        p.  cm.
    Includes bibliographical references and index.
    ISBN 0-312-16254-5
    1. Middle East—Politics and government. 2. Conspiracies—Middle
East. I. Title.
DS63.1.P56 1996
956.05—dc20                               96-18729
                                        CIP

Design by Acme Art, Inc.

First edition: October, 1996
10 9 8 7 6 5 4 3 2 1

*To Beatríz, again, with love*

*We always face conspiracies.*
*—Gamal Abdel Nasser*

# CONTENTS

# LIST OF MAPS AND FIGURES

## MAPS

## FIGURES

# PREFACE

W hy so large a book on seemingly so small a topic? For two reasons. Conspiracy theories are immensely influential; indeed, they provide a key to the political culture of the Middle East. Also, fully to understand the way of thinking they represent requires author and reader alike to thoroughly immerse themselves in the world of the hidden hand. This means mulling over its complexities, always with plenty of examples at hand. I hope to understand conspiracy theories and to convey their importance to others.

The reader will judge to what extent I have achieved these goals; I can only report that writing this book has been exceptionally fascinating. What began as a lighthearted collection of anecdotes quickly turned into something deeper and darker. Deeper because I came to understand that the strange notions floating through the Middle East derive in large part from Western traditions going as far back as the Crusades. In the course of studying these, my attention wandered from the current Middle East to European intellectual history.

Darker because I realized, along with Ervand Abrahamian, that the paranoid style in the Middle East "had produced tragedy as well as comedy." Darker too because I had to spend unforeseen stretches of time exploring the conspiracy theorist's strange and many-mirrored world. The effort to penetrate the conspiracy theorist's mind means replicating his processes of thought. Though never tempted by conspiracism, I tried to order the theorist's assumptions, partake of his obsessions, and draw conclusions as he might.

I have been fortunate to draw on the talents of many capable and energetic research assistants; they much extended my body of quotations and anecdotes by scouring shelves full of materials for conspiracy theories. Special thanks goes to Michael Antonucci, who gave up most of a summer vacation to assist this project and grounded himself so thoroughly in its subject matter that he came up with his own original insights. Kemal Benameur, Eric Eversmann, Chris Strawbridge, Adam Taxin, and Barak Tulin read widely on my behalf. Nick Beckwith, Pam Beecroft, Yoram Borenstein, Lisa Ann Brichta, Anne Gagnon, Michelle Hand, Deborah

Hamilton, Nancy Lisewski, Geeta Nathan, Alison Orenstein, Kimberley Quinn, Allison Schwartz, Josh Segal, Alexander Stillman, and Darian Unger not only helped with reading but also with library work and archiving. Once again, I thank them.

Discussions with Patrick Clawson and Charles Krauthammer helped orient the direction of this study. L. Carl Brown and Bernard Lewis read a very early version and offered helpful comments. C. E. Bosworth and Franz Rosenthal gave me invaluable help on the question of conspiracy theories in premodern Islam.

This topic draws on anecdotes; my thanks to all those who helped by replying to my repeated inquiry: "What's your favorite Middle East conspiracy theory?" As word got around of my collecting conspiracy theories, clippings came in from, among others, Nissim Rejwan, Barry Rubin, Douglas Streusand, and Howard Wiarda. Hilal Khashan very generously sent me batches of clippings from the Beirut press as well as books published in Lebanon and Syria.

I am grateful to the Smith Richardson Foundation and to Middle East Forum's board and supporters, who provided most of the funding to research on and write about conspiracy theories. This book draws on articles of mine that appeared in *The Atlantic, Commentary, The Jerusalem Post, Middle East Quarterly, The New Republic, Orbis, The Wall Street Journal,* and *The Washington Post;* I thank the publishers for granting permission to use those materials.

Unless otherwise noted, all references to radio and television broadcasts derive from the invaluable *Daily Report* put out by the Foreign Broadcast Information Service, an agency of the U.S. government; the same source also provided some news agency items and newspaper articles. For reasons of style, I have taken the liberty here and there slightly to amend FBIS translations.

To lighten the reader's burden, I have usually omitted qualifiers like "alleged," "asserted," and "claimed" in front of preposterous conspiracy theories. To guard from being quoted out of context, I state here that these qualifiers are implicitly present throughout the book. Further for the record, the reporting of conspiracy theories in no way implies my endorsement of them.

*D.P.*

Philadelphia
December 1995

# Introduction

> The history that is dreamed is also
> the historian's terrain.
> —*Alain Demurger*[1]

> The art of being wise is the art of knowing
> what to overlook.
> — *William James*

Just a few minutes' political chat with a sophisticated Middle Easterner makes it clear how much he interprets great public issues through the prism of conspiracy theories. Whereas Westerners see a Syrian government long in conflict with Israel, he perceives Damascus as having surreptitiously worked hand in glove with the Jewish state since the 1960s. In his view, the Western powers built up Saddam Husayn, connived with him to put on Desert Storm, and provided him with the weapons to stay in power after his defeat. Ruhollah Khomeini may have appeared vitriolically anti-Western, but Middle Eastern interlocutors claim this ayatollah faithfully served his British (or American) masters right up to his death. And so forth.

However wrong-headed they may be, these views have great consequence. Indeed, whoever hopes to understand the Middle East must recognize the distorting lens of conspiracy theories, understand them, make allowance for them, and perhaps even plan around them. Conspiracism provides a key to understanding the political culture of the Middle East. It spawns its own discourse, complete in itself and virtually immune to rational argument. It suffuses life, from the most private family conversations to the highest and most public levels of politics. It helps explain much of what would otherwise seem illogical or implausible, including the region's record of political extremism and volatility, its culture of violence, and its poor record of modernization. The conspiratorial mentality also extends beyond the region, skewing both the way outsiders see the Middle East and spurring conspiracism in other parts of the world.

In sum, conspiracism constitutes one of the region's most distinctive political features. Ignore this phenomenon, "almost universal in the Middle East,"[2] and some of the most important features of the Arab and Iranian bodies politic remain elusive. Analyzing the region without taking the hidden hand into account is comparable to studying the American economy without Wall Street or Soviet politics without Marxism-Leninism.

## CONSPIRACISM'S RANGE

Unlike the West, where conspiracy theories are today the preserve of the alienated and the fringe, in the Middle East they enjoy large, mainstream audiences. They flourish on the street and in the palace and everywhere between. If the uneducated and the pious disproportionately fall under their thrall, all strata of society share credulity. Most of the outstanding Muslim thinkers and actors of the twentieth century espoused conspiracy theories. The many startling statements in the pages that follow derive not just from casual conversations with taxi drivers and waiters, but from the solemn pronouncements of the Middle East's great politicians, religious leaders, scholars, and journalists. Ethan Bronner, a journalist for *The Boston Globe*, bears witness to this ubiquity; he tells of repeatedly finding himself "sitting in living rooms and book-lined offices, listening to scholars, businessmen or politicians weave surreal scenarios."[3]

Further, conspiracy theories are not just private fears but public ones magnified in the most authoritative television and radio programs, books, magazines, and newspapers. Noting their presence in a leading Iranian newspaper, a scholar explains: "These paranoid fantasies should not be dismissed as the ranting and raving of the lunatic fringe; *Khayan-e Havai* is a 'highbrow paper' written for graduates studying in Western universities, that is, the crème de la crème of the Islamic Republic."[4] The fear of conspiracy serves as the ubiquitous currency of Middle East political rhetoric, repeated in constitutions, laws, speeches, and communiqués. In a typical example, the Palestinian organization run by Abu Musa closed its fifth general congress in November 1989 with a brief telegram to its sponsor, President Hafiz al-Asad. In just a few boilerplate sentences, the message five times mentioned the hidden hand: "enemy plots," "plots against the central cause of our nation's struggle," "conspiracies," "capitulationist schemes," and "plots of the capitulationists and defeatists."[5]

No occasion is too solemn to air conspiracy theories. At a ceremonial close to Ramadan fasting in 1990, Asad railed against the "dangers facing our nation" and promised that "we in Syria will confront the conspiracy."[6] A few days later, his Mauritanian counterpart, Maaouiya Ould Sid'Ahmed Taya, used the same religious ceremony to call on fellow citizens to be "extremely vigilant" in the face of "the sordid plot hatched against the existence, independence, and sovereignty" of Mauritania.[7]

Nor is any topic too frivolous. Conspiracy theories pollute the world of sports, and especially international soccer matches. British journalist Emma Duncan reports from Pakistan that when that country's national team

> was knocked out of the cricket World Cup in the semi-finals, it wasn't just because the Australians were better than the Pakistanis. There were various theories: one of the Pakistani players had been betting against his own team; the English umpires had favoured Australia because if England won its semi-final it would have to play against either Pakistan or Australia, and Australia was weaker; one of the Pakistani players was an employee of the company sponsoring the game, which had foisted him on to the team.[8]

Fans are not alone in their worries; governments also purvey sports conspiracism. In November 1989, when the Iranian soccer team fared poorly at the Peace and Friendship Cup games, played in Kuwait, an Iranian newspaper read deep significance into the loss. Noting that the Kuwaiti government had helped Iraq in its war against Iran, *Jomhuri-ye Islami* argued that

> the teams in this series of games were chosen in such a way as to facilitate the victory of the Iraqi team with the defeat of the Guinean national team such as that of Yemen. Following this, Iraq was able to advance. This indicates a premeditated plan aimed at ensuring Iraq's superiority in this series of games and at belittling Iran's Islamic revolution.

But the dastardly trick will not work, the newspaper concluded with gravity: "such a nation [as Iran] will not be belittled by losing a soccer game which was the fruit of collusion by the enemies of the revolution."[9] If the Iranians smell soccer conspiracies, who are the Iraqis to resist the same temptation? When a star midfielder's excess fouls forced him to sit out Iraq's make-or-break game to advance to the World Cup finals, the Iraqi Football Federation in Baghdad responded by accusing the international soccer federation and the U.S. government of plotting to keep Iraq from winning the World Cup.

## THIS STUDY

### Subject

They may be a farrago of nonsense, but conspiracy theories have importance. The first chapter documents specific cases where credulity in conspiracy theories affected the course of the Middle East's history, from an event as specific and public as the Six-Day War to something so broad and private as an unwillingness to use contraception.

Part I samples major examples of the conspiracy mentality, with an accent on the specific. We begin with a look at three politicians with outsized conspiratorial legacies, Gamal Abdel Nasser, Shah Mohammed Reza Pahlavi, and Ayatollah Ruhollah Khomeini. Notions of Greater Israel show how a fantasy exacerbates the most contentious political issue in the Middle East. Iran may be the country most under the sway of conspiracism, and the fall of the shah and the Islamic Revolution prompted some particularly striking examples of the mentality. Despite their very different orientations, the paranoid qualities of the Iraqi and Iranian governments, it turns out, are startlingly parallel and very revealing.

Part II analyses the picture of the enemy that emerges from conspiracy theories. What does he aim for, and how does he achieve these goals? Several chapters explore the two dominant figures, the Zionist and the imperialist (aka the Jew and the Christian). The Middle Eastern conspiracy theorist deems the links between these two so close, he often cannot tell who is manipulating whom, with perplexing consequences. In contrast, other possible plotters (Soviets, Japanese, Hindus) hardly register. I conclude with an analysis of the alleged conspirator's identity, characteristics, means, and motives. It is no exaggeration to say that these are all larger than life.

Part III surveys elements common to Middle Eastern conspiracy theorists and theories. I scrutinize the personality of the conspiracy theorist, his assumptions, the nature of the enemy he conjures up, and the type of argument he uses. Do conspiracy theorists share characteristics? Do men (there are but a handful of women's voices here, a reflection of Middle East realities) really believe these notions? I propose that while populations are credulous, leaders have a mix of motives. About the conspiracy theory itself, my analysis shows that they have five basic assumptions in common: conspiracies drive history, everyone seeks power, benefit indicates control, coincidences don't happen, and appearances deceive.

Part IV asks why conspiracy theories have proliferated in the Middle East. Noting the virtual absence of conspiracy theories in the region during premodern times, I conclude that they represent a modern phenomenon and have flourished only in the twentieth century. They spread due to four main causes: the worldly decline of Muslims, the influence of European thought, the plethora of actual conspiracies, and the specific nature of Middle Eastern politics, especially its pan-movements and its autocracy.

The conclusion looks to the future: What chance that Arabs and Iranians will slough off hidden-hand explanations? Anticonspiracist voices, sometimes very eloquent, do make themselves heard, but these have a limited reach so long as conspiracy theories serve important functions. Current trend lines therefore offer little reason for optimism in the short term; eventually, however, the Middle East should outgrow its obsessions.

On the title and subtitle: The "hidden hand" stands in implicit contrast to Adam Smith's "invisible hand." (It is also the title of a journal, *The Hidden Hand: Or the Jewish Peril*, published in the 1920s in London by The Britons, an anti-Semitic society.) The two terms contrast neatly: Smith saw the invisible hand making the market work to everyone's advantage, while conspiracy theorists believe that powerful individuals control the market and direct it to their own advantage and everyone else's detriment. "Fear of conspiracy" derives from David Brion Davis's title for a collection of writings on American conspiracy theories.[10]

The Middle East is not of a piece, least of all in politics, and Middle Eastern countries succumb unequally to the conspiracy mentality. It pervades Iranian political life and in the Mashriq (the Arab East, especially Iraq, Syria, and Jordan) and appears less commonly in the Maghrib (the Arab West). The term "Arab," therefore, refers primarily to Muslim and Christian Arabic speakers living in the Mashriq. Conspiracism has little real impact on the mainstream of public life in Turkey or Israel (on which, see the appendix); Kurds seem less prone to conspiracism than Arabic and Persian speakers. Accordingly, North African, Turkish, and Israeli conspiracy theorists have a small presence in the pages that follow. But conspiracism flourishes in Pakistan (*The Wall Street Journal* finds that

"100% of Pakistanis . . . are conspiracy theorists"),[11] so examples from
there turn up in this study.

Within the Muslim world, influence tends to flow one way, from the
Middle East out. To cover the Middle East, then, is to deal with ways of
thinking that extend from Sarajevo to Brunei. Many of the patterns
discussed here also apply to the rest of the Muslim world. In distant
Malaysia, for example, Prime Minister Mahathir Mohamad echoes the
Middle Eastern leaders when he sounds off about "Jews and Zionists"
trying to oust him and destabilize his country. While some of the descrip-
tions in this study also hold outside the Muslim world, I make no claim to
universality.

## Ignored Subject

Princeton historian L. Carl Brown wrote in 1984 about conspiracy theories
that "this pervasive Middle Eastern attitude has rarely been studied in a
systematic way. The evidence to show that such an attitude exists, while
accessible, has been largely ignored."[12] He is right. While a number of
authors have dealt with the conspiracy mentality in the Middle East
(including Brown himself, Graham E. Fuller, Yehoshafat Harkabi, and
Marvin Zonis), as have some journalists,[13] the topic remains elusive and
for the most part unstudied.

This rudimentary state of research has two implications. For one, it
means looking to European and American studies for ideas and guidance.
I have greatly profited from the writings of Johannes Rogalla von
Bieberstein, Norman Cohn, David Brion Davis, Richard Hofstadter,
Gordon S. Wood, and many others. For another, tackling a new subject
means setting modest goals; this study serves only as a preliminary investigation of a large and complex topic. It does little more than document a
phenomenon and offer a general interpretation. With luck, others will take
up more ambitious questions, such as the origins of prominent conspiracy
themes, changes over time, and reasons for the waxing and waning of the
conspiracy mentality.

The huge numbers of conspiracy theories means that examples
provided here are very far from exhaustive. Still, I have tried to give a
broad sampling, believing that these illuminate the conspiracy mentality,
document it, and establish its general qualities. The following pages
deemphasize constantly repeated but vague generalizations about "international plots" in favor of the highly original formulations that so color
Middle Eastern public life.

## My Goals

The conspiracy mentality, it bears noting, reaches even the world of scholarship, compelling me to state what I wish were obvious but fear is not: I have no covert purpose in writing on this topic. Specifically, I aim not to discredit the Muslim Middle East, much less to embarrass the individuals quoted. Rather, I have several constructive purposes for this study.

First, by analyzing a key phenomenon I hope to help non-Middle Easterners understand the region's political culture. If outsiders are ever to cope with this volatile region, its motivating forces and reigning ideas need to be clarified. The hidden-hand phenomenon lies at its confused heart because it greatly influences the way Arabs and Iranians see themselves and the outside world. Oddly, Westerners tend to study their own attitudes toward the Middle East much more than the reverse.[14] Bernard Lewis, the renowned historian, observes that "Far less attention has been given to the origins and development of Middle Eastern attitudes toward the West, though these are of at least equal importance in determining relations between the two. In the absence of the rather Western habits of self-analysis and self-criticism, they may even be of greater importance."[15]

Second, I hope to increase the possibility, however meager, that Arabs and Iranians themselves will become more aware of the invidious effects of conspiracism. Although nearly all the data in the following pages derive from the rulers and their propaganda machines, it is safe to assume that this study could not (and will not) be published in the Muslim Middle East. Many scholars relied on throughout this study—Walid Mahmoud Abdelnasser, Saïd K. Aburish, Fouad Ajami, Ahmad Ashraf, Khalid Durán, Kanan Makiya—hail from the Middle East. Significantly, these brave individuals live in the West for such frank discussions are at best discouraged in their home countries, at worst completely censored.[16]

This points to an important matter: those who benefit from liberal democracy must expose the dictators' dirty laundry, for no one else will. Again, Lewis:

> [We] have a moral and professional obligation not to shirk the difficult issues and subjects that some people would place under a sort of taboo; not to submit to voluntary censorship, but to deal with these matters fairly, honestly, without apologetics, without polemic, and of course, competently. We who enjoy freedom have a moral obligation to use that freedom for those who do not possess it.[17]

It does no one a favor to suppress an unsavory topic like conspiracy theories; doing so not only constitutes an act of condescension but reduces the chances that Arabs and Iranians will come to terms with their weaknesses.

## Superior Western Attitudes

Condescension rears its ugly head in other ways too. Westerners often dismiss what Arabs and Iranians say and write, implying that they indulge in rhetoric for its own sake. Saddam Husayn's speech on 17 July 1990 threatening force against Kuwait, for example, prompted Don Kerr of the International Institute for Strategic Studies to declare that "Arabic rhetoric always is colorful, so it's natural in the region for people to discount what they are hearing";[18] just two weeks later, Saddam's forces invaded Kuwait. Dismissing what Middle Easterners say constitutes a shameless caricature, an act suggesting little imagination and much ethnocentrism. Middle Easterners do not just bandy words about; far more often, these bespeak sincere beliefs.

Also, Westerners tend to look on Middle East credulity with smug superiority, assuming themselves and their own civilization not susceptible to the puppet theory of politics. Already in 1911 Joseph Conrad wrote that "to us Europeans of the West, all ideas of political plots and conspiracies seem childish, crude inventions for the theatre or a novel."[19] But the record, then as now, emphatically shows otherwise. Conspiracy theories reigned in Western Europe and the United States for about two centuries, 1750 to 1950. Name any date from the Enlightenment to the close of World War II, and the historian can offer a plentiful sampling of phobias about secret societies, banking cartels, and Jewish cabals. Indeed, credence in conspiracy theories has led to incomparably greater disasters in Europe than elsewhere; the tyrannies of Stalin and Hitler caused tens of millions to perish, vastly exceeding all the mischief combined of Middle East conspiracy theorists. The twentieth century's terrible history should expunge the impression that conspiracy theories are trivial or that Westerners are immune to them.

At the same time, conspiracism has been marginalized in the West since about 1950, rarely driving the actions of governments or other major institutions. This helps explain why Westerners tend to see the phenomenon as minor. But conspiracism (like nationalism, another set of ideas that has atrophied in its place of birth) still packs a lot of punch in the rest of the world. Indeed, to make matters worse, today's reigning Middle Eastern phobias about Zionists and imperialists derive in very large part from European sources. Chapter 15 takes this matter up more deeply; here it suffices to note that tidal waves of Western influence reached the Middle East after 1800, changing everything from household furnishings and sexual customs to methods of pedagogy and political institutions; not surprisingly, the Europeans' deepest social fears also got passed along, changing the face of the Middle East in the process.

The rational West, in short, has no moral edge on other civilizations, nor any reason for arrogance when it comes to the matter of political paranoia. Western readers would do well to purge themselves of superior attitudes.

## TERMINOLOGY

The pages ahead distinguish between a *conspiracy* and a *conspiracy theory*. The first describes an actual instance of covert collusion, the latter something that exists only in the imagination of an observer.

### Conspiracy

The word *conspiracy* quaintly derives from the Latin for "breathing together." A conspiracy involves two or more *conspirators* jointly and secretly aiming to achieve a prohibited goal.

Conspiracies do occur. The European powers did conspire to divide up the Middle East during World War I (the Sykes-Picot agreement); the Israelis did bomb American targets in Egypt in 1954 to put the blame on Gamal Abdel Nasser (the Lavon Affair); and the U.S. government did send arms to Iran in the mid-1980s (the Iran/*contra* scandal). The pages ahead (and especially chapter 16) contain many references to individuals who form secret societies and plan clandestinely.

Conspiracies subdivide into *petty conspiracies*, which work within the existing order, and *grand conspiracies*, which aspire to world domination. The former are limited affairs that involve a handful of individuals plotting to make money or to seize power. They aim at transferring money from one pocket to another or replacing one set of rulers with another. With some exceptions, petty conspiracies receive little attention here.

Rather, grand conspiracies are the main topic. (Accordingly, *conspiracy* in the pages ahead is usually a shorthand for *grand conspiracy*.) Larger and vaguer, these go beyond plots for personal gain or for power or money; they seek to destroy religion, subvert society, change the political order, and undermine truth itself. Grand conspiracies involve not duplicitous politicians or evil merchants but covert international movements. They capture the imagination and inflame political passion; they are big enough to cause all the world's ills—and certainly yours and mine.


## Conspiracy Theory

A *conspiracy theory* is the nonexistent version of a conspiracy. Anyone might speculate about the odd conspiracy theory, but the *conspiracy theorist* makes this a habitual practice. He discerns malignant forces at work wherever something displeases him; plots serve as his first method for explaining the world around him. He suspects a plot or cover-up even when other, less malign explanations better fit the facts. We variously call this preoccupation with conspiracy theories *conspiracism*, the *conspiracy mentality*, the *hidden-hand mentality*, or the *paranoid style*.

Just as conspiracies divide into two sorts, the petty and the grand, so do conspiracy theories. Petty theories deal with limited aims, grand conspiracy theories involve fears of world domination. Jasim al-Mutawa, the largest loser in Kuwait's Suq al-Manakh stock bubble of 1982 (he owed something like $10.5 billion), blamed his downfall on the established commercial families who resented his success. As usually the case with petty conspiracy theories, this one was local in dimension and limited in scope. Like petty conspiracies, the mentality associated with them goes back to the earliest social forms and is effectively ageless.

Grand conspiracy theories may also have local manifestations, but they invariably fit into a larger scheme that has the ultimate goal of world hegemony. Such theories have a finite history. They began during the Enlightenment in northwestern Europe, became a major factor with the French Revolution, and peaked in importance in the three decades after 1918. Grand conspiracy theories have a well-established structure and form. The story begins with a small group attempting to benefit itself by clandestinely making plans to take over the government or expand its influence abroad. Its means can be many—spreading lies, destroying a political system, controlling multinational corporations—but the immediate goal is usually economic. Power is a not an end in itself but usually a way to gain wealth, status, or sex. The conspiracy theorist tends toward a Manichean outlook in which the battle zone of Good and Evil has no boundaries. Opponents are agents, mishaps result from plots.

Although grand conspiracy theories surfaced in the Middle East only during the late nineteenth century, their subject matter ranges much farther; indeed, it often extends right back to the time of the Prophet Muhammad. More broadly, conspiracy theorists reinterpret the whole sweep of Islamic history, plundering medieval texts to locate instances of conspiracy, especially on the part of Christians and Jews.

Grand conspiracy theories are the topic here; for simplicity's sake they will in most cases be referred to simply as *conspiracy theories.*

### NOTES TO THE INTRODUCTION

1. Alain Demurger, *Vie et mort de l'Ordre du Temple* (Paris: Seuil, 1985), p. 9.
2. Michael Field, *Inside the Arab World* (Cambridge, Mass.: Harvard University Press, 1994), p.167.
3. Ethan Bronner, "Psycho-Semitic," *The New Republic,* 24 May 1993.
4. Ervand Abrahamian, *Khomeinism: Essays on the Islamic Republic* (Berkeley: University of California Press, 1993), p. 125.
5. The Palestine Liberation Movement—Al Fat'h, Radio Damascus, 9 November 1989.
6. Radio Damascus, 17 April 1990.
7. Agence France Presse, 26 April 1990.
8. Emma Duncan, *Breaking the Curfew: A Political Journey through Pakistan* (London: Michael Joseph, 1989), p. 33.
9. *Jomhuri-ye Islami,* 16 November 1989.
10. David Brion Davis, ed., *The Fear of Conspiracy: Images of Un-American Subversion from the Revolution to the Present* (Ithaca, N.Y.: Cornell University Press, 1971).
11. *The Wall Street Journal,* 10 March 1995.
12. L. Carl Brown, *International Politics and the Middle East: Old Rules, Dangerous Game* (Princeton, N.J.: Princeton University Press, 1984), p. 234.
13. For example, Don Oberdorfer, "Baghdad's Conspiracy View of Recent History," *The Washington Post,* 16 February 1991; Con Coughlin, "Fanciful Anti-Israel Propaganda Reflects Resistance to Mideast Peace," *The Washington Times,* 21 May 1991; "Everything the Other is Not," *The Economist,* 1 August 1992.
14. Edward Said spawned a massive literature on this subject with the publication of *Orientalism* (New York: Pantheon, 1978).
15. Bernard Lewis, *The Shaping of the Modern Middle East* (New York: Oxford University Press, 1994), p. 25.
16. For a noteworthy exception, see Khaldun Hasan an-Naqib, "Al-'Aqliya at-Ta'amuriya 'ind al-'Arab," *Majallat al-'Ulum al-Ijtima'iya,* Winter 1404/1984, pp. 171-81.
17. Bernard Lewis, "Other People's History," *The American Scholar* 59 (1990): 404-05.
18. *The Wall Street Journal,* 18 July 1990.
19. Joseph Conrad, *Under Western Eyes,* part 2, chapter 1.

# 1.

# Changing the Course
# of History

> Unreal conspiratorial traumas leave profound,
> real scars in history.
> —*Henri Zuckier*[1]

> What does it matter what the crackpots believe?
> It matters to the extent that others
> come to believe them.
> —*Daniel Patrick Moynihan*[2]

Conspiracism has a profound impact on life in the Middle East. Credulity in conspiracy theories causes Arabs and Iranians to believe in what is not true; acting on these beliefs then alters the course of events. Ironically, fears of conspiracy also directly lead to the proliferation of actual conspiracies. In the aggregate, the paranoid mentality creates a suspiciousness that impedes modernization in the Middle East.

## CASE HISTORIES

Conspiracy theories have affected the Middle East throughout the twentieth century. We begin with a miscellany of examples, then concentrate on terrorism against U.S. embassies, the 1967 Arab-Israeli war, and developments in Iran.

*Miscellaneous.*  Egypt's Free Officers in 1952 sought out good relations with Washington in the belief that the British and American governments were engaged in a battle for hegemony over the Middle East. Conspiracism gave Mu'ammar al-Qadhdhafi his start in politics: already in secondary school, he impressed other students by alerting them to the inspector of English-language instruction being an imperialist agent. Anwar as-Sadat's seizure of 1,500 opponents in September 1981 on charges of conspiracy caused massive disaffection in Egypt. In March 1990 an eighteen-year-old Muslim girl made up a story about a Coptic man who lured Muslim women to an apartment where a hidden video camera took compromising pictures; as a result, fundamentalist Muslims attacked Coptic houses, stores, and churches.

Ayatollah Khomeini declared in 1979 that the United States "and its corrupt colony, Israel"[3] stood behind the seizure of the Great Mosque of Mecca. His accusation touched a nerve, inspiring a wave of violent anti-American activities in Libya, Turkey, Pakistan, India, Bangladesh, Thailand, and even the Philippines. The rampage in Pakistan cost four lives. A decade later, Khomeini saw *The Satanic Verses,* with its parody of the Prophet Muhammad, as the opening salvo in a cultural assault on Islam. In response, he issued an edict that sent the book's author, Salman Rushdie, into permanent seclusion, caused the deaths of over 20 people, disrupted billions of dollars in trade, and created a lasting wedge between Iran and the West.

Allegations that the Zionists planned to do away with the Mosque of Al-Aqsa, the holiest Islamic shrine in Jerusalem, and replace it with the Third Temple inspired the Western Wall riots of 1929 and poisoned Arab-Jewish relations in Palestine. Forty years later, the same issue gave birth to the Organization of the Islamic Conference, the United Nations of Muslim countries. In August 1969, a deranged Australian Christian by the name of Michael Dennis Rohan (which many Muslims turned into Cohen) set fire to that mosque. Though Israeli firefighters quickly extinguished the blaze and Rohan soon after confessed to setting it, Muslims around the world convinced themselves that the Israeli authorities had paid Rohan between $50,000 and $100 million to burn the mosque. Bellicose pronouncements echoed from all parts of the Middle East and rioting erupted in India, leading to widespread loss of life. King Faysal of Saudi Arabia capitalized on these passions to convene 25 Muslim heads of state at a meeting in Rabat, Morocco. Out of that meeting came the OIC.

***Terrorism against U.S. embassies.*** Recent violence directed against American embassies results from some long-standing ideas about foreign legations. By way of background, historian Peter Avery explained in 1965 the mystique of the British embassy's grounds:

> in the year 1963 it was agreed that most of the high wall which surrounded the British Embassy gardens in Tehran should be demolished, to be replaced by open railings, partly, it must be supposed, in order that neither the Iranian Government nor the British should still be embarrassed by that widespread belief that the walls hid some intangible mystery and that Iranians who were admitted behind them came out with some special authority for use in influencing their compatriots. A story used to be told, and that only six or seven years ago, in Tehran about a man who every morning entered the British compound in the centre of the city, walked thrice around the gardens within and then came out and hailed his friends with a knowing and commanding look, informing them that he had received his "instructions."[4]

Embassies, housing foreign powers in the heart of one's own capital, pose a great threat, one that some Middle Easterners determined to undo. In Iran and the Sudan, fears of conspiracy have led to violence.

Just after the fall of the shah, explains John Stempel, a former diplomat, Iranian worries centered on the huge embassy grounds in Tehran:

> Some factions, particularly the Fedayeen[-e Khalq], were paranoid with fear that the Shah, with the help of the United States, was plotting a counterstrike. In the wake of the revolution, rumors spread that former officials of the Shah had been encouraged to take refuge inside the American compound and were in the midst of helping execute the coup.[5]

Other rumors contended that shah himself was hiding in the compound. To preempt, the Fedayeen and others took control of the U.S. embassy on 14 February—only to be thrown out two hours later by government forces. This proved to be merely a dress rehearsal; the shah's entry to the United States on 22 October 1979 led to a panic that this "was the first step in a counterrevolutionary plot to overthrow the Khomeini regime."[6]

A group calling itself the Muslim Students Following the Line of the Imam captured the embassy, this time staying for 444 days and prompting an international crisis.

Similarly, when the Palestine Liberation Organization (PLO) assaulted the Saudi embassy in Khartoum in March 1973, killing two Americans and a Belgian diplomat, the gunmen acted on the assumptions of two conspiracies. First, they thought one of the dead Americans had directed the Jordanian attack on the PLO in September 1970, and that he would soon return to Jordan to take charge of a secret American missile base there. (Both charges were completely false.) Second, they thought that by taking American hostages, they could pressure the U.S. government to "order" its flunky, Jordan's King Husayn, to release Abu Da'ud, a top PLO operative.[7]

*War in 1967.*    At their most consequential, conspiracy theories can obstruct peace and affect the outcome of wars. President Hafiz al-Asad of Syria, according to an Egyptian official, fears a Syria-Israel agreement because "Israel might maneuver him into a corner. Al-Asad fears the traditional image Israel has in the eyes of the Arabs, according to which Israel is a 'cunning' and plotting country."[8] Just before U.S. troops launched their ground campaign against Iraqi forces in February 1991, Soviet military experts showed satellite pictures to Iraq's Foreign Minister Tariq 'Aziz and explained to him how the Americans were planning a flanking maneuver (what came to be known as the "Hail Mary" strategy). 'Aziz in turn showed the pictures to Saddam, who dismissed them as Soviet plotting in collusion with the United States. He completely ignored the warning and made no changes to bolster positions threatened by the flanking forces.

Even more significantly, conspiracism sometimes contributes to war breaking out. Fears of plots had a key role in the Yemeni and Lebanese civil wars, the Egyptian-Libyan clash in 1977, the Jordanian-PLO conflict in 1970, and the Iraqi invasion of Kuwait. The Palestinian *intifada* began when Gazans interpreted a traffic accident as part of an Israeli plot. The war between the Arabs and Israel in June 1967 has special interest due the complexity of the conspiracy theories surrounding its outbreak.

The causes of that conflict have long mystified observers, for no one sought it and it started so suddenly. In good part, its origins lie in Arab and Soviet fears of an imperialist plot. That several pro-Soviet leaders had been overthrown in the two preceding years set the scene: Ben Bella of Algeria (June 1965), Sukarno of Indonesia (October 1965), Nkrumah of

Ghana (February 1966), and Massamba-Débat of the Congo (June 1966). Rightist colonels, led by Georgios Papadopoulos, took power in Greece in April 1967. The Saudis sought to mobilize an Islamic alignment against radical Arab regimes and fundamentalist Muslims had become newly active in Syria and Egypt.

"According to the Soviets," writes the Israeli author Michel Bar-Zohar, "Washington was pulling the strings" behind these events.[9] Syrian leaders mired themselves in a swamp of paranoia:

> They saw themselves as the victims of plots hatched by rival officers, by religious fanatics, by the propertied classes, all backed in various ways by reactionary monarchs and the Central Intelligence Agency. Above all, they were convinced that Israel had been assigned a special role to destroy their revolution.[10]

In a series of 11 weekly articles during early 1967, Mohamed H. Heikal, President Abdel Nasser's confidant and propagandist, detailed U.S. aggressive intentions vis-à-vis Egypt. He portrayed Washington as the source of Egypt's many woes, both internal (fundamentalist Muslims, economic travails) and external (Israel, civil war in the Yemen, inter-Arab politics), then predicted an American attempt to unseat Abdel Nasser.

Abdel Nasser shared these fears. According to Richard B. Parker, a former American diplomat,

> by the fall of 1966 Abdel Nasser was convinced, or said he was, that the United States was plotting to assassinate him. He let Washington know of this belief through an American lawyer, whom he invited to Cairo for the express purpose of telling him about the plot. Although a high-level [American] effort was made to persuade him that there was no truth to it, he probably did not believe the denials.[11]

Things got worse in early 1967. "After the *coup d'état* in Athens," Eric Rouleau explains, Abdel Nasser "thought that the Americans had decided to rid themselves of all the neutralist or pro-Soviet regimes around the world." Indeed, he became convinced that the Americans had already chosen his replacement and simply awaited the right moment to oust him. Supporting this analysis, Abdel Nasser's party, the Arab Socialist Union, produced a confidential bulletin that parsed the conspiracy in detail and speculated that Egypt would be the "ultimate target" after Greece, Cyprus, and Syria.[12]

Abdel Nasser's expectant state of mind goes far to explain the outbreak of a war nobody planned for or wanted. At a certain point, no matter what the U.S. and Israeli governments did, even when they did nothing, the Egyptians found confirmation of conspiratorial intent. Parker notes that "the Egyptians were responding to phantoms. The crisis was precipitated by a report of nonexistent troop concentrations, given credence by a nonstatement by Israel's Chief of Staff, and made more credible by a belief in a non-existent U.S. plot against the Egyptian revolution."[13] And so the Egyptians took those steps—closure of the Straits of Tiran, expulsion of the United Nations monitoring force, alliance with Jordan and Syria—that led to an unintended war.

Conspiracy theories also affected the Six-Day War's political legacy. To explain the devastating Arab loss, Abdel Nasser charged that U.S. and British forces helped Israel win, touching a raw nerve in Arabic-speaking countries. His excuse was widely accepted and had many consequences. The rout having been caused by American and British forces, demonstrators assaulted the diplomatic facilities of those two states in six Arab countries. Politicians' anger at Washington and London lasted for years, significantly limiting diplomatic options for both sides. Egypt, Syria, Algeria, Sudan, North Yemen, and Iraq broke off relations with the United States; in the case of Iraq, ties were not resumed until 1983. The trumped-up charges inspired an "economic war" against the West in 1967, which included the closure of the Suez Canal and a brief oil cutoff. Although ineffectual, this boycott did serve as a trial run for the much more serious one in 1973. Ironically, the claim of Israeli-American collusion helped justify Sadat's diplomacy after the 1973 war; how could Egypt, he asked his compatriots, fight Israel and America at the same time? He then portrayed his friendly steps toward Washington as a way to break the military alliance against Egypt.

*Iran.*    The three most important Iranian politicians of the later twentieth century each paid a heavy price for his susceptibility to conspiracism. Mohammad Mosaddeq had one preoccupation through his long career: eliminating foreign intervention in Iranian affairs. During his two-year prime ministry, 1951 to 1953, he made nationalization of the oil industry his top priority. At the same time, his suspicion of foreigners led him angrily to turn down a World Bank report with excellent proposals on ways to accomplish this task. Why? Out of fear, as a supporter put it, that the bank was an "agent for British imperialism."[14] Not taking this advice, Mosaddeq embarked on a nationalization effort that deeply alienated the Western powers and eventually led to his own downfall.

Grand conspiracy theories greased the shah of Iran's fall. Mohammad Reza Pahlavi's assumption that foreign powers manipulated his environment led him to neglect domestic issues and to assume that his Iranian opposition consisted not of patriots but of Soviet, British, and American stooges. Intensely scornful of his subjects, he could not imagine they posed a threat to him. Accordingly, he not only underestimated the strength of the Iranian opposition in 1978 but wasted his time trying to discover the external force manipulating them. This wrongheadedness partially explains the mystery of his regime's quick collapse.

Less than two years later, Khomeini made a similar error when he dismissed army intelligence reports warning of Iraqi war preparations, blithely asserting that "No one would dare attack Iran."[15] Those reports were correct, however; and Iranian forces proved unprepared for war in September 1980. Why such assuredness on Khomeini's part? Two explanations have surfaced, both conspiratorial in nature: either the Americans had fed him false assurances about Iraq intentions, or he saw the military reports as a plot to make his government dependent on the army, an imperial institution he mistrusted.

Conspiracy theories affected much else in Iran under the ayatollahs. For example, Iranian scholar Ervand Abrahamian shows, they directly contributed to Iran's worst instance of domestic bloodletting, the mass executions of 1981-82:

> When in June 1981 the [People's] Mojahedin tried to overthrow the Islamic Republic, Khomeini proclaimed that the CIA was planning a repeat performance of 1953 and that the whole opposition, not just the Mojahedin, was implicated in this grand "international plot." In six short weeks, the Islamic Republic shot over one thousand prisoners. The victims included not only members of the Mojahedin but also royalists, Bahais, Jews, Kurds, Baluchis, Arabs, Qashqayis, Turkomans, National Frontists, Maoists, anti-Stalinist Marxists, and even apolitical teenage girls who happened to be in the wrong street at the wrong time. Never before in Iran had firing squads executed so many in so short a time over so flimsy an accusation.[16]

## BLURRING PERCEPTIONS

Conspiracy theories create a tissue of lies so thick that even a sober, clear-sighted analyst finds it hard to distinguish reality from fantasy. The resulting confusion affects both Middle Easterners and those trying to comprehend the region.

For example, in early May 1990, after Syrian troops had been fighting the Lebanese forces of prime minister Michel 'Awn for months, Radio Free Lebanon blithely reported that arms and ammunition were unloaded from Syrian military trucks and passed to 'Awn's forces. True? Who could tell? Ten days later, the same radio station described a rocket launched by 'Awn's forces that did not explode on impact; its exterior bore the inscription "Syrian Arab Republic, 122 mm, Defense Factories." Another eight days later, the station reported the Syrians supplying more materiél to 'Awn,[17] a point subsequently confirmed by Walid Junbalat, the Druze leader. Were these enemies actually cooperating? Or did a radio station make things up and a warlord lie? For murkiness, there's no place like the Middle East.

On 7 March 1990, the U.S. government accused Libya's Mu'ammar al-Qadhdhafi of preparing mustard gas at a plant at Rabta; on 14 March news came from Rabta that a fire had severely crippled the plant. While Libyan authorities blamed sabotage on Americans, West Germans, and Israelis, satellite pictures showed that the fire was about half a mile away from the plant, not inside it.[18] The Libyans apparently set old tires on fire, making it seem that the plant was incapacitated, hoping thereby to divert attention from the Rabta factory. Or so it seemed, for the full truth remained inaccessible.

Even stranger, the Libyan newspaper *Al-Jamahiriya* for three successive days in 1992 criticized Colonel Qadhdhafi; according to many informed sources, including Libyan dissident 'Abd al-Hamid al-Bakkush, the articles "were written by the colonel himself."[19] An observer could be excused for not knowing whether the criticism represented a weakening of Qadhdhafi's power or its revitalization.

On occasion, implausible conspiracy theories turn out to be true, trapping skeptics. The claim by Egyptian antifundamentalists that students and others received Saudi and Libyan money to grow beards has all the hallmarks of unfounded conspiracism; but it happens to be true.[20] Similarly, the Jordanians frequently accused Israel of circulating counterfeited 20-dinar notes to weaken its currency, a claim made even more implausible when endorsed by the notoriously unreliable Victor Ostrovsky, a self-proclaimed defector from Israel's Mossad, Israel's external intelligence service.[21] Who could take seriously the conspiracy-mad Iraqi media echoing this claim in 1992, saying that the U.S. and other foreign governments forged Iraqi money? But this time, reliable American sources revealed, it was true.

Perhaps the most elaborate conspiracy theory in the Middle East of recent years concerned Husni Mubarak's much-discussed Iraqi-Jordanian-Yemeni plan to divide up Saudi Arabia in 1990. The Egyptian president contended that Jordanian and Yemeni leaders knew in advance of the Iraqi plan to invade Kuwait, which they supported in return for a territorial payoff. Iraq was to grab the Saudi oil fields, Jordan would get the holy cities of Mecca and Medina (as well as $200 million in gold), and Yemen would regain those areas it lost to the Saudis in the 1930s. Saudi writ would extend only to a miserable, landlocked rump state in the highlands of Najd, shorn of petroleum and holy places. Saudi officials reportedly took this scheme seriously enough to dispatch a division of Pakistani mercenaries to the Yemeni border region; and it may also have contributed to the Saudi decision to deport some 700,000 Yemenis from the kingdom.

To support Mubarak's claim about these three "lords of conspiracy,"[22] Egyptian officials argued that the Arab Cooperation Council (ACC; an economic and political group set up in February 1989 and comprising Iraq, Jordan, Yemen, and Egypt) was from the start intended to sanction Iraqi aggression. They pointed to three main bits of evidence: persistent Iraqi efforts to make the ACC a military alliance, pressure to share intelligence among the member states, and an offer of $25 billion in bribe money to win the Egyptian government's complicity.[23] Other corroborating points subsequently emerged: Husayn of Jordan's surprising decision to take up the title *sharif*, his family's title during its centuries-long rule of Mecca; a burst of Jordanian military activity days before the Iraqi invasion; the transfer of a squadron of Iraqi MiG-13s to Yemen shortly before the invasion of Kuwait; a Jordanian military alert just after the invasion; Jordanian and Yemeni support for Iraq after the invasion; and the massing of Iraqi troops in the south of Kuwait (suggesting an imminent invasion of Saudi Arabia).

Anti-Saddam polemicists in the Middle East then further elaborated this conspiracy theory, writing whole books on the topic[24] and bringing in a host of new actors: the Palestine Liberation Organization, Sudan, Algeria, and Iran. Kuwaiti officials alleged that the PLO was to receive Kuwait as its reward for supporting Iraq and that Sudanese authorities would get arms to use against the southern rebels. The Saudis came up with further embellishments: the Algerian leader Ahmed Ben Bella supported Saddam in return for Saddam's promise to help him control all North Africa; and Iranian president 'Ali Akbar Hashemi-Rafsanjani met Saddam just four days before the invasion at which time the latter promised to pay reparations for his 1980 aggression.

**FIGURE 1.1.** Perhaps the most elaborate conspiracy theory in the Middle East of recent years concerned an Iraq plan to divide up Saudi Arabia in 1990, following Saddam Husayn's invasion of Kuwait. A book titled *The Conspirators*, published in 1991 in Paris, shows Father Saddam with (from right) his kids, the Yemeni, Jordanian, and Palestinian leaders. *Al-Muta'amirun* (Paris: As-Silah, 1411/1991).

Mubarak's conspiracy theory came to be portrayed as a conspiracy in its own right. The Jordanian government blamed the thesis on "destructive and self-serving elements who stand to gain financial and material profit" by harming inter-Arab relations.[25] Some Arab sources traced the thesis back to an Israeli source.

Foreign analysts differed on whether to believe in Mubarak's conspiracy; to take just one example on each side, *Foreign Report* accepted it while William Safire of *The New York Times* did not.[26] According to Jack Anderson and Dale van Atta, the CIA itself did "not know whether or not to believe The Plot."[27] Thus does a miasma of uncertainty cloud events in the Middle East, making it difficult to know what is actually happening in the region, much less what it means.

## SPURRING PLOTS

Conspiracy theories have another effect: they inspire genuine conspiracies. The pattern recurs regularly. Whoever believes that small cabals run the world will try to join such a group. In this way, the fantasy of a conspiracy spurs a real one. Entering the mental world of conspiracy theories often implies acting like a conspirator, imitating one's opponent's tactics to defeat him. Abundant examples of the conspiratorial temptation exist in the West[28] and also in the Middle East.

Sultan Abdülhamit II (r. 1876-1909) ruled the Ottoman Empire with the brilliance of a paranoid, devoting vast portions of his time to reading spies' reports written by his informers, relatives, and protégés. He kept his military force small, fearful of it turning against him. Abdülhamit also acted like a conspirator, placing opponents in the state bureaucracy so that they would be perceived as agents of the palace, thereby weakening them and making them more pliable. He seems to have preferred a system of offering bribes and selling honors; that way, none of his officials could assert too much independence. Finally, Abdülhamit purposefully promoted evil officials, a policy he explained (with reference to a specific individual) as follows: "I know he is not a bad man, and no harm comes to me from him. But I am good to the bad ones, so as to escape their badness."[29]

King Faysal of Iraq (r. 1921-33) followed Abdülhamit in conspiratorial ploys. He appointed Yasin Pasha to the Iraqi cabinet, a British dispatch explained, "primarily with the object of discrediting him [Yasin] with his supporters." The dispatch continues: "There have been other instances of the fruit of office being used by King Faisal as a carrot to draw inconvenient political opponents to their destruction."[30]

The shah of Iran both feared conspiracies all around him and engaged in conspiracies of his own. During the 1960s, for example, he lavishly praised American foreign policy to foreign politicians and reporters but within Iran he permitted a vicious anti-Americanism. This duality concerned such distant subjects as the war in Vietnam and close ones such as the activities of the Western oil companies operating in Iran.

Gamal Abdel Nasser ruled through a small number of lieutenants in the bureaucracy, the army, and the intelligence services; these three institutions ran the ruling political party and the government. One associate, Kamal ad-Din Rif'at, described him as surrounded with the tools of conspiracy: "No one could prevail upon him, for he pitted one against the other, spread his tentacles everywhere, used little paper, and dealt with various and sundry confidentially, conspiratorially, and face to face."[31] For example, it appears that Abdel Nasser staged the 1954 attempt on his life in Alexandria to enhance his stature and justify a crackdown on the Muslim Brethren, Egypt's main fundamentalist Muslim organization. His biographer sums up Abdel Nasser's career by calling him "a soldier by chance, a politician by instinct and a conspirator by ability and inclination. He contributed little to soldiering or politics. But he elevated the more native art of conspiracy to new technical heights."[32]

Yasir 'Arafat talked conspiracy theories in public and private. Curiously, his conspiratorial career began in connection with that very same alleged 1954 assassination attempt on Abdel Nasser, getting arrested at the age of 25 for complicity in a nonexistent plot. In retrospect, this provided the perfect public debut for a man whose whole career involved conspiring in the shadowy and layered world of Palestinian politics.

Belief in Jewish control of the West prompts some Arabs to aspire to gain the same power. Once this is achieved, writes Kamil Yusuf al-Hajj, "the West would be in our grasp rather than the Zionists' . . . and the fabulous powers of the West would be within our reach instead of the Zionists'."[33] Yet again, belief in conspiracy inspires conspiracy. Taking this argument one step further, Saddam Husayn once declared that Arabs saving the West from Zionist clutches "not only will help liberate ourselves, but . . . will liberate others in the West from the weight of the Zionist pressure they are subjected to."[34] It falls, in other words, on the Arabs to save the West from the Jewish peril.

Saddam Husayn's susceptibility to conspiracy theories increased his inclination to conspire. He saw plots everywhere; one of his half brothers, Barzan at-Takriti, published a whole book on the subject of assassination plots against Saddam Husayn. Conspiracism implied a career full of conspiration: In October 1959, at the age of 22, Saddam participated in an assassination attempt on one ruler, Qasim. In September 1964 he plotted against another ruler, President 'Abd as-Salam 'Arif, and ended up in prison. When ruler himself, Saddam conspired against those in any way suspect, including his closest aides. He showed that Middle Eastern leaders do sometimes engage in the elaborate and far-sighted plots they so much fear others are spinning around them. To justify the purge of his rivals in 1968, he made use of a notebook containing names and telephone numbers taken two years earlier from an alleged Israeli agent captured in a Baghdad hotel. Saddam added to the notebook whichever names suited his interests, then had those individuals arrested. Other of his victims received carefully crafted letters that pointed to their being Israeli agents; minutes later, Saddam's agents arrested them.[35] When Saddam needed an excuse to purge the upper ranks of his party in 1979, he fell back on the expedient of a Syrian conspiracy. "We have treason among us . . . in the party," he announced, then watched as one of his associates publicly denounced some twenty Ba'th Party officials, who were promptly taken from the room and executed.[36]

At other times, the Iraqi dictator favored helicopter or car accidents. (The method seems to have been pioneered in 1966, before Saddam reached power, when President 'Arif went down in a crash.) Yasir 'Arafat was the victim of a planned car accident: A PLO-organized funeral in Baghdad in 1969 celebrated an Iraqi volunteer killed by Israeli forces by paying homage to "Palestine" but not to Iraq's Ba'th Party leadership. Days later, an army truck rammed into 'Arafat's white Pontiac, breaking his arm; apparently 'Arafat correctly interpreted this episode as a signal to pay more deference to his Iraqi patrons, which he subsequently did. During Saddam's tenure, over a dozen important figures left the scene in this manner, most notably 'Adnan Khayrallah, his defense minister and brother-in-law.[37] So common had this former of killing become, shortly after Khayrallah's death, Saddam reportedly received a letter from President Husni Mubarak of Egypt insisting that his be the last such "accident."[38]

Saddam Husayn's career showcases another aspect of the conspiratorial temptation: conspiracy theorists trip up in the underbrush of their own deceits. Saddam justified his invasion of Kuwait by an alleged U.S.-Kuwaiti plot to damage the Iraqi economy. To prove this claim, he cited Washington's decision to terminate credit to Baghdad. While a strange reason to invade a neighbor, yet stranger is that Saddam brought this trouble on himself by conspiring to break American laws. The details are complex, but they boil down to a heist of stunning audacity in which employees at the Atlanta branch of Banca Nazionale del Lavoro (BNL), Italy's largest bank, connived with Iraqi officials to make $2.86 billion in unauthorized loans to the Iraqi government. (The great majority of this money appears to have gone for military purchases.) Discovery of this massive fraud led to an immediate cutoff of American credit to Iraq. Jeff Shear of *Insight* caught the rich irony of this situation: "The conspiracy perceived by Saddam that led to his invasion of Kuwait may have stemmed from a plot to fleece BNL. In which case the conspiracy he so feared was entirely of his own making."[39]

## A FRAME OF MIND

These specifics point to a more general point; conspiracism colors the whole of Middle East politics. By filtering reality through a distorting prism, it fosters anti-Western, anti-Israeli, antidemocratic, antimoderate, and antimodern actions. At the same time, and almost paradoxically, it infuses the region's peoples with a sense of passivity.

Conspiracy theories induce a sense of hopelessness. The enemy looms larger than life, demonic, massively competent, and forever plotting; in contrast, the conspiracy theorist underestimates his own power. The Arabs' instinct after 1967, British journalist Michael Field writes,

> was most often to turn to the West and say, in effect, "we can do nothing, you have put us in this position, now you have to help us, the solution is in your hands." In a sense this position was reasonable, given that the Arabs had failed to defeat Israel in battle and that Israel's willingness to make concessions depended partly on America's willingness to put pressure on it. Yet the Arabs themselves did little diplomatically to make Western governments and public opinion want to help them. . . . the Arabs did not appreciate their own diplomatic and economic potential, except in crude confrontational terms, and overestimated the power of Western governments to put pressure on a country such as Israel without their electorates being fully behind the policy.[40]

The emphasis on a foreign conspirator leads to passivity in another way: letting one's own government off the hook. Poverty and repression seem more overwhelming when they come from a distant capital. The conspiracy mentality makes it harder to face up to reality and deal with it. Lost wars, economic poverty, and medical backwardness are the West's fault. This climate of illusion prompts journalists, academics, and rulers to ignore actual circumstances in favor of imaginary constructions. To the extent that Arabs see Israel's strength based on clandestine international support, for example, Arab military success remains elusive.

The more a government accepts conspiracy theories, the more deadly and aggressive its actions. Verbal violence, however clichéd, does contribute to the volatility and turbulence of Middle East politics. Whenever paranoia drives politics, the urges of extremists vanquish those of centrists. Normal ambitions disappear, replaced by fevered drives to dominate and fears of domination. Diplomatic flexibility falls victim to these fears. To the despair of foreign diplomats, Middle Eastern leaders adopt intensely negative attitudes, due in part to their ceaseless worry about being duped by malevolent outsiders. The accusation of plots incalculably increases fears of Jews and Christians in the general population.

Conspiracism makes it very difficult for Middle Easterners with common interests to work together. Fundamentalists accuse Pan-Arab nationalists of introducing new divisions to turn Muslim against Muslim, thereby doing the imperialists' work. The Egyptian nationalist Mustafa Kamil, for example, is often portrayed as a British agent. The Arab-Israeli conflict offers many instances of this pattern. Despite a shared hostility of Israel among some 20 states and uncounted organizations, they only rarely cooperate; most of the time, conspiratorial suspicions get in the way. One example: Salah Khalaf of the PLO argued that Arab public opinion strongly favors the Palestinian cause, and this pressures Arab governments to mouth pro-PLO statements. At the same time, those governments fear the consequences of a Palestinian victory and so clandestinely undermine the Palestinians by helping their enemies.

Conspiracism engenders a suspiciousness and aggressiveness that spoil relations with the great powers. Blaming the United Kingdom and the United States for much more than the facts warrant stimulates deep animosities. And those who blame all their problems on Britons and Americans then begin terrorizing airplane passengers and abducting college teachers. The paranoid style, Field explains,

> is obviously linked to the theorists' general ignorance of the outside world, and this is clearly a disadvantage for any society. The belief in plots, combined with ignorance, leads the Arabs to exaggerate the power of the West and misjudge its motives, making them believe that it is hostile and manipulative when it is more likely to be morally censorious, occasionally concerned with upholding states' sover-

eignty and/or protecting its oil interests, generally interested in promoting its exports, and often indifferent to Arab issues—or concerned but unable to see how it can influence events.[41]

Conspiratorial anti-Semitism and overwrought fears of Israeli expansionism perpetuate the Arab-Israeli confrontation. For one, suspicion of a covert alliance with Israel prompts rulers to compensate by becoming more anti-Zionist. Because the Sunni Muslim majority of Syria believes in an 'Alawi-Zionist tie, Hafiz al-Asad (the Syrian president of 'Alawi origins) for many years responded by adopting an implacably anti-Israel policy, more hostile than that of most Sunnis.

Second, fears of a grand Zionist plot implies that Israel lacks ordinary state interests, and this discourages diplomacy. Israel might be seen as intent on building a Greater Israel or as the great puppeteer deciding what Western states should do. In either case, conspiracy theorists have built Israel into something so large and monstrous, they cannot imagine making peace with it. Israel becomes too large to fit the Middle East and too threatening to accommodate.

Third, conspiracy theories enlarge the conflict. They explain, for example, why fundamentalist Muslims bombed an innocuous Jewish community center in Buenos Aires, killing nearly 100 persons. As Martin Kramer explains, this "was no mistake" but resulted from their being "in thrall to the idea that Jews everywhere, in league with Israel, are behind a sinister plot to destroy Islam." Fundamentalists end up making war against Jews everywhere.[42] Conspiracy theories also worsen relations with the United States and Britain; seen as "full partners" of Israel's crimes, they have to be fought with "the same level of hostility."[43]

Fourth, and quite the reverse, seeing Israel as a pawn of the United States encourages Muslims to ignore decisions made in Jerusalem. If Israel is nothing but an instrument of U.S. power, then why deal with it? Leonid Brezhnev expressed his surprise to an Arab delegation in July 1967 that it would talk to the Americans but not to Israel ("Israel is not enslaving you but America can"); President Houari Boumedienne of Algeria replied vehemently: "Your words are incomprehensible and ambiguous. . . . Israel is not the problem because Israel is in the hands of the Americans."[44] This mistaken view has blighted Arab-Israeli diplomacy for years.

The specter of conspiracy delegitimates political adversaries, and so rules out many of those features—freedom of expression, freedom of religion, and elections—that constitute civil society. A climate of suspicion among the ruling class prompts mistrust and governmental repression, rendering freedom of expression out of the question. If dissent signals the ugly head of foreign intervention, deviance from the official line must be suppressed. Dictators fearing conspiracies interpret even the meekest attempts to assert an alternate center of power as a sign of treachery and repress it with all their might. The concept of a loyal opposition evaporates when one's opponent is suspect of serving as an agent for malevolent external powers. Conspiracy theorists tend "to equate competition with treason, liberalism with weak-mindedness, honest differences of opinion with divisive alien conspiracies, and political toleration with permissiveness toward the enemy within."[45] In this overwrought atmosphere, political opponents cannot be tolerated; they must be, and often are, killed. If disagreement suggests treachery, meaningful elections cannot take place. Thus do conspiracy theories drive moderation out of Arab and Iranian public life.

Seeing multinational corporations as thieves and foreign investors as saboteurs stunts economic development. It is even less helpful if the middle class is seen as a creature of the imperialists, artificially built up to have a stake in the status quo and to keep revolutions from succeeding. If foreign investment aims to prevent Muslims from achieving self-sufficiency, how will industrialization take place? If foreign visitors are spies, how can normal relations with the outside world exist?

When the Jordanian government attempted to curb the country's very high birth rate, a fundamentalist leader in parliament denounced contraception as "a conspiracy serving Zionist plans to deprive Arab lands . . . of much needed manpower."[46] If oral contraceptives are part of a plot to reduce the number of Muslims, how will Jordan contain its population? If encouraging condoms is really a subtle form of genocide, how will the AIDS virus be stopped?

Ultimately, conspiracy theories obstruct modernization itself. If "modernization is another conspiracy of the West,"[47] Europe's strength appears not to derive not from its own creativity and energy but from deception and trickery. Many Middle Easterners agree with Khomeini that the West stole its accomplishments from the Muslims, a sentiment that obviously gets in the way of respecting or emulating the West. If Europe got where it did merely through chicanery, Muslims have very little to learn from Western civilization; mostly they should avoid it. Seeing European influence as a form of sabotage, fundamentalist Muslims portray Western culture as corrupt; many (including Khomeini) even portray it as a conspiracy against Islam. This in turn prevents them from achieving the advancement they crave.

## NOTES TO CHAPTER 1

1. Henri Zuckier, "The Conspiratorial Imperative: Medieval Jewry in Western Europe," in Carl F. Graumann and Serge Moscovici, eds., *Changing Conceptions of Conspiracy* (New York: Springer, 1987), p. 92.

2. Daniel Patrick Moynihan, "The Paranoid Style in American Politics Revisited," *The Public Interest* 81 (Fall 1985): 119.

3. *The New York Times*, 24 November 1979.

4. Peter Avery, *Modern Iran* (London: Ernest Benn, 1965), pp. 107-08. Similarly, Lebanese politicians are said to want to be seen in the company of CIA agents as a way of flaunting their connections to the mighty. Fascination with the British embassy grounds may recall the fact that 18,000 Iranians took refuge in them in 1906.

5. John R. Stempel, *Inside the Iranian Revolution* (Bloomington: Indiana University Press, 1981), p. 166.

6. Ibid., pp. 225-26.

7. David A. Korn, *Assassination in Khartoum* (Bloomington: Indiana University Press, 1993), p. 152.

8. *Davar*, 1 August 1994.

9. Michel Bar-Zohar, *Histoire Secrète de la guerre d'Israël* (Paris: Fayard, 1968), p. 36. Charles Krauthammer kindly pointed out this reference.

10. Patrick Seale, with the assistance of Maureen McConville, *Asad of Syria: The Struggle for the Middle East* (Berkeley: University of California Press, 1989), p. 114.

11. Richard B. Parker, *The Politics of Miscalculation in the Middle East* (Bloomington: Indiana University Press, 1993), p. 106. Parker was political counselor at the U.S. embassy in Cairo during the 1967 war.

12. Eric Rouleau, Jean-Francis Held, Jean and Simone Lacouture, *Israel et les Arabes: Le 3ᵉ Combat* (Paris: Seuil, 1967), pp. 54-55. See also *Unità*, 25 May 1967. Curiously, Battle Order No. 1, issued on 14 May 1967 by Field Marshal 'Abd al-Hakim 'Amr, portrayed Israel, "urged on by Imperialism," as aiming "to direct military blows at the Arab people of Syria," not Egypt. See *Middle East Record, 1967*, p. 185.

13. Parker, *Politics of Miscalculation*, p. 98. Of course, speculations about a foreign conspiracy causing the Six-Day War are legion; Parker reviews some of them on pp. 11-13, 36-37.

14. Quoted in William H. Forbis, *Fall of the Peacock Throne: The Story of Iran* (New York: McGraw-Hill, 1981), p. 58.

15. Quoted in Abol Hassan Bani Sadr, with Jean-Charles Deniau, *Le Complot des ayatollahs* (Paris: Éditions la Découverte, 1989), pp. 27, 82.

16. Ervand Abrahamian, *Khomeinism: Essays on the Islamic Republic* (Berkeley: University of California Press, 1993), p.131.

17. Radio Free Lebanon, 3 May, 13 May, 21 May 1990.

18. Commercial spy satellites make it possible for Everyman to see the evidence for himself. A photograph taken by the French satellite Spot-1 is reproduced in *The Economist*, 31 March 1990.

19. *Al-Hayat* (London), 13 June 1992.

20. According to Patrick D. Gaffney, *The Prophet's Pulpit: Islamic Preaching in Contemporary Egypt* (Berkeley: University of California Press, 1994), pp. 93-94.

21. *Sawt ash-Sha'b*, 27 August 1988; *Middle East Economic Digest*, 26 July 1991; Victor Ostrovsky and Claire Hoy, *By Way of Deception* (New York: St. Martin's Press, 1990), p. 74.

22. *Ash-Sharq al-Awsat*, 4 March 1991.

23. For details, see Judith Miller, "Egypt Angry at Former Arab Allies," *The New York Times*, 12 November 1990.

24. For example, Anon., *Al-Muta'amirun* (Paris: As-Silah, 1411/1991).

25. Letter from Fouad Ayoub, press secretary to King Husayn, *The Washington Post*, 18 December 1990.

26. *Foreign Report*, 6 September 1990; William Safire, "The Phony War," *The New York Times*, 1 October 1990.

27. *The Washington Post*, 4 December 1990.

28. For a brief survey, see Daniel Pipes, "Plotters," *The New Republic*, 6 July 1992.

29. Quoted in Mahmud Kemal Inal, *Osmanlı Devrinde Son Sadrıazamlar* (Istanbul, 1964-65), vol. 2, p. 1281. Cited in Carter V. Findley, *Bureaucratic Reform in the Ottoman Empire: The Sublime Porte, 1789-1922* (Princeton, N.J.: Princeton University Press, 1980), p. 236.

30. Foreign Office 371/16908, E 1853/105/93, 25 March 1936. Quoted in Mohammad A. Tarbush, *The Role of the Military in Politics: A Case Study of Iraq to 1941* (London: Kegan Paul International, 1982), p. 51.

31. Interview, 1972. Quoted in P. J. Vatikiotis, *Nasser and His Generation* (New York: St. Martin's Press, 1978), p. 291.

32. Vatikiotis, *Nasser and His Generation*, pp. 363-64.

33. Kamil Yusuf al-Hajj, *Hawla Falsafa as-Suhyuniya*, p. 128. Quoted in Sadiq al-'Azm, *An-Naqd adh-Dhati Ba'd al-Hazima* (Beirut: Dar at-Tali'a, 1969), p. 58.

34. Radio Baghdad, 16 April 1990.

35. Adel Darwish and Gregory Alexander, *Unholy Babylon: The Secret History of Saddam's War* (New York: St. Martin's, 1991), p. 206.

36. Quoted in Elaine Sciolino, *The Outlaw State: Saddam Hussein's Quest for Power and the Gulf Crisis* (New York: John Wiley & Sons, 1991), p. 89.

37. For an insider's account of 'Adnan Khayrallah's death, see Mazhar ad-Dulaymi's account in, *Muhattat al-Mawt: 8 Sanawat fi'l-Mukhabarat al-'Iraqiya* (Paris: Dar al-Anbar 1413/1993), pp. 143-56.

38. *The Washington Post*, 26 April 1990.

39. *Insight*, 11 March 1991.

40. Michael Field, *Inside the Arab World* (Cambridge, Mass.: Harvard University Press, 1994), pp. 168-69.

41. Ibid., p. 168.

42. Martin Kramer, "The Jihad against the Jews," *Commentary*, October 1994, p. 38.

43. Leaflet No. 49 of Hamas. Text in Shaul Mishal and Reuben Aharoni, *Speaking Stones: Communiqués from the Intifada Underground* (Syracuse, N.Y.: Syracuse University Press, 1994), p. 267.

44. Quoted in Abdel Magid Farid, *Nasser: The Final Years* (Reading, Eng.: Ithaca Press, 1994), p. 37.

45. Abrahamian, *Khomeinism*, p.130.

46. 'Abd al-Latif 'Arabiyat, spokesman of Islamic Movement deputies in the House of Representatives, *Ad-Dustur*, 14 May 1990.

47. The view of many Indonesian fundamentalists, according to Donald K. Emmerson, "Islam in Modern Indonesia: Political Impasse, Cultural Opportunity," in Philip H. Stoddard et al., eds., *Change and the Muslim World* (Syracuse, N.Y.: Syracuse University Press, 1981), p. 161.

Part I

# CASE STUDIES

Middle Eastern conspiracism turns up in three principal contexts: the Arab-Israeli conflict, Iranian politics, and Iraq's conflicts with the outside world. We review these three topics in some detail because they demonstrate some of the assumptions and themes of Middle East conspiracism. They also provide a factual base for the subsequent inquiry into the region's conspiratorial mentality.

# 2.

# In a League of Their Own

The Englishman leans on a golf stick; the Frenchman
leans on a pretty woman; we Arabs lean on the glories
of the past. And blame others for our failures.
—*Hussein Sumaida, Israeli and Iraqi spy*[1]

Gamal Abdel Nasser (1918-70), Shah Mohammed Reza Pahlavi
(1919-80), and Ayatollah Khomeini (1902?-89) were three of the
most important Middle East politicians of this century. (Kemal Atatürk
and David Ben-Gurion might be the others.) Each of them inhabited a
world of conspiracy theories and actual conspiracies. Together they did
much to make these ideas respectable and to propagate them far and wide.

## NASSER AND THE SIX-DAY WAR

During his nearly two decades as ruler of Egypt (1952-70), Gamal Abdel
Nasser's immensely appealing persona and stances won him a direct connection to the masses throughout the Arabic-speaking world. As a result, he
was widely imitated by Arab contemporaries and successors. His policies
stood as milestones to be accepted or rejected. His rhetoric infiltrated the
language and had lasting importance. His conspiracism had a major role in
making plots into the everyday currency of Middle East politics.

Abdel Nasser was a foremost conspiracy theorist, a leading organizer
of conspiracies, and the victim of many a conspiracy. His first two years
of power were marked by moderation, but the subsequent effort to make
Pan-Arab nationalism dominant throughout the Middle East caused him

to rely heavily on the paranoid style. He deployed the specter of conspiracies with special effectiveness, seeming to bring the Egyptian public into his confidence whenever he spoke. The tactic worked brilliantly; millions of listeners let themselves be seduced into seeing the world his way.

His accusations were legion. He habitually called Arab adversaries (such as King Husayn of Jordan and King Faysal of Saudi Arabia) "agents of Western imperialism" and "CIA agents." Egypt's union with Syria collapsed due to the efforts of Western stooges. Israel he deemed "America's forward base in Western Asia"[2] and "the tip of imperialism's bayonet inside the Arab nation."[3] The West he portrayed as intent on destroying his government, partly to regain control of Egypt, partly out of fear that his principles would spread through the Arab world and the membership of the Non-Aligned Movement.

Conspiracy theories provided a base for Abdel Nasser's strategy. "The size of the plot against us is big and we have to plan our moves."[4] Foreigners who met Abdel Nasser frequently commented on his conspiratorial mentality; for example, U.N. Secretary General Dag Hammarskjöld found him "pathologically suspicious of everybody."[5] These accusations came together and culminated in Abdel Nasser's initiating the Six-Day War in June 1967 (see chapter 1, "Case Histories"), then taking action in response to his crushing loss.

*Military defeat.*    Israel's devastation of the Egyptian air force on Monday, 5 June 1967 was quick and complete: between 8:45 A.M. (Egyptian time) and 11:35 A.M., Israeli planes destroyed over 300 of the 340 serviceable Egyptian combat aircraft, including bombers, fighters, and transports. Israel's years of planning had paid off, as did its excellent machinery, well-trained pilots, superior intelligence, highly proficient ground crews, and effective $C^3I$ network.

From an Egyptian point of view, however, the destruction of the air force looked very different. As he explained in his resignation speech on 9 June, Abdel Nasser found three facts most suspicious. The first of them—that the Israeli fighters had been expected to come from the east and the north, but instead came from the west—only revealed the Egyptian military's lack of ingenuity; but the other two points were more substantial.

The second concerned the fact that a mere 12 aircraft had been left behind to protect the Israeli home front. "The enemy attacked at one time all military and civil airports in the United Arab Republic [Egypt]. This means he relied on some force other than his normal force to protect his skies from retaliation from our side."[6] Egyptians could not imagine that

Israelis would leave their country defenseless. Someone else's planes, they concluded, must have covered it.

Third, Abdel Nasser knew the size of the Israeli air force and calculated that it could not have carried out the operation on 5 June. The number of sorties over Egypt required a much larger air force than the Israelis possessed. "It can be said without emotion or exaggeration that the enemy was operating an air force three times stronger than his normal force." The other two thirds, obviously, must have been provided by outside powers.

In fact, these two points resulted from the daring and skill of the Israeli military. To maximize air force strike capabilities, it took the chance of exposing Israeli airfields and civilians. Israeli ground crews had learned how to turn fighter planes around between sorties in as little as 7 1/2 minutes. This meant that their planes could complete a full sortie in less than an hour; and each aircraft flew three sorties during the 170 minutes after 8:45 A.M. In contrast, the Egyptians required something like two hours to turn a plane around, meaning that each sortie required about three hours, or three times what the Israelis required. Projecting their own capabilities on to the Israelis, Egyptians counted an air force three times its actual size.

Abdel Nasser responded to Israeli daring and skill not by probing to find out what happened; instead he jumped to conclusions. In this, he typified a Middle Eastern pattern.[7]

*Accusing the United States and Great Britain.* Whoever was to blame for the destruction of the Egyptian air force, it certainly was not Egyptians. The Egyptian reaction to the calamity went through several stages. Anwar as-Sadat recounts that Field Marshal 'Abd al-Hakim 'Amr accused the U.S. Air Force of having attacked the Egyptian planes as soon as he learned what had happened on 5 June. In contrast, Abdel Nasser initially rejected the U.S.-British gambit in a "firm and unyielding" way, replying: "I am not prepared to believe this, or to issue an official statement that the U.S.A. has attacked us, until you've produced at least one aircraft with a wing showing the U.S. ensign."

No such wing turned up, of course, but by early the next morning Abdel Nasser came to see matters very differently. In Sadat's words: "Having realized the magnitude of the disaster . . . he changed his mind" and decided to blame the U.S. government.[8] On 6 June at four o'clock in the morning Abdel Nasser telephoned King Husayn of Jordan and, according to an authenticated intercept of this now-notorious conversation, the two leaders agreed to blame the United States and Britain for the loss of the Egyptian air force. They contrived a story about Western fighter planes flying into Egypt from aircraft carriers:

> Abdel Nasser: Should we say the United States and Britain, or only the United States?
>
> Husayn: The United States and Britain.
>
> AN: Does Britain have aircraft carriers?
>
> H: [Garbled answer]
>
> AN: As God is my witness, I tell you that I shall publish a communiqué and that you will publish a communiqué. And we'll see to it that the Syrians also announce that American and English aircraft are attacking us from their aircraft carriers. So, we will publish this communiqué. We'll really emphasize this point and we'll do it together.
>
> H: Good, perfect.[9]

About an hour after this conversation, Radio Cairo accused the U.S. government of collusion with Israel, a charge rapidly echoed by radio stations in Amman and Damascus, then by the media in other Arab and Muslim countries.

Later that morning, 'Amr called in the Soviet ambassador and launched into a tirade against Moscow for providing intelligence to Israel and colluding with the United States against Egypt. To lessen the ambassador's astonishment, 'Amr retreated, saying this was not his opinion but "a common view among the officers."[10] Abdel Nasser saw the ambassador that same day and told him "it was evident that the United States of America was with all its force behind Israel."[11]

Over the next three days, Abdel Nasser elaborated on his conspiracy theory. On the seventh, he sent a letter to King Husayn informing his ally that the Egyptian Supreme Command had verified British and American air force assistance for Israel, thereby allowing Israel to recover from its "severe losses."[12] On the eighth, he suggested to Husayn that the Arab leaders announce that Israel could not have won without "constant and concentrated" military help from the United States, Great Britain, and "those states sympathetic to them."[13] In his resignation speech on the ninth, Abdel Nasser took these conspiratorial theses public: "It is now established that American and British aircraft carriers were near the enemy's shores helping his war effort. British aircraft raided positions on the Syrian and

Egyptian fronts in broad daylight, while a number of American aircraft mounted reconnoitering operations over some of our positions."[14]

***Dropping the charges.*** Eventually, the perpetrators of this conspiracy theory withdrew their charges. Already on 24 June 1967, King Husayn admitted in a television interview that he had no proof of Western military intervention.[15] Abdel Nasser needed nine months, but he, too, acknowledged that the claim was a "misunderstanding based on suspicion and faulty information."[16] Both Husayn and Abdel Nasser, it should be noted, made their admissions to Western, not Arab, media; while regaining their credibility in the West, they apparently preferred to keep the accusation alive in the Middle East, where it does still surface to this day. The Syrian government dropped the charges without ever admitting their falsity.

Of course, retractions lack the impact of accusations; a great many Arabs and Iranians continue to believe that Israel relied on Western help in 1967, fed by a literature regularly confirming this point. The charges grew both more imaginative and more restrained with time. A 1984 study titled *The Fifth of June: Catastrophe or Conspiracy?* accuses Field Marshall 'Amr of colluding with the U.S. Department of State to "finish with Abdel Nasser."[17] Some years later, a leading Egyptian journalist, Mahmud Sa'dani, wrote that the war in 1967 "was not a defeat . . . but a multiple conspiracy in which the American president Mr. Johnson himself participated" by agreeing to meet an Egyptian diplomat on 5 June, the very day of the Israeli attack, thereby fooling Abdel Nasser into thinking that mediation was still possible.[18]

## SHAH MOHAMMED REZA PAHLAVI

Shah Mohammad Reza Pahlavi, Iran's ruler from 1941 to 1979, featured in a myriad of conspiracy theories during his long reign. Sometimes he propagated theories, sometimes he was seen as the conspirator, and other times he was seen as the victim of others' machinations.

***A conspiracy theorist.*** "I am all alone. Nobody understands my problems. Everybody is in a conspiracy against me."[19] The shah reportedly made this pathetic statement in 1951, but the sentiment characterized his long reign (1943-77). He worried constantly about staff and allies conspiring against him. He suspected his own prime minister of instigating unrest in the country to distract attention from the government's shortcomings. To ascertain the loyalty of his officers, the shah insisted on personally interviewing every candidate for military promotion above the rank of major. No one was immune from these fears. General Fazlollah Zahedi's heroic efforts did much to return the shah to his throne in 1953; but (according to the shah's wife), the shah "harbored a suspicion that Zahedi had his eye on the throne itself," so he eventually exiled this aide to Switzerland.[20] Speaking of the shah's wife, she too came under doubt. In the fall of 1978, at the height of the revolution,

> The Shah ordered his personal guards to admit no one to his presence without a thorough body search, to ensure against weapons being brought into the imperial presence. The empress learned of the Shah's new ruling when she called on him in his private quarters. To her horror, his guards insisted on searching her before she was allowed to enter the Shah's rooms.[21]

For the shah, most Middle Easterners served as Western agents. It mattered not whether they were friendly to the West (such as the United Arab Emirate ambassador in London) or hostile to it (Qadhdhafi or Iraq's President Hasan al-Bakr). He believed London controlled Iran's mullahs and that both London and Washington employed many of his closest aides. The British demand for the removal of Prime Minister Mossadeq camouflaged its collusion with him. The shah interpreted virtually all contacts between foreign embassies and the opposition as a conspiracy against himself.

The same paranoid outlook guided the shah's understanding of foreign countries. Sometimes he assumed that the British and American governments controlled their own media; at other times he assumed that the Jews did. He believed the United States to be "guided by some hidden force; an organization working in secrecy, powerful enough to dispose of the Kennedys and of anyone else who gets in its way."[22]

*A conspirator.*    To understand how Iranians viewed the shah as a superhuman conspirator, we are fortunate to have a vivid description recorded by the American anthropologist Grace E. Goodell; her observations deserve quotation at length.

To assess the shah's rural development projects, Goodell lived in two rural locations in Iran between 1972 and 1975: first at Rahmat Abad, a traditional village, then at Bizhan, a new model town (*shahrak*) designed by American technocrats. She came away struck by the contrast: the village brimmed with human vitality, the model town overwhelmed her with a sense of devastation. Among many other symptoms of this difference, Goodell found herself readily accepted in Rahmat Abad but the subject of intense suspicion in Bizhan—reflecting the model townsman's fears of the state. The Bizhan population put great store in the ancient legend of the king learning what was going on in his realm by sending out inspectors in disguise. Indeed, Goodell learned that this story applied directly to herself:

It made sense to assume that I was either such a spy or the Shah's twin sister carrying our similar work. If a spy, I would have to be a man, because the Shah would never have a woman perform important work; everything the townsmen associated with the *shahrak* reeked of masculine power. On the other hand, Princess Ashraf could present an exception. Being his twin she would be clever as well as trustworthy. Whichever I was, the model townsmen's paranoia resulting from their traumatic experiences after land reform, and their desperate hope to find a way through to the King, immediately focused on me as a direct link to the Shah. Everyone from the outside who was not a kinsman had to be from *dulat* [state]. Although the villagers from Rahmat Abad had helped me move into the model town and had assured their handful of relatives in Bizhan as well as my neighbors there that I was a student, "pure of heart," and although they often came to visit me, publicly verifying my "village" connections, it took months to convince most of the workers I was not a spy. They would make me leave my windbreaker outside in the yard when I visited their homes, thinking the zipper was a television camera beaming whatever it photographed instantly to the King who sat at home watching it. Frequently I had to leave my glasses at home for the same reason (although they all had seen glasses, and had zippers on their own clothes). Mothers forbade their children to go near me; if the children said as much as "darn it!" the King watching his screen might have them killed. In contrast to this massive fear in Bizhan (as though the slightest irregularity in their environment might once again overturn their world), the villagers in Rahmat Abad had felt so much in control of their world that by the third day Musa [the headman] had told me *he* was appointed to spy on *me*, making me the dependent.

This treatment not only took a toll on Goodell, but it led to aberrant behavior.

In the *shahrak* I became very discouraged. Hardly several days would
pass without someone pleading with me, "Tell the King this . . . when
you talk to him tonight." Some people were extreme in what they
wanted me to tell His Imperial Majesty, my twin brother! A woman
in whose home I had enjoyed tea upon.occasion came up to me one
day at the street faucet where I was washing clothes with neighbors.
"You've taken our land, then our house, now our sons, our life and
our peace, our hopes, our garden and cows, *now* what have you come
for? *Now* what more do you want? What have you come to take from
us now? Have it! *Take it*! Take it away!" she screamed. *"Chizi nist
diger. HICH!* There isn't anything more! Nothing!" Almost weeping
myself, I fled to a wise old neighbor woman. "I'm not a spy!" I pleaded
with her, asking her how I could convince people. "But we *want* you
to be a spy," she replied.

One afternoon, Rahim, one of the several teenage boys whom
I had come to know, walked right up to me in public, reached out at
my breasts, looked at me with pained courage and a bewildered sneer,
and put his hands on me firmly. "They're foam rubber?" he exclaimed,
with a question. Since he and others had ruled out my being Princess
Ashraf, my credibility as a friend and not a spy had come to hinge on
my being a woman. By physically acting out the turmoil in their
minds, in a manner so crude to their sensibilities, Rahim demonstrated the extent of social and cultural erosion that had taken place
between the villagers' world and that of the workers of Bizhan.

Goodell ponders the town's curious obsessions and mistrust:

It is difficult to know what is hallucination in another culture, but the
extravagance of these anxieties about my spying and these assumptions about the King's attentiveness could find nothing but contrast
in the down-to-earth village culture that these same people shared
but a few years earlier in Rahmat Abad. It was as though their trauma
had come to be projected upon me, a single non-Iranian woman, in
endless contradictory, fabulous, often pathetic ways. That my zipper
was a camera, that I was the Shah's sister come to live in a cinder
block room in their midst for a year just to check on their children's
language, that every night His Majesty cared to hear about Bizhan
town on his hot line showed the bizarre distortion of power, politics,
technology, and paternalism that had made them at once bitter and
worshipfully dependent, like people who idealize the man who has

hijacked the plane they are in. Mingled with their fear and rancor that I was a spy was the new townsmen's longing that I was.

When in later months we discussed these attacks and demands that I must tell the King their loss, the workers and their wives themselves pointed out the nightmarish jumble of inconsistencies in their suspicions about me. Still, they never really could appreciate the wildness of their fantasies, the frenzy that had led some of them to break all rules of their customarily dignified reserve, and above all the unreasonableness of their visions and anticipations, so opposite the villagers' stolid self-containment and empiricism.[23]

In addition to illustrating the shah's role in the life of ordinary Iranians, Goodell's account hints at the profound needs that conspiracy theories satisfy, the confusion of the conspiracy theorist, and the state of turmoil in which so much of the Middle East finds itself.

*A victim of conspiracy theories.*      Iranians widely believed that the shah was victimized by conspiracies, primarily from abroad. In 1988, Iranian television broadcast the purported confession of General Hosayn Fardoust, a childhood friend of the shah who for many years directed the Imperial Inspectorate, the second security agency after SAVAK. His statement dwelt on the royal court's foreign connections. Ervand Abrahamian summarizes some of the highlights:

> He claimed that Reza Shah had been a secret Bahai; Foroughi, the wartime premier, was a Freemason and therefore a British agent; and the royal palace was so full of British spies that even the shah could not speak freely there. Fardoust also claimed that over 30 percent of the leaders of the National Front were secret Tudehis [Soviet-backed Communists]; the British secretly favored [Mohammad] Mosaddeq and his campaign to nationalize the oil company; the National Front was "linked" to the United States; the British arranged the young shah's marriage to and divorce from Princess Fawzieh of Egypt; Queen Elizabeth had personally ordered the shah to set up the Imperial Inspectorate; and Ernest Perron, another of the shah's childhood friends, had been placed by the British in Le Rosey School in Switzerland to establish ties with the future shah.

In the more detailed memoirs published three years later by *Kayhan-e Hava'i*, Fardoust purportedly provided even more information. On the last point, about Ernest Perron, the son of the handyman at Le Rosey school,[24] he held that

> Perron had been planted by the British in Le Rosey to seduce the young shah; that Perron headed a homosexual clique among the courtiers and the Freemasons; and that he continued to work for MI6 until his death in 1961, when his espionage role was taken over by Dr. [Karim] Ayadi, a Bahai veterinary surgeon who had cured the shah of a psychosomatic ailment.

Fardoust also insisted on seeing Mosaddeq serving as a British agent.

> Mosaddeq could not have attained high positions in the 1920s without London's support and . . . his [the shah's] close friend [Asadollah] Alam was a "well-known" British agent. To top it all, the memoirs claimed that Mosaddeq, because of these foreign ties, had consciously helped the MI6 and CIA carry out the coup against himself.[25]

Seeing a prime minister orchestrate his own overthrow seems like a fitting place to the leave the twisted tale of the shah and his courtiers.

## KHOMEINI AND THE FUNDAMENTALISTS

Of all Middle Easterners, fundamentalist Muslims present the most cohesive conspiratorial thesis. Others spew out accusations without grounding these in a theoretical context; in contrast, Khomeini and all those who propose "Islam is the solution" tend to see the whole course of modern history as a single conspiracy against Islam. What Martin Kramer writes about Lebanon's leading fundamentalist group applies more generally: "the reality of a conspiracy of falsehood to corrupt Islam is so crucial to Hezbollah's understanding of Islamic truth that no contemporary event is subject to interpretation outside of its context." Israeli historian Emmanuel Sivan sees this tendency to worry about infiltration by a fifth column as "a sort of mortar joining the bricks of self-image and the image of the [nonfundamentalist] outside."[26]

Here, in brief, is their argument: Muslim strength follows directly from living by the sacred law of Islam (known in Arabic as the *Shari'a*). A millennium ago, when the faithful lived scrupulously by God's commandments, the Muslim world flourished, enjoying military strength, wealth, and sparkling cultural attainments.[27] But then came external influence, Jewish according to some, European according to others, and it lured Muslims away from close adherence to Islamic ways as adumbrated in the Qur'an—or Koran—and the other guides to Islamic behavior. Zionists and imperialists targeted the Shari'a knowing that it underlies the Islamic way of life and that its precepts would fatally obstruct their efforts to vanquish Muslims.

Fundamentalists almost unthinkingly premise their understanding of modern history on Western plots against Islam, seeing the expansion of European power around the world resulting not from Europe's power but from the successful sabotaging of Islam. Muhammad al-Ghazali, a leading fundamentalist thinker from Egypt, explains that "there is a conspiracy against Islam . . . by Western secularism because it claims that Islam is a dangerous religion."[28] Khomeini, as ever, goes further, writing that "In the interests of the Jews, America, and Israel, we [Muslims] must be jailed and killed, we must be sacrificed to the evil intentions of foreigners."[29]

Conspirators got their way: Muslims strayed from the law. Predictably, Muslims lost their strength. They now lag the rest of the world. Regimes are undemocratic, people poor, and culture derivative. Literacy is low and life-spans short. To return to the grandeur of centuries past, fundamentalists insist, Muslims must implement the law in its entirety, thereby protecting it from foreign meddling. A wholehearted return to the Shari'a means extirpating foreign influence and resisting non-Muslim ways.

Fundamentalists see the need to return to the law as so self-evident that every loyal, righteous Muslim must seek this course; not to do so implies knowing treachery, a wish to enfeeble the Muslim world. A Muslim who neglects the law or, worse yet, encourages others to do so, must be working on behalf of a non-Muslim power. Promoting a secularized version of Islam or taking up antireligious credos like Marxism-Leninism points to agency for the Jews or the Europeans. Leaders who claim to be Muslim but do not apply the Shari'a are also traitors; thus did Ayatollah Khomeini accuse the shah of trying to eliminate Islam from Iran.

Fundamentalist Muslims tend to see Islam as a fragile growth easily imperilled by the acts of its enemies. Khomeini called the shah's granting women the right to vote "an attempt to corrupt our chaste women" and a plot against Islam "perhaps drawn up by the spies of the Jews and the Zionists" with an intent to destroy the "independence of the state and the economy."[30] Salman Rushdie's fantastical novel *The Satanic Verses* he saw as a mortal threat to the religion.

Nearly all the most influential fundamentalist thinkers (Hasan al-Banna, Sayyid Qutb, Abu'l-A'la al-Mawdudi) accept the premise of anti-Islamic conspiracy by Jews and Europeans, as do most of the preachers, scholars, journalists, and politicians who follow their lead. For example, a review of Egyptian fundamentalist views of the outside world in the years 1967 to 1981 concludes that "The notion of the international conspiracy was applied on virtually all specific issues in the period under study."[31]

## NOTES TO CHAPTER 2

1.  Hussein Sumaida, with Carole Jerome, *Circle of Fear: My Life as an Israeli and Iraqi Spy* (Washington, D.C.: Brassey's, 1994), p. 29.

2.  *Nasser's Interviews with the Foreign Press 1968-70* (Cairo), pp. 116-17. Quoted in P. J. Vatikiotis, *Nasser and His Generation* (New York: St. Martin's Press, 1978), p. 258.

3.  Statement of 24 June 1960. Quoted in Vatikiotis, *Nasser and His Generation*, p. 252.

4.  Quoted by Ahmad Jibril, *Ash-Shuruq* (U.A.E.), 3-9 December 1992.

5.  Foreign Office 371/121724 from Paul Gore-Booth (Rangoon), 9 February 1956, VR 1073/55. Quoted in Keith Kyle, *Suez* (New York: St. Martin's Press, 1991), p. 106.

6.  Text of the speech in Faruq Fahmi, *I'tarafat Shams Badran wa Mu'amarat 67* (Cairo: Mu'assasat Amun al-Haditha, 1989), pp. 169-74.

7.  S. Abdallah Schleifer of the American University in Cairo points out that when an event takes place, an American journalist goes to the scene to make inquiries and get firsthand information. In contrast, his Arab counterpart goes to a café and asks the habitués for opinions about what happened.

8.  Anwar el-Sadat, *In Search of Identity: An Autobiography* (New York: Harper & Row, 1977), p. 175. Sadat himself blamed the U.S. government not for military collusion with Israel but for helping the Israelis deceive Egyptian leaders.

9.  Quoted in Hussein of Jordan, *My "War" with Israel* (New York: William Morrow, 1969), pp. 82-83.

10. Muhammad Hasanayn Haykal, *1967, Al-Infijar: Harb ath-Thalathin Sana* (Cairo: Markaz al-Ahram, 1411/1990), p. 728.

11. Ibid., p. 730. The Soviets were not convinced. Shortly after the war, Aleksei Kosygin remarked in private that "no forces — that is non-Israeli forces — or aircraft took part with Israel. Why? The answer is because Israel was strong." Quoted in Abdel Magid Farid, *Nasser: The Final Years* (Reading, Eng.: Ithaca Press, 1994), p. 26.

12. Sa'd Jum'a, *Al-Mu'amara wa-Ma'rakat al-Masir* ([Beirut]: Dar al-Katib al-'Arabi, 1968), p. 247.

13. Jum'a, *Al-Mu'amara wa-Ma'rakat al-Masir*, p. 253-54.

14. Fahmi, *I'tarafat Shams Badran*, p. 171.

15. La Monde, 25-26 June 1967.

16. *Look*, 19 March 1968.

17. Sa'd at-Ta'a, *5 Yunyu: Naksa am Mu'amara?* (Beirut: Dar an-Nidal, 1404/1984), p. 21. Major General Hasan al-Badri's memoirs are indicated as the source for 'Amr's incriminating statements. Abdel Nasser himself said "there was an attempted coup against me in 1962 . . . led by Marshall Amer." Quoted in Farid, *Nasser*, p. 127.

18. *Al-Musawwar*, 4 April 1995, quoted in *The Jerusalem Post International Edition*, 6 May 1995.

19. Mohamed Heikal reports this from Princess Ashraf's husband in *Iran: The Untold Story* (New York: Pantheon, 1981), p. 59.

20. Quoted in William H. Forbis, *Fall of the Peacock Throne: The Story of Iran* (New York: McGraw-Hill, 1981), p. 61.

21. Marvin Zonis, *Majestic Failure: The Fall of the Shah* (Chicago: University of Chicago Press, 1991), p. 139.

22. Spoken 9 September 1970. Quoted in Asadollah Alam, *The Shah and I: The Confidential Diary of Iran's Royal Court, 1969-1977*, edited and translated by Alinaghi Alikhani (New York: St. Martin's, 1991), p. 169.

23. Grace E. Goodell, *The Elementary Structures of Political Life: Rural Development in Pahlevi Iran* (New York: Oxford University Press, 1986), pp. 164-66.

24. On Perron, see Zonis, *Majestic Failure*, pp. 116-20.

25. Ervand Abrahamian, *Khomeinism: Essays on the Islamic Republic* (Berkeley: University of California Press, 1993), pp.129-30.

26. Emmanuel Sivan, "The Enclave Culture," in Martin E. Marty and R. Scott Appleby, eds., *Fundamentalisms Comprehended*, vol. 5 of *The Fundamentalism Project* (Chicago: University of Chicago Press, 1995), p.19.

27. An objective review of the Muslim experience shows a far more complex picture. The Shari'a makes exceedingly difficult demands, for example, prohibiting interest on loans. Indeed, the historical record since the seventh century suggests that the law asks too much and cannot be implemented in its entirety. In premodern times, Muslim religious authorities took this problem into account by reducing standards, finding ways for interest to be paid on loans. But fundamentalists insist on Islamic regulations being fulfilled exactly and entirely, insisting, for example, that no interest at all ever be paid on money.

28. *'Aqidati* (Cairo), 6 December 1994.

29. Quoted in Bernard Lewis, *The Shaping of the Modern Middle East* (New York: Oxford University Press, 1994), p. 121.

30. Quoted in ibid., p. 120.

31. Walid Mahmoud Abdelnasser, *The Islamic Movement in Egypt: Perceptions of International Relations, 1967-81* (London: Kegan Paul International, 1994), p. 254.

# 3.

# "Greater Israel"

> To your descendants I give this land from the River of
> Egypt to the Great River, the river Euphrates.
> —*Genesis 15:18*

> Every place where you set the soles of your feet shall
> be yours. Your borders shall run from the wilderness
> to the Lebanon and from the River, the river
> Euphrates, to the western sea.
> —*Deuteronomy 11:24*

Even before the State of Israel came into existence, Arab leaders accused Zionists of seeking to rule most of the Middle East. This notion of a Greater Israel, quite distinct from the one understood by Zionists (which includes only the West Bank), eventually became so routinized and accepted, it by now serves as the conventional wisdom in all the Arabic-speaking countries and Iran. However farfetched, the fear has real significance, virtually guaranteeing misunderstanding, poisoning attitudes toward Israel, and making resolution of the Arab-Israeli conflict more difficult.

## PROOFS: COIN, FLAG, INSCRIPTION, AND MAP

### Coin

On 25 May 1990, the United Nations Security Council left its permanent quarters in New York City and moved its representatives and staff the whole way to Geneva, Switzerland, so that Yasir 'Arafat, who had been prohibited from entering the United States, could address the Council. And what did 'Arafat have to say on this momentous occasion? One of the subjects he chose to highlight for this august body was his proof that the Israeli government sought to expand far beyond its present borders. "Please allow me to show you this document," he told the assembled diplomats. "This document is a 'map of Greater Israel' which is inscribed on this Israeli coin, the 10-agora piece." Producing a map, 'Arafat elucidated in detail the boundaries of Israel purportedly represented on the coin: "all of Palestine, all of Lebanon, all of Jordan, half of Syria, two-thirds of Iraq, one-third of Saudi Arabia as far as holy Medina, and half of Sinai."[1]

This was hardly the first time 'Arafat had displayed such a map. Indeed, throughout 1990 he made a practice of carrying 10-agora coins in the shirt pocket of his uniform. On occasion he would hand them out. "Look, look," he would exclaim, taking out a coin.

> This is a 10-agora piece. It is a new Israeli coin. And what does it show? The Jewish seven-branched candelabrum [menorah] against the background of an incredible map: an outline shows the region which goes from the Mediterranean to Mesopotamia, from the Red Sea to the Euphrates. It is a glaring demonstration of Zionist aspirations.[2]

Sometimes 'Arafat claimed that these boundaries showed the map of Israel after the immigration of 3.5 million Jews.

Except to someone predisposed to find clues of Zionist expansionism, the 10-agora piece has only the vaguest resemblance to a map of the Middle East. It was closely patterned after a coin issued in 37 B.C., during the Roman siege of Jerusalem, by Mattathias Antigonus II, the last Hasmonaean king. According to Professor Ya'acov Meshorer, head of the antiquities section of the Israel Museum, the artist Nathan Karp used only the general outline of the ancient coin in his design of the 10-agora piece. "Karp was astounded," said Meshorer, "that anyone could see the coast of the Land of Israel there."[3]

'Arafat rejected this explanation. As further proof of his assertion, he produced a second document, a map from a scholarly article titled "Developing Perspectives Upon the Areal Extent of Israel: An Outline Evaluation." Despite its jargon-laden title, this article by Dr. Gwyn

**Figure 3.1.** Coin issued in 37 B.C.E., during the Roman siege of Jerusalem, by Mattathias Antigonus II, the last Hasmonaean king. The seven-branched menorah has for over two millennia served as a symbol of Judaism. Note that this unique example of the Hasmonaean coin did not survive in its entirety, but only in the odd shape pictured here.

**Figure 3.2.** Israeli 10-agora coin. The modern coin incorporates the Hasmonaean menorah, then adds the word "Israel" (in the Hebrew, Arabic, and English languages) and a miniature representation of the State of Israel's seal, itself a menorah. For months, Yasir 'Arafat carried this 10-agora coin in the shirt pocket of his uniform. He described the shape on it as "an incredible map . . . a glaring demonstration of Zionist aspirations." In fact, the coin contains no map; the outline behind the menorah traces the shape of the surviving Hasmonaean coin.

Rowley of the University of Sheffield in England[4] contained a diagram of spectacular utility for 'Arafat's argument: a map of the Middle East with a superimposed outline reaching from the Sinai peninsula to the Iraq-Iran border. (See Map 3.1.) According to the legend accompanying the map, it provides "The real dimensions of Israel according to the current (1989) Israeli 10 Agorot coin." 'Arafat rested his case on the basis of Dr. Rowley's scholarship.

The story about the map on the 10-agora coin took on a life of its own. Mahmud 'Abbas, a member of the PLO Executive Committee, turned the coin into a bill and the map into a political slogan: "The slogan

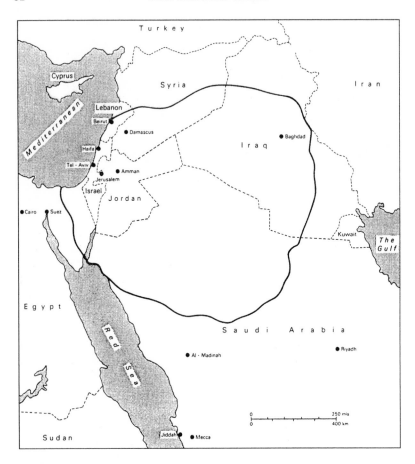

MAP 3.1. "The areal dimensions of Israel according to the current (1989)
Israeli 10 Agorot coin." In Gwyn Rowley, "Developing Perspectives Upon
the Areal Extent of Israel: An Outline Evaluation," *Geo-Journal*, 19 February
1989, p. 109. Yasir 'Arafat relied heavily on Rowley's article to forward his
claim that Israel intends to conquer much of the Middle East.

of an Israel extending from the Euphrates to the Nile is now being
discussed in a concrete and realistic way [in Israel]. For instance, this
slogan has been printed on the Israeli 10-agora note."[5] Such stories built
on themselves and spread widely.

### Flag, Inscription, and Map

In another imaginative argument, 'Arafat discerned a hidden symbolism of expansionist intent in the Israeli flag: its two horizontal blue lines represent the Nile and Euphrates rivers, he told a *Playboy* interviewer, "and in between is Israel."[6] (In fact, the blue lines derive from the design on the traditional Jewish prayer shawl.) Mu'ammar al-Qadhdhafi saw in the Star of David "the Israeli state with its borders."[7]

The claim for a Greater Israel also asserts that Israel's parliament, the Knesset, contains an inscription or map asserting Israel's right to rule from the Nile to the Euphrates. Syria's president and defense minister as well as Iran's president have all claimed that "The Land of Israel from the Euphrates to the Nile" is chiseled over the Knesset's entrance.[8] That the Knesset has hosted millions of visitors and not one has yet laid eyes on either inscription or map seems not to affect the rumor; they can always be removed in anticipation of a given person's visit.

On one occasion, addressing the Arab League's Jerusalem Committee, 'Arafat declared that the Knesset's inscription had been gone for 32 years but then went back up in 1990. Here is his muddled but determined explanation:

> Last year [1989] they stamped on its face the Israeli menorah, directly under which there is the map of Greater Israel. This has attracted our attention, especially since talk about Greater Israel had commenced with the establishment of Israel, when they put a sign on the entrance of the Israeli Knesset that said: "This is your land Israel, from the Nile to the Euphrates." This sign remained for ten years. They were advised to remove it, but now they have put it back up. They have returned to it following the agreement of the two giants in Malta [a reference to the Bush-Gorbachev summit of December 1989].[9]

As if this were not enough, a few days later, 'Arafat offered an alternate conclusion: "They were advised to remove this plaque, [which they did,] but they have engraved this map on this coin under the menorah."[10] On another occasion he added that the American Israel Public Affairs Committee has "published maps on this issue,"[11] although again no one has laid eyes on them.

### THE IDEA

Whence comes this notion of Greater Israel? What validity does it have?

## Origins

The idea has five main sources. First, and by far most important, the Jewish Bible contains two passages that point to Israeli domination of the Middle East. In describing God's covenant with Abraham, Genesis 15:18 reads: "To your descendants I give this land from the River of Egypt to the Great River, the river Euphrates." More ominously, Moses announces to the Jews in Deuteronomy 11:24 that "Every place where you set the soles of your feet shall be yours. Your borders shall run from the wilderness to the Lebanon and from the River, the river Euphrates, to the western sea."

Second, some Westerners expected modern Israel to recapitulate the ancient state's borders; the British ambassador in Istanbul, for example, predicted as early as 1910 that "The domination of Egypt, the land of the Pharaohs, who forced the Jews to build the Pyramids, is part of the future heritage of Israel."[12]

Third, early Zionist leaders referred to a Jewish intent to rule large territories. Around 1900, Theodor Herzl and Isidore Bodenheimer routinely referred to Jewish settlement in "Palestine and Syria," as did organizations like the Jewish National Fund and the Zionist Congress. In 1898 Herzl planned to ask the Ottoman sultan for a territory stretching from the Egyptian frontier to the Euphrates.[13] Four years later he spoke of settling Jews in Mesopotamia. Vladimir Jabotinsky, the founder of Revisionist Zionism, was quoted in 1935 stating "We want a Jewish empire."[14]

Fourth, a number of thinkers from the "Whole Land of Israel" movement, starting with Israel Eldad, espoused notions of a Greater Israel that at times reached from the Nile to the Euphrates.[15]

Finally, Israeli leaders are quoted having made ambitious claims. Moshe Dayan's visit to the Golan Heights soon after its capture by Israeli troops in 1967 has become the stuff of legends. According to Hafiz al-Asad, Dayan announced that "the past generation established Israel within its 1948 borders; we have established Israel within the 1967 borders; and you have to establish a Greater Israel from the Nile to the Euphrates."[16] An Iraqi writer recounts the speech somewhat differently: "We have taken Jerusalem . . . and are now on our way to Yathrib [Medina] and Babylon"[17]—two other cities of ancient Jewish habitation. Whatever the specifics, Arabs agree that Dayan spurred a new round of Israeli expansionist fervor. Prime Minister Menachem Begin was later quoted to the effect that the Bible predicts the Israeli state will eventually include portions of Iraq, Syria, Turkey, Saudi Arabia, Egypt, Sudan, Lebanon, Jordan, and Kuwait.[18]

## Validity

How valid are these arguments, how accurate these quotes? The second and third sources—statements by European Christians and early Zionists—clearly have only limited importance. External predictions can hardly serve as authoritative sources for the Zionist movement. Territorial musings before the Balfour Declaration of 1918 were uttered when the Zionist movement was still embryonic; in any case, Herzl did not in fact request the Nile-to-Euphrates region from the Ottoman king or anyone else. The "Whole Land of Israel" movement is a fringe phenomenon that has as yet had very little impact on the actual conduct of Israeli policy. As for the bellicose statements attributed to Jabotinsky, Begin, and Dayan, they are all secondhand and at best somewhat dubious. In all probability, opponents simply invented them. The first was quoted by Robert Gessner, a hostile writer; the second by enemy leaders of proven unreliability; and the third by a friendly source (the American television evangelist Jerry Falwell), yet the claim to the Sudan and Kuwait strains credulity.

The passages in the Bible are a more complex matter. Four considerations have to be taken into account to understand their meaning.

First, the "River of Egypt" almost certainly refers not to the Nile but to Wadi al-Arish on the north coast of the Sinai Peninsula. The lack of parallel between the two formulations "the Great River, the river Euphrates" and "the River of Egypt" seems to corroborate this interpretation. In any case, the principal Jewish commentaries on this text, notably that of Rashi, identify the River of Egypt with Wadi Al-Arish. These commentaries, it bears noting, have for centuries accompanied the biblical text itself in published editions of the Bible and thus predisposed Zionists to understand "the River of Egypt" along these lines.

Second, by "Euphrates," the biblical command undoubtedly refers not to that river in Iraq but in Syria, just east of Aleppo, for that marked the farthest reaches of King David's empire.

Third, the rules of biblical exegesis hold that specific laws always take precedence over general ones. Accordingly, the detailed, and geographically far more constrained, delineation of *Eretz Yisra'el* (the Land of Israel) in Numbers 34:1-12 ("It shall then turn from the south up to the ascent of Akrabbim and pass by Zim, and its southern limit shall be Kadesh-barnea. . . . ") and Ezekiel 47:13-20 supplant the much vaguer ones in Genesis and Deuteronomy. For this reason, Jewish tradition has long viewed the Genesis statement as nonoperational.

Fourth, in the biblical account, Abraham's "descendants" include not just the Jews through Isaac but also their "cousins," the Arabs through Ishmael—in which case the covenant was long ago amply fulfilled.

To assess correctly the contemporary importance of the biblical injunctions, a number of points need to be kept in mind:

- *Greater Israel* is an inexact translation of *Eretz Yisra'el Hashlemah*, Hebrew for "the Complete Land of Israel." The English term implies a geographical expansion not present in the original.

- Early Zionists considered a wide range of lands for Jewish colonization, including Cyprus, Sinai, Mesopotamia, East Africa, and Argentina. In addition, the Soviet regime made Birobidzhan, a region of distant Siberia, into its version of a Jewish homeland. These territories should be understood as alternatives to, not extensions of, Palestine.

- For decades, the Zionist debate centered on how much to emphasize Jewish control over the whole of *Eretz Yisra'el*. Labor Zionists thought this less important than the objective of establishing a sovereign Jewish state; Revisionist Zionists made it their first priority. Until 1977, it bears noting, Revisionists lost out in nearly all cases to their Labor rivals.

- The Israeli government has not adopted the Bible as a policy document. Middle Easterners are predisposed to think this, for some majority Muslim states (such as Saudi Arabia) call the Qur'an their constitution and virtually every other one derives some of its legislation from the Qur'an. Yasir 'Arafat actually makes this comparison: "They use the Torah as a reference. We use what is much more recent, the Covenant of 'Umar."[19] Similarly, Vice President 'Abd al-Halim Khaddam of Syria imagines that "Zionist ideology is based on the Jews' Torah."[20] But nationalist and socialist goals, not religious ones, inspired the founders of Israel. And really, isn't it faintly preposterous to assume that passages dating from three millennia ago would guide the actions of modern democratic polity? Indeed, Israeli politicians at times explicitly repudiate this notion. Prime Minister Yitzhak Rabin declared in 1995: "The Bible is a book of values and heritage but not an atlas."[21]

- While Revisionist Zionists did claim Jordan and parts of Lebanon[22] and Syria as a part of *Eretz Yisra'el* during the

Mandatory period, no Zionist ever laid claim to or sought to control Egypt, Sudan or Iraq, much less Mecca and the Persian Gulf.

- The notion of *Eretz Yisra'el* subsequently shrank, to the point that today it includes just the territory of Mandatory Palestine. As proof, note that Revisionists in recent decades have viewed the Sinai, the Gaza Strip, the Golan Heights, and southern Lebanon in strategic terms only, not historic ones, confirming that they now see these areas outside of *Eretz Yisra'el.*

- No Israeli political party today (not even Meir Kahane's Kach) aspires to Israeli rule over all *Eretz Yisra'el*; rather, Revisionists only demand now that Israel not give up any part of *Eretz Yisra'el* already under Jewish control. All Israeli factions, clearly, right and left alike, "have long disregarded a literal reading of the divine promise. They have done so despite the fact that, unlike some visionary prophecies, it is territorially specific."[23]

- Difficulties with less than 2 million Muslims in the West Bank and Gaza surely put to rest the grandiose notion of 4 million Jews ruling a Muslim population 25 times larger. How would the Israel Defense Forces handle an *intifada* in Cairo?

- The Israelis did have a chance to choose their ideal borders in June 1967, and they stopped far short of the Nile and the Euphrates. Had they plans to expand to those rivers, they could have done so with virtual impunity at that time.

- The Israelis thrice won part or all of the Sinai peninsula (in the 1948-49, 1956, and 1967 wars) and thrice they returned captured territories to Egypt. (They kept the Gaza Strip after 1979 because the Egyptians did not want that territory back.) How can this fact be reconciled with supposed plans of wanting to rule from the Nile to the Euphrates?

In fact, Israelis tend to register surprise when they learn about Nile-to-Euphrates fears. Ron Ben-Yishay writes in *Yedi'ot Ahronot* that "We [Israelis] sometimes find it hard to comprehend, but the Arab states still have a deeply rooted belief that Israel is trying to expand its borders from the Nile to the Euphrates."[24] To the average Israeli, this is simply baffling.

For these many reasons, the whole idea of a Greater Israel from the Nile to the Euphrates has to be dismissed as groundless fantasy.

## ELEVEN STATES

Fantasy or not, leading politicians from the major Muslim states of the Middle East (with the important exception of Turkey) volubly express themselves on the subject of Greater Israel. Here are some statements, both typical and extravagant:

*Saudi Arabia.*    King 'Abd al-'Aziz ibn Sa'ud of Saudi Arabia (r. 1902-53) seems to have been the first important politician firmly to believe in Greater Israel. Confiding to a retired British diplomat in October 1937, he explained his expectation of a Zionist invasion of his kingdom: "the Jews contemplate as their final aim not only the seizure of all Palestine but the land south of it as far as Medina. Eastward also they hope some day to extend to the Persian Gulf." Why as far as Medina, the second holiest city of Islam? The Saudi king recalled the Jewish presence in that city during the Prophet Muhammad's lifetime and assumed they wanted to return to what he called "their old stronghold."[25]

*Egypt.*    Gamal Abdel Nasser of Egypt picked up this theme and spread it through the region. He argued tirelessly that Israelis sought a Greater Israel to include the whole central Middle East and thereby to turn the Arabs into "a horde of refugees."[26] The Israelis would never give up this aspiration, he affirmed: "Even if they do not expect to realize their talk today or tomorrow about an Israeli state or a Kingdom of Israel from the Nile to the Euphrates, they will persevere in this goal until they find an opportunity [to attain it]."[27] At times he agreed with the Saudi king and declared that "the Jews intend to conquer Mecca and Medina."[28] Or he would accuse them of planing to annihilate all Arabs. Abdel Nasser's aide, Hasan Sabri al-Khuli, went further and portrayed Greater Israel as a way to implement "Zionist aspirations for world domination."[29] Indeed, Greater Israel often slips into the old thesis about a Jewish conspiracy to take over the world.

Long after Abdel Nasser's death, and through years of Egypt's peace with Israel, his acolytes continued to warn against Greater Israel. General Saad El-Shazly flatly asserted that Ariel Sharon would "aspire to conquest over an area greater even than the biblical dreams of a land from the Nile to the Euphrates."[30] A 1990 editorial in *Al-Akhbar* held that the immigration of Soviet Jews to Israel would cause the expulsion of Palestinians from the West Bank and Gaza Strip — "an important step toward fulfilling the old dream of Greater Israel, stretching from the Nile to the Euphrates."[31]

This theme keeps reappearing in print, sometimes extending even further: "The road is completely open before Israel and others to devour the Arab world from the [Persian] Gulf to the [Atlantic] Ocean."[32]

*Libya.*    The Libyans, ever short of water, brought a different sensibility to the issue, transforming the biblical injunction into a hydraulic dream of "dominating water sources in the region, from the Euphrates to the Nile."[33] Jews covet the Nile and Euphrates Rivers, Mu'ammar al-Qadhdhafi asserted, "to control Arab waters," and are ready to settle millions of Jews in the Arab countries.[34] Controlling the sources of these waters would take the Israelis from Turkey to Central Africa.[35] Thus fired up, Qadhdhafi conjured up the greatest Greater Israel of them all: "The Israelis have said their home is from ocean to ocean, from the Indian Ocean to the straits of Bab al-Mandib, straits of Hormuz, the Red Sea . . . to the Atlantic Ocean together with the straits of Gibraltar and the Mediterranean."[36] Qadhdhafi imagined an Israel headquartered in Cairo stretching from Pakistan to Spain, from Turkey to Yemen. In his most paranoid moments he presented Greater Israel as a joint Zionist-American plot "to occupy the Arab world and the Islamic world," with special emphasis on the control of Mecca and Medina.[37] In other words, Greater Israel serves as an instrument to eliminate Islam.

*Syria.*    In contrast, the Syrian fear appears relatively modest. After 1985, Hafiz al-Asad often raised the Greater Israel theme, presenting it as an imminent danger that he single-handedly stopped, calling on Arabs "to prevent the establishment of Greater Israel."[38] Defense Minister Mustafa Tallas told a military audience that, "Had it not been for Hafiz al-Asad, Greater Israel would have been established from the Nile to the Euphrates." If that were not achievement enough, he claimed Asad's forces "prevented Israel from occupying the sources of oil."[39] Vice President Khaddam made the geographically curious charge that "Israel aims to border Iraq, Iran, and Pakistan."[40] Syria's ambassador to Egypt, 'Isa Darwish went further: unless the Syrian strategy of creating "a new Arab order" works, he said, "the future will one of Israeli hegemony. Israel's ambitions will grow. It will seek control of the area extending from the [Persian] Gulf to the Atlantic Ocean, not only the area from the Nile to the Euphrates."[41]

In a distinct interpretation of Greater Israel, Syria's leaders portray its achievement as a Jewish religious duty. Asad has spoken of this; the minister of information reiterates the agreement of "religious rhetoric" and "political theory" on the issue; and even the army chief of staff speaks about "the Israeli rulers" being "driven by Talmudic dreams of containing and controlling the region."[42] If Israel's leaders don't raise these subjects, that's because they are "talking mildly to deceive world opinion."[43]

The Syrians also broke ground by being the first state to give Greater Israel a diplomatic role. In January 1992, during peace process talks, the Syrian delegation displayed a map of Greater Israel and claimed it represented the Jewish state's territorial goals. Needless to say, the Israeli delegation quickly rebutted this assertion.

*Iran.*    Since the Islamic Revolution of 1979, Iranian propaganda has strongly emphasized the threat of Greater Israel, often in connection with accusations of Jewish plans to control the world. A 1985 Tehran reprint of *The Protocols of the Elders of Zion* included a map, the "Dream of Zionism," purporting to show Greater Israel's ideal boundaries. It contains the whole of inhabited Egypt, Saudi Arabia down to Medina, all of Syria, Iraq, and Kuwait, the oil-producing region of Iran, and a good-size slice of Turkey. To make matters complete, the boundary is drawn in the shape of a snake; and the scales are represented by a Freemason's Eye drawn repeatedly along the snake's back.

The Iranian media deprecates Israel by referring to it as a "tribe" that "considers its geographical boundaries" to extend from the Nile to the Euphrates.[44] A 1990 newspaper report warned that because of Greater Israel, "six Arab countries around Palestine will be destroyed, or their inhabitants will be reduced to refugees."[45] Rafsanjani noted the emigration of "millions of Jews from all over the world" (foremost the Soviet Union, but also Argentina and other countries), and interpreted this in terms of a Greater Israel "from the Euphrates River to the Nile River." Included in this vast area, he speculated, would be the north of Saudi Arabia and a large section of the Red Sea coast. The Zionists hoped to settle 10 to 12 million people, Jews and others, to make Israel "a mighty and invincible state." Rafsanjani portrayed the last major advance toward this goal taking place in 1967, with the security zone in Lebanon a finishing touch.[46]

*Other countries.*    Occasional echoes of these statements come from Arabs in other states, and not always from government officials. Just weeks before the Iraqi invasion a Kuwaiti newspaper accused the Zionist movement of planning to reach the Nile River, which it termed "the southern border of the Torah's Israel."[47] This subject, understandably, has not been broached again in the Kuwaiti media. Instead, the Iraqis have picked up on the idea: Muhammad Subayh, Iraq's ambassador to the Arab

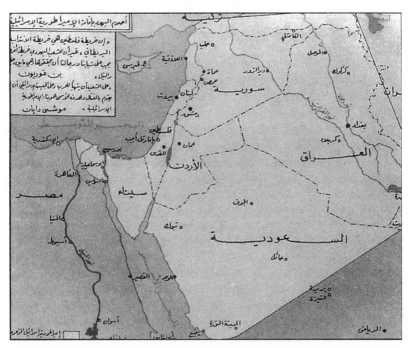

**Map 3.2.** Syrian map portraying "Jewish dreams of establishing an Israeli Empire." This map comes from a wall hanging, "Know Your Enemy," published in the 1980s by Maktab Ibn Hayyan al-'Alami of Dayr az-Zawr. The hanging has six maps, portraying the Levant from Ottoman times through the British mandate and several Arab-Israeli wars. The final map offers alleged quotes from David Ben-Gurion and Moshe Dayan about the need for an "Israeli Empire." Curiously, the area included in Greater Israel goes well beyond the Euphrates River but includes only a tiny portion of the Nile.

League, asserted that the Likud Party "advocates the establishment of a Greater Israel extending from the Nile to the Euphrates."[48]

In Jordan, Sultan al-Hattab, editor of the newspaper *Sawt ash-Sha'b*, wrote that "Greater Israel means Jordan, Syria, and Iraq as an immediate target and the entire Arab homeland as Israel's *Lebensraum.*"[49] The Israelis are said to see Lebanon as a no-man's land and intend to annex it to a location north of Sidon.[50] Layth Shubaylat, a fundamentalist leader, speaks vitriolically on "the daily Jewish claims to alleged rights in Jordan":

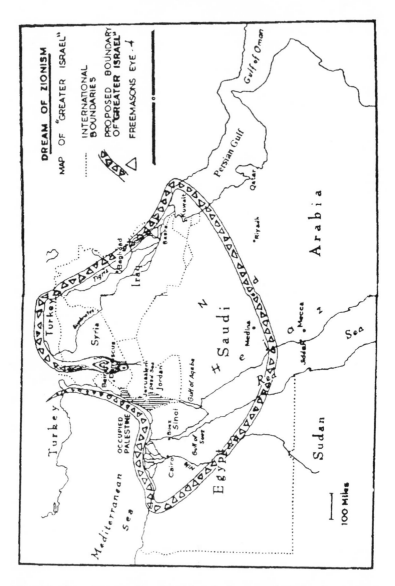

**Map 3.3.** Map of Greater Israel, dubbed the "Dream of Zionism," contained in an English-language edition of *The Protocols of the Elders of Zion* published in Iran (Tehran: Islamic Propagation Organization, 1405/1985). Curiously, the Iranians see Greater Israel including Medina but not Mecca; the oil fields of Kuwait but not those of Saudi Arabia; and more of Turkey than Iran.

All Zionists believe in this doctrine, and any differences [between them] are not between racists and humanists but between reformist racist such as [Binyamin] Netanyahu, the Likud Party, and the religious parties, which want a purely Jewish state on all the 'land of Israel,' including Jordan, and between a racist secularist that does not accept less than complete control of the land of 'Greater Israel' politically and economically as a fulfillment of the promise their alleged god has made.

Shubaylat goes on to express shock that the Jordanian government "is not angered by the successive statements that Jordan is part of Greater Israel and does not seek an apology or an explanation."[51]

The all-but-nonexistent government of Lebanon occasionally stirs the conspiratorial pot from time to time. President Ilyas al-Hirawi declared in early 1990 that a plot existed for Soviet Jews emigrating to Israel to settle in Lebanon, where they would further the Greater Israel aspiration. Not to be left out, the League of Arab States, reflecting the views of its members, posits not just the existence of a Greater Israel plan but the existence of precise Israeli maps showing its reach.

The Greater Israel thesis has also reached Turkey. In a statement of conventional paranoia, the columnist Ahmet Kabaklı writes: "Considering Turkey progressive, secular, and democratic, Israel is preparing it for cooperation against the Muslim states in its cause for the Promised Land, that is, the great Jewish land from the Nile to the Euphrates."[52] But Mustafa Necati Özfatura, another columnist, adds a distinctly Turkish twist.

Israel will never give up its dream of thousands of years. A Greater Israel cannot exist without the Tigris and Euphrates water sources. . . . The world's seven greatest oil companies belong to Jews from the United States. . . . During 1951-1968, they covered up the fact that they had discovered oil in southeast Anatolia by claiming "there is no oil" and "it is not productive." They overlaid the oil wells with cement and went as far as burying the Turkish engineers in those cemented wells. . . . Those wells were designated for Greater Israel. . . . Even the PKK is part of the Greater Israel plan.[53]

Arabs and Iranians, who have plenty of oil but not enough water, accuse Israel of hydrodreams; Turks, who have plenty of water, wield Greater Israel as an explanation for Turkey's lack of petroleum.

Even in distant Bangladesh a newspaper analyst writes that, with the help of their "Christian friends," the Jews "plan to expand the frontier of their state" from the Nile to the Euphrates.[54]

## CONCLUSIONS

### Contradictions

Contradictions abound in the Greater Israel thesis. To begin with, the borders keep changing. The eastern frontier, for example, ranges anywhere between central Iraq and Pakistan. Even the same speaker might offer different borders. In late April 1990, 'Arafat announced that the Zionists aspired to (among other territories) the whole of Lebanon, three quarters of Iraq and the majority of Sinai.[55] Less than two weeks later, his Greater Israel included just two thirds of Iraq and no part of Lebanon or Sinai.[56]

Damascus is even less consistent. Radio Damascus envionsed Greater Israel as merely "double the size of the Zionist entity."[57] In 1989 Asad defined a larger polity extending from the Nile to the Euphrates. Syria's Prime Minister 'Abd ar-Ra'uf al-Kasm warned a Turkish audience that Israelis intend to occupy everything "from the sources of the Nile [in Ethiopia and Uganda] to the sources of the Euphrates [in central Anatolia]. . . . Greater Israel includes Turkey, Iran, and Africa."[58] And in 1992 Asad declared that Israel "wants to extend wherever there are Jews."[59] Which is it?

Arabs also contradict themselves about their future under Israeli rule. Sometimes they see themselves dominated and exploited, sometimes expelled so that Greater Israel becomes a place "where only Jews can live."[60] Sometimes they foresee a single giant Jewish polity, other times they expect today's Arab states to be replaced by "illegitimate cardboard entities" that would eventually accept the existence of Israel.[61]

So confused is this whole issue, Arab leaders even trip over their own nomenclature. Taha Yasin Ramadan, the Iraqi first deputy prime minister, postulated on one occasion that "Greater Israel" implies "a new expansionist policy much more serious than the past slogan, 'From the Nile to the Euphrates.'"[62] In fact, the two expressions are synonymous.

## Ubiquity

An article in the Egyptian magazine for the tourism trade asserts that Israelis visiting Egypt "talk all the time about . . . Israel from the Nile to the Euphrates."[63] The reverse actually approaches the truth: fear of Greater Israel is common coin on the Arab street. When tens of thousands of Palestinians participated in May 1990 in a "march of return" (a walk to Jordan's border with Israel), they chanted slogans against Greater Israel. So widespread is talk of Greater Israel, it need not even be spelled out. When a Jordanian sought to blame Jerusalem for sedition at Yarmuk University in December 1989, he merely blamed plotters "who plan day and night to ruin this nation and to extend their country from the Nile to the Euphrates."[64] Everyone knew exactly who he had in mind.

The PLO laid the scholarly basis for the notion of a Greater Israel by publishing two detailed books on the subject in Beirut during the early 1970s.[65] The theme now appears occasionally in academic work, even in European languages. Muhsin D. Yusuf, a historian at Birzeit University, concludes an article implying that Israel's government has territorial ambitions to a Greater Israel stretching from the Sudan to Kuwait.[66] The idea has spread outside the Middle East, too. Patrick Seale, a British journalist of considerable reputation, has flatly asserted that "some nationalist Israelis (especially those in the Herut Party) dream of a Jewish state extending 'from the Nile to the Euphrates.'"[67] Foreign Minister Claude Cheysson of France in 1983 called the division of Lebanon between Greater Syria and Greater Israel "our nightmare."[68]

## Recent Developments

After years of immobility, the Greater Israel thesis has undergone several potentially significant changes of late. These result from the emergence of Israeli Arabs as a political force of some importance and the success of the Arab-Israeli peace process.

In contrast to the unconstrained statements just quoted, Palestinians living in Israel show caution, at least in public, about the notion of Greater Israel. 'Abd al-Wahhab ad-Darawsha, a leading Israeli Arab politician, sidestepped a question from an Arab journalist asking him if most Israelis supported a Nile-to-Euphrates Greater Israel, mumbling instead about Israel's lack of constitution and disagreement about Israel's final borders.[69]

While no Zionist, Darawsha knew firsthand the falseness of claims about a Greater Israel. But then, when Darawsha traveled to Syria and appeared on Syrian television, he reverted to the standard line, reporting that some of Likud's members raise the slogan of "from the river to the river."[70]

As peace treaties with its neighbors make territorial expansion by Israel less likely, Arab opinion appears to be more divided. Some antiZionists put less stress on the specter of Israeli borders expanding, more on the fear of economic domination by Israel. For them, Shimon Peres's "new Middle East" is but a code for this vision. Ibrahim Ghawsha, the spokesman for the Palestinian fundamentalist group Hamas (as reported by the Dutch correspondent Solomon Bouman) predicts that

> Israel would misuse what he saw as the predominantly economics-based agreement with the PLO economically to dominate the Middle East from the Nile to the Euphrates, as a variant to military dominance. "We know the Jews well," he said. "They are hard workers. With their modern industry, they make the best products at low prices. We are afraid of economic domination."[71]

An Egyptian newspaper laid out this argument in April 1994: "What it [Israel] has failed to achieve by war it will achieve by peace. A Zionist empire will spring up between the Nile and the Euphrates, one in which the mighty Zionists will be masters and the inept, misguided, and dysfunctional Arabs the underdogs."[72] Even more alarming, an Arabic translation of Peres's book, *The New Middle East* contained an introduction claiming his text provided "irrefutable proof" that *The Protocols of the Elders of Zion* — a century-old Russian forgery claiming that Jews seek to take control of the world — are truthful. How's that? "Peres's book is nothing but an additional step," asserted the introduction, "toward implementation of the dangerous plots" outlined in *The Protocols.*[73]

These writers keep the same geography, the same interpretation of Israeli motives, and merely change the mechanism from military to economic. In this reading, Greater Israel provides an added reason not to make peace with Israel. This fear has had great importance, undermining Peres's hope of trade replacing war. Israel television notes that "even Yitzhak Rabin has admitted that the declarations about a 'new Middle East' aroused old fears among the Arabs about the international

Jewish conspiracy to take over their countries. A new Middle East? Not here."[74]

But another, more optimistic, reading also exists, one that sees the Greater Israel project winding down. Faruq Qaddumi, the PLO's "foreign minister," came to this surprising conclusion in April 1994. "A new reality is now emerging in the arena of the Palestinian-Israeli struggle, making all the Zionist dreams vanish and the Greater Israel concept something of the past."[75] Muhammad Husayn Fadlallah, Hizbullah's spiritual guide, offered a similar analysis some weeks later, declaring Greater Israel to be "a finished dream." Instead, he speculated that Israel would become a partner of Europe and the United States.[76]

These two assertions stand out not just because any denial by Arabs of the Greater Israel ambition is so rare, but especially because both speakers had earlier been associated with the Greater Israel thesis. Take Fadlallah: in 1985 he interpreted Greater Israel to mean Arabs cannot live in peace with Israel. "Israel's ambitions to extend from the Euphrates to the Nile are known. . . . We can never have any security, whether military, economic, or political, so long as Israel is harboring its expansionist designs."[77] In 1990 he talked about Soviet immigrants to Israel settling in Lebanon as part of the Greater Israel scheme.

The Greater Israel concept, then, can change over time. This points to the happy possibility of conspiratorial arguments being adjusted to real circumstances.

## Credence

Do Arabs really believe what they say about Greater Israel? Yitzhak Shamir of Israel thinks not, telling an interviewer in 1989 that Hafiz al-Asad knows such talk to be "sheer nonsense."[78] But Patrick Seale, Asad's confidant, holds that the Syrian president truly believes vast expansion to be the long-term Israeli goal.[79] There is no reason to doubt Seale's verdict. Shamir ignores the self-reinforcing impact of repetition; rulers and populations alike eventually do become convinced by their own propaganda machines.

Foreign reporters who encounter the Greater Israel mentality understand it to be genuine among the populations they encounter. Take the Syrian case. *The Wall Street Journal* reports that "Just as Israelis fear Damascus's old dream of a 'Greater Syria,' encompassing Israel, Syrians believe that Tel Aviv craves an 'Eretz Israel' stretching from the Nile to the Euphrates."[80] Indeed, Mamdou Adwan, a leading Syrian poet, used almost these exact words in asserting that "We are as afraid of Greater Israel as they are of Greater Syria." According to Larry Cohler, an American journalist, Adwan is not alone: "most Syrians support these huge outlays [on the military] out of a genuine fear of Greater Israel." Cohler reports that he "encountered this fear repeatedly from people who earnestly believe that the Zionist goal is to expand from the Nile to the Euphrates." As his Syrian handler saw it, "Jews tend to lay claim to any part of the region they have dwelled in historically." One Syrian woman summed up the dangers of the Greater Israel accusation: "All the time we hear about Israel's claim, from the Nile to the Euphrates. How can we trust them when they act like that and say they want peace?"[81] There is no reason to doubt the sincerity of these statements.

Survey research confirms this impression. A poll of 5,000 Egyptians in 1994 showed 17 percent of them thought Israel "should disavow its 'from the Nile to the Euphrates' claim as a condition for cooperation and joint efforts."[82] Asked about Israel's long-term intentions toward the Arabs in 1993, 16 percent of a sample of Levantine Arabs chose Greater Israel as their first fear, 18 percent chose it as their second fear, and 17 percent as their third.[83] When asked the same question a year and a half later, a similar sample (though now with Maronite respondents added), chose Greater Israel 12, 20, and 25 percent of the time, respectively.[84] About one sixth of Israel's neighbors, it appears, take the Greater Israel notion very seriously and half worry about it somewhat.

## Consequences

These fears have significant consequences. Belief in Israel's plan to expand from the Nile to the Euphrates, and perhaps beyond, makes the Jewish state's very existence a threat to the entire Middle East and increases the already substantial paranoia in the Middle East to even higher levels. Arab and Iranian leaders who entertain these delusions conclude that they must destroy Israel before it devours them. An Egyptian opines that the battle with Israelis "will continue until they establish their 'promised' kingdom from the Euphrates to the Nile."[85] The Greater Israel myth also justifies anti-Israel behavior as a defensive act. When

'Arafat asserts, "There will not be a Greater Israel,"[86] he legitimates almost any action against Israel.

These extravagant fears of Israeli expansionism prevent Middle Easterners from seeing Israel as a country with normal security concerns. In addition, the fears transform the Jewish state into something too threatening to coexist with. Just as the demonization of Jews in Europe caused uncounted pogroms and culminated in the Nazi holocaust, so making the Jewish state out to be a menace to the whole Middle East creates a parallel danger of unremitting conflict that could someday terminate in nuclear warfare. Only when Israel comes to be regarded as a state like any other is there a chance that its neighbors will deal with it in accordance with conventional diplomatic norms. There is little prospect of this happening soon, however, if wild claims about Israeli expansionism remain integral to the fabric of Arab mainstream political life.

The Greater Israel calumny bounces back to harm Arabs, too. By exciting Arab hatred of Israel, it persuades many Israelis to hold on to the territories they won in 1967 and not take a chance on peace treaties. Trading land for peace poses enough problems in its own right, without gratuitous Nile-to-Euphrates complications.

Nearly every polity's rhetoric contains statements of geographic grandeur that practical experience renders nonoperational. It serves no one—least of all the Arab and Iranian populations—for their leaders to dredge out a religious pronouncement from three millennia back and transform it into a statement of aggressive intent.

### NOTES TO CHAPTER 3

1. Radio Monte Carlo, 25 May 1990.
2. *La Repubblica,* 3 April 1990. 'Arafat made the same point again in a speech to the Jerusalem Committee of the Arab League on 9 April 1990.
3. *The Jerusalem Post,* 9 June 1990.
4. *Geo-Journal,* 19 February 1989, pp. 99-110.
5. Petra-Jordan News Agency, 28 March 1990.
6. *Playboy,* September 1988.
7. Libyan Television, 4 October 1995.
8. *Al-Jazira,* Jan. 17, 1982.
9. Sawt Filastin (Sanaa), 9 April 1990.

10. Amman Television, 25 April 1990.

11. *Ad-Dustur,* 17 April 1990.

12. Secret letter from Gerard Lowther to Charles Hardinge, 29 May 1910, Foreign Office 800/193A (Lowther Papers). Quoted in Elie Kedourie, *Arabic Political Memoirs and Other Studies* (London: Frank Cass, 1974), p. 256.

13. Theodor Herzl, *Zionistisches Tagebücher, 1895-1899,* edited by Johannes Wachten et al. (Berlin: Ullstein, 1983), vol. 2, p. 650. For a catalogue of Zionist and Israeli statements, real and alleged, see Ass'ad Razzouq, *Greater Israel: A Study in Zionist Expansionist Thought* (Beirut: Palestine Liberation Organization Research Center, 1970), especially pp. 83, 87-90, 92, 96-97, 99-103, 144-45, 167-69, 178-81, 187, 209, 212-14, 230, 234, 240, 243-45, 249-52, 264, 278-82, 286 as well as Maps 3 and 4.

14. Robert Gessner, "Brown Shirts in Zion," *New Masses,* 19 February 1935, p. 11.

15. Ian Lustick, *For the Land and the Lord: Jewish Fundamentalism in Israel* (New York: Council on Foreign Relations, 1988), pp. 104-110.

16. Damascus Television, 18 February 1986.

17. Sa'd al-Bazzaz, *Gulf War: The Israeli Connection,* transl. Namir Abbas Mudhaffer (Baghdad: Dar al-Ma'mun, 1989).

18. *Tyler Courier-Times-Telegraph,* 5 February 1983; reported in *The Los Angeles Times,* 6 February 1983.

19. *Al-Quds,* 8 June 1994. 'Umar I supposedly set out the relations between Muslims and *dhimmi*s soon after the Prophet Muhammad's death. For the text (and reasons to consider it apocryphal), see S. D. Goitein, "Ha-Omnam Asar ha-Khalifa 'Umar 'al ha-Yehudim la-Shevet bi-Yerushalayim," *Melila,* 3-4 (1949-50): 158-62; Antoine Fattal, *Le Statut légal des non-Musulmans en pays d'Islam* (Beirut: Imprimerie Catholique, 1958), pp. 60-69.

20. *Sawt al-Kuwayt,* 4 August 1991. Jews are sometimes accused of rewriting the Torah to serve their current political interests.

21. *Davar,* 12 September 1995. More colorfully, he subsequently deemed the Bible "not just a collection of old property deeds" (Qol Yisra'el, 30 September 1995). Earlier, Rabin had explained his views more fully: "I do not suggest that we view the Bible as the book of maps of the Jewish state. To me, the Bible is the book of religion, real values, real codes, tradition, and history of the Jewish nation. This is how I studied it. Not as the book of the precise maps of the Jewish state" (Qol Yisra'el, 13 April 1994).

22. Joshua 19:28 alots one of the tribes of Israel land "as far as Greater Sidon."

23. Jack Miles, "Promised Land?" *The New York Times,* 6 December 1995.

24. *Yedi'ot Ahronot,* 16 September 1994.

25. Conversation on 25 October 1937 with H. R. P. Dickson, Foreign Office 371/20822 E7201/22/31. Text in Elie Kedourie, *Islam in the Modern World* (New York: Holt, Rinehart and Winston, 1980), pp. 72-73.

26. Speech, 26 March 1964. Quoted in Y. Harkabi, *Arab Attitudes to Israel,* trans. by Misha Louvish (London: Valentine, Mitchell, 1972), p. 73.

27. Ibid., p. 74. The translation has been slightly altered.
28. Radio Cairo, 22 July 1965 and *Al-Ahram* 23 July 1965. Quoted in Eliezer Be'eri, *Army Officers in Arab Politics and Society* (Jerusalem: Israel Universities Press, 1969), p. 399.
29. Hasan Sabri al-Khuli, *Qadiyat Filastin* (about 1966), pp. 19, 24. Quoted in Harkabi, *Arab Attitudes*, p. 82.
30. Saad El-Shazly, *The Arab Military Option* (San Francisco: American Mideast Research, 1986), pp. 17, 31.
31. *Al-Akhbar*, 31 January 1990.
32. Ibrahim Dassuqi Abaza, in *Al-Wafd*, 25 May 1995.
33. *Al-Jamahiriya*, 19 July 1991.
34. *Al-Ahram*, 23 February 1990.
35. More imaginatively yet, some Arabs suggested Israel would alter geography: according to one Egyptian, "Sadat even offered to divert the waters of the Nile into Israel" (quoted in Sana Hassan, "Egypt's Angry Islamic Militants," *The New York Times Magazine*, 20 November 1983, p. 138).
36. Jamahiriya Arab News Agency, 6 January 1990.
37. Tripoli Television, 20 March 1990.
38. Radio Damascus, 12 March 1985. Asad has on several occasions (1985, 1989, and 1990) emphasized Greater Israel in his annual 8 March address commemorating the Ba'th Party reaching power in 1963, his most formal and important speech of the year. For several mentions earlier than 1985, see Moshe Ma'oz, *Syria and Israel: From War to Peace-making* (Oxford: Clarendon Press, 1995), pp. 32, 80, 82, 143, 186.
39. Damascus Television, 7 March 1990.
40. Radio Monte Carlo, 20 November 1995.
41. *Al-'Arabi* (Cairo), 8 August 1994.
42. Radio Damascus 8 March and 7 May 1990; *Al-Musawwar*, 22 July 1994; Syrian Arab Republic Radio, 30 November 1994.
43. Radio Damascus, 8 March 1989.
44. *Kayhan International*, 30 May 1991.
45. *Kayhan International*, 8 May 1990.
46. Radio Tehran, 20 April 1990.
47. *Ar-Ra'y al-'Amm*, 14 June 1990.
48. Iraqi News Agency, 13 June 1994.
49. *Sawt ash-Sha'b*, 16 January 1990.
50. Amman Television, 25 April 1990.
51. *Al-Bilad*, 14 June 1995.
52. *Türkiye*, 7 November 1994.
53. *Türkiye*, 7 August 1994. For more on Özfatura, see the appendix.
54. *Inqilab* (Dhaka), 4 May 1995.
55. Amman Television, 25 April 1990.

56. Iraqi News Agency, 7 May 1990.
57. Radio Damascus, 8 March 1989; 12 April 1990.
58. Damascus Television, 2 March 1986.
59. Syrian Arab Republic Radio, 1 April 1992.
60. The Grand Mufti of Palestine [Hajj Amin al-Husayni], *Memorandum Submitted to His Holiness Pope Paul VI*, Beirut, 28 February 1964.
61. *Al-Jumhuriya* (Baghdad), 2 March 1991.
62. Iraqi News Agency, 3 May 1990.
63. *As-Siyaha* (Cairo), May 1991.
64. Nayif al-Hadid, quoted in *Jordan Times*, 17 December 1989.
65. Khalid Kishtainy, *Whither Israel? A Study of Zionist Expansionism* (Beirut: Palestine Liberation Organization Research Center, 1970); Ass'ad Razzouq, *Greater Israel: A Study in Zionist Expansionist Thought* (Beirut: Palestine Liberation Organization Research Center, 1970), translated into Arabic as As'ad Razuq, *Isra'il al-Kubra* (Beirut: Markaz al-Abhath at-Tabi' li-Munazama at-Tahrir al-Filastini, 1973).
66. Muhsin D. Yusuf, "The Zionists and the Process of Defining the Borders of Palestine, 1915-23," *Journal of South Asian and Middle Eastern Studies* 15 (1991): 39.
67. Patrick Seale, "La Syrie et le processus de paix," *Politique Etrangère*, Winter 1992, p. 785.
68. Reuters, 7 February 1983.
69. *Ash-Sharq al-Awsat*, 9 June 1992.
70. Damascus Television, 10 March 1994.
71. *NRC Handelsblad* (Rotterdam), 9 November 1993. The Hamas Charter, it bears noting, mentions the Zionists' plans from the Nile to the Euphrates, after which "they will look forward to more expansion" (article 290).
72. *Al-Wafd*, 7 April 1994.
73. *The Jerusalem Post International Edition*, 2 September 1995.
74. Channel 2, Jerusalem, 18 April 1995.
75. *Sawt ash-Sha'b* (Amman), 18 April 1994.
76. *Ash-Sha'b* (Cairo), 3 June 1994.
77. *An-Nahar al-'Arabi wa'd-Duwali*, 1 July 1985. Quoted in Martin Kramer, *Hezbollah's Vision of the West* (Washington, D.C.: Washington Institute for Near East Policy, 1989), p. 55.
78. *'Al Hamishmar*, 17 January 1989.
79. Patrick Seale, "Madha Yurid Hafiz al-Asad?" *Al-Majalla*, 23 July 1982, p. 22.
80. *The Wall Street Journal*, 27 September 1990. Greater Syria is in fact a serious proposition, as I have argued in *Greater Syria: The History of an Ambition* (New York: Oxford University Press, 1990).
81. Quoted in Larry Cohler, "Rethinking Syria," *Tikkun*, September/October 1992, p. 33.
82. *Akhbar al-Yawm* (Cairo), 9 April 1994.

83. Hilal Khashan, "Are the Arabs Ready for Peace with Israel?" *Middle East Quarterly,* March 1994, p. 25.

84. Hilal Khashan, "The Levant: Yes to Treaties, No to Normalization," *Middle East Quarterly,* June 1995, p. 9.

85. *Al-Ahram,* 28 February 1994.

86. Radio Madrid, 26 February 1991.

# 4.

# Iran's Islamic Revolution

Rumours flow so freely in my country.
*—Mohammed Reza Pahlavi*[1]

Every day we face a fresh conspiracy.
*—Ayatollah 'Abdolkarim Musavi-Ardebeli*[2]

The Islamic Revolution of 1978-79—a movement that mobilized millions of citizens to defy a seemingly all-powerful regime—ranks as one of the great public acts of will in history. Iranians actively took control of their destiny and created an Islamic Republic no outside power wanted to see. The U.S. government showed itself helpless to prevent Khomeini's ascent to power. He then promoted an enormously combative ideology, and his troops performed credibly in a grueling eight-year war with Iraq. Powerful industrial states paid his government billions of dollars annually for oil purchases.

An outsider might suppose that this spectacular event sounded the death knoll for conspiracism in Iran. Hardly. Regardless of political complexion, Iranians interpret the revolution not as an act of will but as the manifestation of mysterious forces. They debate less the causes of the upheaval than the identity of those forces. This view profoundly colors their understanding of Iran's place in the world and points to a more general likelihood: that Iran is the world's most conspiracy-minded country.

## THE WORLD'S MOST
## CONSPIRACY-MINDED COUNTRY?

From the most private relationship to the affairs of state, from the lowliest peasant to the king of kings himself, suspicion of plots is endemic. As Ervand Abrahamian explains, the vocabulary of conspiracism is ubiquitous in Iranian public life:

> Political polemics in Iran are replete with such terms as *tuteah* (plot), *jasouz* (spy), *khianat* (treason), *vabasteh* (dependent), *khatar-e kharejeh* (foreign danger), *'ummal-e kharejeh* (foreign hands), *nafouz-e biganeh* (alien influence), *asrar* (secrets), *naqsheh* (designs), *'arosak* (marionette), *sotun-e panjom* (fifth column), *nokaran-e este'mar* (servants of imperialism), *posht-e pardeh* (behind the curtain), and *posht-e sahneh* (behind the scene).[3]

Conspiracism has suffused Iranian life since the nineteenth century. According to Firuz Kazemzadeh, an historian of Iran, it was usually the case then that "internal Persian political forces do not operate until there are assurances that external political forces will support and legitimize them."[4] Under the Qajar dynasty, historian Ann K. S. Lambton observes, "Intrigue and corruption . . . were the constant concomitants of public life. Both derived from the prevailing insecurity and both in turn fostered that insecurity."[5] Observers in this century have often observed similar patterns. Widespread Iranian distrust, a 1966 Tehran newspaper noted,

> begins with the people themselves. People are no longer sure of their own ideas, beliefs, attitudes, or even their decisions. This distrust in oneself, gained through actual experience, extends, naturally, to others too. They do no longer trust anyone. They have heard so many lies, have seen so much creeping and crawling. . . . Whom can they trust? The people do not even trust "the people."[6]

So strong and entrenched is the conviction that foreign powers are intriguing, a former official of the shah's regime notes, that "any alleged motives—no matter how farfetched—and any circumstantial evidence—no matter how flimsy—is readily accepted as fact."[7] Homa Katouzian points to "the universal myth—believed by almost every order of urban Iranian society—that any event of the slightest political significance must be the result of a carefully conceived and meticulously executed conspiracy by foreign powers."[8] Sattareh Farman Farmaian, an Iranian aristocrat in exile, observes that she and her countrymen are prone to see "foreign poison in every bottle and foreign treachery behind every tree."[9]

Foreigners discern the same pattern. Sociological research led Norman Jacobs to conclude that

> Iranians claim that it is not that they basically are distrustful or that they prefer the interpersonal relations to be the way they are, but that since no basis for altruistic trust exists in Iranian society, they can but respond accordingly to protect themselves; or, as more than one Iranian has expressed himself on the matter, "If I am trustful, I will only be taken advantage of by others."[10]

Similarly, Marvin Zonis's research during the mid-1960s revealed that Iranians, by a factor of over 0.7, believed political power in their country to be "really controlled by certain foreign governments."[11]

The conspiracy mentality is not easy to quantify or compare, but many Iran specialists believe it more deeply felt in Iran than anywhere on earth. Ervand Abrahamian finds the paranoid style "much more prevalent in modern Iran than in most Western societies."[12] Graham E. Fuller of the RAND Corporation notes that while conspiracy-mindedness is "widespread in the Middle East as a whole and in almost any cultures where weakness and suffering at the hands of powerful exterior forces encourage similar attitudes . . . , the art would seem to be raised to a higher level in Iranian culture than in most other countries." So widespread is the assumption of conspiracy, Fuller explains, for an Iranian to ignore it is "(a) to indicate ignorance of the superior forces around oneself or one's nation and (b) to demonstrate the stupidity, naivete, or insensitivity not to perceive the hidden motives of others." Fuller sees a penchant for the conspiratorial mentality being "a central feature of Iran's political outlook, particularly in international politics" and concludes that "paranoia threatens to insinuate itself into the qualities of a national trait."[13]

## WHO OVERTHREW THE SHAH?

Three events spawned the most intense conspiracy theories of recent Iranian history: the fall of the shah, opposition to the Islamic Republic, and the Iraq-Iran war.

Never was the Iranian imagination more active than during the Islamic Revolution of 1978-79. Conspiracy theories multiplied in the fever of political change: the implausibility of an old mullah overthrowing a gilded and bemedaled shah prompted Iranians of all persuasions to search for intrigues. The revolution then brought fundamentalist Muslims, with their special penchant for hidden-hand explanations, to office. A welter of confusion resulted. The same individual would blithely make opposite interpretations of the same facts, and political opponents would mutually interpret the same incident as directed by the other side against themselves.

In 1978, as power slipped from his grasp, Mohammed Reza Pahlavi sought solace in the merest whips of an explanation. He refused to see the mass demonstrations in the Iranian streets as signaling hostility to his rule; even after his fall from power, Pahlavi persisted in holding that "popular support for the crown ran strong and deep."[14] Of course, this meant blaming all the disturbances on foreign plotters. The closest he came to admitting Iranian involvement was when, talking with President Jimmy Carter, he blamed his troubles on a "well-planned diabolical plot by those who were taking advantage of his liberalization program."[15] Otherwise, he contemptuously rejected Ayatollah Ruhollah Khomeini's claim to be a genuine opposition leader, arguing that he had emerged as a political leader in June 1963 only due to "secret dealings with foreign agents" and that he thereafter remained a proxy for foreign interests.

Which interests? Here the shah could not make up his mind. In 1971 he mentioned the possibility of the Iraqis sponsoring Khomeini. Sometimes he held the Western media responsible for his problems; they "of course, never let an opportunity go to play up acts of violence and make them reflect badly on my rule." He saw the international oil companies as "long-time adversaries" and sometimes accused them of seeking revenge for his leadership in the early 1970s, which caused them to lose their Middle East power and wealth. Most of the time, however, he blamed the great powers—the Union of Soviet Socialist Republics, the United Kingdom, and the United States. For good measure, he sometimes included Israel, too.

*Israel.*    No matter how attenuated, every major Middle Eastern event has an Israeli angle. Why would Israelis oust their most helpful ally in the Middle East in favor of a regime that loudly proclaimed its intention root and branch to extirpate the Jewish state? Because, according to some pro-shah and anti-Israel Iranians, the shah's Iran presented Israel with its one significant rival in the Middle East. The Islamic revolution knocked off Iran, thereby increasing Israel's power and enhancing its value to the United States. The shah himself believed that his support for the Palestinians led to Zionist anger, and that explained why the Western press criticized him for the practices of his secret police, SAVAK.

*The Soviet Union.* The Kremlin ousted the shah as revenge for his services to the West. It found a demagogic mullah and made him a force to be reckoned with. Pahlavi claimed that "radio stations run by atheist *émigrés* belonging to the Tudeh [Communist] Party" bestowed the title of ayatollah on Khomeini.[16] He had "little doubt" that the riots of 7 January 1978, which kicked off the year-long campaign that brought him down, included a combination of "communist elements" and "religious students and their supporters." Many of the veiled female demonstrators, he maintained, were actually male Communists. His downfall resulted from an "unholy alliance of the red and the black"—the mullahs and the Marxists.

Others shared the shah's views. Prime Minister Ja'far Sharif Imami claimed he had evidence to prove that a East European government had caused the disturbances. Princess Ashraf, the shah's twin sister, maintained that Khomeini merely served as a front man for Iranian Communists.[17] The former chancellor of Tehran University accused Khomeini and his colleagues of being "terrorists disguised as ayatollahs" trained in Moscow, Prague, Cuba, as well as in PLO camps.[18]

*The United Kingdom.* As early as 1949, the shah suspected London of trying to get rid of him. The lone assassin who tried to kill him on 4 February of that year turned out to be associated with both "religious fanatics" (as the shah described them) and the Tudeh Party. "And strangely," the shah told Kermit Roosevelt of the CIA, "his mistress was the daughter of a gardener at the British Embassy!" Smiling, he added: "I attach no significance to that."[19] Thirty years later the shah and his entourage were still convinced that the British wanted him out, and they often blamed Perfidious Albion for his precipitous fall from power.

To dispose of Pahlavi, London relied on its traditional agents, the mullahs. A newspaper account that appeared in *Ettala'at* on 7 January 1978—the article that actually precipitated the Islamic Revolution—portrayed Khomeini as "an agent of Britain." This was not pure disinformation but rather reflected a widespread assumption that the mullahs had for over a century been in the British pay. Along these lines, the British ambassador was rumored in the late 1970s to have stopped off in the Iraqi town of Najaf to give Khomeini his instructions. As further evidence of collusion, pro-shah sympathizers pointed alternately to the activities of the intelligence services or the massive BBC coverage of the ayatollah's activities.

This line of thinking strongly appealed to the shah. "If you lift up Khomeini's beard," he declared, "you will find MADE IN ENGLAND written under his chin."[20]

*The United States.* "Why do they pick on me?" the shah lamented about Americans to his aides in mid-1978.[21] Given the topsy-turvy logic of conspiracy theorists, it stands to reason that the power most closely associated with the shah's government should take the lion's share of the blame for his deposition. The U.S. campaign against him supposedly began in 1959, when the oil companies and the CIA jointly organized Iranian student demonstrations against his rule. The two joined forces again during his visit to San Francisco in 1962, when they arranged for an airplane to drag a streamer across the sky accusing the shah of drug trafficking: "Need a fix, see the Shah."

But why would the Americans want to harm their ally, then or later? Typical of the conspiracy theorist, the shah offered flatly contradictory explanations. Sometimes he feared (as he confessed to the American ambassador, William H. Sullivan) a "grand design" of the Soviets and Americans to divide Iran.[22] To ex-vice president Nelson Rockefeller he wondered out loud whether riots in Iran and a coup d'état in Afghanistan meant that "the Americans and Russians have divided the world between them?" (He reports Rockefeller's response as "Of course not. . . . At least as far as I know.") Similarly, he asked Edward Heath, the former British prime minister, for more information on U.S.-Soviet efforts to plot his overthrow.

Sometimes the shah saw America's betrayal motivated by exactly the opposite purpose—to strengthen its effort against the Soviets. As the old strategy of building military alliances against Communism had had only modest success, Pahlavi worried that Washington found a new ally, fundamentalist Islam, with which to form a spiritual alliance against Communism. The shah stood in the way of this partnership, so he had to go. Alternatively, he worried about the Americans seeing him as having become too friendly with Moscow. Whatever the exact motive, he remained "convinced that the Western governments had some plan in mind, some grand conception or overview" that would explain his ouster.

Princess Ashraf pointed to a connection between Khomeini and the CIA, while the shah's son Reza held that the CIA had begun killing his father ten years before his death. According to Reza, the Americans bombarded him with radiation while he vacationed in Europe during the early 1970s, bringing on malignant lymphoma.[23]

Nor were the Pahlavis alone in their fears of Washington. Gary Sick, the National Security Council official who handled Iranian affairs during the Carter administration, tells of the many "sophisticated, well-educated Iranians" who invariably asked him, "Why did the United States want to bring Khomeini to power?"[24] Some of the shah's former officials saw the revolution as the joint handiwork of Robert Huyser (the American general who served as a liaison to the Iranian military in January 1979) and Mohammed Beheshti (one of Khomeini's chief lieutenants). Others of the shah's courtiers held that Western pressure prevented the timely arrest of a few hundred troublemakers, a step they believed would have aborted the revolution. That so many of Khomeini's top aides had an American connection—Amir Entezam, Sadeq Qotbzadeh, Ibrahim Yazdi—confirmed the suspicion of some pro-shah Iranians that the U.S. government sponsored the Islamic Revolution.

Unsure of whom to worry about, the shah generally told Americans of his fears about British collusion with Khomeini; and he told Britons about American collusion with Khomeini. After the fall, he wrote of a joint U.S.-British effort to oust him, to which the French and West Germans assented. And sometimes he blamed everyone at once—Soviets, Americans, Britons, and oil companies.[25]

## THE KHOMEINI REGIME AND ITS ENEMIES

### Khomeini and After

If possible, conspiracy theories had an even more central place for Ayatollah Khomeini than for the shah.

Khomeini and his followers could not make up their minds about the shah's relations with the West. On the one hand, they saw him as a puppet of the United States, and derisively dismissed long-standing tensions between Tehran and Washington as camouflage. Khomeini repeatedly referred to the shah's entry into the United States as a "plot." On the other hand, and quite contradictorily, they understood the shah's exit from the country as a result of an American and British decision to end his rule. More: as the shah lay dying in Egypt in June 1980, Radio Tehran speculated that President Carter had paid Anwar as-Sadat to eliminate the shah; perhaps Sadat "has made another deal with Carter and his friends to get rid of the White House's disgrace in these pre-election days."[26]

Iran's new leaders also relied on conspiracy theories to account for the existence of opposition to themselves. Khomeini introduced the portmanteau concept of "enemy of God" into public life, then discerned enmity to God in any activity he deemed harmful to the Islamic Revolution, from drug trafficking and prostitution to disagreement about the mullahs' proper role in politics. Enemies of God engaged in a host of conspiracies against the regime. Ervand Abrahamian catalogues some of them:

> "Satanic plots" lurked behind liberal Muslims favoring a lay, rather than a clerical, constitution; behind conservative Muslims opposed to his interpretation of *velayat-e faqih*; behind apolitical Muslims who preferred the seminaries to the hustle-and-bustle of politics; behind radical Muslims advocating root-and-branch social chances; behind lawyers critical of the harsh retribution laws; behind Kurds, Arabs, Baluchis and Turkomans seeking regional autonomy; behind leftists organizing strikes and trade unions; and, of course, behind military officers sympathetic to the Pahlavis, the National Front, and even President Banisadr.[27]

Khomeini liked to call the pro-Soviet leftists "Russian spies," anti-Soviet leftists "American Marxists," and conservatives "American Muslims."[28] Everyone in the opposition, in short, served one or other foreign power.

Curiously, even those who might expect help from foreign powers blamed those very powers for their failures. When a plot to overthrow Khomeini (codenamed the Mask) failed in 1980, some of the plotters suspected that Mossad had learned of the operation and told the CIA, which in turn informed the Iranian authorities as a way of garnering favor with the mullahs.

### Romania and Mecca

Khomeini intellectually dominated Iran during the decade of his rule, 1979 to 1989. His death did not, however, lead to any diminishment in conspiracism. Two incidents showed how Iranian authorities had become completely accustomed to seeing world events through the prism of conspiracies.

In December 1989, just as the Romanian populace began the sequence of events that led to the overthrow of Romania's President Nicolae Ceausescu, he happened to be visiting Iran. On Ceausescu's last day in Iran, 20 December, a Tehran daily noted the news reports coming out of Timisoara and pointed to a conspiracy against the Islamic Revolution.

Before the visit had even begun, the Western propaganda machinery embarked on a vast attempt to broadcast the news of skirmishes in the tiny town of Timisoara. The American and British radios, on the one hand, and Associated Press, Reuters, and France Presse news agencies, on the other, were sending hourly reports of serious unrest (!) in the town and of pitched battles between the troops and demonstrators. . . .

Contradictory remarks by these agencies made clear the dimensions of the Western propaganda conspiracy. . . . What is clear is the unmistakable attempt by the Western mass media to create an anti-Romanian feeling during the state visit by the country's president to Iran.[29]

Of course, just two days later those "skirmishes in the tiny town of Timisoara"[30] led to Ceausescu's overthrow — and to some awfully red faces in Tehran. Iran's embarrassment prompted a second round of conspiracism: some Iranians pointed to two facts (Ceausescu's similarity to Shah Mohammed Reza Pahlavi and the red-carpet treatment for him in Iran days before his sanguinary collapse) and concluded that someone had put together a plot to make the Islamic Republic look bad.

The death of over 1,400 pilgrims in July 1990 stimulated a no less implausible Iranian response. The Saudi authorities explained the disaster in the pedestrian tunnel of al-Mu'aysim near Mecca as a simple accident: the passageway had been overcrowded, so the fall of some pilgrims from a bridge precipitated panic. King Fahd attributed the deaths by trampling and suffocation to "God's unavoidable will."[31] In accordance with Islamic law, the Saudi authorities buried the corpses within 24 hours.

The Iranians rejected out of hand this innocent explanation and elaborated three malign scenarios. In the first, a group of pilgrims spontaneously began chanting loudly and in unison "Death to Israel" and "Death to America." To quell the demonstration, Saudi police trapped the offending pilgrims in a tunnel, then slaughtered them. What exactly they used to kill the innocent pilgrims is a matter of dispute. A Tehran radio station mentioned tear gas canisters and rifles; a newspaper wrote of poison gas and automatic weapons.[32] Having no place to flee, over 4,000 pilgrims died. The Saudis expeditiously buried the incriminating evidence.

The second explanation began with the premise that Washington desperately fears the politicization of the *hajj* rituals, for this spreads radical Iranian ideas throughout the Muslim world. Eager to find a pretext to intimidate radical pilgrims, the Americans pressed their Saudi lackeys to engage in violence. More than that, the Americans actually took charge of security for the *hajj.*

Third, and most ominously, some Iranians accused Riyadh of massacring pilgrims with an eye to cancelling the *hajj* ceremonies altogether. Alternately, others speculated that, prompted by American intelligence, the Saudis plan to restrict access to Mecca and thereby turn the *hajj* into a "recreational tour." They conjectured that the pilgrimage might be limited to a few hundred persons who would content themselves with exalting the Saudi leadership and engaging in some commerce.[33]

In explaining the Meccan tragedy, Iranians often implicated Israel and the United States. According to one Tehran newspaper, "the Zionist regime is evidently very pleased not to see more anti-Israeli protest rallies in Mecca and Medina"; on another occasion, the same paper observed that "the criminal hands of the U.S." were ultimately responsible for the massacre.[34] 'Ali Akbar Mohtashemi, invariably the most extreme Iranian leader, interpreted the deaths as a clever attempt by "world apostasy" to control Muslims by infiltrating Zionism into the Hijaz (Western Arabia).[35]

Before leaving the shah and Khomeini, it bears noting that these men and their partisans fully agreed on the importance of foreign intrigues against Iran as well as the cast of villains and the favored repertoire of tricks. Agreeing on so much, the two leaders battled in effect over the mantle of victimhood. Where the shah saw the United States using Khomeini as an instrument to harm himself, Khomeini offered precisely the opposite explanation—himself the victim and Pahlavi as the instrument of American power. In an even more striking way, the same parallelism applied to the leaderships of Iran and Iraq.

## NOTES TO CHAPTER 4

1. Mohammed Reza Pahlavi, *Mission for My Country* (London: Hutchinson, 1961), p. 318.

2. Voice of the Islamic Republic of Iran, 22 November 1991.

3. Ervand Abrahamian, *Khomeinism: Essays on the Islamic Republic* (Berkeley: University of California Press, 1993), p.111.

4. Quoted in Marvin Zonis, *Majestic Failure: The Fall of the Shah* (Chicago: University of Chicago Press, 1991), p. 170.

5. Ann K. S. Lambton, *Qajar Persia: Eleven Studies* (Austin: University of Texas Press, 1988), p. 102.

6. *Sahar* (Tehran), 30 July 1966. Quoted in Marvin Zonis, *The Political Elite of Iran* (Princeton, N.J.: Princeton University Press, 1971), p. 13.

7. Jahangir Amuzegar, *The Dynamics of the Iranian Revolution: The Pahlavis' Triumph and Tragedy* (Albany, N.Y.: State University of New York Press, 1991), p. 79.

8. Homa Katouzian, *The Political Economy of Modern Iran: Despotism and Pseudo-Modernism, 1926-1979* (New York: New York University Press, 1981), p. 65.

9. Sattareh Farman Farmaian, with Dona Munker, *Daughter of Persia: A Woman's Journey from Her Father's Harem Through the Islamic Revolution* (New York: Crown, 1992), p. 201.

10. Norman Jacobs, *The Sociology of Development: Iran as an Asian Case Study* (New York: Praeger, 1966), p. 260.

11. Zonis, *Political Elite*, p. 253.

12. Abrahamian, *Khomeinism*, p.112. For more quotes testifying to the power of Iranian conspiracism (from Lord Curzon, Ann Lambton, Herbert Vreeland, Andrew Westwood, Hooshang Amirahmadi, Marvin Zonis), see ibid., pp. 113-14. For an impressive compilation of Iranian conspiracy theories, see Ahmad Ashraf, "Conspiracy Theories," *Encyclopedia Iranica*.

13. Graham E. Fuller, *The "Center of the Universe": The Geopolitics of Iran* (Boulder, Col.: Westview, 1991), pp. 21, 22, 19.

14. Mohammad Reza Pahlavi, *Answer to History* (New York: Stein and Day, 1980), p. 154. Unattributed quotes in the following paragraphs derive from this book, especially pp. 145-55.

15. Gary Sick, *All Fall Down: America's Tragic Encounter with Iran* (New York: Random House, 1985), p. 51.

16. Ibid., p. 104.

17. Ashraf Pahlavi, *Faces in a Mirror: Memoirs from Exile* (Englewood Cliffs, N.J.: Prentice-Hall, 1980), p. 215.

18. Iran Press Service, London, 28 April 1983.

19. Kermit Roosevelt, *Countercoup: The Struggle for the Control of Iran* (New York: McGraw-Hill, 1979), p. 73.

20. Anthony Parsons, *The Pride and the Fall: Iran 1974-1979* (London: Jonathan Cape, 1984), p. x.

21. Quoted in Mansur Rafizadeh, *Witness: From the Shah to the Secret Arms Deal* (New York: William Morrow, 1987), p. 264.

22. William H. Sullivan, *Mission to Iran* (New York: W. W. Norton, 1981), pp. 156-57.

23. Rafizadeh, *Witness*, p. 327.

24. Sick, *All Fall Down*, p. 34.

25. John K. Cooley quotes him to this effect in *Payback: America's Long War in the Middle East* (Washington, D.C.: Brassey's [US], 1991), p. 3.

26. Radio Tehran, 17 June 1980.

27. Abrahamian, *Khomeinism*, p.122.

28. Ibid., p.122.

29. *Abrar*, 20 December 1989.

30. Timisoara then had a population of 270,000.

31. Saudi Press Agency, 3 July 1990.

32. Sawt al-Mustad'afin (Iran), 6 July 1990; *Jomhuri-ye Islami,* 5, 9 July 1990.

33. Sawt al-Mustad'afin (Lebanon), 4 July 1990.

34. *Kayhan International,* 5, 8 July 1990.

35. *Kayhan,* 8 July 1990.

# 5.

# Iran versus Iraq
# versus the World

Each time Iraq comes under aggression
or is subject to a conspiracy,
it emerges stronger than before.
—*Radio Baghdad*[1]

We always have an enemy lying in ambush.
—*Mohammed Javad Larijani, a leading member of Iran's parliament*[2]

The governments of Iran and Iraq are two of the most highly attuned to conspiracy theories. Shared experiences—especially eight years of war and poor relations with the West—sharpened a general susceptibility to conspiracism, making it central to the politics of both countries. They number among the very few states whose constitutions specifically refer to plotting. The constitution of the Islamic Republic of Iran describes the White Revolution (the shah's land-reform program) as an "American plot . . . a ploy to stabilize the foundation of the colonialist government [of the shah] and strengthen Iran's . . . ties with world imperialism." It also promises that non-Muslim Iranians will be well treated if they refrain from getting involved "in conspiracies hatched against the Islamic Republic of Iran."[3] The Iraqi constitution refers more vaguely to "malicious circles among the great powers and even among countries of this region" plotting against the Ba'th Party.[4]

Four major events show the direct consequences of conspiracism on policy: the Iraq-Iran war, the Rushdie affair, the invasion of Kuwait, and Operation Desert Storm.

## THE IRAQ-IRAN WAR

As any reasonably well-informed American knew, his government had poor to terrible relations with both Iran and Iraq in the years after 1978. During this period, the Iranian authorities sanctioned the seizure of the U.S. embassy, suicide bombings, hostage-takings, and airline explosions. On occasion they threatened terrorism on United States territory. While relations with Iraq were not hostile before the seizure of Kuwait, the brutal and aggressive regime of Saddam Husayn represented exactly the kind of rule Americans deplore. The Kuwaiti adventure prompted the U.S. government to lead a coalition of states to defeat Iraq in war during the first two months of 1991.

So much for reality; propaganda emanating from Tehran and Baghdad tells an entirely different story. In what may have been a historical first, each side blamed the same third party—the U.S. government— for inciting a war and then keep it going. These uncannily similar accusations resulted from concentrating only on the enemy's bonds to the United States, no matter how meager they were, and ignoring all sources of enmity. Further straining the bonds of credulity, each party portrayed the other as Israel's close ally.

*The view from Baghdad.*    Iraqi propaganda depicted a Western world deeply fearful of a fully modern Iraq. Westerners who benefited from control over the oil reserves of the Persian Gulf would, Saddam Husayn told his citizens time and again, do anything to prevent Iraq from attaining its potential military, industrial, and scientific strength. The Zionist-American-British conspiracy aimed to "block Arab progress and cultural renaissance by keeping Arabs in the grip of backwardness, fragmentation, and foreign domination."[5]

Toward this end, the conspirators called in their well-known agent, the Ayatollah Khomeini, who initiated a war of conquest. Israel and Iran often colluded against Iraq, most notably in the Israeli air strike against the Osirak nuclear reactor in June 1981. The Iran/*contra* affair, of course, gave Iraqi propagandists a field day. For years afterward, they accused the West of engaging in "immoral methods"—spies, tendentious media campaigns, lies, false accusations, and plots.[6] Rather than see this for what it was—the exception to an otherwise hostile relationship—the Iraqi Information Ministry painted it as the visible portion of a much larger intrigue. Saddam Husayn deemed great-power assistance to Iran's war effort nothing less than "the biggest conspiracy in modern history."[7] Also, in return for Iranian help, the West sanctioned Tehran's efforts to export the Islamic revolution (just as it paid off Israel by permitting its drive for Greater Israel).

To destroy Iraq's economy and break its military forces, Europeans and Americans had their Iranian minion try and try, keeping the brutal Iraq-Iran war going for eight years. But the population stayed loyal to Saddam Husayn and Iranian aggression failed. The powers finally gave up when they understood the Iraqi people's indomitable will.

*The view from Tehran.* The Iranian government portrayed the war similarly, explaining that "global arrogance" and "international blasphemy" (i.e., the West, sometimes including the Soviet Union) panicked on seeing Iranians assert Muslim power. The Iranians and their allies tended to see the non-Muslim world as a single whole. Thus, Hizbullah's newspaper contained a headline that described a moment in the Iraq-Iran war as "an attack of unbelief in its entirety against faith in its entirety."[8] The White House and Kremlin rightly feared the Islamic Republic as a threat to their highly favorable but ill-gotten positions. To stop the Islamic movement, they tried to subvert the Islamic Revolution. "All the West's plots," explained President 'Ali Hoseyni Khamene'i, "are aimed at stopping Islam and the revolution from becoming a world model."[9]

Anti-Iranian efforts initially took the form of a military assault. According to Mohtashemi, Americans and Soviets "believed that if they could defeat Islam in Iran with military warfare . . . they could then easily confront the Muslims and the Islamic world."[10] Sadeq Qotbzadeh claimed to buy for $200,000 a plan agreed on by Americans, Israelis, and Iranian exiles to bleed the revolutionary regime through external war.[11] Rather than attack directly, however, the great powers decided instead to task their Iraqi minion, Saddam Husayn, to take on this task.

Saddam was a natural choice for the job: not only did he rule a strong state adjoining Iran, but he was a covert ally of the U.S. and Israeli governments who (the Iranians claimed) had secretly signed the Camp David Accords. Relying on Israeli and American intelligence, he launched hostilities in September 1980. The Soviets also connived in Iraqi plans to invade Iran; Rafsanjani once asserted that they "knew well in advance" what Saddam was planning.[12] American, British, and Soviet forces fought alongside the Iraqis.

The West made a grievous mistake, however, in attacking Iran. The forces of iniquity had no chance against Iranians inspired by genuine Islamic fervor. These stymied Iraqi military aggression and in 1988, Saddam's Western sponsors finally called the war off.

## THE RUSHDIE AFFAIR

With the end of the war, Tehran and Baghdad both claimed victory over each other and the West. The Americans and Europeans, the line went out in both capitals, realized that brute force would not work, and so shifted emphasis. The Westerners came up with a second strategy, a more indirect one that would sap the very foundations of the country's strength. Iranians hypothesized Western cultural warfare; Iraqis worried about economic warfare. In both cases, the revolution was portrayed as threatened from within; and in both, the response was rapid, innovative, and dramatic.

For Iran, round two meant contending with a cultural assault. Ayatollah Khomeini had forewarned this danger already in 1987: "the oppressors give priority to military and economic conspiracies, and if they do not succeed, they set their hopes on cultural conspiracies." While "devilish experts and mercenaries"[13] had tried to undermine the Khomeini regime since its inception, the West made this a priority only after the Iraq-Iran war. Its chosen instrument was *The Satanic Verses,* a book first published in London just one month after the end of the Iraq-Iran war.[14]

Presented as a magical realist novel to gullible Westerners, it actually consisted of a terrible and sustained insult against Islamic verities and historical figures. Prostitutes mimic the Prophet Muhammad's wives, the Qur'an originated with Satan (rather than God), and a figure reminiscent of Khomeini is maliciously caricatured. Not for a minute did Rafsanjani believe that Salman Rushdie, the immigrant novelist ("a mad Indian"), had written the book; rather, he blamed the British and other Western governments.[15] Rafsanjani commended the British for choosing Rushdie as a shill, for he provided an ideal front for Iran's enemies. In him, they found

a person who seemingly comes from India and who apparently is separate from the Western world and who has a misleading name [i.e., a Muslim name]. . . . All these advance royalties were given to that person. One can see that they appointed guards for him in advance because they knew what they were doing. . . . All this tells us of an organized and planned effort. It is not an ordinary work. . . . I believe there has not previously been such a well-planned act as this.[16]

In return for lending his name, Rushdie received world renown and a payoff of $1.5 million.

In the imaginative tradition of conspiracy theorists, Iranians conjured up a wealth of detail about the writing of *The Satanic Verses*. They established official British patronage by noting that Rushdie belonged to the Royal Society of Literature, and that Home Secretary Douglas Hurd had belonged to the Whitbread Prize committee in 1988 when Rushdie won that honor. European Union solidarity with Rushdie showed the width of the Western conspiracy. "From the way all the Western leaders suddenly entered the scene in haste and fervor," Rafsanjani explained, "we can see that they wanted to have such an incident and they welcomed it."[17] These accusations took yet more vivid form in the summer of 1990 with the release of a three-hour Pakistani feature film, *International Guerrillas*, which showed the Elders of Zion commissioning *The Satanic Verses* and the police chief of Islamabad (whose forces in February 1989 shot and killed six anti-Rushdie rioters) receiving a suitcase stuffed with a million rupees ($50,000) in cash immediately before giving the order to shoot.

Transforming Rushdie from an independent novelist writing about matters of immigration and identity into an agent of Zionism and imperialism went far to explain the Iranians' hysterical reaction to his writings. That a born Muslim ostensibly stood behind this challenge to Islam itself made it all the more imperative to make an example of him, and so Khomeini did. In an edict issued on 14 February 1989, he declared Rushdie an apostate on the grounds that *The Satanic Verses* was "compiled, printed, and published in opposition to Islam, the Prophet, and the Qur'an." He then called for the execution of Rushdie and "all those involved in its publication who were aware of its contents." More, they were to be killed "quickly, wherever they may be found, so that no one else will dare to insult the Muslim sanctities."[18]

In short, Khomeini recognized the Western plot and nipped it with a "tooth-smashing answer to all such imperialist-Zionist conspiracies."[19] In addition to spurring an unprecedented international debate about freedom of speech and secularism, the edict led to deaths, disrupted diplomacy, and lost trade. Viewed from Tehran, these costs were well worth it. If not for the vigilance shown, President Khamene'i predicted, "in a few years you would have seen the sacred name of the prophet and allies and wives . . . being broadcast in the ugliest, most offensive, and distasteful manner."[20]

The West's cultural campaign did not end with Rushdie. Years later, top politicians continued to warn about cultural subversion. Minister of Islamic Culture and Guidance 'Ali Larijani directly blamed Iranian youth's love of television and sports to Westerners, who "try to weaken religious feelings in the Islamic societies."[21] Speaker of the Parliament 'Ali Akbar Nateq-Nuri called on religious officials, seminarians, and other devoted Khomeinists to "put the enemy's cultural onslaught at the top of their agendas."[22] Khamene'i warned that "The enemy carries out its cultural onslaught against the Islamic Republic of Iran in an organized way. If our response is not organized, the danger of the enemy's onslaught increases."[23] Television satellite dishes (which permit individuals to receive programs directly from the sky, bypassing their governments) have provoked many worries. An Egyptian fundamentalist writes that "The West has directed these dishes at us."[24] Why so? Because, an Iranian ayatollah explains, the television fare amounts to a "cultural onslaught" that undermines the sanctities of Islam: "The satellite is exactly against the honorable Prophet, exactly against the Qur'an."[25]

This Iranian response clearly touched a nerve in the Muslim world, for even some of those unsympathetic to the mullahs of Tehran adopted their argument. A Palestinian newspaper editorial, for instance, had this to say when President Clinton met Salman Rushdie: "The United States behaves as though it wants to subdue and force the Islamic nation down to its knees. It is waging a real war against us — an international legal war, an economic war, and a cultural war. This is an all-out war against our existence with the aim of eliminating us."[26]

## THE INVASION OF KUWAIT

*The view from Baghdad.*    For Iraq, round two (which started in late 1989) meant staving off economic collapse. Realizing that the Iranians could not defeat Iraq on the battlefield, the Western powers had no choice but to enter the fray themselves, "playing the game directly."[27] Frustrated, fearful of Iraqi pan-Arabism, the imperialists shifted gears and decided to attack the bases of Iraqi strength. Iraqi authorities claimed that Israelis designed the "chain of conspiracies"[28] that followed — cutting off aid and trade to Iraq, stealing its resources, and encroaching on its territory. Late in 1990 Saddam Husayn alleged that he had warned the U.S. government a year earlier to "stop perpetrating conspiracies" against Iraq and specifically to desist from their plots against what the dictator grandly dubbed "the personal life of Saddam Husayn."[29]

But the main means of attack was through the oil market. Iraqi officials provided documents (doctored, it later turned out) to prove the existence of an economic conspiracy. Saddam Husayn publicly detailed these plots in a speech commemorating the twenty-second anniversary of the 17 July 1968 revolution. In it he offered an extended description of the "large-scale, premeditated campaign by the official and nonofficial imperialist and Zionist circles against Iraq." As he portrayed it, the campaign began when those circles realized the hopelessness of waging war against a country with Iraq's scientific, industrial, and economic accomplishments. They gave up threatening Iraq militarily and adopted a new method, one

> which produces results that are more dangerous than those produced by the old direct methods. This new method, which has appeared within the ranks of the Arabs [a reference to Kuwait], seeks to cut off livelihood while the old method, which has already been contained, sought to cut off necks. . . . They hope to achieve their aim by this new method and through the Arabs themselves.

At this point, Saddam pointed the finger at his neighbors, attacking "the new oil policy which certain rulers of the Gulf states have for some time intentionally been pursuing to reduce oil prices." Noting that each drop of $1 per barrel meant a loss of $1 billion to Iraq each year, he complained that the Arab states that should have rewarded Iraq for staving off the Iranian menace were instead thrusting a "poisoned dagger" in its back. Saddam also included a threat: "If words fail to afford us protection, then we will have no choice but to resort to effective action to put things right and ensure the restitution of our rights."[30]

Iraqi forces entered Kuwait 16 days later. Plots had a large part in the formal justification for the conquest of Kuwait. Just hours after the occupation, the first communiqué of the "Provisional Free Kuwaiti Government" attacked the prior Kuwaiti authorities for a conspiracy in league with Zionism and imperialism "against the steadfast brother, Iraq."[31] A few weeks later Saddam Husayn put it more bluntly: "The rulers of Kuwait wanted to destroy Iraq."[32]

Kuwait digested, Saddam Husayn turned his attention to Saudi Arabia. Some of his verbal attacks recalled the language hurled against Kuwait (King Fahd was part of "a big U.S.-Zionist conspiracy aimed at carrying out an aggression against Iraq"),[33] but he also adopted a radically different justification—one more suited to his old enemies in Tehran than to himself. Describing Saudi rule as unjust, corrupt, and treasonous, he called on Muslims everywhere "to stand up to defend Mecca, which is the captive of the spears of the Americans and the Zionists."[34]

*The view from Tehran.* So long as Iraq had a working relationship with the West, the Iranians could plausibly blame Saddam Husayn's actions on the West. But those relations plummeted in 1990: the U.S. government arrested an Iraqi diplomat for the attempted murder of a dissident; the Iraqis executed Farhad Bazoft, a correspondent of Iranian origins who reported for London's *Observer*; the British caught Iraqi agents exporting nuclear triggers; several European governments intercepted parts for a giant Iraqi canon; Saddam made a bellicose speech about Iraqi chemical weapons destroying half of Israel; and then his forces seized Kuwait, an event that precipitated the most unanimous public outrage in modern history. Even before the aggression on Kuwait, *Newsweek* called Saddam Husayn "Public Enemy No. 1" and *U.S. News & World Report* called him "The World's Most Dangerous Man."[35] After it, Western politicians and media routinely compared him with Hitler.

In the face of all this, could the Iranians portray Saddam as a Western and Israeli agent? Of course. Indeed, this challenging assignment permitted Tehran's spin doctors to show their mettle. Most commonly, they presented the Iraqi and Western governments as merely pretending to disagree. The British shammed outrage over Bazoft's execution. "Muslims of the world will not be fooled," intoned the Tehran media, "by [Margaret] Thatcher's scenario of defending Bazoft."[36] Iraqi threats to attack Israel with chemical weapons amounted to a "charade" and a "trap"[37] intended to extract the Iraqi regime from its domestic and international isolation. When the Israelis responded with plans to distribute gas masks, the Iranian media portrayed this as posturing to deceive the outside world.

The case of Iraqis arrested in Great Britain for attempting to smuggle out 95 krytrons, or nuclear triggers, inspired some particularly convoluted examples of conspiratorial thinking. Saddam Husayn responded to the arrests with a classic blame-the-victim maneuver, announcing that Western *agents provocateurs* had in fact been trying for five or six years to sell enriched uranium to Iraq. "They used to come to us every day and ask us: 'Don't you want enriched uranium for an atomic bomb?'" Saddam quoted his own response to this alleged offer: "By God, spare us your evil. Pick up your goods and leave."[38] Tehran read this incident differently, as an example of Iraqi leaders colluding with the British, permitting the mock arrest of their own people on charges of exporting nuclear triggers from Britain as a way of burnishing Saddam's anti-Israel credentials: "Reports of the seizure at London's Heathrow Airport of nuclear triggers destined to Baghdad, and the propaganda which portrayed Iraq as a threat to Israel look as though they were intended for publicity purposes in favor of the

Baathist regime."[39] Tehran chose to believe Saddam's claim that Western states tried to foist nuclear weapons on him, then used this incident as evidence of the tight relations between Baghdad and the Western powers: so tight, they had even offered him nuclear weaponry.

Nor did the Iraqi invasion of Kuwait and the dispatch of an American-led expeditionary force to Saudi Arabia much impress the Iranians, who dismissed the crisis over Kuwait as an American-run conspiracy. The conspiracy theorists differed only on the conspiracy's purpose — religious, economic, political, or military.

- Religious: Jerusalem was already under the Jews; now the dispatch of American soldiers to Saudi Arabia brought Mecca and Medina under Christian rule. Some saw the U.N. expeditionary force as part of a long-term plot to extirpate Islam. According to 'Abd al-Fattah Fahmi, an Islamic preacher in Egypt, it also meant the establishment of a Greater Israel, Maronite rule in Lebanon, Christian rule in the southern Sudan, the elimination of such anti-American rulers as Saddam Husayn, control over petroleum resources, and the subjugation of the Islamic revival.[40]
- Economic: Washington sought to improve the U.S. economy, either by selling more arms or raising oil prices. Talk spread of a U.S. plan dating back to 1975 to control such Muslim oil-exporting states as Saudi Arabia, Libya, and Algeria.
- Political: The crisis slowed the tempo of unification in Western Europe or provided a "ballyhoo" to allow Saddam Husayn, a U.S. lackey, to portray himself as anti-American. Others saw it as a way for the U.S. government to get its European allies to remain obedient to its will.
- Military: The invasion created a state of fear in Saudi Arabia and the other oil sheikhdoms, inducing their leaders to accept a U.S. security umbrella.[41] As a result, Washington attained "the long-cherished American dream" of dispatching American troops to the Persian Gulf.[42]

At times, Tehran acknowledged Iraqi differences with the West, but only within the context of the West punishing a wayward agent. When Saddam went "out of control," his Western sponsors took steps to remind him who was calling the shots.[43] Thus, Israel's 1981 destruction of the Iraqi nuclear reactor occurred when Washington, "having lost hopes about

Saddam's ability to survive the war he started against Iran, decided to annihilate the atomic energy facilities near Baghdad."[44] Similarly, the attack on Kuwait "was a trap to strip Saddam of his arrogance"; by inducing him to take steps that exposed him to international condemnation, Iran's Deputy Foreign Minister 'Ali Mohammed Besharati, maintained, the U.S. government found a measure by which to control him more tightly.[45]

## OPERATION DESERT STORM

The total defeat of Iraqi forces during Operation Desert Storm inspired a whole new round of conspiracy theories from Baghdad and Tehran.

*The view from Baghdad.*    Out went allegations of a Kuwaiti effort to undermine the Iraqi economy; in came an American effort to lure Saddam Husayn into a trap. Iraq's former ambassador in Washington, Muhammad al-Mashat, promoted the idea that Americans prompted Kuwait to challenge Baghdad. He interpreted Kuwait's "stiff-necked" behavior as a sign of conspiracy; only U.S. backing could have made a weak state so arrogant.[46] That the U.S. ambassador in Baghdad, April Glaspie, left Baghdad for Washington one day before Saddam invaded Kuwait pointed to foreknowledge of the invasion. The notion of a trap quickly spread among Saddam's supporters, becoming an article of faith that supported them through a difficult time.

*The view from Tehran.*    War between the United States and Iraq in January-February 1991 temporarily silenced those who hated both Saddam and the United States. But when Saddam Husayn survived the war still in power, they returned in legion. Iranians claimed that the West kept Saddam to guarantee Western influence in the Persian Gulf; because he would be too weak to stand in the way of an Arab peace with Israel; or because he promised President Bush to forgo further international ambitions if he could remain in power. Some charged the Americans with providing fuel for Iraqi tanks and helicopters to crush the postwar rebellions; Hosayn Hashemian, vice speaker of the Iranian parliament, accused the U.S. and British governments of actually massacring Shi'is in Iraq.[47] Syria's Defense Minister Tallas speculated that the U.S. government kept Saddam in power "to reward an agent" and "turn him into a bogeyman."[48] Others suspected the two leaders had a deal right from the start and plotted out the whole war as a means to lure the anti-Saddam elements of Iraq into the open, then eliminate them.

These conspiracy theories, it bears noting, did not just circulate in Iran, but also in Iraq. The regime's many enemies not only believed that the Allied troops wanted Saddam Husayn to remain in power (thereby guaranteeing that Western troops would remain in the Persian Gulf), but they even "reached Baghdad at the end of the war and formed a defensive circle around the presidential palace to protect Saddam." According to this reasoning, "Iraq and the US may have been in cahoots from the start."[49]

A variant conspiracy theory emerged in Arab circles, according to which Washington encouraged the Iraqi invasion so as to use it as a model and a precedent for other countries. Dare defy America, the message went out, and you, too, will suffer a fate like Iraq's—complete with economic isolation and destruction of weapons. Saddam Husayn, in his evil stupidity, fell into the American trap and thereby disserviced all those trying to resist American hegemony. He was a dupe, not an agent, who fell neatly into an American trap, thereby providing "an invaluable service to the United States."[50]

Iranian and Iraqi perceptions followed uncannily parallel paths from 1980 on. Both leaderships portrayed their accomplishments (a modern economy in Iraq, genuine Islam in Iran) as so threatening to imperial interests that America and West Europe had to overturn their regime. Rather than do this directly, the West called on its local agent. That agent (read Iran or Iraq) battered itself for eight long years against the unbeatable will of righteousness. Eventually the West acknowledged the futility of the military effort, so it called off its proxy and the war came to an end in 1988.

Unable to tolerate the example of Iraq (or: Iran), the West switched to a second and more subtle way of undermining its revolution. This time it struck at the heart of the enemy's strength—Islam in the case of Iran, the economy in the case of Iraq. Once again, the West located a Muslim agent to do its dirty work: Salman Rushdie in the Iranian case, Kuwait in the Iraqi one. Each of these agents was rewarded with a death sentence—a Khomeini edict for Rushdie, conquest and annexation for Kuwait. Western opinion feigned outrage at each of these incidents; but Tehran and Baghdad disdained this emotionalism as the purest hypocrisy.

The closely matching patterns of Iran and Iraq call for an explanation. Was there some underlying structure that they shared and that impelled them down similar paths? Or did something influence both of them? Both explanations seem plausible.

The two leaderships shared so much—hostility toward the West, epic ambitions, a repressive government system, an economy tied to oil sales—that they found themselves frustrated by similar developments and responded in similar ways. In the end, structural similarities outweighed ideological differences in the way they chose to define challenges and failures. When looking at the outside world, the incompatible ideologies of these two states mattered less than their shared vocabulary of bellicose fear.

In addition, the two states may have drawn from the same intellectual well. Consider this statement by Gamal Abdel Nasser, Egypt's president until 1970:

> the American plans against us . . . have gone through three stages. In the first stage, the military defeat was supposed to destroy the entire regime and to replace it by a pro-American regime. . . . In the second of these stages they estimated that we would run out of money in December [1967] and be unable to provide the wheat for making bread for the people. . . . The third and last stage is the one in which the Americans have turned to attempts to overthrow us internally through domestic instability.[51]

This closely anticipates Iranian rhetoric of a quarter century later.

> At one time, the enemy decided to embark on a military war with us. He lost the military war and did nothing. He embarked on political war. . . . He made some trouble with economic war; but, thank God, our nation endured that and still does. But now he has entered a cultural war [i.e., television satellite dishes]. The cultural war, God forbid, will wreak blight on our young.[52]

The Iraqi and Iranian regimes, in other words, both seem likely to have been inspired by Abdel Nasser specifically, and more generally by the intense conspiracism of Middle Eastern political culture.

### NOTES TO CHAPTER 5

1. Radio Baghdad, 9 March 1991.
2. *Ettala'at*, 5 July 1990.
3. "Constitution of the Islamic Republic of Iran," *The Middle East Journal* 34 (1980): 184, 190.
4. Text in *Al-Jumhuriya* (Baghdad), 30 July 1990. In addition, Article 201 of an Iraqi penal code promulgated in the mid-1980s imposed the death penalty on "any person

who propagates Zionist or Masonic principles or who joins or advocates membership of Zionist or Masonic institutions." Quoted in Middle East Watch, *Human Rights in Iraq* (New Haven, Conn.: Yale University Press, 1990), p. 28.

5. *Ath-Thawra* (Baghdad), 12 April 1990.
6. *Ath-Thawra* (Baghdad), 4 April 1990.
7. "*Statement* made by President Saddam Hussein," Baghdad, 2 April 1990.
8. *Al-'Ahd*, 24 July 1987. Quoted in Martin Kramer, *Hezbollah's Vision of the West* (Washington, D.C.: Washington Institute for Near East Policy, 1989), p. 42.
9. Radio Tehran, 12 March 1989.
10. Radio Tehran, 16 February 1989.
11. Abol Hassan Bani Sadr, with Jean-Charles Deniau, *Le Complot des ayatollahs* (Paris: Éditions la Découverte, 1989), pp. 23, 25.
12. Iran Press Service, London, 28 April 1983.
13. Islamic Revolution News Agency, 15 February 1989.
14. And in early 1989, in New York, by Viking.
15. Radio Tehran, 24 February 1989.
16. Radio Tehran, 15 February 1989.
17. Radio Tehran, 24 February 1989.
18. *Kayhan Hava'i*, 22 February 1989.
19. Hizbullah, quoted by the Islamic Revolution News Agency, 18 February 1989.
20. Radio Tehran, March 3, 1989.
21. *Kayhan*, 23 September 1993.
22. *Resalet*, 21 July 1992.
23. IRIB Television (Tehran), 10 December 1992.
24. *'Aqidati* (Cairo), 17 May 1994.
25. Ayatollah Mohammad Emami-Kashani, Voice of the Islamic Republic of Iran, 12 August 1994.
26. *An-Nahar* (Jerusalem), 28 November 1993.
27. "*Statement* made by President Saddam Hussein."
28. *Al-'Iraq*, 22 July 1990.
29. ITV Television (London), 11 November 1990. Each side of the Kuwait War, in other words, had its central organizing conspiracy theory: Iraq purveyed a Kuwait-U.S. plot while the other side had the one about Iraq and its three minions (detailed in chapter 1, "Blurring Perceptions").
30. Radio Baghdad, 17 July 1990. Several months later, Iraqi authorities termed the invasion "a preemptive act designed to avert a sure danger represented by American plans to dispatch U.S. troops to Kuwait and to occupy it" (Ilyas Farah of the Ba'th Party, quoted by the Iraqi News Agency, 19 December 1990).
31. Sawt ash-Sha'b (Baghdad), 2 August 1990.
32. Radio Baghdad, 30 August 1990.
33. *Al-Jumhuriya* (Baghdad), 15 August 1990.
34. Radio Baghdad, 10 August 1990. This became a common, if secondary, theme of Iraqi propaganda. For example, a Baghdad newspaper, *Ath-Thawra,* asserted on 20

May 1994 that Iraq's opponents "are targeting true Islam as expressed by Iraq. They want finally to liquidate Arabism and pan-Arab hopes in a new war of the Franks."

35. *Newsweek*, 9 April 1990; *U.S. News & World Report*, 4 June 1990.

36. *Kayhan*, 18 March 1990.

37. *Ettala'at*, 19 April 1990; 'Ali Akbar Mohtashemi, quoted in Agence France Presse, 28 April 1990.

38. "*Statement* made by President Saddam Hussein." The trouble with lying is that you forget what you said earlier. In an interview almost three months later (*The Wall Street Journal*, 28 June 1990), Saddam Husayn declared that he would accept an American gift of nuclear weapons.

39. *Kayhan* (Tehran), 4 April 1990.

40. *Ash-Sha'b*, 4 September 1990.

41. Iran's Deputy Foreign Minister 'Ali Mohammed Besharati, quoted in *Jomhuri-ye Islami*, 6 August 1990.

42. *The Muslim*, 4 August 1990.

43. *Jomhuri-ye Islami*, 5 April 1990.

44. *Kayhan International*, 4 April 1990.

45. *Jomhuri-ye Islami*, 6 August 1990.

46. *Newsweek*, 28 January 1991.

47. Islamic Revolution News Agency, 22 May 1991.

48. *Ruz al-Yusuf*, 25 December 1995.

49. Ayad Rahim, "Attitudes to the West, Arabs and Fellow Iraqis," in Fran Hazelton, ed., *Iraq Since the Gulf War: Prospects for Democracy* (London: Zed, 1994), p. 179.

50. *As-Safir* (Beirut), 7 April 1992.

51. Quoted in Abdel Magid Farid, *Nasser: The Final Years* (Reading, Eng.: Ithaca Press, 1994), p. 96.

52. Ayatollah Mohammad Emami-Kashani, Voice of the Islamic Republic of Iran, 12 August 1994.

Part II

# THE CONSPIRATOR

The reader may have noted that the case studies repeatedly point to the same two culprits—Jews and Christians, Zionists and imperialists, Israelis and Europeans. The time has come to analyze these two main bogeymen. Part II considers their activities, their interrelations, their characteristics, motives, and methods.

# 6.

# Zionists and Imperialists

Zionism is behind everything [bad] that befalls you.
—*Saddam Husayn*[1]

The British are the greatest enemies of Islam.
—*M. Sıddık Gümüş*[2]

America is behind all our catastrophes.
—*Hizbullah*[3]

Middle Easterners fear two main conspirators, Zionists and imperialists.

In the dictionary, *Zionists* are persons who believe the Jews should have a nation of their own in their historic homeland. In the Middle East vocabulary, however, the word means something quite different—an attempt to "unite the world's Jews under a central leadership and to direct them to work for making Israel the foremost power and the Jews the leading people in the world."[4] The dictionary refers to an overt nationalist movement of modest aspirations; the Middle East transforms this into a covert attempt to rule the world.

The same distinction applies to *imperialists*, conventionally anyone seeking to extend a state's authority by territorial acquisition. In the Arab and Iranian conspiratorial imagination, however, the word is virtually synonymous with Britons and Americans, and it refers to their alleged attempts to take over the world. Rarely does the term refer to other Western peoples, much less to non-Western ones. Seen from the Middle East, Britons and Americans share much: an obsessive hatred of Islam, an ambition to exploit Middle Eastern economic resources, and a joint sponsorship of Israel. Indeed, so closely does the Middle East imagination link Great Britain and the United States, these two sometimes meld into a single entity.

## THEIR POWER

When Mu'ammar al-Qadhdhafi refers to Napoleon's invasion of Egypt as the Ninth Crusade and the establishment of Israel as the Tenth, he makes explicit a parallel that underlies a great deal of Middle Eastern conspiratorial thinking.

## The Zionists

That a Jewish population in Israel of less than 5 million has repeatedly defeated an Arab population 40 or 50 times its size provides the premise for "Zionist" conspiracy theories. If Jews can achieve this remarkable feat, what can they not do?

Jews get accused of causing a large proportion of the Middle East's ills. Some Arab and Iranian accusations—the strength of local Communist parties, the absence of tourists, dominating international sports organizations—are slightly plausible; but most stretch the imagination. How can Israel be held to account for political instability and extremism, violence in public life, the absence of democracy, water problems, infestations of disease, or failures of the Aswan High Dam? Other accusations veer into the preposterous. Israel allegedly caused the depletion of the ozone layer over Arab countries (but presumably not that over Israel). It somehow caused 200,000 Lebanese residents of West Africa to be maltreated. Saddam Husayn charged it with infiltrating propaganda into the school textbooks used in Arab countries.[5] Jews secretly manipulate the opponents in an intra-Muslim conflict; a Pakistani newspaper saw them directing the fighting in the Kuwait War "from both sides—visible on one side, hidden on the other."[6]

Some Middle Eastern conspiracy theorists end up blaming Zionists for every ill in the region. "Anyone who insists on causing harm to people," Saddam Husayn once remarked, "cannot but be linked to Zionism, regardless of where he comes from, and irrespective of his name, be it Arab, foreign, Eastern, or Western."[7] Mu'ammar al-Qadhdhafi also vilified Zionism as a universal abomination and the source of all evil.

Middle Eastern leaders sometimes portray Jews as a threat not merely to them but to all of humanity. They specialize in the abortions of non-Jews and killed Presidents Lincoln, McKinley, and Kennedy. "By their own admission," says Syria's Defense Minister Mustafa Tallas, they assassinated Dag Hammarskjöld.[8] They caused the French and Russian revolutions, and more recently the Soviet collapse. The charter of the fundamentalist Palestinian group, Hamas, provides details:

> The enemies . . . accumulated a huge and influential material wealth which they put to the service of implementing their dream. This wealth [permitted them to] take over control of the world media. . . . they stood behind World War I. . . . They also stood behind World War II. . . . They inspired the establishment of the United Nations and the Security Council to replace the League of Nations, in order to rule the world by their intermediary.[9]

President Asad of Syria sees Zionists as "invaders who are threatening not just the Arab nation but the entire human race."[10] Likewise, senior Palestine Liberation Organization figures portray themselves doing battle on behalf of all humanity. Saddam Husayn declares that "Zionism is behind everything [bad] that befalls you,"[11] Amal, the moderate Shi'i movement in Lebanon, calls Zionism a continuing danger "to the whole of humanity."[12]

These charges against Jews so exceed the plausible, they point not to a way of dealing with the world as it is, but to a mental condition; not to an objective set of conditions but to an imaginary construct. Antony Lerman calls exaggerated accusations of this sort "fictive anti-Zionism," for they bear no relationship to anything actually in existence. Rather, they serve as a crutch to fulfill the speaker's psychological needs.[13] Robert S. Wistrich concludes that for the Muslim Brethren in Egypt, "Of all the myriad enemies of Islam (the crusading West, Communism, secularism), Jewry represents the ultimate abomination, evil in its purest ontological form";[14] and the same applies for many other Muslims.

In the end, if every party accused of abetting the Zionists actually did so, there would be no one left to oppose Israel.

## The Imperialists

Others ascribe all problems to the imperialists. The Iranian historian Sheykh al-Islami writes that

> The imperial powers interfered in everything, even the personal affairs of leading statesmen. Britain and the United States are over-

whelmingly the most important imperialist states, but before telling
about them, it bears note that when others are perceived as threatening, they fit the same roles. Absolutely nothing could be done without
their permission.[15]

During World War I, the German case also fit this pattern:

> In the bazaars [of Istanbul], where there was a grave meat shortage,
> it was whispered that this was because, on Berlin's orders, all supplies
> were being sent to Germany. Indeed, very soon almost everything
> that went wrong was being blamed on the Germans.[16]

We concentrate on Iranian views of the British and American conspirators,
for Iranians most elaborately developed this myth.

*The United Kingdom.*    "Perhaps the most bitter memories of our
country and the Islamic world in the past century have been due to the
various actions and plots hatched by Britain."[17] Iranians commonly believe
the British government manipulated all their major institutions, including
those associated with the Islamic faith, in its effort to control the country.
London is ascribed a "nasty catalogue" of "crimes against Islam and the
Muslim people of Iran,"[18] most of which would come as a complete surprise
to Britons. To create dissension among eighteenth-century Muslims, it
foisted the Wahhabi doctrines on the House of Saud and helped the Saudis
expand their desert empire. In the nineteenth century, it conjured up the
Baha'i religion to confuse Shi'i Muslims and set them to fighting each
other. In the twentieth century, it foisted the 1905 Constitutional Revolution and liberalism on unsuspecting Iranians. Other links in the "chain of
crimes" included: destroying the Ottoman Empire; inciting Iran's enemies
to bite away portions of its territory; fomenting the Constitutional Revolution of 1905-06; stealing Iranian oil; and placing the Pahlavi dynasty on
the throne. At various times, London stage-managed the mullahs, the
Russians, the Qajar dynasty, the Tudeh Party, the Feda'iyan-e Islam,
Mossadeq, and Khomeini. Hoseyn Malek, a follower of Mosaddeq and the
National Front, goes so far as to deem Islam an "Arab ideology." Why?
Because the English controlled the Arab world, and this made Islam a tool
of London's.[19]

   In Iranian eyes, historian Richard Cottam, observes, "No conspiracy
was too elaborate, too intricate, and too demanding in terms of orchestra-
tion to be impossible for the British."[20] Hyperbolic fear about the British

extended from the most humble rural dwelling to the palace. "If a poor woman in Khurasan found a dangerous snake one morning in her kitchen, she would as likely as not think the English had planted it there."[21] At the other extreme, Reza Pahlavi (as remembered by his son) "regularly accused his opponents of being tools of foreigners, especially of the British."[22]

A Middle Easterner's particular phobia often betrays his age: those born before 1935 tend to be more worried about Great Britain, those born after that date focus on the United States. Their views are very similar; what differs is the specific identity of the conspirator.

*The United States.* Whatever Washington does is automatically suspect, whether taking a stand against Khomeini or making overtures to him. (The latter are a trick "to lull the mullahs into a sense of security while it planned new attempts to unsettle the regime.") Both leftists and conservatives are American agents. According to Abol Hassan Bani Sadr, Khomeini's one-time ally and Iran's first president, Americans so thoroughly infiltrated the key institutions of the shah's state that they "knew all about our army, even those things the shah did not."[23] If the identities of those killed in the April 1983 bombing of the U.S. embassy in Beirut were not instantly made available, the reason had to be that Washington purposely kept silent "so that their anonymous deaths can be mourned longer and patriotic feelings . . . can be led and excited . . . by the gangs governing American politics."[24] When a monarchist group in exile, Azadegan, succeeded in boarding an Iranian patrol boat of the coast of Spain and hijacking it, the Foreign Ministry announced that "following an investigation, the hands of the CIA became obvious in the recent piracy."[25] More broadly, the Americans sought to control Iran by dominating its neighbors, a process some saw completed by the war against Iraq in early 1991.

Iranian media blame the "bloodthirsty hyena" in Washington for all Iran's tribulations. Restricting himself to just the recent era, 'Ali Akbar Mohtashemi, a leading hard-liner in the Islamic Republic, comes up with the following litany:

> World-devouring America was the one who plundered Iran's oil and other resources for over thirty years, who imposed capitulations on Iran, on whose orders the 5 June 1963 massacre took place, and who shed the blood of hundreds of this country's children during the fifteen years after the imam [Khomeini] was exiled to Turkey and Iraq and then during the revolution. America was the one who, after

the victory of the revolution, organized the incidents in Kordestan and Azerbaijan, the operation by small groups, the direct attack on Tabas [in April 1980], the Nowzheh coup attempt, the imposed war [with Iraq], the intervention by its warships in the Persian Gulf, the downing of the [Iran Air] airbus and the martyrdom of 290 of its defenseless passengers, the dispatching and using of spies, and dozens of other efforts to overthrow the Islamic Republic.[26]

In brief, Mohtashemi blames every piece of bad news on the United States: "All the afflictions of Islam, the Muslims, and the nation of Iran come from the Great Satan, criminal America."[27] This happens also to be the official viewpoint, as Foreign Minister 'Ali Akbar Velayati explained: "any problem that is now being faced by Muslims, be it in Bosnia, Palestine, Lebanon, or Iran, has been caused by the United States."[28] The street too shared this fear. Marking the fourteenth anniversary of the Islamic Revolution in Iran, a mob called the United States "the main culprit behind all crimes and ploys against Muslims and world Islamic movements."[29] An Iranian youth put it more succinctly: "America controls everything."[30]

Everything includes internal matters, of course. The U.S. government came up with the idea for Iran to have a single-party system in 1963. When the presidential campaign of 1980 attracted a field of 124 candidates, the Students Following the Imam's Line discerned in this profusion a Zionist and imperialist conspiracy "to destroy the nation from within." Musavi Kho'ini described the situation as "an American inspired plot . . . intended to subvert Iran's revolutionary dignity."[31] When squatters rioted in Mashhad to protest the razing of their houses, the government ascribed the violence to American efforts to destroy Iranian relations with Central Asia.

CIA conspiracies reach down into the very most mundane areas of daily life. It stands behind Iranian marital spats, at least when one spouse is an American.[32] It permeates the school system: "Anything that stands between the [university] student and the degree is a plot."[33] Khomeini blamed Tehran's high drug consumption on a superpower scheme, reasoning that "a heroin addict cannot think about politics" and would be useless in time of military invasion.[34] At a time when the Iranian currency was dropping, President Rafsanjani blamed the problem on moneychangers, saying that "They have acted in full harmony and synchronized their actions with the trade ban of the United States and the actions of the Israelis."[35] Nor is traffic immune from the CIA's machinations:

A Teheran taxi driver explained that he thought the city's notorious traffic jams were the handiwork of American agents. "They get people to do unnecessary things and make the drivers frustrated and lose their temper," he said. When shopkeepers complained that itinerant vendors were setting up tables in front of their stores and demanded their removal, there were allegations that the Central Intelligence Agency was behind the frictions.[36]

In brief, Iranians see virtually every aspect of life in their country dictated by a foreign master, an outlook leaving precious little scope for Iranian initiative.

The United States looms very large for others in the Middle East beside Iranians. South Yemen's President Salim Ruba'i 'Ali told a visiting American in 1974, claiming to report on the views of his countrymen, that "All suffering, all damage caused by subversives, is really the work of the United States government."[37] Twenty years later, when civil war broke out in Yemen, editorials were quick to blame Washington: "The concealed U.S. hands, and the United States's flagrant involvement in fomenting the Yemeni war, have now begun to appear."[38] Egyptian fundamentalists echoed this theme and more explicitly put the blame on the Saudis: "The conspiratorial role played by Saudi Arabia against fraternal Yemen is part of an orchestrated campaign led by the United States and carried out by its agents in the region."[39] The same goes for Lebanon. According to the Hizbullah's leader, "all the political, financial, economic, and security complications in Lebanon are American ones."[40]

Mu'ammar al-Qadhdhafi of Libya captures this spirit with his usual flamboyance: "America is now fixing the price of bread in the Arab countries through the World Bank. . . . Who is fixing the value of your currencies? America." He goes on to advise Arabs not even to aspire to independence: "Never mind about saying who will rule and who will be foreign minister and who will be minister of the economy—this is a foregone conclusion. No person can form a government unless he consults the American Embassy."[41]

In a perverse testimony to imperialist power, both sides to a conflict sometimes finger the same party as the conspirator behind the other side's aggression. The outstanding case must be the Iraq-Iran war, when for eight years leaders in two capitals looked beyond the immediate enemy and saw, in almost the same terms, Washington's nefarious influence. On a lesser scale, the war in Bosnia inspired Muslims and Serbs alike again to blame the U.S.

government. Nateq-Nuri spoke for many when he asked, "Is not the hand of America evident in the massacre in the Balkans and Bosnia-Herzegovina and in support of the Serbs? Is not the hand of America evident in the amount of time wasted by international organizations?"[42] Bosnian Serbs saw an identical United Nations and CIA plot arrayed against them.

## THE "NEW WORLD ORDER"

George Bush first used the phrase "new world order" in 1990 in the course of rallying friendly states against Iraq; he then used it a second time in the context of an appeal to the United Nations to ban select chemical weapons. But it never amounted to more than a dimly conceived, anodyne notion about politics after the cold war, lacking operational importance, and was quickly forgotten by most Americans.[43] In the Middle East, however, the phrase was widely understood as signaling a plan for "the United States, master of the new world,"[44] to establish hegemony over the entire globe. Whole books[45] are devoted to understanding its ominous and programmatic connotations.

A Damascus newspaper declares that World War III is already underway and that it will continue until "every U.S. ministry becomes a ministry of the whole world."[46] Ahmad al-Banna, leader of the Egyptian Muslim Brethren, sees "a plan to impose a single civilization on the entire world."[47] Libya's quirky Qadhdhafi goes a step further, seeing Islam as just one of several religions to be dominated: "The New World Order means that Jews and Christians control Muslims and if they can, they will after that dominate Confucianism and other religions in India, China, and Japan."[48] In all, as Qadhdhafi's news agency puts it, the New World Order will achieve "the American dream of Americanizing the world."[49]

The regimes in Iran and Iraq disagree on just about everything—except their fear of an American order. Iran's Ahmad Khomeini (son of the late ayatollah) says Americans are establishing a "mastery and domination over the world."[50] Using almost identical language, Iraq's Ramadan accuses Americans of seeking to impose a "unilateral U.S. hegemony over the world."[51]

Middle Easterners proffer three main explanations for why Washington seeks world hegemony. Predictably, perhaps, fundamentalist Muslims discern hatred of Islam as the key motive. For the Muslim Brethren, "The New World Order simply aims at crushing Islam and its people in the Islamic world, in fact in the entire world."[52] This enmity results from a mix of a Jewish plan for a Greater Israel and a Christian "spirit of the Crusades."[53]

Nationalists stress colonialist motives. According to the Libyans, the Central Intelligence Agency is putting together "a world dictatorial police system under the control of the United States where freedom, justice, and democracy have no worth and where colonialism will be restored."[54] A Jordanian newspaper reports from an alleged National Security Council Document (No. 2,000) that the U.S. government, in effect, has plans to turn "Arabs and Muslims into the new Red Indians under the hegemony of the New World Order."[55]

Oil potentates fear American lust for Middle Eastern petroleum resources. Baghdad media reports that Washington dreams of "securing complete and total control over the Arabian Gulf oil fields and rearranging the international scene without any obstruction or real crises."[56]

These three themes — anti-Islam, colonialism, and oil avarice — recur when Middle Easterners look at specific cases.

*Somalia.* Americans may think their troops went to Somalia in 1992 to save lives in that forlorn country, but Middle Easterners suspected a far more menacing purpose. A Jordanian newspaper saw mass starvation as a new U.S. "scheme aimed at creating further tension" to justify "the dispatch of its war machine."[57] Iraqi media accused the U.S. government of having "exploited the Somali people's tragedy"[58] in Somalia and giving American soldiers "a license to kill at will."[59] The People's Arab and Islamic Congress, a fundamentalist group, claimed the U.S. purpose was not feeding people but just the reverse: "genocide" against the Somali people.[60]

Many groups and governments accused Washington of establishing a new colonialism in Somalia. They differed only in the extent of their fears. The Iraqi news service portrayed an American entry "through the gate of death and starvation" leading to control over Somalia.[61] A Beirut newspaper saw the tragedy as an "excuse to intervene to reshape the political situation in the Horn of Africa and the entire center of Africa."[62] Lebanon's fundamentalist organization Hizbullah went further, seeing a global menace. "On the pretext of providing food aid and achieving peace, the United States is conducting a new colonial policy in a world approaching the twenty-first century, using UN institutions for the plan."[63]

Others smelled oil. Somalia being in the general vicinity of the Persian Gulf suffices for the Jordanian news agency to call Somalia an "important strategic region"[64] and for Iranian radio to refer to its "strategic location."[65] Likewise, the editors of a Palestinian newspaper in Jerusalem concluded that the Somalia expedition's objective was to tighten an American "grip over Arab oil."[66] As usual, Qadhdhafi went further and announced that "America knew that there was oil in Somalia" and so, "to serve Israel's interests," rushed in to exploit it before Arabs could.[67]

*Cairo population conference.*    The United Nations' International Conference on Population and Development held in Cairo in September 1994 aroused strong reactions among Muslims who saw it as a stage for the West to weaken Islam by undercutting Muslim birth rates. 'Adil Husayn, a leading Egyptian fundamentalist polemicist, argued that the West's promotion of birth control "is not aimed at developing the poor world. It is a racist plan designed to continue looting and weakening us in favor of the dominating white race. . . . The conference is the culmination of a scheme aimed at annihilating mankind and Muslims."[68]

A spokesman for the Muslim Brethren read much meaning into the conference locale: "It is no coincidence that they chose Cairo, the heart of Islam, to unleash this attack. . . . An attempt is underway to change the world, starting with an attack on Islam."[69] According to a Cairene newspaper, the roots of this conference went back to a CIA-funded study of 1989, which noted the threat of Arab population growth to Israel and emphasized the need to put a stop to it. The Jewish lobby then struck a deal with Bill Clinton: it would support his presidential candidacy if he promised to organize an international conference calling for limits on the population growth of Arabs and Muslims — under the cover of dealing with the Third World in general so as to hide his real motives.[70]

Others took the Third World dimension seriously. A Muslim Brethren spokesman saw the conference related to the West's "sole concern . . . to halt the growth of the Third World countries."[71] Jordan's Islamic Action Front read the conference aims as "perpetuating the colonialist and expansionist lust of pillaging the wealth of the Third World."[72] Some analysts went beyond the issue of birth rates to see a looming apocalypse. If the conference succeeded, an Iraqi daily stated, the West would destroy the Muslim world "by flaring wars and crises, causing famines, spreading fatal epidemics, disintegrating the family system, and encouraging the collapse of social values."[73] In a similar spirit, 'Adil Husayn wrote that the final goal of the conference was "annihilating mankind."[74]

## MULTIPLE ENEMIES

Within their agreement on Zionists and imperialists being the main enemies, Middle Easterners still have plenty of room for disagreement. Did a Zionist or an imperialist carry out a particular crime? If an imperialist, which nationality? For what reason? Because each conspiracy theorist typically sees himself as the intended victim (on which, see chapter 13, "The Conspirator Always Gains"), he usually offers an explanation that dwells on himself. Victimization leads to the odd situation in which several parties concur on a plot, sometimes even on the culprit's identity, but disagree on who the intended target might be.

This can lead to surprising results, For example, mutual enemies are held responsible for the same problem. The 1948-49 and 1967 Arab losses to Israel prompted accusations against both the Western powers (for helping Israel) and against the Soviet Union (for supplying the Arabs with shoddy weapons). In addition, conspiracy theorists blamed Middle Eastern Jews (for serving as a fifth column) and God himself (for caprice). Five episodes in recent history show the full extent to which Arabs and Iranians find a multitude of conspirators.

***Musa as-Sadr.*** The August 1979 disappearance in Libya of the Lebanese Shi'i leader Musa as-Sadr stirred up a wide number of conspiracy theories, many of them mutually contradictory.

> Saudi authorities: Qadhdhafi did it.
>
> Iranian authorities: Qadhdhafi did it; but when subsequently Tehran allied with Libya, it changed to accusing Zbigniew Brzezinski, Jimmy Carter's advisor, of masterminding a plot.
>
> Anti-Khomeini politicians (such as Shahpour Bakhtiar of Iran and the Iraqi government): Ayatollah Khomeini killed Sadr, his own relative and disciple, because Sadr rivaled Khomeini as leader of the Shi'a.
>
> Hizbullah: Imperialists killed Sadr, fearing he would turn Lebanon into a truly independent state.
>
> Libyan authorities: (1) Iranian and American intelligence, (2) German terrorist organizations, (3) the Italian intelligence and the Red Brigades together, (4) Zionists and imperialists jointly plotting to harm Libyan relations with Iran, (5) Iranian revolutionaries, or (6) Yasir 'Arafat.
>
> Pro-Qadhdhafi Middle Easterners: An amorphous conspiracy intent on harming Sunni-Shi'i relations, distracting attention from the Camp David Accords, and harming the Palestinians by weakening their truest ally.

To this fearsome brew, Musa as-Sadr's own organization replied with simple dignity: "Imam Sadr was the victim of an Arab conspiracy and is still in Arab hands."[75]

*Lebanese civil war.*    Lebanon's civil war unleashed many and contradictory accusations as Lebanese sought to find foreigners to blame for their predicament.

> Their explanations [writes the journalist Thomas Friedman] for why someone was killed or why a certain battle broke out were usually the most implausible, wild-eyed conspiracy theories one could imagine. These conspiracies, as the Lebanese painted them, featured either the Israelis, the Syrians, the Americans, the Soviets, or Henry Kissinger—anyone but the Lebanese—in the most elaborate plots to disrupt Lebanon's naturally tranquil state.[76]

Here follows a partial listing of foreign scapegoats for the fighting:

> Maronite views: (1) A Syrian plot to rule all of Lebanon. (2) a Palestinian plot to militarize Lebanon for use against Israel, with the Libyans, Soviets, and Iranians also suspect. (3) An American plot to empty Lebanon, turning it into an "alternative" country.[77]

> Shi'is: "an American decision not to leave a trace of Islam in Lebanon."[78]

> A Greek Catholic figure: Henry Kissinger sent a letter to the French in 1976 in which he wrote that "there would be no peace in Lebanon until all the political leaders were killed."[79]

> A Palestinian intellectual: (1) "[R]egional and world powers" permit the militias to bomb civilians. (2) Arms merchants use the Lebanese as "the guinea pigs on whom new weapons are being tried out and obsolete ones used up lest they go to waste." (3) Great powers and arms merchants twirled into a single grand conspiracy, with the former "allowing, or even encouraging, the endless supply of weapons and armaments" flooding into Lebanon.[80]

But most Lebanese blamed Israel. Interestingly, their explanations all differed:

> Walid Junbalat, the Druze leader: Israelis supplied arms to all factions in Lebanon, hoping these would "fight and destroy each other."[81]

Raymond Eddé, a Maronite leader friendly to the PLO: Israel, helped by the CIA, destroyed the Lebanese model of multisectarianism within one country, thereby reducing the pressures on it to accept a "secular democratic" Palestine.

PLO: Israel plotted to weaken Palestinian legitimacy, thereby excluding the PLO from diplomacy.

Hafiz al-Asad, president of Syria: The Israelis developed a plot "against Islam and Arabism."[82]

Egypt's Muslim Brethren: Israelis sought a Christian state that could gather in all the Christians of the Middle East; they would fight Islam and humiliate the Muslims.

Iranian government: Israelis wanted to disrupt Lebanese life; "statistics show that whenever internal clashes between Lebanese Islamic groups become less frequent, or cease completely, the number of Zionist attacks increases."[83]

*Ta'if accord.*    When Lebanese legislators, meeting in the Saudi city of Ta'if in late 1989, rewrote the Lebanese constitution, conspiracy theorists from all points on the Lebanese political spectrum blamed the decision on an outside faction. Here are five voices: Walid Junbalat ascribed the success to Riyadh's purchasing votes for $1 billion.[84] Michel 'Awn called it an "American plot" against the Lebanese to "give up their country"; he also charged the Syrians of a conspiracy to take over Lebanon.[85] Damascus replied by accusing 'Awn of carrying out a "Zionist scheme" to control the country.[86] Hizbullah, the pro-Iranian party, agreed with Damascus and called the Ta'if meeting a conspiracy to "bolster Israel's presence in Lebanon."[87] Sa'id Sha'ban, a fundamentalist Sunni leader, ascribed the accord to "an American plot . . . to waste fifteen years of steadfastness by Lebanese Muslims and the war they waged to achieve majority rule."[88] As usual, each actor read his own fears into the Ta'if accord and saw himself as the target of the conspirator's plans.

*Salah Khalaf.*    On 14 January 1991, just two days before the Kuwait war began, the PLO leader Salah Khalaf (who went by the *nom de guerre* Abu Iyad) was assassinated. Everyone agreed on two facts: Hamza Abu Zayd, a member of his own bodyguard, had carried out the murder; and Abu Zayd had previously been a member of Abu Nidal's gang, known as the Fat'h Revolutionary Council. But who had prompted Abu Zayd to carry out the execution and what were his motives?

Analysts fingered several culprits. (1) Israel: The Mossad had infiltrated Abu Nidal's group and were "manipulating" Abu Zayd.[89] (2) Iraq: Khalaf had become Saddam's most prominent Palestinian critic, so the Iraqi dictator called on Iraq's Palestinian agents to dispose of him. Or, more Machiavellian, Saddam killed Khalaf to increase Palestinian suspicion of Israel (for the operation resembled the Abu Jihad assassination of 1988, universally ascribed to Israel). (3) Yasir 'Arafat: The PLO chairman murdered his trusted lieutenant of four decades, Kuwaiti media hypothesized, because Khalaf decided to dissolve the PLO terrorist apparatus.[90] (4) Both 'Arafat and Israel: Syria's Defense Minister Mustafa Tallas maintained his reputation as a man of unusual imagination by blaming Khalaf's demise on both these parties. 'Arafat plotted the assassination with the Mossad because he wanted "to escape from Baghdad" before the 15 January 1991 war deadline; Khalaf's funeral in Tunis provided him a perfect pretext to get out.[91]

*World Trade Center.*    A New York court of law found a gang of six Middle Easterners guilty of bombing the World Trade Center in February 1993. For whom, Middle Easterners debated, did they work? One faction contended that "'Umar 'Abd ar-Rahman, their spiritual leader, was a CIA agent"[92] who served his master well by discrediting Islam. Another faction pointed to Israeli intelligence: The mother of prime culprit Muhammad Salama told a reporter: "The Jews. This is from the Jews, who have done this and blamed my son."[93] Salama's father expanded on the same theme, explaining that Israeli agents bombed the building to make Arabs and Muslims look bad. The Muslim Brethren in Jordan agreed: regardless of Salama's passport or his place of birth, "we believe the hands of Zionist agents were behind the bombing."[94] But Hasan at-Turabi, the Khomeini of the Sudan, contended that an "Egyptian agent" working for the U.S. Department of Justice framed the five Sudanese nationals connected to this and another New York bombing conspiracy.[95]

Conspiratorial explanations pile up higher and higher, the one at odds with the other, and nobody seems to notice the inherent contradictions. But if conspiracy theorists are open to so many potential enemies, why do they so often limit themselves to Zionists and imperialists?

## NOTES TO CHAPTER 6

1. Republic of Iraq Radio, 4 May 1993.
2. M. Sıddık Gümüş, *British Enmity Against Islam*, 3rd ed. (Istanbul: Hakikat Kitabevi, 1993), p. 104.
3. *Ar-Risala al-Maftuha Allati Wajjaha Hizbullah ila al-Mustad'afin fi Lubnan wa'l-'Alam.* English text in Augustus Richard Norton, *Amal and the Shi'a: Struggle for the Soul of Lebanon* (Austin: University of Texas Press, 1987), pp. 105, 170.
4. *The Pakistan Times*, 4 February 1991.
5. Iraqi News Agency, 26 June 1990.
6. *The Pakistan Times*, 4 February 1991.
7. Republic of Iraq Radio, 4 May 1993.
8. *Ash-Sharq al-Awsat*, 4 December 1995.
9. Article 22, quoted in Bernard Reich, ed., *Arab-Israeli Conflict and Conciliation: A Documentary History* (Westport, Conn.: Praeger, 1995), pp. 208-09.
10. Radio Damascus, 2 August 1973.
11. Republic of Iraq Radio, 4 May 1993.
12. Charter of the Amal Movement. English text in Norton, *Amal and the Shi'a*, p. 146.
13. Antony Lerman, "Fictive Anti-Zionism: Third World, Arab and Muslim Variations," in Robert S. Wistrich, ed., *Anti-Zionism and Antisemitism in the Contemporary World* (New York: New York University Press, 1990), pp. 121-22. Lerman provides (pp. 127-36) many examples of Middle Eastern reliance on conspiracy theories about Zionism.
14. Robert S. Wistrich, *Antisemitism: The Longest Hatred* (New York: Pantheon, 1991), p. 228.
15. *Ettela'at Siyasi va Eqtesadi* 35 (Mar.-Apr. 1990): 5. Quoted in Ervand Abrahamian, *Khomeinism: Essays on the Islamic Republic* (Berkeley: University of California Press, 1993), p.117.
16. Peter Hopkirk, *Like Hidden Fire: The Plot to Bring Down the British Empire* (New York: Kodansha International, 1994), p. 128
17. *Kayhan Hava'i*, 8 July 1992.
18. *Kayhan International*, 3 October 1990. For an overview of the British specter in the Iranian psyche, see Ahmad Ashraf, "Conspiracy Theories," *Encyclopedia Iranica*, especially the long section entitled "Conspiratorial schemata focused on the British."
19. Hoseyn Malek, *Nabard-e Pruzheh-ha-ye Siyasi dar Sahneh-e Iran* (n.p., 1982). Quoted in Abrahamian, *Khomeinism*, p.126.
20. Richard W. Cottam, *Iran and the United States: A Cold War Case Study* (Pittsburgh: University of Pittsburgh Press, 1988), pp. 41-42, 59.
21. Peter Avery, *Modern Iran* (London: Ernest Benn, 1965), p. 107.
22. Mohammed Reza Pahlavi, *Mission for My Country* (London: Hutchinson, 1961), p. 65.
23. Abol Hassan Bani Sadr, with Jean-Charles Deniau, *Le Complot des ayatollahs* (Paris: Éditions la Découverte, 1989), p. 116.

24. Radio Tehran, 19 April 1983.

25. Radio Tehran, 15 August 1981.

26. *Kayhan* (Tehran), 29 April 1990.

27. *Resalat,* 26 January 1991. Mohtashemi then provides a listing of American crimes from 1963 on.

28. Voice of the Islamic Republic of Iran, 21 June 1995.

29. Islamic Revolution News Agency, 11 February 1993.

30. Quoted in Tony Horwitz, *Baghdad Without A Map and Other Misadventures in Arabia* (New York: Dutton, 1991), p. 249.

31. Radio Tehran, 11 January 1980; *Tehran Times,* 12 January 1980. Both quoted in *Middle East Contemporary Survey, 1979-80,* p. 447.

32. Betty Mahmoody with William Hoffer, *Not Without My Daughter* (London: Corgi, 1989), pp. 173, 195, 267, 357.

33. William H. Forbis, *Fall of the Peacock Throne: The Story of Iran* (New York: McGraw-Hill, 1981), p. 196.

34. *The New York Times,* 6 January 1980.

35. *The New York Times,* 16 May 1995.

36. *The New York Times,* 6 January 1980.

37. Quoted in Paul Findley, *They Dare to Speak Out: People and Institutions Confront Israel's Lobby,* revised edition (Chicago: Lawrence Hill, 1989), p. 8.

38. *Akhbar al-Usbu',* 2 June 1994.

39. *Ash-Sha'b* (Cairo), 17 June 1994.

40. Muhammad Fadlallah, Sawt al-Mustad'afin (Lebanon), 15 August 1992.

41. Libyan Television, 29 July 1995.

42. Voice of the Islamic Republic of Iran, 8 August 1993.

43. But not all: for the right-wing conspiratorial fringe, the "new world order" is no less real and terrifying than for Middle Easterners. Curiously, these two groups understand the term in exactly opposite terms: to American conspiracy theorists "new world order" means a foreign takeover of the United States; to Arabs and Iranians, it means a U.S. takeover of the world.

44. *An-Nahar* (Jerusalem), 8 March 1995.

45. For example, Salah Waqi', *Al-Mu'amara wa'n-Nizam al-'Alami al-Jadid* (London: Dar ar-Rafid, 1994).

46. *Al-Ba'th* (Damascus), 22 June 1992.

47. *Correire della Sera,* 29 August 1994.

48. Great Jamahiriya Radio, 13 March 1994.

49. Jamahiriya News Agency, 29 April 1995.

50. Voice of the Islamic Republic, 3 February 1992.

51. *Akhir Khabar* (Amman), 20-21 September 1994.

52. Sawt Suriya al-'Arabiya (Baghdad), 22 February 1994.

53. Quoted in Sylvia Haim, "Sayyid Qutb," *Asian and African Studies* 16 (1982), pp. 154-55.

54. Jamahiriya Arab News Agency, 18 May 1994.

55. *Ad-Dustur* (Amman), 1 September 1994.
56. *Al-Jumhuriya* (Baghdad), 2 August 1994.
57. *Sawt ash-Sha'b*, 9 December 1992.
58. Iraqi News Agency, 10 December 1992.
59. *Ath-Thawra* (Baghdad), 17 June 1993.
60. Sudanese News Agency, 13 June 1993.
61. Iraqi News Agency, 10 December 1992.
62. *As-Safir*, 3 December 1992. And if Somalia appears to be an unlikely place for Americans to take over, the Libyan Great Jamahiriya Radio Network reported on 30 April 1994 an even less likely one: Rwanda, where the Western states had fabricated problems "with the aim of military intervention" there.
63. Sawt al-Mustad'afin (Lebanon), 15 June 1993.
64. Petra, 9 December 1992.
65. Voice of the Islamic Republic of Iran, 9 December 1992.
66. *Al-Quds*, 4 December 1992.
67. Libyan Television, 6 April 1995. In fact, no oil had been found in Somalia.
68. *Ash-Sha'b*, 12 August 1995.
69. Ma'mun al-Hudhaybi in *La Repubblica*, 7 September 1994.
70. *Al-Ahrar* (Cairo), 14 August 1994.
71. Hudhaybi in *La Repubblica*.
72. *Jordan Times*, 30 August 1994.
73. *Babil*, 28 August 1994.
74. *Ash-Sha'b* (Cairo), 26 August 1994. A year later, these same writers responded with almost exactly the same words about the U.N. World Conference on Women held in Peking. 'Adil Husayn, for example, saw in it a "strategy of controlling population increase among non-white nations, notably Islamic nations" (*Ash-Sha'b*, 18 August 1995).
75. Muhammad Mahdi Shams ad-Din, quoted in Peter Theroux, *The Strange Disappearance of Imam Moussa Sadr* (London: Weidenfeld and Nicolson, 1987), p. 92.
76. Thomas L. Friedman, *From Beirut to Jerusalem* (New York: Farrar Straus Giroux, 1989), p. 36.
77. Antun Khuwayri, *Al-Harb fi Lubnan*, part 3 (Junya: Dar al-Abjadiya, 1977), p. 933.
78. Subhi at-Tufayli on Sawt al-Mustad'afin, 15 January 1989.
79. Quoted in Charles Glass, *Tribes with Flags: A Dangerous Passage Through the Chaos of the Middle East* (New York: Atlantic Monthly Press, 1990), p. 433.
80. Jean Said Makdisi, *Beirut Fragments: A War Memoir* (New York: Persea Books, 1990), pp. 218, 231, 243.
81. Sawt al-Jabal, 5 July 1990.
82. Radio Damascus, 20 July 1976.
83. Radio Tehran, 9 July 1990.
84. *Le Figaro*, 23 October 1989.
85. *Le Figaro*, 25 October 1989; Radio Free Lebanon, 17 October 1989.
86. Radio Damascus, 13 October 1989.

87. Sawt al-Mustad'afin (Baalbek), 25 October 1989.

88. Radio Tehran International, 8 October 1989.

89. Agence France Presse, 15 January 1991.

90. *Sawt al-Kuwait*, 21 June 1991.

91. *Al-Akhbar al-Yawm*, 26 January 1991.

92. *Al-Jumhuriya*, 8 July 1993.

93. *The New York Times*, 8 March 1993. Curiously, the same page and column of the *Times* contains a quote from a man from Salama's home village of Biddiya, on the West Bank, who offered a nearly opposite explanation: "if anything like this happens, America should realize that it's because of its relations with Israel."

94. Hamza Mansur of the Muslim Brethren, *Jordan Times*, 7 March 1993.

95. Quoted in Judith Miller, "Faces of Fundamentalism: Hassan al-Turabi and Muhammed Fadlallah," *Foreign Affairs*, November/December 1994, p. 134.

# 7.

# Why Only Zionists and Imperialists?

> In the twilight world of popular myths and images,
> the West is the source of all evil.
> — *Bernard Lewis*[1]

The Bank of Credit and Commerce International (BCCI) was founded by an ostentatiously pious Pakistani, Aga Hassan Abedi. Muslims dominated its staff, and Urdu, the national language of Pakistan, served as its primary language. The bank made much of advancing Third World development. Seen by all as a Muslim institution, BCCI represented Pakistani power and Muslim aspirations.

So, when Western banking authorities shut down BCCI in July 1991, citing rampant corruption and a Ponzi-scheme method of operations, Pakistanis suspected darker motives. Jashed Omar, the head of a construction company, believed the bank "was a threat to some powerful people outside this country, and it was singled out unfairly."[2] Some smelled a plot to "drive the Pakistani bankers from international banking."[3] But who were those "powerful people"? Japanese bankers who disposed of far more capital than their American counterparts? Hindu Indians long in conflict with Pakistan? Communists taking revenge for Pakistan's role in Afghanistan? A Vatican eager to discredit Muslim financiers?

Not for a minute. The suspects fell into two and only two categories: Zionists and imperialists. The chief minister of Sindh, Jam Sadiq 'Ali, offered up classic anti-Semitic language when he portrayed BCCI as a challenge to "the hegemonistic control of the Jewish lobby on the world's financial institutions."[4] Others fingered imperialists. Mohammed Salim, a Pakistani garment exporter and BCCI customer, suggested that the bank's success "provoked the jealousy of the West."[5] The imperialists first destroyed Middle East military power in its war on Saddam Husayn, then went on to wreck its economic power by closing BCCI. Others yet saw both Zionists and imperialists behind the crackdown. Pakistan's *Daily News* blamed "Jewish pressure" for the U.S. crackdown,[6] while *Newsline* pointed to "America's Jewish-controlled financial and media circles."[7]

As this illustration shows, Jews and imperialists so dominate the Middle Eastern imagination that they leave other little scope to other potential conspirators, whether Communist, religious, or nationalist. Rome, Moscow, New Delhi, and Tokyo virtually disappear. Fellow Muslims have a minute role, being seen mainly as dupes of the West. More accurately, these other potential conspirators come into view only when they ally with one of the two archplotters. Why is this the case and what does it tell about the Middle East?

## COMMUNIST ASSISTANTS

The Union of Soviet Socialist Republics, the one force that plausibly mounted a genuine grand conspiracy in the half century after 1940, hardly worried Arabs and Iranians; they had no inordinate fear of Communism. In Egypt, for example, the last student demonstration of an anti-Soviet cast took place in 1943. If anything, Middle Easterners worried more about post-Soviet Russia, which might join forces with the United States and thereby make Western efforts at global domination closer at hand. Indeed, to the extent that Arabs and Iranians did worry about Moscow, it almost always concerned Soviet collusion with Zionists and imperialists. Communists threatened only when helping one, the other, or both of these main conspirators.

### Helping Zionists

During the 1920s, extreme right-wingers in the West tended to portray Moscow as a tool of other groups, usually of bankers or Jews. Some saw the Russian Revolution as a joint Jewish-German conspiracy, others as a Jewish-Jesuit effort. Echoing these views, Muslims, especially fundamentalists, sometimes see Communism as a Zionist plot. An Egyptian daily maintains that "only the U.S.S.R. has derived benefit" from the establishment of Israel.[8] The Muslim Brethren of Egypt understood Gamal Abdel Nasser's close relations with the Soviet Union as his way of serving Israel. More accurately, fundamentalists noted that Jews founded the Communist parties in many Muslim countries. Less accurately, they accused Communist parties in the Arab countries of taking orders from their Israeli counterpart.

Conspiracy theorists took the Zionist-Communist link in imaginative directions. Some drew a parallel between Marx's socialism and Herzl's Zionism, portraying both as mechanisms to solve Europe's Jewish problem. Exponents of this thesis played up Marx's Jewish origins; as one writer put it (letting his enthusiasm overwhelm historical accuracy), "Mordechai Karl Marx, as well as Lenin, Stalin, and Beria, were all Jews."[9] Several Communist leaders worked for the Elders of Zion. Jews placed Tito of Yugoslavia in power and ran him as "a puppet of world Zionism."[10] One commentator dubbed Mikhail Gorbachev a "faithful servant of Zionism and Israel."[11]

King Faysal of Saudi Arabia (1906-75) stood out as the premier exponent of these notions, having perhaps picked them up during his European travels after World War I. In keeping with *The Protocols*, Faysal saw Communism as a Jewish invention intended to further Zionist power. He found evidence for this thesis in arcane and dubious bits of information, claiming, for example, that Leonid Brezhnev's first name derives from *Leon*, a Jewish name, so he had to be Jewish. (In fact, it does not and he was not.) Why, then, did the Soviet Union side with the Arabs against Israel? "They are only pretending to work against each other," came Faysal's reply.[12]

Faysal's obsession caused him to lobby world leaders on the matter whenever he could, no matter how unsettling the effect. At a White House dinner in his honor, he spent much of the occasion explaining to Richard Nixon that Bolshevism is an offspring of Zionism and came away gratified with his success. "The President," he reported to Mohamed Heikal, "had shown great interest and had asked him to repeat his remarks to Vice-President Spiro Agnew and to the Director of the CIA, Richard Helms, which he did." Heikal reports that "The King was obviously pleased at having, as he felt, convinced these powerful figures of a profound and neglected political truth."[13] (In his memoirs, however, Nixon wrote only one dismissive sentence on this topic — "Faisal saw Zionist and Communist conspiracies everywhere around him.")[14]

Kissinger's famous account of his conversation with King Faysal at a state dinner in a Riyadh palace in his honor is worth quoting at length:

It was like an eerily rehearsed symphony. When the King spoke, all was silent; my comments were drowned out in a buzz of conversation. The silences for the King heightened my awareness in my first exposure to what throughout the Arab world, and in many more outlying regions, was immediately recognizable as Faisal's standard speech. Its basic proposition was that Jews and Communists were working now in parallel, now together, to undermine the civilized world as we knew it. Oblivious to my ancestry—or delicately putting me into a special category—Faisal insisted that an end to be put once and for all to the dual conspiracy of Jews and Communists. The Middle East outpost of that plot was the State of Israel, put there by Bolshevism for the principal purpose of dividing America from the Arabs.

Deeply embarrassed, Kissinger tried to change the topic by asking the king about a picture on the wall. This gambit "threw Faisal into some minutes of deep melancholy, causing conversation around the table to stop altogether."[15]

## Helping Imperialists

Communism and capitalism appear to Muslims as variants of the same civilization, an approach that renders plausible the notion of Soviet-American collusion. To be sure, Americans and Soviets promoted rival ideologies and competed for power, but their confrontation lacked the cultural depth of the one between the West and the Muslim world. Where others saw rivalry, these Muslims discerned cooperation.

At times, they imagined the two sides physically getting together in the same room to conspire. An American television correspondent recounts how Lebanese spoke of Reagan and Brezhnev "huddled over maps of Beirut ordering aides to set a bomb off on this corner or provoke a clash on that street."[16] Jalal Al-i Ahmad, the Iranian thinker, envisioned Soviets and Americans sitting "quite comfortably at the same table,"[17] divvying up Middle Eastern spoils.

Capitalist and Communist worked together on many issues. In Afghanistan, they cooperated during the 1980s to damage Muslim interests. In the Persian Gulf, Moscow aided the allied operation against Iraq in the Kuwait war by feeding false information to Baghdad. In the Arab-Israeli conflict, they cooperated against the Arabs from 1967 on. Outside the Middle East, they joined forces to eliminate Islam from such countries as the Philippines, Cyprus, Eritrea, Somalia, and Chad.

In Iran, this notion of Western and Soviet collusion flourished on all sides of the political spectrum. Shah Mohammad Reza Pahlavi believed that the British government "had a hand" in founding Tudeh, the Iranian Communist party. Why? Because "it was and is their policy to have their people everywhere, hoping to exercise some control no matter what happens."[18] Khomeinist leaders perceived a joint White House-Kremlin effort to destroy the Islamic Republic via Iraq and Afghanistan. The Soviet occupation of Baku in January 1990 had been planned at the U.S.-Soviet summit in Malta a few months earlier — Moscow's payoff for approving Washington's decision to invade Panama.

The West used the Communist bogeyman for its own purposes. Hasan al-Hudaybi, leader of the Muslim Brethren after 1949, portrayed the Soviet danger to Egypt as a myth conjured up by London to preserve its position in that country. Similarly, Anwar as-Sadat saw détente as a Soviet-U.S. conspiracy to prevent Arabs from taking back their territories from Israel.

## Helping Both

The prospect of Americans, Israelis, and Soviets working together, dubbed by Egyptians the "destructive triad," or the colonial "trinity,"[19] inspired responses akin to panic in the Middle East. This suspicion has deep roots in the Islamic precept (*hadith*) that "unbelief is one religion." For example, Sayyid Qutb (1906-66), the influential Egyptian who presaged much of the fundamentalist thinking that followed his death, alluded to this when he wrote of "the solidarity of the unbelievers";[20] as did Ayatollah Khomeini when he portrayed Western powers as multiple facets of a single hostile force.

Such fears arose already during the Cold War, for example, as an explanation for the June 1967 war. More generally, the three parties were seen as engaging in "colonialist diplomacy"[21] with an eye to keeping the Arab-Israeli conflict going and the region poor, generating weapon sales, and using Middle Easterners as guinea pigs for advanced arms. But fear of collusion by this trio became an abiding concern only as Soviet-American hostility came to an end about 1990. Rafsanjani declared that "East and West have joined forces" against Islam, while Khamene'i saw the United States as the leader of an "anti-Islamic front of arrogance."[22]

Jewish emigration to Israel in 1990 by the tens of thousands prompted widespread talk of a "trilateral drive": Soviet authorities permitted Jews to leave, Israelis welcomed them, and the U.S. government helped cover their settlement costs. Yasir 'Arafat described the U.S. and Soviet roles in terms of "one of them providing human beings and the other providing money and weaponry."[23] Some Arabs added the German and British governments to this scheme. Near panic set in. 'Arafat inflated the numbers tenfold and more, telling of "3 million Jews coming from East Europe."[24] Tariq 'Aziz of Iraq portrayed the emigration as Israel's third catastrophe for the Middle East (after its creation and the war of 1967). 'Ali Akbar Mohtashemi termed the Jewish immigrants a "tidal wave" and the "most dangerous" issue facing Muslims.[25] Rafsanjani went furthest, calling it "one of the most significant calamities of our century."[26] Only the outsized fear of an all-forces coalition of Zionists and imperialists explains this alarmist reaction to a minor population movement.

## OTHER POTENTIAL CONSPIRATORS

If the Communist threat amounts to so little, who else can scare the Middle East? Many high-profile conspirators in the West receive little or no attention in the Middle East. Other than Great Britain and the United States, foreign states pose little danger. Other than Jews, adherents of religions hardly register. If possible, fellow Muslims have even less of a role.

### Secret Societies

Non-Jewish secret societies, a European preoccupation since the mid-eighteenth century, hardly scare Arabs and Iranians. The Templars came into existence in 1118 as an anti-Muslim order and continue to capture the imagination of conspiracy theorists in the West, but the Middle East knows them not. Rosicrucians and Bavarian Illuminati are similarly absent. The Council on Foreign Relations, Trilateral Commission, and other bogeymen of the right are nowhere to be found. Nor those of the left: conspiracy theorists pay little attention to multinational corporations (despite the oil companies' especially large and visible presence in the Middle East) and bankers are almost entirely missing. "Fascist" and "Nazi" are epithets, not the source of serious concerns.

Freemasons, a great scourge of European conspiracy theorists and also a mildly consequential force in the Middle East, especially in Iran,[27] do sometimes rank as an independent force. Thus, the Jordanian fundamentalist leader Layth Shubaylat spoke of "our humiliation before the Americans, the Zionists, and Masons."[28] But this is unusual; for the most part, they rate as nothing more than an adjunct to the Zionists or imperialists, who found, control, and deploy this organization for their own purposes. The Elders of Zion told the Freemasons to bring down the Ottoman Empire. The cover of a booklet issued by the UAE Ministry of Defense in the 1980s portrays a Jewish figure pulling the strings of the Freemasons, Lions, and Rotary.[29] The Hamas Charter repeatedly portrays Freemasonry as a tool of Jewry (articles 17, 22, 28). A history professor at Al-Azhar University, Salih Hasan al-Maslut, goes into more detail: "the Masons is a Jewish international organization seeking to destroy non-Jewish nations and governments. The Masons' ultimate goal is to rebuild Solomon's Temple over the ruins of Al-Aqsa Mosque" in Jerusalem and to "establish a global Jewish government as defined by the Zionists' *Protocols*." The professor goes on to explain that, "not content" with the Masonic instrument, Jews established another public body, the Rotary Clubs.[30]

## Foreign States

Two German attempts in this century to dominate the Middle East have disappeared down the memory hole. Only in Turkey do suspicions of Germany remain significant (on which, see the appendix).

The French, who once commanded an empire of Muslims second only to the British, have also dropped from Middle Eastern consciousness. The occasional phobia might yet arise (Pieds Noirs are suspected of wanting to get back their holdings in Algeria), but these are but the feeble vestiges of an imperial presence. Paris's invisibility may result from its diminished power, its persistent differences with Washington, and its efforts not to upset commercial partners, actual or potential. Other European states are virtually absent, except for an eccentric appearance. (Scandinavian pornography companies are said to be investing heavily in Bangladesh.)

Neither Japan's imperialist legacy in South East Asia nor the present reality of its economic strength scare Muslims; to the contrary, from the Russo-Japanese War of 1905 on, Muslims have tended to associate themselves with Japanese success against the West. Middle Easterners do not even suppose the Japanese can be responsible for their own problems: a Tehran daily speculated that the U.S. government "may have been behind" the spread of poison gas on a Yokohama subway train, "in view of Japan's growing economic power." In a particularly imaginative analysis, the newspaper editorial pointed out the similarity of the names Yokohama and Oklahoma and noted that cultists are "superstitiously steeped in rhymed words."[31]

Chinese, other East Asians, Africans (even South Africans), and Latin Americans almost never appear in Middle East speculations. International organizations (the International Monetary Fund, World Bank, United Nations) figure in conspiracy theories only as agents of Western power; otherwise they are ignored.

## Members of Other Religions

Christianity, archrival to Islam for over a millennium, today retains only minor importance. Its representatives—missionaries, Jesuits, the Vatican, Christians of the Middle East—do turn up, but again as agents of Zionism or imperialism, rather than autonomous actors working for specifically Christian ends. Missionaries make an interesting case. Though openly working to win converts for openly religious reasons—hardly a conspiracy—conspiracy theorists tend to discount these explicit aims and see them working surreptitiously on behalf of imperialism. A Turkish writer holds that "religion is a trade in the eyes of [Christian] missionaries."[32] A spokesman for Hizbullah, the Iranian-backed fundamentalist movement in Turkey, says there "in no difference between missionaries and spies."[33] The Egyptian intellectual Muhammad al-Ghazali sees "a vast conspiracy being plotted by missionary aggressors and cultural imperialists. Its purpose is obtain the place which Islam occupies in the hearts of its sons."[34] Hasan at-Turabi of the Sudan considers missionaries to be intriguers against Islam.

Other Christians also serve as agents. The World Council of Churches depends on its funding from the Western intelligence services, especially the American and German. Abu Nidal raised the scenario of a Vatican plot against the Palestinians, possibly in league with Middle Eastern Christians, acting on Israel's behalf. When Yasir 'Arafat warned of Christian plans to destroy Pakistan's nuclear reactor and Sudanese unity, he portrayed these acts as part of an "imperialist-Zionist plot."[35] Along these lines, the Sudanese government accused the Christian rebel Isaias Afwerki of being "a dictator led by international Zionism and used by imperialism."

Equally telling, Pope John Paul II's travels to Muslim lands raised fears not of his attempting to spread the Catholic faith but of a political plot.[36] A trip to northern Nigeria prompted Iranian fretting about "the pope's suspicious visit to Islamic countries."[37] In November 1979, one and a half years before he shot John Paul, Mehmet Ali Ağca wrote a letter to an Istanbul newspaper in which he decried the pope's forthcoming visit to

Turkey. "Western imperialists sent John Paul II to Turkey as commander of the crusades out of fear of seeing Turkey and its Muslim brothers create a new political, economic, and military force across the Middle East."[38] Nor was this view confined to the lunatic fringe. *Milli Gazete*, a publication of Turkey's mainstream fundamentalist Muslim party, saw that visit in light of a need "to set a strategy against the Muslim world." In 1990 the same paper perceived a Christian plot against Islam that included the pope, the United States, West Europe, and the Soviet Union.[39]

Orthodox Christians are a source of confusion. They sometimes rate as fellow victims of Zionist and imperialist plotting. Libya's Qadhdhafi, responding to the situation in Bosnia, addressed the Serbs in this unexpectedly friendly manner: "You Serbs have been our friends since Tito's day, the Orthodox doctrine is similar to Islam; you should not fall into the plot of the Catholics, the Protestants, the Christians, and the Israelis."[40] At other times, and more accurately, the Orthodox Church is seen as the inspiration behind anti-Muslim policies of the Soviet and Russian governments.

Middle East Christians become actors in their own right only when Muslim-Christian strife erupts. In Imbaba, a conflict-ridden district of Cairo, a fundamentalist Muslim leader spun a theory about this enemy:

> There is a Christian conspiracy. They have control of most of the businesses in Egypt, including the gold shops. They use their money to buy weapons and explosives that they hide in their churches, and they have control of the Government. Why are the police around the churches and not the mosques? Why do you think those churches burned up so quickly? Their goal is to take over Egypt and our goal is to stop them.[41]

Muslim-Christian tensions in Lebanon prompted similar suspicions of local Christians working on their own behalf. These flourished during the civil war, but had an impact even before then. For example, Lebanese jealousy of Palestinian success prompted the conspiracy that caused the Palestinian-owned Intra Bank to collapse in 1965.

Hindus should be a major concern. In contrast to their more tolerant attitude toward Judaism and Christianity, Muslims look at Hindu beliefs and practices with revulsion. The Hindu confrontation with Islam goes back a thousand years; today, 100 million Muslims live tensely in India among 700 million Hindus (in contrast, 2 million Palestinians live among 5 million Jews.) Muslim Kashmir's attempt to slough off the control of Hindu India has made that province an emotional flashpoint for Muslims everywhere. India and Pakistan have already gone to war three times and continue to skirmish (in the dramatic but obscure "Glacier War"). India had a prominent role in the splitting of Pakistan in 1971 and the emergence of an independent Bangladesh. Looking to the future, the two states' nuclear capabilities may well end in the first-ever exchange of atomic weapons.

Despite this record, Hindus very rarely turn up as conspirators in Muslim eyes. In December 1992 extremist Hindus swarmed over a sixteenth-century mosque, the Babri Masjid, and demolished it by hand, brick by brick, to clear the space for a Hindu temple. Muslims across India responded with fury at the mosque's destruction, leading to thousands of deaths. This incident did lead to retribution (the Saudi authorities reportedly banned Hindus from employment in their country) but not to conspiracy theories. Iran's leaders interpreted the Babri incident not as the cutting edge of a Hindu plot against Islam but as "another chapter . . . of the great conspiracy fomented by the United States, the West, the Zionist enemy, and their client regimes in our Islamic world."[42] Ayatollah Mohammad Emami-Kashani contended that destruction of the Babri Mosque "was a pre-planned plot by world arrogance, which includes Zionism among its members."[43] A Tehran newspaper linked the demolition to atrocities in Bosnia-Herzegovina and referred to "the hidden and obvious hands of arrogance,"[44] while Ayatollah 'Abdolkarim Musavi-Ardebili saw the mosque incident as a Western plot to divert the Muslims' attention from their true problems.

Hindus also turn up in other small incidents. A Muslim figure from Singapore spoke of a Hindu conspiracy to destroy 123 mosques in New Delhi. Rumors spread that it was not a fundamentalist Muslim group fighting for Kashmir that beheaded a Norwegian hostage in the fall of 1995, but rather the Indian government. But these are minor matters; in general, Hindus are not conspirators in their own right, merely agents of Zionist-imperialist plotting. As Sayyid Qutb noted, although "the intensity of the struggle between the Hindu idol-worshippers and Islam is vividly apparent, . . . it does not equal the viciousness of world Zionism."[45] Confirming this, when Hindus are mentioned as conspirators, they are often linked to one or other of the main culprits. Thus, the murder of a prominent Shi'i in Pakistan provoked suspicions of "Hindu and Jewish agents" being behind the crime.[46]

Other religious groups feature even less prominently in the conspiratorial imagination. Buddhists tangle with Muslims in Burma, Thailand, and Sri Lanka, but they inspire few conspiracy theories. The same goes for adherents of minor religions — Baha'is, 'Alawis — who worry Muslims not in their own right but as agents of others.

Hoary fears of pre-Islamic religions surface occasionally. Egyptian fundamentalists see celebration by Muslims of the ancient spring holiday of *Shamm an-Nasim* as a way to destroy Islam in Egypt. Pious Sunnis sometimes fear that Zoroastrians converted to Islam with an intent of subverting the faith from within. Rashid Rida (1865-1935), the Syrian writer, held Zoroastrians responsible for a secret plot that brought Sufism (Islamic mysticism) into existence; this is a way "to corrupt the religion of the Arabs and pull down the pillars of their kingdom by internal dissension, so that by this means they could restore the rule of the Zoroastrians and the domination of their religion to which the Arabs had put an end in Islam."[47] Rather unbelievably, the Pakistani writer Sayed Abdul Wadud presented the *hadith* (accounts of the Prophet Muhammad's sayings or doings) and Sufism as part of a Persian conspiracy against Islam.[48]

## Fellow Muslims

What about Muslims? The ferocity and duplicity of such Middle Eastern states as Iraq and Syria should make local conspiracy at least as great a concern as the activities of a few Zionists or the distant imperialists. Not so; Muslims consistently play a subsidiary role in conspiracy theories. When Muslims betray family, country, and religion, they do so as the dupes and stalking horses of non-Muslims. Asad colludes with Israel. Saudis helped Israeli war planes strike the Iraqi nuclear reactor in 1981 but did not initiate this aggression. Saddam fell into an American trap; or was it that Muslim participants in Operation Desert Storm served imperialist interests?[49] It seems never to be the other way around, with Muslims luring non-Muslims into evil plots.

Among fundamentalist Muslim groups, the more mainstream ones generally tend to blame foreigners for the ills of their society and tend to attack foreign interests. In contrast, the more radical groups focus on their rulers, seeing them serving as local agents of the foreign powers, and so more often target the government. Thus, while Hizbullah made a speciality of assaulting foreigners resident in Lebanon, a secret group killed Anwar as-Sadat.

Conspiracy theorists portray Muslim agents not just as traitors but as losers, used and then discarded by their foreign sponsors. Shah Reza "placed himself at the disposal of the enemy," then got dumped by the British when he no longer served;[50] his son Mohammad Reza Pahlavi worked for the Americans and lost his job when Washington no longer needed his services. He reportedly told Anwar as-Sadat: "No one in the Middle East has served the Americans as much as I have. The result has been that they have colluded with Khomeini against me. While Carter was dancing with my wife and I with his, the chief of the CIA was waiting to meet Khomeini."[51] As for Sadat, America's favorite Arab, he was murdered when he had served his purpose for the U.S. government. He "had become expendable.... It was time for him to be replaced by someone more liberal and more acceptable."[52] Husni Mubarak, Sadat's successor, proved himself embarrassingly pro-American, so Washington would have to dispose of him, too—or at least, so the Iraqi media predicted in late 1991.[53] That did not happen, but years later a leading Iraqi polemicist warned Mubarak that "America, should it continue to exist, will not protect you, rather it will sell you."[54] According to Syria's Tallas, Saddam reasonably expected Kuwait as a reward for his efforts on behalf of the U.S. government, but instead he got duped when Washington turned against him.

The near absence of Muslims as conspirators is not entirely surprising, for misfortune has always been seen to derive mainly from non-Muslims. For one, blaming foreigners closes ranks; in contrast, accusing locals has a divisive effect. By linking the Jews and Kurds of Iraq to Zionism and imperialism, for example, Baghdad whitewashes indigenous problems. For another, the ideal of Muslim brotherhood causes believers to reject the idea of an inner demon. Evil comes from without. A foreign master makes aberrant Muslim behavior slightly more comprehensible. Reactionary Muslims represent British and American economic interests. Fundamentalists sabotage efforts to modernize. Leftists forward Soviet goals. Apostates undermine the faith. Sunni and Shi'i chauvinists introduce religious divisions. Pan-Arabists import European nationalist passions. In short, evil acts by Muslims imply the hidden hand of an infidel enemy; if not for this, Muslims would not do evil. They are not instigators but traitors.

At the same time, only rarely admitting Muslims to the ranks of the conspirators has the ironic effect of denying their competence, intelligence, and political autonomy. While Muslims view Western governments with awe, they look upon fellow Muslims as hapless. When an Iraqi fighter struck the U.S. frigate *Stark*, killing 37 sailors, a Syrian paper asserted that this must have resulted from a scenario "drawn up in advance through joint coordination" between Iraqi and American forces. Why so? Because the Iraqi plane could not have hit the American ship without American permission.[55] Never blaming Muslims, in other words, has the odd implication of derogating them.

## WHY ONLY ZIONISTS AND IMPERIALISTS?

Why, of all the possible conspirators, do Middle Easterners dwell so much on Zionists and imperialists? Why not Japanese, Hindus, and fellow Muslims? The answer lies partly in the fact that Europeans see these two as the archconspirators, partly in the role of Jews, Britons, and Americans as paragons of modernity.

### Imitating the West

The Zionist and imperialist archenemies derive straight from European demonography; indeed, fears of conspiracy constitute one aspect of the West's historic impact on Muslim civilization.

*Two Western traditions.*     The West developed two traditions of grand conspiracy, a mainly right-wing version concerned with Jews and a mainly left-wing version fearful of secret societies. Each phobia ascribes its nemesis a very long and impressive lineage.

Anti-Semites trace a single conspiracy beginning with Herod and including the Sanhendrin, medieval rabbis, Karl Marx, Theodor Herzl, Sigmund Freud, and the "Elders of Zion." Secret society theorists trace an alternate tradition that includes such names as the Assassins, Templars, Jesuits, Freemasons, Illuminati, Jacobins, Rosicrucians, Philosophes, Carbonari, Catholics, and the Council on Foreign Relations.

While fears of Jews and secret societies both originated in the Crusader era, anti-Jewish and anti-secret society ideas developed into coherent intellectual concepts around 1800. Religiously-based animosity toward Jews turned into a political animosity, even as Augustin de Barruel's four-volume *Studies in the History of Jacobinism* systematically and rigorously established secret societies as a menace.[56] Full-blown anti-Semitic and antisecret society theories emerged simultaneously in Russia during the 1890s, again with two publications. Just as the Okhrana (tsarist secret police) were forging *The Protocols of the Elders of Zion*, anti-Semitism's standard text, Lenin was composing his main theoretical writings on imperialism. These publications then became the definitive twentieth-century statements of the rightist and leftist versions of conspiracism.

Anti-Semites and anti-Templars have much in common. Both fear a centuries-old clandestine attempt to control the world in which a benign, open affiliation shelters a malign, covert conspiracy. The one sees Jews as the universal problem, the other looks to secret societies. A World

Masonic Council parallels the fictive Elders of Zion as the ultimate authority. Seen to represent roughly the same forces, Jews, Britons, and Americans tend to attract the same enemies: anti-Semites easily fear and hate Anglo-Americans, too.

*Muslims copy the West.*    With only slight modifications, Arabs and Iranians imported intact these two European traditions of grand conspiracy; as a result, the conspiracy theories developed in Russia during the 1890s remain surprisingly potent in today's Middle East. Indeed, just as anti-Semitic and antisecret society ideas fell out of the European mainstream, they gained strength in Muslim lands, giving the Middle East a time-warp quality. Europe's phobias of a century back persist there, as if preserved in amber. Just as Marxists remain mired in the economic battles of mid-nineteenth-century Britain, Middle Easterners are yet entangled in distant European anxieties about Jews and secret societies.

Middle Easterners tend to accept the intellectual baggage that accompanies these two mythic forces, no matter that it contradicts their own traditions. Never mind that Muslims once saw Jews as weak and vestigial; now, under Western influence, they fear Zionists as potential rulers of the world. In contrast, the historic fear of Hindus has faded. "Imperialism" now applies only to Europeans and Americans, not to Mongols or Russians. Never mind the historic Muslim idea that "unbelief is one religion": now they see Zionists and imperialists each out for themselves, ultimately seeking total power. Middle Easterners also adopted the Western notion of two great chains of conspiracy, the Jewish and the non-Jewish:

> Sayyid Qutb, the Egyptian fundamentalist thinker: "Through the lengthy centuries — regretfully — [the Jews] poisoned the Islamic heritage in a way that may itself be revealed only with the effort of centuries."[57]
>
> Saddam Husayn's son 'Udayy: "The devil has taken the form of idols, such as Lat and 'Uzza [pagan Meccan goddesses]. At other times, the devil became a group of Tatars to obliterate the Islamic and Arab identity. At still other times, the devil took the form of British and French colonialism. Finally, the devil has taken the shape of the Americans."[58]

These views derive from Western ideas, not from anything coming out of the Middle East.

Further, Muslims now reread their own history under European impress and discover plots where they had not existed before. Stories of Jewish provenance about the Qur'an *(the Isra'iliyat)* have always been looked on with skepticism by Muslim scholars; at the same time, they were seen as innocuous. In modern times, they came to be seen as part of a plot to subvert Islam. In a similar spirit, historical events changed their character completely. Ahmad al-Hifnawi's *Opposition Movements and Conspiracies in Islamic History* considers the murder of caliphs 'Umar, 'Uthman, and 'Ali to have all been conspiracies. Take the murder of the second caliph, 'Umar, in A.D. 644. The early chronicles record Abu Lu'lu', a slave from Iraq, formerly Christian but a convert to Islam, going to 'Umar with a complaint about his master and, displeased with the scant concern 'Umar paid him, returning to stab the caliph.[59] In modern times, this incident gets turned into a "treacherous conspiracy" in which the slave represents those Persians, Jews, and Christians upset by the Arab conquest and trying to sabotage the nascent Muslim state.[60] Like many Muslim authors, Hifnawi places great stress on Ka'b al-Ahbar, the renowned Jewish convert to Islam, seeing him as the first to sabotage Islam from within.[61] Again, this reads European-style conspiracism back into history.

There is something deeply ironic (and not a little humiliating) about Arabs and Iranians depending on Europeans to define their own enemies. Emulation of the West meant that the West's enemies became the Middle East's enemies. Because Westerners focus on Jews and secret societies, so too do Arabs or Iranians. This also means that the Chinese and the Muslims themselves have as little role in the Middle Eastern imagination as they do in the European one. Even as Muslims decry the West as the source of their problems, they look to the West to tell them whom to fear and why to do so. Thus did the Middle East become an acolyte of Europe. Or, as Kenneth Minogue points out, "It is Americans themselves who supply most of the materials of anti-Americanism."[62] This dependence points to a cultural and political subservience more total than even the most ambitious imperialist would aspire to. On reflection, however, such emulation is not entirely surprising. The West influenced nearly every aspect of human existence in the Middle East; why not the substance of its paranoid thinking, as well?

At the same time, conspiracy theories did change on reaching the Middle East. Cut off from their cultural sources, anti-Semitic and anti-secret society biases changed in the Middle East; a new religion, a new region, and a new era meant twists and embellishments. Europe's ideas traveled more easily than its memories and its attitudes. Arabs and Iranians elaborated rococo flourishes on plain European themes. They turned anti-Semitism into anti-Zionism; secret societies transmogrified into national governments. Put another way, "Zionists" and "imperialists" resonate so deeply because they are code words for two traditional opponents, Jews and Christians. Not all Jews are Zionists, of course, and even less so are all Christians imperialists, but the categories overlap closely enough to touch a profound Muslim nerve.

### Fear of More Advanced Peoples

A conspirator must be more advanced than oneself to inspire the deepest fears. Jews and Anglo-Saxons exactly fit this bill, symbolizing the enormous power (and threat) of modern ideologies and technologies. That is a second reason why Muslims look to Jews, Britons, and Americans as the archconspirators.

*Jews.*    Jews have had disproportionate presence in world history during the past two centuries, to the point that the Jewish role over the past 100 years has served as a symbol of the secularization and pluralism so hateful to conspiracy theorists. Jews include thinkers such as Karl Marx, Sigmund Freud, and Albert Einstein; financial dynasties such as the Rothschilds and Warburgs; political figures such as Benjamin Disraeli, Leon Trotsky, and Henry Kissinger. The Zionist project succeeded not only in creating a state but a powerful one with many international connections.

In this frame of mind, Sayyid Qutb accused Jews of "decorating" such anti-Islamic principles as sensualism and amorality in high-minded, modern ways, thereby hiding their anti-Islamic quality.[63] Other Muslims accused them of devising the theory of evolution; spreading the practice of usury around the world (i.e., modern finance); and standing behind "materialism, animal sexuality, the destruction of the family and the dissolution of society."[64] Egypt's Muslim Brethren insist on Émile Durkheim and Jean-Paul Sartre being Jews and hold Jews accountable for the consequences of their ideas. Mustafa Mashhur, the number-two official in Egypt's Muslim Brethren, sees Jews behind "every weird, deviant principle" in history.[65]

*Anglo-Saxons.*    Arabs and Iranians devote enormous attention to the United Kingdom and the United States, the richest and most powerful countries of the modern era. Middle Easterners, and especially fundamentalists, reject the West not just for the things it does wrong, but also for the things it does right. They are outraged by bourgeois society, with its unabashed pursuit of happiness, its commercialism, and its military preeminence. Qutb wrote that the growth of Western ideas "is the most dangerous *jahiliyya* [barbarism] that has ever menaced our faith."[66] This sentiment leads a Tehran newspaper commentary to assert that "the Iranian public hates Britain and America."[67] That's not true for the population at large, but it does capture the rage of fundamentalist Muslims.

Perhaps the most intimidating development in the West is unabashed atheism. Most Muslims simply cannot imagine a society not premised on religious foundations. While not admirers of Christianity, fundamentalist Muslims infinitely prefer it to a nonreligious order. The subject of the West having forsaken its roots comes up repeatedly with fundamentalists. 'Ali Akbar Hashemi-Rafsanjani of Iran declares that "In the West Christianity does not govern,"[68] and sees that fact as self-evidently damning. Hasan at-Turabi speaks for many Muslim appalled by the free-thinking experiment called Western civilization.

> You say that you believe in God, but you have closed Him up, imprisoned Him in your churches, your tabernacles. And yet you only listen to Him on Sunday morning, for a half hour, during the mass. The rest of the time God does not exist, you think you are strong enough to do without Him, to no longer listen to Him! You are crazy! The separation of God and the state of which you are so proud is totally mad. It is a . . . diabolical absurdity. Or—but you do not dare to say it—the fact is that you do not believe in God.[69]

The number-two official in Egypt's Muslim Brethren adds: "the West has shifted from a religion that opposed knowledge to a knowledge that fights religion, from a religion without culture to a culture without religion, from a religion that exalts the world hereafter to a religion inclined toward materialism, and from a religion that revered God and disparaged man to one that glorifies man and disregards God."[70]

The answer to the chapter's title is simple. Muslims pay little attention to Communist, Hindu and other non-Western conspirators because (1) Europeans historically have not worried about Communists and Hindus, and (2) because Communists and Hindus are not appreciably more modern than Muslims. The implication is clear. Had Westerners developed serious conspiracy theories about Japanese, presumably Middle Easterners would have emulated them. If Westerners feared conspiracies by fundamentalist Muslims, Arabs and Iranians would presumably follow suit. For example, it was only after the World Trade Center bombing in February 1993 that the Egyptian government made a strong case for an Iranian plot in Egypt.

## NOTES TO CHAPTER 7

1. Bernard Lewis, *The Middle East and the West* (London: Weidenfeld and Nicolson, 1963), p. 135. In the reissue of this book as *The Shaping of the Modern Middle East* (New York: Oxford University Press, 1994), Lewis on p. 158 (surprisingly) changes the verb tense in this sentence to the past.
2. *The New York Times*, 5 August 1991.
3. *Time*, 29 July 1991.
4. *The Jewish Week*, 9-15 August 1991.
5. *The New York Times*, 5 August 1991.
6. Quoted in *Time*, 29 July 1991.
7. Quoted in Agence France Presse, 30 July 1991.
8. *Al-Jumhuriya*, January 1984. Quoted in David Shipler, *Arab and Jew: Wounded Spirits in a Promised Land* (New York: Times Books, 1986), p. 258.
9. 'Umar Muftizadeh, quoted in Reinhard Schulze, *Islamischer Internationalismus im 20. Jahrhundert: Untersuchungen zur Geschichte der islamischen Weltliga* (Leiden: E. J. Brill, 1990), p. 398.
10. Mohamed H. Heikal, *Cutting the Lion's Tail: Suez Through Egyptian Eyes* (New York: Arbor House, 1987), p. 118.
11. Editorial, *Ad-Dustur*, 16 June 1992.
12. Quoted in Robert Lacey, *The Kingdom* (London: Hutchinson, 1981), p. 386.
13. Mohamed Heikal, *The Road to Ramadan* (New York: Quadrangle/The New York Times Book Co., 1975), p. 139.
14. Richard Nixon, *Memoirs* (New York: Grosset & Dunlap, 1978), p. 1012.
15. Henry Kissinger, *Years of Upheaval* (Boston: Little, Brown, 1982), p. 661.
16. Larry Pintak, *Beirut Outtakes: A TV Correspondent's Portrait of America's Encounter with Terror* (Lexington, Mass.: Lexington, 1988), p. 39.
17. Jalal Al-i Ahmad, *Gharbzadagi*, trans. by R. Campbell as *Occidentosis: A Plague From the West* (Berkeley, Calif.: Mizan, 1984), p. 29.
18. Mohammad Reza Pahlavi, *Answer to History* (New York: Stein and Day, 1980), p. 73.
19. "Destructive triad": Muhammad 'Atiya Wakid, *Isra'il Waqr al-Isti'mar* (Cairo: Kutub Siyasiya, 1959), p. 19; quoted in Y. Harkabi, *Arab Attitudes to Israel*, trans. by Misha Louvish (London: Valentine, Mitchell, 1972), p. 239. Colonial "trinity": quoted in

Walid Mahmoud Abdelnasser, *The Islamic Movement in Egypt: Perceptions of International Relations, 1967-81* (London: Kegan Paul International, 1994), p. 222.

20. Sayyid Qutb, *Ma'rakatna ma'a'l-Yahud*, edited by Zayn ad-Din ar-Rakkabi. Text translated in Ronald L. Nettler, *Past Trials and Present Tribulations: A Muslim Fundamentalist's View of the Jews* (Oxford: Pergamon, 1987), p. 87.

21. *Jomhuri-ye Islami*, 20 July 1991.

22. Rafsanjani: Radio Tehran, 6 April 1990; Khamene'i: Islamic Revolution News Agency, 7 June 1992.

23. Sawt Filastin (Sanaa), 9 April 1990.

24. *Al-Ittihad al-Usbu'i*, 5 April 1990.

25. *Kayhan*, 21 April 1990.

26. Radio Tehran, 6 April 1990.

27. On which, see Hamid Algar, *Mirza Malkum Khan: A Study in the History of Iranian Modernism* (Berkeley: University of California Press, 1973), pp. 36-53.

28. *Shihan*, 17-23 June 1995.

29. Khalid Muhammad ash-Shabih, *Haba'il ash-Shaytan* (Dubay: Wizarat ad-Difa', n.d.).

30. *'Aqidati*, 13 June 1995. For Freemasonry in earlier writings, see Harkabi, *Arab Attitudes to Israel*, pp. 240-41. For a detailed exposition of this conspiratorial view, see Sabir Ta'imi, *Al-Masuniya dhalika'l-'Alim al-Majhul: Dirasa fi'l-Asrar at-Tanzimiya li'l-Yahudiya al-'Alimiya* (Beirut: Dar al-Jil, n.d.).

31. *Kayhan International*, 1 May 1995.

32. M. Sıddık Gümüş, *British Enmity Against Islam*, 3d ed. (Istanbul: Hakikat Kitabevi, 1993), p. 102.

33. *Tempo*, 29 March 1995.

34. Muhammad al-Ghazali, *Min Huna Na'lam*, 5th ed. (Cairo: Matba'at as-Sa'ada, 1965), p. 14.

35. Sudan News Agency, 26 April 1991.

36. This is part of a common tendency in modern times to view other religions not as faiths but as rival forms of ideology.

37. *Al-Wahda al-Islamiya*, June 1982.

38. *Milliyet*, 26 November 1979.

39. *Milli Gazete*, 26 January 1990.

40. Libyan Television, 16 February 1994.

41. *The New York Times*, 22 October 1991.

42. Voice of the Islamic Republic, 7 December 1992.

43. Voice of the Islamic Republic, 19 February 1993.

44. *Jomhuri-ye Islami*, 8 December 1992. "Arrogance" is Iranian code for the U.S. government.

45. Qutb, *Ma'rakatna ma'a'l-Yahud* p. 84.

46. Pakistani senator Syed Jawad Hadi, Voice of the Islamic Republic, 7 March 1995.

47. *Al-Manar* 28 (1927-28): 177. Quoted in Albert Hourani, *Arabic Thought in the Liberal Age, 1798-1939* (London: Oxford University Press, 1970), p. 232.

48. Sayed Abdul Wadud, *Conspiracies Against the Quran* (Lahore: Khalid Publications, 1976), pp. 61, 59.

49. Though one Iraqi-financed newspaper did give the Saudis some credit: "Saudi circles and powerful elements in the royal family close to the king [believe] that the entire Kuwait war was fabricated: a trap into which they drew Iraq so that they could lay hands on the oil; which they did" (*Al-Muharrir*, 1 May 1995).

50. 'Ali Hoseyni Khamene'i, Voice of the Islamic Republic of Iran, 12 August 1992.

51. Anis Mansur claims he conveyed this message between the heads of state, *Al-Ahram*, 24 August 1995.

52. Mohamed Heikal, *Autumn of Fury: The Assassination of Sadat* (New York: Random House, 1983), p. 268.

53. *Babil*, 19 October 1991.

54. Salah al-Mukhtar, writing in *Babil*, 27 June 1995.

55. *Tishrin*, 23 May 1987.

56. Augustin de Barruel, *Mémoires pour servir à l'histoire du Jacobinisme*, 4 volumes (London: De l'imprimerie françoise, chez P. le Boussonnier, 1797-98).

57. Qutb, *Ma'rakatna ma'a'l-Yuhud* p. 75.

58. *Babil*, 9 June 1992.

59. For an account of this incident, see William Muir, *The Caliphate: Its Rise, Decline, and Fall*, 3d ed. (London: Smith, Elder, 1899), pp. 198-203.

60. Ahmad al-Hifnawi, *Harakat wa-Mu'amarat Munahida fi Ta'rikh al-Islam* (Mansura, Egypt: Dar al-Wafa', 1986), pp. 101-02.

61. Ibid., p. 108.

62. Kenneth Minogue, "Anti-Americanism: A View from London," *The National Interest*, Spring 1986, p. 47.

63. Qutb, *Ma'rakatna ma'a'l-Yuhud* p. 77.

64. Quoted in Sylvia G. Haim, "Sayyid Qutb," *Asian and African Studies* 16 (1982), p. 156.

65. *Ash-Sha'b* (Cairo), 19 April 1994.

66. Sayyid Qutb, *Ma'alim fi't-Tariq* (n.p., n.d.). Quoted in Emmanuel Sivan, *Radical Islam: Medieval Theology and Modern Politics* (New Haven, Conn.: Yale University Press, 1985) p. 25.

67. *Jomhuri-ye Islami*, 3 December 1994.

68. *Le Figaro*, 12 September 1994.

69. *Le Figaro*, 15 April 1995.

70. *Ash-Sha'b* (Cairo), 19 April 1994.

# 8.

# Who Controls Whom?

Everything that happens in the region emanates
from the United States and Israel.
—*Talal Naji, deputy secretary general of the PFLP-GC*[1]

Sometimes inconsistents seemed to possess them
[Arabs] at once in joint sway; but they never
compromised: they pursued the logic of several
incompatible opinions to absurd ends, without
perceiving the incongruity.
—*T. E. Lawrence*[2]

## CONTRADICTIONS

In March 1990, the U.S. Senate passed a nonbinding resolution deeming Jerusalem the capital of Israel. This event inspired interestingly contradictory responses from Iraq. *Ath-Thawra*, a Baghdad newspaper, declared that the resolution "outspokenly" reflected Zionist influence.[3] Three weeks later, Saddam Husayn adopted precisely the opposite tack, arguing that the resolution proved how Washington made the real decisions.

> If the politicians in Israel had dignity, and were really convinced that they were right, how would they accept that any country says from far away, "We have decided Jerusalem be the capital of Israel"? That

they accepted this decision from another country indicates that they know they have no right to reach this decision on their own.[4]

The newspaper interpretation chose to see the congressional act as a sign that Israelis tell Americans what to do; but Saddam read it as a sign of Israeli weakness.

This points to a common contradiction at the heart of Middle Eastern political culture. Is Israel an outpost of imperialism or the headquarters of a conspiracy? Two schools of thought coexist in the Middle East. Arabs and Iranians sometimes portray Israel as a puppet run by Washington. At other times, they reverse the power relationship and portray Israel as the puppeteer behind American policy. Logic suggests that either Washington tells Jerusalem what to do or the other way around; both cannot use the other at the same time. But what the outside observer finds flatly self-contradictory creates few problems in the Middle East; these two cherished interpretations exist in blithe simultaneity—even in the same individual and in the same speech—without so much as a hint of intellectual strain or inconsistency.

Indeed, Iraq offers other contradictions of this sort, especially at the time of the Kuwait crisis. On 28 June 1990, a month before Iraqi troops entered Kuwait, a Baghdad newspaper proclaimed that the United States has for decades "used the Zionist entity as a tool to safeguard its interests in the region." Just four days later, another Baghdad daily flatly proclaimed that the U.S. government merely echoed decisions made in Israel and that it lacked an "independent policy" on the Arab-Israeli conflict.[5]

As the first bombs began to fall on Iraq in mid-January 1991, Saddam Husayn and his partisans offered two strikingly contrary interpretations of their war with the U.S.-led alliance. When they wanted to paint President Bush as the "arch-Satan" in the White House, Israel shriveled into America's "evil cat's-paw."[6] But on other occasions—and especially when Iraqi authorities sought to justify their missile attack on Israel—they presented the conflict as a great conspiracy hatched by the Zionists and executed by their American stooge. "This war that is being waged against us is a Zionist war," Saddam Husayn declared at the end of January, "only here Zionism is fighting us through American blood."[7]

The same contradiction persisted in subsequent years. In mid-1992, an Iraqi daily asserted that "Israel is the West's tool to retaliate against the Arabs because of the defeats which the Arabs inflicted on their enemies."[8] Not long after, Deputy Prime Minister Tariq 'Aziz blamed Israel: "U.S. policy in the Middle East has only two reference points: Oil and Israel.

Oil was making us stronger and stronger; too strong. So the Israelis started turning President Bush against us."[9]

Baghdad is not alone in its forwarding two contrary messages. Many other states and the PLO do the same.

*Egypt.*    Gamal Abdel Nasser, the charismatic Egyptian leader, used to declare that, if not for British help, the idea of a Zionist state would have remained a "madman's fantasy."[10] At the same time, he subscribed to an extreme form of Jewish conspiracy theory: "three hundred Zionists, each of whom knows all the others, govern the fate of the European continent."[11] Sadat's aides echoed his ambivalence. Chief of Staff Saad El-Shazly saw Israel as "America's cudgel, its baseball bat to beat and punish any Arab country which has the temerity to challenge American hegemony. When propaganda fails, the killing begins. And Israel is willing to do the job."[12] In contrast, Foreign Minister Ismail Fahmy asserted that "In effect the United States has given Israel power of veto on its Middle East policy."[13] Another Egyptian, the leading intellectual Anouar Abdel-Melek, also saw things this way, calling Zionism "the most absolute imperialism the Middle East has ever known."[14]

Even more interesting, on one page in his memoirs, President Anwar as-Sadat portrayed Zionism as a subcontractor for imperialism; "Israel," he wrote, "had come to assume the role of the only 'power' guarding U.S. interests in the Middle East." Then, eleven pages further in the same book, he maintained that American policy puts "Israel's interests before those of the United States herself."[15]

*Iran.*    Ayatollah Khomeini declared that "the source of all our troubles is America. The source of all our troubles is Israel. And Israel also belongs to America."[16] At the same time, Khomeini saw Jews "as the real power behind the imperialists plotting to take over the whole world."[17]

*Jordan.*    One newspaper reported that, during Operation Desert Storm, "all of the Western media were put under the control of the CIA upon orders from President Bush."[18] But others in Jordan built a case around Zionist manipulation of the U.S. media swaying the good Americans to move a half million troops halfway around the globe to protect Israel.

*Palestine Liberation Organization.*    "The Zionist entity," PLO chairman Yasir 'Arafat announced in April 1990, "represents the head of the body of hostile world forces inside the Arab nation; its role is to protect the interests of those forces."[19] But Hani al-Hasan, a top 'Arafat aide, claimed that the United States "is governed by the Zionist lobby."[20]

How can Middle Easterners see Israel as the forward bastion of Western interests and also the covert power behind Western decision making? It is tempting to conclude that Arabs and Iranians have a different logic; but there is only one logic. A closer look at each argument reveals the reasoning behind this contradiction.

## AN IMPERIALIST CONSPIRACY? . . .

### Israel Created and Sustained by the West

The notion that Zionism serves as a tool of the Western powers is an old one, going back at least as far as Abdülhamit II, the Ottoman king who ruled between 1876 and 1909. His was a reasonable idea: after all, St. Petersburg looked after the interests of Armenians living in his realm, Paris sponsored the Maronites, and London was allied with the Druze; so why not assume the Jews, or the Zionists, were sponsored, too? A reasonable idea, perhaps, but not a true one.

Nevertheless, it persisted. Arab leaders differ in their assessment of what exactly the imperialists supply to Israel—manpower, military support, or funding. Egypt's Muslim Brethren claim that the British assembled "thousands of vagabonds and aliens, bloodsuckers and pimps, and said to them, 'Take for yourselves a national home called Israel.'"[21] If Washington would only keep their forces away, Mu'ammar al-Qadhdhafi believes, the Palestinians would need "just 24 hours" for a complete victory.[22] The PLO's Faruq Qaddumi holds that Israel is "an artificial state that can only survive with American and European money."[23]

During the Mandatory period (1918 to 1947), Muslims primarily interpreted the British endorsement of a Jewish national home in Palestine as a way to protect the Suez Canal and the route to India. They saw British and American help making it possible for Israel to come into being. The British occupation of Palestine nurtured Zionism before it could survive on its own. The 1929 massacre of Jews in Hebron "never took place," according to a resident of that city. Rather, it was "a fictitious massacre engineered by the British to make sure the Jews would be able to come and take over Palestine."[24] A whole literature has grown up around the notion of secret agreement between the Zionists and Jordan, arranged by the British to partition Palestine and to rob the Palestinians of their due. With India's independence in 1947, its importance faded and British commerce in the Middle East, especially the Persian Gulf, came to be seen as paramount, so that Israel's utility was now seen in the light of oil and gas imperatives.

When the U.S. government replaced Britain as chief culprit, it got the bulk of blame for the establishment of Israel. Mu'ammar al-Qadhdhafi of Libya has flatly asserted that "the United States created Israel," supplying it with the weapons and intelligence Israelis to kill Arabs.[25] This change of patron, Saad El-Shazly of Egypt claims, makes Israel unique: "It was created to serve the ends of one empire; it survives as the creature of another."[26]

The British and Americans provided the edge in every one of Israel's successes against its Arab enemies; Israel could not have survived on its own. Israel won the war of 1948-49 because Soviets and Americans armed the Jewish state, then pushed the ill-prepared Arab states into battle. In the case of Jordan, the imperialists actually had King 'Abdallah help establish the State of Israel: Colonel John Bagot Glubb and the other British officers in the Arab Legion made sure their men did not fight the Jews (this according to someone in the know, Colonel 'Abdallah at-Tall, who turned against the king in January 1950). London subsequently pressured the Arab states to accept a truce with Israel, thereby allowing Israel to consolidate its military advantage.

In 1956, British and French support assured Israel's military success. In 1967, American and British aircraft carriers made all the difference. In 1973, American military personnel operated some of Israel's most advanced materiel. The U.S. government may have condemned Israel's 1981 bombing of the Iraqi nuclear installation at Osirak, but an Egyptian general insisted that it really supported the action and was even "an accomplice in the raid."[27] In 1982, the PLO faced "the full might of the U.S. and Israel."[28]

## Israel's Uses

What utility does Israel have to British and American imperialists? Arabs have a rich assortment of answers to the question. Israel provides intelligence: *Ash-Sha'b*, a leftist Egyptian newspaper, portrays Israel as a branch office of the Central Intelligence Agency, one that requires CIA "approval and support" before taking almost any step.[29] It provides military help: Ahmad Jibril (leader of the Popular Front for the Liberation of Palestine—General Command) dubs Israel "America's Mideast aircraft carrier"[30] while Iranian president 'Ali Akbar Hashemi-Rafsanjani believes

Westerners see Israel as a "military base."[31] And it has an economic use: Khalid al-Hasan, a PLO leader, sees Israel as "something like a conglomerate — General Motors, for example."[32]

What functions does this intelligence office/aircraft carrier/multinational corporation serve? To jeopardize whatever it may be the speaker holds most dear.

*Power base.*    Some Middle Easterners see Israel providing a generally useful purpose for the United States. Qadhdhafi sees Washington pushing a Greater Israel plan to bring the whole Middle East under Jewish rule. Ibrahim Ghawsha, the spokesman for Hamas, explains that the objective of American assistance to Israel is "the economic and social development of the Zionist regime so that it can become predominant in the region."[33] Using more colloquial language, Linda Blandford reports the same feeling from Saudi Arabia, where Israel is known as "America's 52nd precinct — the cop shop where Yanks can keep an eye on the rumbling Mideast."[34]

*Colonialist.*    For Abdel Nasser, the Pan-Arab leader, Israel "was created to destroy Arab nationalism."[35] His 1962 Charter of National Action dubbed Israel "the tool of imperialism" and "a whip" in the hands of imperialists.[36] Israel's value to the West lies in two areas: it forms a "barrier dividing the Arab East from the Arab West," making a unified Arab state that much more difficult to achieve; and it serves as a drain on "the energy of the Arab nation," thereby holding it back. Gamal Abdel Nasser variously explained Israel's purpose as "breaking the Arabs' vigour," giving "a death-blow to Arab nationalism,"[37] and preventing Egypt from becoming truly independent.

An extremely powerful influence in his time, Abdel Nasser succeeded to make this imperialist interpretation the dominant one among Arab leaders in the 1950s and 1960s. Typically, the PLO's *Covenant* accused Israel of being the "spearhead" and "pillar" of colonialism in the Middle East as well as "a geographic base for world imperialism placed strategically in the midst of the Arab homeland to combat the hopes of the Arab nation for liberation, unity and progress."[38] This outlook persisted after Abdel Nasser's death in 1970. The final communiqué of an Arab League summit meeting in February 1974 warned of "a serious resurgence of the colonial system" and interpreted Israeli actions within "the framework of imperialist strategy" to resurrect just such a colonial system. Saddam Husayn, Abdel Nasser's would-be successor, sees Israel as the "base and method" for neocolonialism to suppress the Arabs after World War II.[39]

Another epigone, Mu'ammar al-Qadhdhafi, declares that "America trusts the Israelis; it relies on them to control the Middle East on its behalf."[40]

*Oil.*    For Nasser's confidant, Mohamed Heikal, Israel's main role was to control the oil trade. He held in 1964 that "the flow of Arab oil is one of the important factors in the establishment of Israel on the soil of the Arabs."[41] Shortly afterward, Yahya Hamuda, 'Arafat's predecessor as head of the PLO, portrayed Israel as "an instrument of American imperialist colonialism which seeks to appropriate our oil."[42] This view remained strong, if recessive, over the next decades.

*Economic backwardness.*    Some Middle Easterners see Israel as a U.S. instrument to prevent Arabs from developing an independent economy, thereby breaking their ties of servitude to the West. "The international power which created Israel wanted chaos for us, so that its manufacturing and agriculture would grow."[43] In a variant on this theory, Saad El-Shazly of Egypt interpreted the U.S.-Israel free trade agreement of April 1985 as intended to "enable Israel to penetrate the Arab market beneath an American cloak."[44] Fat'hi ash-Shiqaqi, the first leader of Islamic Jihad, saw Israel as "an imperialist entity" that helps the West penetrate the Arab-Islamic fold, "dominate it and loot its wealth."[45] Saddam Husayn asserted that Americans deploy Israel to prevent the Arabs from becoming a powerful and modern nation. It conducts smear campaigns (rendering innocent research centers into weapons factories) and military aggression to keep the Arabs backward.

*Anti-Islam.*    For fundamentalist Muslims, Israel is a vehicle to suppress true Islam. Hizbullah, the pro-Iranian Lebanese group, characterized Israel as the "American spearhead in our Islamic world" and (along with that other devil, the shah of Iran) one of the "two watchdogs of American imperialism."[46] Hamas accused the Jews of trying to "liquidate Islam."[47]

*Judaize the Middle East.*    Others speculate about Israel serving the West by converting the Middle East to Judaism.[48] When bombs went off in Cairo in 1993, Egyptian media worked up a complex scenario of $200 million in CIA money going to Mossad to establish a "Committee for Reviving Judaism in the Middle East" and to carry out operations against fundamentalist groups.[49] In a related fear, Tariq Masarwa of Jordan sees Israel not coming into existence because of "the oppression of the Jews in

Europe" but as a mechanism to extend "Western Judeo-Christian civilization in the east."[50]

*Other.*    Israel also stands accused of serving other purposes. In 1979, Edward Said of Columbia University, then an unofficial spokesman for the PLO, called Israel "a device for holding Islam—and later the Soviet Union, or Communism—at bay."[51] Others point to Israel's alleged part in fomenting counterrevolutionary activities and acting as a center for a psychological warfare. Its existence is seen as forcing the Arabs to invest in war rather than economic development; or diverting their attention from domestic issues; or providing reactionaries with the means to stay in power.

## Washington Makes Decisions

Washington is either the principal nemesis or the path to a solution, depending on an Arab leader's strategy toward Israel. Those who plan militarily to destroy Israel are implacably hostile to the United States. To Qadhdhafi, Washington is "the bitter enemy until doomsday"; Asad deemed it "the main enemy of the Arab nation"; and Baghdad Radio's Voice of the PLO chimes in calling it "the major enemy . . . both in the past and in the present."[52] But Arab leaders intent on dealing diplomatically with Israel draw the opposite conclusion; if Washington makes the key decisions, they had better cultivate it. Sadat and 'Arafat followed this course in the hope that the Americans would compel Israel to do their bidding.

Whether it casts the U.S. government as enemy or ally, the imperialist theory causes Arab leaders to focus too much on the United States and too little on Israel. With the single exception of 1957 (when President Dwight Eisenhower compelled the Israelis to evacuate the Sinai Peninsula), the expectation of American pressure on Israel has invariably been disappointed. Still, the illusion lives on that the Americans might again, as 'Arafat puts it, "do what Eisenhower did."[53] Sadat thought that Americans held "99 percent of the cards" but eventually discovered that he had to negotiate with Menachem Begin, not Jimmy Carter. Alexander Haig was considered pro-Israel; therefore, when he resigned as secretary of state in June 1982, during Israel's war in Lebanon, the PLO was elated. One of 'Arafat's aides even acknowledged, "I felt as if we had won the war that night."[54] But as the next few months showed, he was mistaken.

Too little attention to Israel leads the Arabs into serious blunders. Nasser concentrated so intently on extruding American influence from the Middle East, he virtually ignored the effect of his actions on Israel; this partially explains how he blundered into the Six-Day War. Similarly, leaders of the *intifada* on the West Bank and Gaza Strip designed their insurrection to win the sympathy of Western television audiences and did not notice the damage this did to their cause among the Israeli electorate.

### Jewish Lobby a Mirage

If Israel is merely Washington's pawn, a cherished slogan has to be discarded—that the Jewish lobby drives American policy. Surprisingly, Arab opinion leaders do sometimes draw this conclusion, especially when they are very much at odds with the U.S. government. Deputy Prime Minister Khaddam of Syria put it clearly in 1981: "There is a deep and organic link between the United States and Israel. We are under no illusions about this. The link is not due to the 'Zionist lobby' in the United States but to the fact that it is the only friend of the United States in the area and because it represents a major base for protecting U.S. interests."[55] Khaddam reiterated this point in 1995, speaking about negotiations with Jerusalem: "Washington is playing a major role but the issue depends on a decision by Israel."[56]

'Arafat echoed this view. In 1988 he announced that "The so-called Zionist lobby has no influence on U.S. policy."[57] A year later, the Kuwaiti News Agency paraphrased him to the effect that "the Israeli public wants peace but the PLO's major problem is with the U.S. Administration, noting that it's the U.S. and not Israel that determines the American policy in the region, dismissing as baseless the myth of the Zionist lobby in the United States."[58] Tariq 'Aziz of Iraq mused at length on this subject in 1994:

> I am not one of those analysts, writers, or politicians who agree fully with the notion that U.S. political decisionmaking is in the hands of the Jewish lobby in the United States. . . . the Jewish lobby in the United States is part of the establishment and not a foreign power exercising pressure and influence. As long as the United States has interests and strategies in the Arab homeland and the surrounding area, 'Israel' and, consequently, its agents and supporters inside the United States are an inseparable part of these interests and strategies. . . . some Arabs have the illusion that the United States and "Israel" have different objectives, and that the poor United States is victim to the very powerful and devious Jewish lobby.[59]

But, of course, this is not the only point of view.

## . . . OR A JEWISH ONE?

In the other myth, Americans do not use Israel but instead are its dupes. "The Jews want to be a world superpower. . . . No one should imagine that the Jews act on behalf of any super or minor power."[60] American institutions are hollow, comparable to the Polish and Hungarian façades during the Cold War, with all the trappings of power but little of its substance.

### Jerusalem Makes Decisions

The press constantly declares Israel to be the decision making power. A Libyan editor explains: "the real capital of the United States is not Washington but Tel Aviv."[61] A London-based newspaper editorializes that "American foreign policy is formulated in Tel Aviv and not in Washington."[62] The United States "is a great country," a Syrian editor muses, "except that everything in America is subject to the will of the Zionist lobby."[63]

Scholars concur. Writing about U.S. politics in his 1951 book, *From Here We Learn,* Muhammad al-Ghazali asserted that "the rudder of higher politics is in the hands of the Jews."[64] Rana Kabbani is a sophisticated Syrian woman who lived in Washington and studied at Georgetown University; the novelist Salman Rushdie praised her study, *Europe's Myths of Orient,* as "an important, fierce and judicious book"; married to the British journalist Patrick Seale and living in London, she has been described in *Mother Jones* as having "star quality: beauty, brains, and a social position."[65] And what did this highly intelligent woman learn during her years in proximity to the institutions of American power? That the simple prejudices bandied about in her homeland are valid. "Every Arab believes that American policy towards the Middle East is made in Tel Aviv, but to discover that this was indeed the case, and not mere paranoia, was a great shock."[66]

Politicians repeat this charge. At the United Nations debate on the partition of Palestine, Faris al-Khuri, dean of the Arab diplomats, held that although Zionists formed only one-thirtieth of the U.S. population, "they have extended their influence into all circles." He warned Americans to "be careful for the future which awaits them."[67] Anwar as-Sadat wrote in his memoir about events in early 1971: "It was obvious that the United States . . . was still adopting the Israeli line of thinking, under the influence of Zionist propaganda, and that America gave Israel's interests priority even over her own."[68] "U.S. policy toward the Arabs," declared the Iraqi first deputy prime minister, Taha Yasin Ramadan, "is drawn up by Zionist circles."[69] Hafiz al-Asad told the U.S. envoy Robert McFarlane in a private conversation in August 1983 that "Israel's policy is in fact executed by the U.S. We suffer the consequences." A leading Iranian ayatollah flatly declared that Israel "has taken control of the American government."[70] Nor is Jewish power limited to foreign affairs: a counterterrorism bill drawn up in the wake of the Oklahoma City bombing "was drafted in cooperation with the chairmen of Zionist organizations."[71]

President Clinton's announcement of a near-total ban on trade with Iran from the podium of the World Jewish Congress in May 1995 prompted an outburst of angry declarations in the Middle East. Iranian radio declared that "The White House is the executor of the plans of international Zionism. The source of this Punch and Judy show is in Israel."[72] One Cairene newspaper wrote that, "To the state of the Jews, the United States can only say: I hear and obey."[73] Another observed that "No one knows for sure whether the U.S. Congress works for Israel or the United States."[74] Fat'hi ash-Shiqaqi of Islamic Jihad wryly commented how "we used to say Israel was the 51st state and today we can say it is the state that leads America."[75] Ramzi Yusuf, in jail in New York charged with bombing the World Trade Center, stated that "Clinton is insolent, a Zionist and the son of a Zionist."[76]

Others see Jewish influence going beyond America to the whole of the West. Houari Boumedienne, the president of Algeria, claimed that "Zionism controls America, Western Europe, and Britain" and concluded: "This is why their opinions always reflect those of Israel."[77] A fundamentalist magazine fills in the historical details: a century or two back, the Zionists organized Christiandom to combat Islam, assigning North Africa to France, Indonesia to Holland and Portugal, the former Soviet bloc to Russia, and so forth. The United States and Great Britain joined Israel in taking care of the residual countries.[78] Zionists don't forget the details either: in 1939, they caused Paris to cede Hatay to Turkey, thereby "spoiling relations between Arabs and Turks."[79]

More recently, the Kuwait crisis struck many Arabs and Iranians as an Israeli-devised episode. A Jordanian flatly asserted about George Bush that "Israel convinced him to launch war against Iraq."[80] In the view of *The Pakistan Times*, the U.S. government is "an instrument in unseen hands. The Gulf crisis, the ongoing war, the catastrophes that will still come, are not the work of America but the scheme of the Zionists."[81] Then, when Saddam Husayn survived the war, that, too, resulted from a Jewish plot. "The real explanation for Saddam's remarkable survival, she [a well-to-do Iraqi woman in her early sixties] went on, was the larger plot of the Zionists to rule the world. 'Whatever the Israelis want, the Americans will do. The Israelis need Saddam Hussein because through him, they want us to suffer.'"[82]

## A "Strange Hypnotic Influence"

Why does the U.S. government favor 4 million Jews in Israel over some 200 million Arabs? Syria's Khaddam articulated this enduring Arab mystification: "What has Israel given the United States? Obviously, nothing, neither oil nor money. The reverse is true. Israel takes everything from the United States. At a time when the Arabs provide the United States with oil, money, and political support, what is the result? U.S. aid to Israel."[83]

The answer: 5 million Jews in the United States dominate a country of 260 million. And how does that happen? Via the Jewish conspiracy. Some Muslim writers find the Jewish hold on the West so strange, they revert to spiritual causes. Back in 1937, King 'Abd al-'Aziz ibn Sa'ud of Saudi Arabia discerned a "strange hypnotic influence" of the Jews over Great Britain.[84] Mawdudi, the preeminent fundamentalist Muslim of Pakistan, asserted that Jews rule the United States just as the *jinn* (spirits) rule mankind. On a more mundane level, Jews dominate key positions in the arts, the universities, and the great corporations. But three institutions stand out for their part in the Jewish conspiracy: the media, the Christian church, and the government.

*The media.*    Speculations about Jewish control of the American press abound. Khamene'i of Iran calls Zionists the "ringleaders of the world's media" and says that Zionists run the "world propaganda network."[85] Muhammad Salman, Syrian minister of information, states simply that "the Zionist media is everywhere."[86] A tirade in *The Pakistan Times* explains what this means: "The information media including publishing and book trade is its [Zionist Jewry's] leading instrument of deception, disinformation, hiding truth, confusing facts and yet conditioning the minds of the public and the policy makers to perceive things the way it wants."[87] That Zionists dominate the media means it is on the wrong side not just on the Arab-Israeli conflict, but on every issue. In the words of a Baghdad daily, "Throughout their history, the U.S. media have never sided with any just cause in the world."[88]

Jews control the press by staffing and owning it. That Jews have a disproportionate presence in news rooms results not from personal predilection or skill, but from a concerted Zionist effort that includes salary supplements from Jewish organizations. According to Iraqi television, "the Western media establishments, particularly those hostile to Iraq, are companies which need funding, and this funding, most of the time, is supplied by the Zionist entity."[89]

*The church.* In one of their more startling beliefs, Middle Easterners commonly assume that Jews control the Christian religion. In a particularly colorful example of this thinking, the English-language *Syrian Times* published an article in May 1994, just before Secretary of State Christopher arrived in Damascus, asserting the usual blather about American cultural life being under Jewish control. The article then went on to make three astonishing claims: Jews by law pay no U.S. taxes; some prominent journalists receive salaries from Jewish organizations; and "30 percent of Protestant bishops in the U.S. are originally Jews who did not quit Judaism."[90] In response to the ensuing uproar, the Syrian authorities a few days later weakly "expressed regret about the content and tone" of the article to the American ambassador.

That this nonsense was not the strange notions of a subeditor, but the thinking of Syria's leadership, is clear from the fact that it closely echoes what leading politicians say. Foreign Minister Faruq ash-Shar' had stated a couple of years earlier that Israel has had the ability, through the media, to "brainwash" American public opinion into forgetting the greatest Jewish conspiracy of all, the murder of Jesus (and thereby cause a reduction in anti-Semitism).[91] Other Arab leaders concur with this view. A PLO spokesman once explained that "Zionism has succeeded not only in infiltrating into all the institutions of society in the West, but also in penetrating the Christian Church."[92] Qadhdhafi went further yet, calling Christianity a "branch of Judaism" and arguing that Jews use Christianity as a mechanism to dominate Muslims.[93]

*The U.S. government.* Already in 1944, the Palestinian leader Amin al-Husayni noted (in a broadcast on Nazi-controlled Radio Berlin) the strong support for Zionism found in the U.S. Congress. His comment: "No one ever thought that 140,000,000 Americans would become tools in Jewish hands."[94]

Henry Kissinger, along with Richard Nixon the dominant American foreign policy figure in the period from 1969 to 1977, stands out as the Jewish American who Middle Easterners most often suspect of being a Zionist agent. They see Kissinger's Jewish background as a mechanism for Israeli control over the American body politic. Ismail Fahmy wrote in his memoir that Kissinger "was in fact always acting on behalf of Israel." If ever he dared disagree with the Israeli government, it "brought him quickly into line."[95] The honeymoon in U.S.-Israel relations that occurred under Bill Clinton prompted another round of suspicions, articulated by Muhammad Husayn Fadlallah, one of the most thoughtful of fundamentalist Muslims. "[T]he current U.S. administration is an Israeli administration supervised by a president who has U.S. citizenship," he observed; "the United States is the police for Israel. . . . there is no U.S. policy on the Middle East; it is an Israeli policy."[96]

But Kissinger and Clinton are only individuals; Arab and Iranian conspiracy theorists tend to dwell on the American Israel Public Affairs Committee (AIPAC) as the main institution that maintains Jewish control over Washington. AIPAC can "tamper with political decision making . . . from the top" by planting its friends in the structure of the ruling establishment.[97] With this power, AIPAC diverts attention from U.S. interests to those of the "parasitic" Zionist entity.[98] It also infiltrates the Zionist dream of global domination into American thinking. The Jews cajole and threaten recalcitrant politicians with large amounts of money. Syrian radio has argued that Israeli power in Washington results from "the Zionists' gold and dollars." According to it, "the Zionists financed election campaigns [of senators], gave them their racist votes, and continued to provide them with bribes to raise their hands whenever a decision desired by the Zionists needed to be made." And as if that were not enough, the Israeli government "slips dollars into their pockets."[99]

David Steiner, briefly president of AIPAC in 1992, confirmed what conspiracy theorists long suspected when he boasted to a potential contributor about his organization's clout. Clandestinely recorded in a telephone conversation just before the 1992 presidential election, he claimed to be "negotiating" with Bill Clinton over his secretary of state and national security advisor. "We have a dozen people in [Clinton's] headquarters," he went on, "and they are all going to get big jobs." Steiner also told of secret negotiations with Secretary of State James Baker in which "I got almost a billion dollars in other goodies [besides stated U.S. aid to Israel] that people don't even know about."

On resigning his AIPAC position when these quotes were made public, Steiner apologized and termed his recorded statements "simply and totally untrue"; hoping to win a new donor, he had got carried away with boasts.[100] (The billion dollars "people don't even know about," for example, turned out to be $700 million in U.S. Army equipment and $200 million in prepositioned military supplies, both of which were public knowledge.)

Conspiracy theorists paid no attention to his later statements. From their point of view, Steiner had inadvertently leaked the hidden truth. As a Saudi-backed newspaper put it, "whether real or exaggerated," his statements confirmed AIPAC's true influence.[101]

## Not Just Israel

Some Middle Eastern analysts criticize the notion of blaming Israel alone, leaving out the imperialists. Sayyid Qutb, the Egyptian fundamentalist thinker, noted the mistake of blaming Zionists alone:

> Those who believe that the financial influence of the Jews in the USA and elsewhere is what directs the West in its materialistic and imperialistic approach, or that Anglo-Saxon hypocrisy, or the struggle between East and West, are the main factors, ignore a real factor to be added to all these, [that] Western blood carries the spirit of the Crusades within itself. It fills the subconscious of the West.[102]

Similarly, a hardline Iranian magazine criticized the Iranian parliament for placing more stress on Israel than on the United States, arguing that a stand against Washington includes Israel too, whereas the reverse does not. Therefore, it concluded, the Jewish conspiracy is either a blunder or a devious attempt to mislead opinion away from the main enemy.[103]

### FRIENDS OR ENEMIES?

Middle Easterners contradict themselves on another matter too, this time saying that Israel and the United States are a single entity, that time portraying them as deadly rivals.

## Israel Equals the United States

In one view, the U.S.-Israel alliance transcends either country to become a single malevolent entity. What they call "the joint conspiracies of the U.S. and the Zionist regime"[104] have existed at least since the dawn of Islam. The caliphate was "brought down by Zionism and the Crusades."[105] In the nineteenth century, "Zionists joined hands with other arrogant powers to give a grant to Karl Marx to go and study in Britain."[106] A member of the Muslim Brethren in Egypt portrayed Atatürk and Gamal Abdel Nasser as two "agents of the same power, Crusader [imperialism] and Judaism."[107] Shortly after World War II, "Anglo-American imperialism" allied with Israel and the resulting cooperation is sometimes referred to as the "troika," the "Crusader-Zionist alliance," or the "the joint conspiracies of the U.S. and the Zionist regime."[108] In recent times, the two parties induced rich Arabians to import Asian labor, thereby de-Arabizing the population of those states. Mossad agents protected Husni Mubarak from a plot of "free officers" against him in October 1990; a few months later, the CIA helped him, too.

Each side covertly helps the other in war. The U.S. government aided Israel in all of its major confrontations with the Arabs; in particular, it sent airplanes during the Six-Day War of 1967. The Israelis returned these favors by quietly providing assistance to the Allies in Operation Desert Storm. Indeed, so embarrassed was Washington about this that when General Norman Schwartzkopf indicated disagreement with the Bush administration on ending the war as soon as it did, Iraqi media claimed that Bush silenced Schwartzkopf, fearing he would expose the deeply buried secrets about Israeli involvement in the war on Iraq.

Fundamentalist Muslims, who see things in a larger context than others, go beyond specific countries and view the problem in civilizational terms. A Muslim Brethren leader discerns "full cooperation between Zionism and the Western world against Islam and the Muslims,"[109] while Khomeini refers to a "Judeo-Christian plot." For Hamas, the U.S. role in the peace process is identical to Israel's: "Kissinger, Shultz, and Shamir . . . are one body and a single spearhead. . . . Things have reached a pass where it is Shamir who is visiting Arab capitals in the guise of the American Shultz."[110] Along similar lines, Egypt's Muslim Brethren declares that variances between Israel and the United States are "differences in tactics rather than in objectives."[111]

Even when Middle Easterners see Israel as an instrument of imperialism, they nonetheless depict the Jewish state as active and willing to do its part. 'Arafat, for example, saw Israel as the "beast's claws" that "wants a share of the beast's kills."[112]

This alleged cooperation leads some Middle Easterners to see the two parties as strangely intertwined. For Saddam Husayn, "the essence of the conspiracy" lies in the convergence of U.S. efforts to dominate the world and Israeli desires to create a Greater Israel.[113] Mu'ammar al-Qadhdhafi says that "America is the protector of Israel, Israel is the protector of America. They are friends and protectors to each other."[114] Radio Damascus also portrays matters in this complex way. The bond "between Israel and the United States," it pronounced in 1986, "makes Israel a U.S. tool directed against national liberation movements in the region, and also makes U.S. foreign policy a tool for implementing Israeli policy."[115]

Others go beyond this to see the United States and Israel as tied organically to the other. Zionists and imperialists become the twin manifestations of a single, horrible evil. They "are two heads of the same spear."[116] They can no longer be separated from each other: "The United States and Israel are the same thing."[117] The two forces meld in Iraqi propaganda. Saddam spoke of "America, together with Zionism, or Zionism, together with America — or any of these two alternatives."[118] The first military communiqué from Iraq on 17 January 1991 reflected such thinking, referring to criminal aggression carried out by "the treasonous Zionist-American enemy"; the fourth communiqué was even more explicit, announcing that "Israel and the United States are one and the same."[119] Taha Yasin Ramadan of Iraq came up with a more enigmatic formulation of the same thought, telling of "Israel's protégés—who created and nurtured it."[120]

Fundamentalists also see the two combining into one. Ramzi Yusuf, the bomber on several continents, refers to the "so-called United States," preferring the name "the Israeli States" on the grounds that "it supports Israel in everything, as if it were subordinated to Israel and not vice-versa." At the same time, he would use the term "American Israel" on the grounds that Israel is "like any" of the fifty states.[121]

## Israel vs. the United States

At other times, Middle Easterners reverse themselves and portray the U.S.-Israel relationship as fundamentally hostile.

*The U.S. as victim.* Arabs and Iranians widely assume that Jews killed John F. Kennedy and his brother Robert F. Kennedy. As John had done much to advance U.S. relations with Israel, it was nearly inevitable that Edward Kennedy would hear in a Palestinian refugee camp three years later, "The Jews killed your brother just as they killed Christ."[122] That Jack Ruby, a Jew, had murdered Lee Harvey Oswald was somehow taken as proof positive of this speculation. When Robert Kennedy died in 1968 at the hands of a Palestinian protesting his pro-Israel politics, the PLO portrayed the assassination as part of a Zionist plot. Why would the Zionists murder a friend? Reaching for any straw, a Beirut newspaper postulated the Jewish fear that he would reveal the Zionist role behind John's assassination in 1963.[123]

Some Arabs go so far as to see the Arab-Israeli conflict as a symptom of tensions between the United States and Israel: "the dispute in the region is not an Arab-Israeli conflict as much as it is a U.S.-Israeli conflict over spheres of influence in the Middle East."[124] Consistent with this, Salah Khalaf of Al-Fat'h, claimed that his organization received notice in March 1968 about an imminent Israeli attack from the CIA, via the Jordanians.[125] In other words, Washington deceived its Israeli ally to help its PLO enemy.

This interpretation became common in late 1991, after the American-led victory over Iraq and as the Soviet Union collapsed. Noting that Israel's close relations with Washington put it in good stead in the new era, anti-Zionist governments developed fantastical allegations about Israel's hostile acts toward the United States, perhaps hoping to sabotage that bond. The Syrian Arab News Agency revealed a secret U.S. government report that held Israel responsible for trying to bomb an American civil airliner. The Syrian media held that Israeli settlements in the disputed territories "are part of a conspiracy against the United States."[126] Syrian vice president 'Abd al-Halim Khaddam mused on this topic: "Although Washington and Israel are allies and it assists, nourishes, supports, and defends Israel, the Israelis do not want the [Arab-Israeli] negotiations to be held in Washington. That gives us food for thought."[127] 'Arafat blamed Israelis for the explosion on Pan Am 103 which killed 271 persons, seeing this as their way "to undermine the peace march."[128] A Pakistani newspaper carried this theme further, revealing that "The state of Jewish involvement in the KGB covert operations in the U.S. is so serious . . . that if the KGB secrets are revealed, the U.S. might either expel the American Jews or declare war against Israel."[129]

*Israel as victim.*    Curiously, there is also a recessive view that has Israel not an adjunct of imperialism but as its victim—a place to which a people not wanted in Christian Europe was expelled. (This approach may derive from long-ago Soviet claims: in late 1948, the Soviets supported Israel at the United Nations on the grounds that it was a victim of a conspiracy between British imperialists and their Arab agents.) Yasir 'Arafat's father is quoted as observing in the late 1940s, "What is going on is colonialism. It is not the Jews. This is a game of high stakes."[130] Khalaf held that the British engaged in all sorts of dirty tricks in Palestine in the 1940s, such as attacking both Arabs and Jews, thereby inciting them to armed clashes, as a way to prolong their mandate.

This line of thought inspires some eye-opening speculations. Muhammad Mahdi at-Tajir, ambassador of the United Arab Emirates in

Great Britain, once explained to a British writer: "It is not the Jews who created the state [of Israel]. It is an invention of their enemies, especially the British. When you wanted to get rid of them because you were afraid they would rule Britain, you put the idea in their head of creating a homeland."[131] This from an ambassador to the Court of St. James's! Qadhdhafi took the notion one step further, calling the creation of Israel "a big international conspiracy against the Jews." Addressing Jews, he warned them that the Europeans "want to get rid of you and throw you in Palestine for the Arabs to eliminate you some day." To avoid this fate, Qadhdhafi urged Israelis to "leave Palestine immediately and return to [your] own countries."[132]

To be sure, the notion of Jews as victims has never enjoyed a wide following among Muslims, possibly because it is much less useful than portraying Israel as a monstrous and all-powerful agent of imperialism. This latter view deepens hatred for the enemy, inflates the threat he poses, stimulates xenophobia, and rallies citizens to the government. It turns Israel from a parochial Middle East concern into a global problem, universalizing the Arab cause. It also makes the Arabs' defeats that much more palatable; how can they beat an Israel enjoying British and American support?

## REFLECTIONS

Several points about U.S.-Israel relations bear noting.

***Kernel of truth.*** Each of these two contrary themes contains an element of truth, but conspiracy theorists draw bizarre readings from simple facts.

The great powers then and now have expected to benefit from Israel. As early as 1840, British foreign minister Lord Palmerston, wrote that the return of the Jewish people to Palestine would serve to check "any future evil designs of Mehemet Ali [the ruler of Egypt] or his successor."[133] The British government did endorse a national home in Palestine for the Jewish people in the Balfour Declaration. The U.S. government formed a strategic partnership with Israel in the 1980s. But all this has to be put in context. Palmerston's ideas were stillborn; London quickly regretted the Balfour Declaration; and American support for Israel comes much less from putative imperialists (such as business interests or the military) than from those who feel moral or spiritual ties with the Jewish state.

Conversely, Israel and American Jews do affect the U.S. government's policy in the Middle East. The great Zionist leader Chaim Weizmann had access to the highest circles of British officialdom, while AIPAC has rightly been called "perhaps the most effective pressure group in Washington."[134] Still, the idea of a Zionist plot rests on the faulty premise that Jews are the only Westerners favoring strong ties to Israel; in fact, of course, this "special relationship" draws on many sources—theological, moral, political, and strategic—and enjoys wide support among the Christian majority. Americans have consistently viewed good relations with Israel as an important aspect of U.S. foreign policy. In the aftermath of the Jewish holocaust in World War II, they wanted to help protect the fragile Zionist enterprise. This initial impulse evolved into a wide-ranging moral commitment and celebration of common values, cultural and political. In the 1980s, an all-but-formal military alliance emerged, built on the two countries' complementary assets and skills. Indeed, while the U.S. public is skeptical about foreign aid in principle, a review of 40 years of history shows that "most Americans strongly support" economic and military aid to Israel.[135] Conspiracy theorists tend to ignore these inconvenient details.

Middle Eastern perceptions of Israel's place in the world suggests that, even after a century of the Zionist enterprise, Muslim peoples cannot understand the Jewish state's relations with the Western world. As Muslims, they fail to understand the emotional resonance of a common Bible and a host of Judeo-Christian features. As Middle Easterners, they cannot see beyond the clash of nationalisms to comprehend shared interests between countries. As citizens of authoritarian states, they miss the importance of personal, cultural, and political bonds between free peoples. In short, the "special relationship" between the United States and Israel mystifies Arabs and Iranians. Perplexed by an alliance that makes no sense, they fall back on conspiratorial explanations.

*Armenia.*    Independent Armenia, newly emerged from the former Soviet Union, like Israel is sometimes seen as Washington's cat's paw, other times as its boss. As an example of the first, an Iranian newspaper held that the U.S. government "provoked Armenia into a conflict with Azerbaijan and Nakhichevan [as a means] to thwart Iran's peace efforts, and thinking that it can harm Iran's popularity."[136] Azeri leaders, in direct contrast, see Armenia as all-powerful; they "argue that the West, especially France and the United States but also Russia, is controlled to one extent or the other by an organized Armenian lobby."[137] This wins Armenia great benefits. The Pan-Turkish nationalist Mustafa Necati Özfatura claims that the Armenian president, in a secret meeting with George Bush, got the U.S. government to agree on an Armenia stretching from the Mediterranean Sea to the Black Sea to the Caspian to the Persian Gulf[138] — or roughly the area of Greater Israel.

The connection between Armenia and Israel is sometimes made explicit. Bülent Ecevit, the leftist Turkish leader, accused Washington of encouraging Armenians to make territorial demands on both Azerbaijan and Turkey. Why? Because "the United States is planning to give Armenia a role in the Caucasus similar to that played by Israel in the Middle East."[139] Nakhichevan's President Haydar Aliyev, seeing Armenia as the U.S. base in the Caucasus, also drew the analogy to Israel. This embryonic parallel to the U.S.-Israel nexus suggests that Israel need not be unique in the Middle Eastern imagination; any non-Muslim state with a lobby in Washington can enter the same twilight of puppet and puppeteer.

*Useful.*    Each view has its own uses. When ties to Moscow were strong, Damascus stressed the dangers of imperialist plots and variously derided Israel as "a U.S. base,"[140] America's "big stick,"[141] and "a mere U.S. aircraft carrier."[142] In contrast, when Damascus sought to improve relations with Washington, it blamed "world Jewry" for subverting American decision making. "The United States does not have a policy of its own in the Middle East," but blindly follows directives issued in Tel Aviv.[143] Similarly, Sa'd Jum'a, a Jordanian prime minister known for his pro-U.S. views, found it convenient to blame Washington's policy on Zionist agents, whose "constant efforts mislead the ordinary American citizen."[144]

Each explanation has other uses, too. The imperialist thesis helps explain away Israel's military success against the Arab states. As the British writer, David Pryce-Jones observes, "to have been defeated by Jews is humiliating, but to have been defeated by a conspiracy of all the powers is clearly unavoidable."[145] In contrast, the Zionist thesis accounts for American reluctance to adopt the Arab cause against Israel; however just that cause, it cannot compete with the machinations of a conspiracy.

*Derived from Europe.*    Neither the imperialist or the Zionist interpretation is original to the Middle East; both come from Europe. The notion of Israel as a tool of imperialism goes back to Vladimir Ilyich Lenin and the early Bolshevik state. A Soviet document from July 1919 called Zionism "one of the branches of the imperialist counter-revolution,"[146] an idea subsequently repeated *ad nauseam* by the Soviet propaganda apparatus and also in private by Soviet leaders. Leonid Brezhnev told two Arab rulers in 1967 that "Israel by itself was nothing. It depended for its existence on American aid, and the reason why the Americans kept Israel alive was because they wanted the oil of the Middle East. . . . The Americans could not themselves attack the Arab nation, but they could attack through Israel."[147]

As for the notion of Israel as part of a Jewish world plot, it derives from Nazi ideology. As early as the mid-1920s, Adolf Hitler wrote in *Mein Kampf* of his suspicions about the Zionists' ultimate goals: "They do not think at all of establishing a Jewish state in Palestine to live in it someday; rather, they want a central organization for their international world cheating, withdrawn from others' reach—a refuge for convicted dregs and a college for aspiring swindlers."[148] The Nazis found an eager audience in the Middle East for their anti-Semitic message. Hitler's ideology appealed to many there. Already in the mid-1930s, one Arab recalls, Palestinian Arabs "lapped up Fascist and Nazi lies. They saw the Zionists as the sinister world-menace of the Nazi legend, and England as a puppet power in their clutches."[149] Leading Arab intellectuals such as Michel 'Aflaq, Shakib Arslan, Sati' al-Husri, and Antun Sa'ada adopted Nazi ideas, as did politicians like Rashid 'Ali al-Gilani and Anwar as-Sadat.

In brief, Middle East politicians still today routinely echo the ideas of Lenin and Hitler, the men who initiated this century's most appalling political experiments. In keeping with the origins of these ideas, leftists tend slightly more to fear an imperialist plot, while those on the right worry more about Zionist conspiracies. Leftists find it natural to make common cause with the Soviet, Chinese, and other bastions of anti-Americanism. The rightist emphasis on the prominent role of American Jews, especially their presence in business, the media, and politics, makes it natural for them to link up with anti-Semitic groups in the West.

***Contradiction.*** Having it two contradictory ways at once recalls *The Protocols of the Elders of Zion* and *Mein Kampf*. Those writings portray Jews as both the capitalists and middlemen who steal from the workers and as socialists who threaten the bankers. For example, Hitler declared in 1922 that "Moses Kohn on the one side encourages his [employers'] association to refuse the worker's demands, while his brother Isaac in the factory incites the masses [to strike]."[150] Just as Germans seemed not to note the inconsistency of these claims, so Middle Easterners believe simultaneously in opposite conspiracy theories about Israel and the United States. How can this be?

***Explaining the paradox.*** The two conspiracy theories share many premises. Both dismiss disagreements between Jerusalem and Washington as charades to fool the gullible. Both discern a hidden agenda. Both transform mutual influence into terrifying manipulation. Both turn a powerful foe into a conspirator of global proportions. Both theories take a basic truth and distort it beyond recognition. Both twist the essential balance of U.S.-Israel relations into something skewed. Both postulate lock-step agreement between the two sides, implying that only one party makes decisions; the other takes orders. As Mu'ammar al-Qadhdhafi explains, "there is no ordinary friend in the U.S. lexicon; one is either an agent or an enemy."[151]

We see here two opposite conspiracy theories reconciled by a yet larger conspiracy theory: (1) The Jews' economic power permits them to run American foreign policy, and (2) this power is used for imperialist ends. It then follows that: (3) the Zionists run U.S. policy and Washington depends heavily on Israel. Or, more succinctly: Jews rule America; Israel serves as part of its mechanism for world control. Of course, this train of thought assumes that both Lenin's and Hitler's ideas are correct—a rare combination in the West but commonplace in the Middle East.

At this point the theories converge, the double conspiracy becomes one, and exact roles hardly matter. One government is in charge, the other has betrayed its national interests. Americans and Israelis are working together to rule the world, so who cares which of them is dominant, which is subservient? There's only one seat of decision making: one is the ventriloquist, the other the dummy. It may not be clear which is which, but that hardly matters. Not being able to discern their real roles only makes the alliance that much more sinister.

## NOTES TO CHAPTER 8

1. An-Nahar (Jerusalem), 20 June 1994.
2. T. E. Lawrence, *Seven Pillars of Wisdom: A Triumph* (Garden City, N.Y.: Doubleday, Doran & Company, 1935), p. 38.
3. *Ath-Thawra*, 28 March 1990. Sulayman 'Arar, speaker of the lower Jordanian house of parliament concurred, seeing the vote as proof that "the U.S. Senate is controlled by the Zionist lobby" (*Jordan Times*, 25 March 1990).
4. Radio Baghdad, 19 April 1990.
5. *Al-Qadisiya*, 28 June 1990; *Al-Jumhuriya*, 24 June 1990.
6. Radio Baghdad, 17 July 1990.
7. Cable News Network, 28 January 1991.
8. *Al-Ba'th* (Baghdad), 5 June 1992.
9. *Europeo* (Milan), 16 October 1992.

10. Quoted in P. J. Vatikiotis, *Nasser and His Generation* (New York: St. Martin's Press, 1978), p. 250.

11. 28 September 1958 interview. Text in *President Gamal Abdel Nasser's Speeches and Press Interviews During the Year 1958* (Cairo: U.A.R. Information Department, 1959), p. 402. Abdel Nasser's statement closely echoes Walther Rathenau's famous 1909 assertion ("Three hundred men, all of whom know each other, guide the economic destinies of the Continent"), except that he adds a anti-Semitic twist. See Walther Rathenau, *Zur Kritik der Zeit* (Berlin: S. Fischer, 1919).

12. Saad El-Shazly, *The Arab Military Option* (San Francisco: American Mideast Research, 1986), pp. 94-95.

13. Ismail Fahmy, *Negotiating for Peace in the Middle East* (Baltimore: Johns Hopkins University Press, 1983), p. 297.

14. Anouar Abdel-Melek, "Introduction à la pensée arabe contemporaine," in Anouar Abdel-Melek, ed., *La pensée politique arabe contemporaine* (Paris: Editions du Seuil, 1970), p. 37.

15. Anwar el-Sadat, *In Search of Identity: An Autobiography* (New York: Harper & Row, 1977). pp. 288-89, 300.

16. *Gozideh Payam-ha Imam Khomeini* (Tehran, 1979), quoted in Amir Taheri, *The Spirit of Allah: Khomeini and the Islamic Revolution* (Bethesda, Md.: Adler & Adler, 1986), p. 152.

17. Ervand Abrahamian, *Khomeinism: Essays on the Islamic Republic* (Berkeley: University of California Press, 1993), p.123.

18. *Ar-Ra'y*, 7 December 1991.

19. Iraqi News Agency, 3 April 1990.

20. *Al-Anba'* (Kuwait), 12 April 1990.

21. Fathi 'Uthman al-Mahlawi, "A Spearhead Against Arab Nationalism," *Journal of Arab Nationalism*, January-March 1959.

22. Tripoli Television, 24 March 1990.

23. Agence France Presse, 23 July 1993.

24. Muhammad Ayyubi in *The New York Times*, 28 March 1994.

25. Tripoli Television, 24 March 1990.

26. El-Shazly, *The Arab Military Option*, p. 1.

27. Ibid., p. 45.

28. Rashid Khalidi, *Under Seige: P.L.O. Decisionmaking During the 1982 War* (New York: Columbia University Press, 1986), p. 128.

29. *Ash-Sha'b*, 13 March 1990.

30. *U.S. News & World Report*, 10 July 1989.

31. Radio Tehran, 20 April 1990.

32. *Al-Musawwar*, 20 January 1989.

33. *Kayhan* (Tehran), 31 October 1992.

34. Linda Blandford, *Super-Wealth: The Secret Lives of the Oil Sheikhs* (New York: William Morrow, 1977), p. 87. It's not clear what they consider the fifty-first precinct to be.

35. 22 April 1958 interview. Text in *President Gamal Abdel Nasser's Speeches . . . 1958*, p. 390.

36. *The Charter* (Cairo: U.A.R. State Information Service, [1962]), pp. 79, 27.

37. Al-Lajna ath-Thaqafiya bi-Hay'at at-Tahrir, *Hadhihi as-Sahyuniya*, introduction by Jamal 'Abd an-Nasir (Cairo: Ikhtarna Lak: 1954); and speech of 22 July 1961. Both quoted in Y. Harkabi, *Arab Attitudes to Israel*, trans. Misha Louvish (London: Vallentine, Mitchell, 1972), pp. 158-59.

38. Articles 19 and 22, in Y. Harkabi, *The Palestinian Covenant and its Meaning* (London: Valentine, Mitchell, 1979), pp. 110, 117.

39. Republic of Iraq Radio, 8 August 1994.

40. Libyan Television, 4 October 1995.

41. *Al-Ahram*, 19 June 1964. Quoted in Harkabi, *Arab Attitudes to Israel*, p. 160.

42. Text in Hussein of Jordan, *My "War" with Israel* (New York: William Morrow, 1969), p. 133.

43. Sa'd Jum'a, *Al-Mu'amara wa-Ma'rakat al-Masir* ([Beirut]: Dar al-Katib al-'Arabi, 1968), p. 204.

44. El-Shazly, *The Arab Military Option*, p. 101.

45. *Ash-Sharq al-Awsat*, 17 March 1995.

46. Anon., *Nass ar-Risala al-Maftuha allati Wajjahaha Hizbullah ila al-Mustad'afin fi Lubnan wa'l-'Alam* (Beirut, 16 February 1985), p. 28; 'Abbas al-Musawi, cited in the *La Revue du Liban*, 27 July 1985. Both quoted in Martin Kramer, *Hezbollah's Vision of the West* (Washington, D.C.: Washington Institute for Near East Policy, 1989), p. 51.

47. Article 28 of the Hamas Charter, quoted in *Contemporary Mideast Backgrounder*, October 1988, pp. 8-9.

48. *Ash-Sha'b*, 6 July 1993.

49. Ibid.

50. *Ar-Ra'y* (Amman), 23 October 1993.

51. Edward W. Said, *The Question of Palestine* (New York: Times Books, 1979), p. 29.

52. Tripoli Television, 24 March 1990; *Tishrin*, 15 July 1980; Baghdad Voice of the PLO, 14 April 1990.

53. *Ar-Ra'y*, 9 January 1989.

54. Director of the archives, office of the chairman of the PLO, interviewed on 11 March 1984. Quoted in Khalidi, *Under Seige*, p. 123.

55. *Al-Majalla*, 4-10 July 1981.

56. Middle East News Agency, 10 July 1995.

57. Reuters, 9 December 1989. Quoted in Barry Rubin, "The PLO Between Anti-Zionism and Antisemitism," *Analysis of Current Trends in Antisemitism* (Jerusalem: Hebrew University, 1993), p. 16.

58. Kuwaiti News Agency, 6 March 1989.

59. Iraqi News Agency, 7 September 1994.

60. Muhammad Fadlallah, quoted in Martin Kramer, "The Jihad against the Jews," *Commentary*, October 1994, p. 40.

61. Libyan Television, 9 June 1994. Of course, Jerusalem and not Tel Aviv is Israel's capital; odd that in this context, the international affairs editor of the Jamahiriya Arab News Agency should pretend otherwise.

62. *Al-Quds al-'Arabi* (London), 2 August 1995.
63. Fayiz as-Sayigh, managing editor of the Syrian Arab News Agency, quoted in *The Wall Street Journal*, 27 September 1990.
64. Muhammad al-Ghazali, *Min Huna Na'lam*, 5th ed. (Cairo: Matba'at as-Sa'ada, 1965), p. 107.
65. Clark Blaise and Bharati Mukherjee, "After the Fatwa," *Mother Jones*, April-May 1990, p. 62.
66. Rana Kabbanni, *Letter to Christendom* (London: Virago, 1989), p. 52.
67. Quoted in J. C. Hurewitz, *The Struggle for Palestine* (New York: Schoken, 1976), p. 308.
68. Anwar el-Sadat, *In Search of Identity: An Autobiography* (New York: Harper & Row, 1977), pp. 278-79.
69. *At-Tamaddun*, 30 April 1990.
70. Voice of the Islamic Republic of Iran, 29 December 1995.
71. *Al-Muharrir* (Paris), 8 May 1995.
72. Voice of the Islamic Republic of Iran, 8 May 1995.
73. *Al-Akhbar* (Cairo), 11 May 1995.
74. *Al-Ahram* (Cairo), 13 May 1995.
75. Voice of the Islamic Republic of Iran, 10 May 1995.
76. *Al-Majalla*, 28 May 1995.
77. Quoted in Abdel Magid Farid, *Nasser: The Final Years* (Reading, Eng.: Ithaca Press, 1994), p. 32.
78. *Crescent International*, 16-31 October 1994.
79. Sa'd Jum'a, *Al-Mu'amara wa-Ma'rakat al-Masir* ([Beirut]: Dar al-Katib al-'Arabi, 1968), p. 206.
80. *The Star* (Amman), 31 January-6 February 1991.
81. *The Pakistan Times*, 4 February 1991.
82. John Wallach, "Visiting Baghdad," *Middle East Insight*, May-August 1994, p. 34.
83. *Tishrin*, 17 May 1980.
84. Conversation on 25 October 1937 with H. R. P. Dickson, Foreign Office 371/20822 E7201/22/31. Text in Elie Kedourie, *Islam in the Modern World* (New York: Holt Rinehart and Winston, 1980), p. 71.
85. Voice of the Islamic Republic, 14 February 1993, 3 September 1993.
86. *Ad-Dustur* (Amman), 23 November 1992.
87. *The Pakistan Times*, 4 February 1991.
88. *Al-Qadisiya*, 11 July 1990.
89. Iraq Television Network, 19 June 1995.
90. *Syrian Times*, 14 May 1994.
91. *The Economist*, 25 January 1992. This is an even stranger statement than may initially appear, for Islam holds that Jesus did not die on the cross at all; accordingly, the Jews did not kill him.
92. Speech given on 7 May 1970. Text in *International Documents on Palestine 1970* (Beirut: Institute for Palestine Studies, 1973), p. 797.

93. Libyan Television, 2 March 1992.

94. Statement dated 1 March 1944, quoted in Joseph B. Schechtman, *The Mufti and the Fuehrer* (New York: Thomas Yoseloff, 1965), p. 150.

95. Fahmy, *Negotiating for Peace*, pp. 31, 53.

96. Sawt al-Mustad'afin (Baalbek), 3 August 1995.

97. *Ash-Sharq al-Awsat,* 7 November 1992.

98. Ibid.

99. Radio Damascus, 25 March 1990.

100. *The Washington Times,* 4 November 1992.

101. *Ash-Sharq al-Awsat,* 7 November 1992.

102. Quoted in Sylvia Haim, "Sayyid Qutb," *Asian and African Studies* 16 (1982), pp. 154-55.

103. *Tehran Times,* 19 June 1990. The Soviets encouraged their allies to concentrate on the United States. In Leonid Brezhnev's words: "If the United States stops loans and aid to Israel, it will wither and vanish within a short period. So, why is America so interested in Israel? The answer lies in America's ambition in the Arab region, which contains 60 per cent of the world's oil reserves." Quoted in Abdel Magid Farid, *Nasser,* p. 22.

104. *Jomhuri-ye Islami,* 12 January 1991.

105. *An-Nur* (Cairo), 29 June 1994.

106. Voice of the Islamic Republic, 19 February 1993.

107. Quoted in Emmanuel Sivan, *Radical Islam: Medieval Theology and Modern Politics* (New Haven, Conn.: Yale University Press, 1985), p. 57.

108. *Ar-Ra'y* (Amman), 25 December 1990; *Ad-Dustur,* 30 January 1991; *Jomhuri-ye Islami,* 12 January 1991.

109. Deputy Leader Mustafa Mashhur, *Ash-Sha'b,* 27 September 1994.

110. Leaflet No. 10 of the Unified National Command. Text in Shaul Mishal and Reuben Aharoni, *Speaking Stones: Communiqués from the Intifada Underground* (Syracuse, N.Y.: Syracuse University Press, 1994), pp. 67-68.

111. Walid Mahmoud Abdelnasser, *The Islamic Movement in Egypt: Perceptions of International Relations, 1967-81* (London: Kegan Paul International, 1994), p. 162.

112. *An-Nahar,* 8 May 1991.

113. Iraqi News Agency, 27 December 1990.

114. Great Jamahiriya Radio, 13 March 1994.

115. Radio Damascus, 27 January 1986.

116. Libyan Television, 16 February 1994.

117. As'ad 'Abd ar-Rahman, member of the Palestine National Council, quoted in *Svenska Dagbladet,* 5 September 1990.

118. Radio Baghdad, 25 December 1990.

119. Communiqué no. 1, issued by the Armed Forces General Command, 17 January 1991; communiqué no. 4, 18 January 1991.

120. Iraqi News Agency, 18 April 1990.

121. *Al-Majalla,* 28 May 1995.

122. Quoted in Hussein, *My "War" with Israel*, p. 166.

123. *Al-Kifah* (Beirut), 6 June 1968; cited in Harkabi, *Arab Attitudes to Israel*, p. 186.

124. *Sawt ash-Sha'b*, 29 March 1990.

125. Abou Iyad, *Palestinien sans Patrie* (Paris: Fayolle, 1978), p. 98.

126. Syrian Arab Republic Radio, 29 September 1991.

127. Sawt Lubnan, 3 December 1991.

128. *Ar-Ra'y* (Amman), 9 January 1989.

129. Shahid Aziz, writing in *The Muslim*, 1 October 1991.

130. Quoted by Fat'hi 'Arafat in Janet Wallach and John Wallach, *Arafat: In the Eyes of the Beholder* (New York: Lyle Stuart, 1990), p. 67.

131. Quoted in Andrew Duncan, *Money Rush* (Garden City, N.Y.: Doubleday, 1979), p. 250.

132. Jamahiriya Arab News Agency, 6 January 1990.

133. Palmerston to Ponsonby, 11 August 1840, no. 134, Foreign Office 78/390. Quoted in Frederick Stanley Rodkey, "Lord Palmerston and the Rejuvenation of Turkey, 1830-41," *The Journal of Modern History* 2 (1930): 215.

134. *The Washington Post*, 10 April 1984.

135. Eytan Gilboa, *American Public Opinion Toward Israel and the Arab-Israeli Conflict* (Lexington, Mass.: Lexington Books, 1987), p. 308.

136. *Kayhan*, 12 July 1992.

137. Mark Saroyan, "Azerbaijan Looks 'West': New Trends in Foreign Relations with Iran and Turkey," *The Iranian Journal of International Affairs*, Spring 1992, p. 187.

138. *Türkiye*, 29 September 1991.

139. *Milliyet*, 6 March 1990.

140. Prime Minister 'Abd ar-Ra'uf Kasm, quoted in *Ar-Ra'y al-'Amm*, 17 May 1980.

141. Editorial, *Tishrin*, 9 July 1981.

142. Editorial, *Al-Ba'th*, 14 June 1987.

143. Radio Damascus, 15 August 1985; editorial, *Ath-Thawra* (Damascus), 1 February 1986.

144. Jum'a, *Al-Mu'amara wa-Ma'rakat al-Masir*, p. 47.

145. David Pryce-Jones, *The Closed Circle: An Interpretation of the Arabs* (New York: Harper & Row, 1989), p. 216.

146. Quoted in Ran Marom, "The Bolsheviks and the Balfour Declaration 1917-1920," *The Wiener Library Bulletin*, 29, nos. 37/38 (1976): 22.

147. Paraphrased in Mohamed Heikal, *The Sphinx and the Commissar: The Rise and Fall of Soviet Influence in the Middle East* (New York: Harper & Row, 1978), p. 186. Farid, *Nasser*, p. 23, has a slightly different version: "A direct imperialist attack against the Arab countries is almost impossible but an attack through Israel will always give it an appropriate solution."

148. Adolf Hitler, *Mein Kampf* (Munich: Zentralverlag der NSDAP, 1935), p. 356.

149. Edward Atiyah, *An Arab Tells His Story: A Study in Loyalties* (London: John Murray, 1946), p. 203. Paradoxically, Arab leaders were also spouting the opposite accusation. Already in 1943, while the gas chambers were operating at full capacity, Faris

al-Khuri of Syria asserted that "Zionists are *Nazis.*" (Quoted in Freya Stark, *The Arab Island,* New York: Alfred A. Knopf, 1946, p. 141.) This calumny spread with the decades, becoming almost commonplace by 1982.

150. Speech of 12 April 1922, in Norman H. Baynes, ed., *The Speeches of Adolf Hitler, April 1922-August 1939* (London: Oxford University Press, 1942), vol. 1, p. 29.

151. Libyan Television, 15 January 1992.

# 9.

# The Conspirator's Nature

> Havoc and spoil and ruin are our gain.
> —*Jedidiah Morse's notion of the conspirator's credo*[1]

> The majority of conspirators act
> out of love for the game.
> —*The Protocols of the Elders of Zion*[2]

Who carries out grand conspiracies? Just about anyone can be complicit, but the leaders are usually Jews or Christians, with Muslims providing the footsoldiers. These are not pleasant people, but satanic, ubiquitous, and very clever foes. While *The Protocols* discerns a "love for the game," purely malicious inspiration hardly ever figures in Middle Eastern perceptions. Rather, Arab and Iranian theorists usually explain a conspirator's motives by pointing to some aspect of three main drives: love of money, love of power, and hatred of Islam.

## PERSONNEL

While the ultimate conspirators are but a handful of elders or tycoons sitting around elegant boardrooms, plots are carried out by a wide range of individuals. For convenience sake, we can divide these into Jews, Christians, and Muslims. Each of these religious groups then further divides into two: overt and covert Jews, orientalist and traveling Christians, fundamentalist and antifundamentalist Muslims.

## Jews
***Overt.***    Every last Jew works on behalf of Zionism: "Israel has eleven million ambassadors, spies, financiers, and company representatives in the world."[3] The spokesman for Hamas, Ibrahim Ghawsha, puts it even more absolutely: "A Jew is always loyal to his Jewishness and state."[4]

Israelis in the Arab countries inspire special concern. Egypt's 'Adil Husayn tells of Israelis who entered his country with false passports and posing as tourists: "what are they doing now? The security services arrested many of these people while they were carrying out acts of sabotage."[5] News reports soberly asserted in 1993 that the Israeli Cultural Center in Cairo was used for stockpiling arms to use in terrorist incidents against Egyptians.

Even the trampled and elderly remnants of Jewish communities in Arab lands are accused of taking an active role in renting the fabric of society. In Iraq after June 1967 war, the abuse of local Jews took on special importance, as Samir al-Khalil explains in *Republic of Fear*:

> The ghosts of tens thousands of Egyptian, Syrian, Jordanian, and Palestinian casualties, to say nothing of the occupation of territories, the collapse of whole armies, and the destruction of equipment—all of this was summoned up in the fantasies of ordinary men and women as the responsibility of Iraq's tiny Jewish community.[6]

Building on this precedent, the Ba'th Party spun a story in December 1968 about efforts of three states—Israel, Lebanon, and Iran—to use Iraqi nationals, especially Jews, to get access to Iraqi military secrets. The Jewish owner of a kitchen-utensils shop turned out to be the key figure in this sinister scheme, sending messages to Israel via a radio set located in a church. The regime transformed his court case into a massive public event that led to the imposition of a reign of terror on Iraq.

***Covert.***    Virtually every important powerholder in the Middle East has come under suspicion of being a covert Jew. Kemal Atatürk was a *dönme* (or crypto-Jew) who imposed a secularist program in Turkey in revenge for the Ottomans not ceding Palestine to the Jews. Mohammad Reza Pahlavi was either born a Jew or converted to Judaism. The ruling families of Saudi Arabia and Kuwait are both Jewish. Michel 'Aflaq, the

Ba'th Party founder, was a Jew. PLO leaders Yasir 'Arafat and Salah Khalaf were Jewish-born. Queen Noor of Jordan, the former Lisa Halabi of Princeton University, is a Jewess sent by the CIA to poison her husband, King Husayn. Not only are they Jews, but they actively help Israel. Thus, Mu'ammar al-Qadhdhafi of Libya is a secret Zionist who uses the funds from oil sales to subsidize Israel's government.

(In addition, many powerful figures around the world are covert Jews who help Israel, including Lavrenti Beria, Leonid Brezhnev, Lyndon Johnson, and Nelson Rockefeller.)

Jews often put on disguises to present themselves as the armed forces of Muslim states; according to Ayatollah Khomeini, Israeli soldiers disguised themselves as Iranians and killed his followers on the streets of Iran in 1978. They also penetrate the armed forces; Iraqi officials privately told an Arab president, "Do not cooperate with Egypt in anything involving weapons, because the [Egyptian] armed forces are all deeply infiltrated by Israeli intelligence."[7] In like fashion, Khomeini deemed the shah's television station "a Jewish spy base."[8]

Sayyid Qutb takes this further, portraying all nonfundamentalist Muslims as Jewish agents. Their genius lies precisely in their appearing to be Muslim: "And so are they Muslims!! Do they not carry Muslim names?"[9] Retaining a Muslim identity and hiding their Jewish affiliation, these agents act with great effectiveness. They amount to "a massive army of agents in the form of professors, philosophers, doctors and researchers — sometimes also writers, poets, scientists and journalists — carrying Muslim names because they are of Muslim descent,"[10] though working for the Jewish conspiracy. Precisely the opposite argument is sometimes made; a Syrian diplomat claimed that fundamentalists who seduce the young "are, in fact, Jews, who secretly converted to Islam with the aim of corrupting the nation's youth."[11]

Not all Israel agents are human. When a falcon was captured near the Sudanese border with Chad and bore a tag with Hebrew lettering, Sudan's military intelligence took great interest in the bird and studied it closely. Word got out that it was an Israeli spy, complete with a miniature transmission device, on a mission over a 1,000 miles away from Israel. Eventually, however, its innocence was established. The falcon bore a in Hebrew tag because Israel, located at the confluence of Africa and Eurasia, is thick with birds traveling between continents. To track migration patterns, Israeli zoologists at Tel Aviv University catch and label some of the birds landing in their country.

## Christians

*Orientalists.*     Scholars of the East serve imperial interests by probing the Muslims' weak spots, exposing them, and informing Western governments of the results. Why else would students spend years learning a language and culture of little obvious use to them? Why do scholars pry into sensitive topics? Sayyid Qutb worried that "Hundreds and thousands have infiltrated the Muslim world, and they still do in the guise of orientalists."[12] He warned Muslims to be on their guard: "it would be extremely short-sighted of us to fall into the illusion that when the Jews and Christians discuss Islamic beliefs or Islamic history, or when they make proposals concerning Muslim society or Muslim politics or economics, they will be doing it with good intentions."[13]

Archaeologists and anthropologists arouse especially intense worry, precisely because their work pretends not to bear on power and politics. To xenophobes in the Yemeni court in 1952, archaeology "seemed to be just a pretext for Western entanglement in their country's affairs," and the Yemeni official who supervised a dig hinted in reports to the palace that American archaeologists were engaged in espionage.[14]

Middle Easterners sometimes have their suspicions confirmed by the information that Westerners (and their Muslim assistants) acquire. When an American anthropologist returned to an Egyptian Bedouin community to show off her published study on them, an elder responded with less than delight: "knowledge is power. The Americans and the British know everything. They want to know everything about people, about us. Then if they come to a country, or come to rule it, they know what people need and they know how to rule."[15] Khomeini thought along the same lines. He regaled audiences about British and American spies who, long before the advent of motorized travel, gathered information on Iran, to the point that they knew more about the country than Iranians. On occasion he would recall how once when he was in the city of Hamadan,

> a former student of the religious sciences, a man who had forsaken the religious garb but persevered in his Islamic ethics, came to see me and showed me a map on which certain places had been marked in red. He told me that those red symbols indicated all the mineral resources existing in Iran that had been located by foreign experts.[16]

The Committee for the Defense of Legitimate Rights, a fundamentalist Muslim group, discerned far deeper American control in Riyadh:

The Americans draw up all the [Saudi] Kingdom's policies including international relations, military policies, social policies, financial and economic policies in their entirety. The plans implemented in the Kingdom since the mid-1970's have been designed by Harvard University professors. The military strategies have been designed by the American Defence Ministry and those strategies even include the designation of those states deemed to be enemies of the Kingdom, namely neighbouring Muslim countries, and the Saudi population itself. The economic policies were designed by the Americans to enable them to achieve the largest operation of embezzlement in history.[17]

The study of Islam raises special fears for those who see faith as the key to power. Shabbir Akhtar, a British Muslim intellectual, holds that the "consistency and vigour" of Western expert bias against Islam suggests a conspiracy.[18] Again, Khomeini explains it best:

The British imperialists penetrated the countries of the East more than three hundred years ago. Being knowledgeable about all aspects of these countries, they drew up elaborate plans for assuming control of them. . . . They felt that the major obstacles in the path of their materialistic ambitions and the chief threat to their political power was nothing but Islam and its ordinances and the belief of the people in Islam. They therefore plotted and campaigned against Islam by various means. . . . The agents of imperialism, together with the educational, propaganda, and political apparatuses of the anti-national puppet governments they have installed, have been spreading poison for centuries and corrupting the minds and morals of the people. . . . They are destroying Islam![19]

Consistent with this fear, Iran's media accused orientalists (Jewish ones, this time) at Tel Aviv University of inspiring *The Satanic Verses* (which several intelligence services then proceeded to write). As if in response, the Iranian opposition claimed that a Princeton professor wrote Khomeini's book, *Islamic Government*.

Leftists are less impressed by the information collected by orientalists than by the attitudes that they help shape. Edward Said articulated the professorial version of this suspicion in *Orientalism*;[20] the Middle East press daily publishes vulgar renditions. For example, a Kuwaiti daily contends that a "thoroughly prepared" U.S.-Zionist plan to subvert the Middle East drew "on the expertise of social scientists and researchers."[21] Mention is made from time to time of a "Bernard Lewis plan" to fragment the Middle East into states so small they cannot pose a danger to outside interests.

*Travelers.*     Travelers are really spies, sent out to bring home secrets. Why else would tourists wend their way slowly across the Middle East, taking pictures of tribal peoples and poor neighborhoods? Curiosity, romanticism, and a flair for adventure being largely incomprehensible to locals, they assume malign motives. In a typical case of projecting, their own lack of curiosity about Western countries makes Middle Easterners suspicious of Westerners who travel off the beaten track or inquire about institutions; they must be up to no good. Michael Field observes that, "Having no interest in any other country themselves, the officials are only too ready to believe that anyone who is interested in theirs must have a dubious motive, probably as a spy."[22] Tal'at Fu'ad Qasim, an Egyptian fundamentalist living in Denmark, offered three ulterior purposes for tourism. It "spreads prostitution and AIDS via female Jewish tourists. It is a vile means of spreading all forms of immorality. Tourism is also used to collect information on the Islamic Groups for foreign intelligence services."[23]

Resident foreigners of all professions are believed routinely to report to their authorities at home, who pass details on to Jerusalem. Relief workers are too good to be true: they come from their fine houses in the West to do good in some backwater? They must have an ulterior purpose in mind—presumably a malign one that fits someone's grand conspiracy theory. Business corporations work hand-in-glove with their governments, serving as field agents. Journalists routinely file private reports with their intelligence agencies. In this spirit, a Lebanese woman at a dinner party very pleasantly but without apology asked her guest, a British reporter, if it is true "that all foreigners are spies?"[24]

Gamal Abdel Nasser concluded that "Israel has detailed information on Egypt through the Americans, French and Italians who are in our country."[25] A Libyan newspaper dug the deepest. It first noted a suspicious phenomenon:

> Many Westerners have been entering our Arab region legally and for public purposes. They are traders, tourists, commercial representatives, businessmen, diplomats, or workers in the so-called humanitarian agencies. They all claim that they are in love with the East. Arab countries open their doors for them by extending to them the renowned Arab hospitality.

Then the paper revealed their true missions, and how it knew what these are:

> The West reveals its true identity when it happens that one of them becomes involved in a road accident, an aggression, a disappearance, or a kidnapping by unknown persons. Then the state of the person involved hurriedly reveals his true identity and announces that the person in question is a spying intelligence officer or the head of a spying network for his country, or an official of an administration of this network. . . . Why does the West send us only its intelligence officers and men? Americans entered Lebanon for apparently innocent and humanitarian causes, including religious purposes, and after their kidnapping, America announced that they were intelligence men on a spying mission."[26]

## Muslims

Only rarely are ordinary Muslims accused of selling out. In one example, Hamas accused "hypocrites and cowards from among our people" of aiding Israel by convincing would-be warriors "to neglect *jihad*."[27] Unemployed individuals of weak character were said to have fomented violence in Egypt for Israel's Mossad, presumably for money.

Far more commonly, politicians get accused of being in the pay of Zionist and imperialist paymasters. Muhammad 'Abduh, the innovative Egyptian thinker on topics Islamic, is said to have been a stooge of Lord Cromer, the country's British ruler. King Husayn's middle name is "CIA." According to a Cairene newspaper, "Hashemi-Rafsanjani is known to be the United States' man" in Iran.[28] The Saudi ambassador in Washington, Prince Bandar bin Sultan, is an employee of the State Department and the CIA. A book cover shows Saddam Husayn's face superimposed on the American Statue of Liberty.[29] More generally, Qadhdhafi told of Westerners controlling "a small number of hireling and cowardly rulers who came to power against the will of their people and through a series of coups d'état and conspiracies."[30]

Interestingly, the fundamentalist and antifundamentalist camps trade charges, each accusing the other of selling out to the conspiracy. Sayyid Qutb accused modernists and secularists who reject his stringent vision of Islam of being Zionist agents. Whether they know it or not, they lead innocent Muslims away from their religion, and so are in fact working for the Jews.

Antifundamentalist Muslims throw this accusation right back. According to Muhammad Sa'id al-Ashmawi, an outspoken Egyptian enemy of fundamentalism, "Islamic extremism serves Israel's goals by distorting the image of Islam and weakening the Egyptian state."[31] But Qadhdhafi most consistently portrayed fundamentalist Muslims as agents of the West. "I do not trust organizations that call themselves Islamic. We are worried that the West might be behind them, especially when we see their leaders under the protection of the American, British, French, and German intelligence services."[32] Specifically, he discerned "a Zionist-Jewish-Christian plot to balkanize Egypt and divide it into several states. . . . Orders are given from Christian and Jewish capitals to destroy Egypt and Algeria."[33] In a characteristically eccentric statement, Qadhdhafi claimed that Communists and Muslim Brethren collude "in the same alliance against the [Libyan] revolution."[34]

Middle Eastern traitors carry out a number of tasks for their foreign masters. First, they sell precious resources at a discount and buy up the West's shoddy goods at inflated prices. Khomeinists accused first the shah of having "given away" Iranian oil, then berated their Persian Gulf neighbors for allowing the West "easy and cheap access" to oil.[35] Worse, because of the Arab leaders' "complicity with the international plundering thieves, oil has today become a tool in the hands of the consumers instead of serving the interests of the oil-producing states."[36]

Second, they make war on the righteous. The Kuwait war prompted each side to accuse the other of agentry. Iraqi media told of the Saudis and Kuwaitis providing $300 million to Israel for an advanced radar center near Eilat, which Cairo used to monitor troop movements in Iraq. The Syrian government countered by portraying Saddam Husayn as a loyal U.S. agent from 1962 on; in the words of Mustafa Tallas, he expected Kuwait as his reward for "his unjust war against Iran."[37]

Third, rich Middle Easterners keep the West afloat. An unnamed PLO official explained that Arab money "permits the United States to control the world." He argued that while the Soviet bloc collapsed for want of less than $50 billion, "the United States borrows annually, through various means, $100 billion from the Arabs, Japan, and Europe, and particularly from the Arabs. Without doing so, it would have collapsed before the USSR and the eastern bloc."[38] This bizarre reading of Soviet history is matched only by its wildly inflated notions of Arab financial power.

Finally, Middle Eastern leaders sell territory or secrets to Israel for personal gain. Israel won its war of independence because King 'Abdallah and Glubb Pasha sold it the Arab armies' battle plans. And Jordan's loss of the West Bank in 1967 to the Israelis prompted the comment, "They sold it to them furnished."[39] When Soviet Azerbaijan became independent, its good relations with Israel led to Iranian accusations that the ruling People's Front Party intended "to hand Baku over to the Jews."[40]

The claim that Hafiz al-Asad (then Syrian defense minister) evacuated the Golan Heights in June 1967 in collusion with the Israelis has had unusual force, in part because Khalil Mustafa, a Syrian intelligence officer present when the Golan fell to Israel, wrote an influential Arabic book, *The Fall of the Golan!?* on the subject[41] How else to explain that Israeli forces took this highly fortified area, including the town of Qunaytra, almost without a fight? (The real reason for the Syrians prematurely announcing the loss of the Golan had to do with an effort to induce the great powers to arrange a cease-fire.) Mustafa's calumny stuck. For 30 years, Asad's enemies made it an article of faith that he handed the Golan to Israel. When Arab heads of state met in February 1974, King Faysal of Saudi Arabia publicly accused Asad of allowing Qunaytra to fall without resistance in exchange for $300 million from the Israelis. Years later, the Iraqi government still routinely charged him with "surrendering the Golan to the Zionist enemy without a fight" and called him "the seller of the Golan."[42]

As for Mustafa, the Syrian leadership showed its sensitivity to his charges by abducting him in 1970 from Lebanon and, after a cursory trial, sentencing him to 15 years in prison. When his sentence ended in August 1985, he did not leave jail but disappeared.

## CHARACTERISTICS

Conspiracy theorists definitely do not underestimate their opponents. Quite the reverse; the enemy is ascribed a host of impressive attributes. Smarter and craftier than the forces of good, the conspirator treats them as a criminal would a child. Or, in the words of an imaginary Elder of Zion telling his fellow conspirators: "The *goyim* are a flock of sheep, and we are their wolves."[43]

*Satanic.* The conspirator, who enjoys evil for its own sake, is beyond the bounds of morality. All ill falls on the broad shoulders of this universal scapegoat. Middle Easterners frequently refer to the conspiratorial enemy as "satanic" or as an "enemy of God," by which they seem to mean that he intends to control all mankind. Most notably, Khomeini called the United States and Israel the Greater and Lesser Satans. Iranian officials use this

language in their everyday speech. Thus, Mehdi Karrubi, the speaker of
the Iranian parliament, informed government employees that their first
duty lay in promoting Khomeini's ideology "against the satanic actions of
the conspirators."[44]

*Omnipotent.*    The conspirator never rests, never falters, never makes
mistakes, and never shows fear; word to the contrary is disinformation. He
is tireless: "Whenever the American-Atlanticist-Zionist alliance finds that
Iraq has foiled one chapter of its aggressive conspiracy, it opens a new one."[45]
He is relentless: "Every day they [the enemies of Islam] plot new conspiracies and schemes."[46] He has many tools: the Zionist conspiracy "has enormous resources at its disposal: money, media, industry, technology, oil,
military hardware, and the intelligence agencies led by Mossad and CIA."[47]
He is also rich: Gamal Abdel Nasser instructed a Sudanese official to
"remember that while Sudan's annual budget is 100 million pounds, American intelligence has a budget of 2 billion pounds every year."[48] When the
conspirator pleads poverty, he must have a motive: Said El Jamal, a leader
of the Palestinian staff of the United Nations Relief and Works Agency
(UNRWA), insisted that the organization's "financial deficit is nothing but
a mere fabricated or concocted pretext for political aims."[49]

Abdel Nasser believed that "the Americans know perfectly well what
we will say, where we will proceed, and what we will do."[50] Sattareh
Farman Farmaian tells of the servants in her family's Iranian home that
they "believed that the *englis-ha* [English] were so diabolical that they
could even cause floods, droughts, and earthquakes. And it was true that
to Iranians, the British seemed almost supernaturally clever. They took
nearly all the money from Iran's oil while we stayed poor."[51] Speaking of
earthquakes, this is a quite common theme. Cairo's devastating earthquake
of October 1992 prompted speculation in the Iraqi press of Israeli or
American nuclear devices unsettling the earth's interior.[52] And what
Jerusalem and Washington can do, so can Moscow: by the end of 1988,
anti-Soviet feeling was so strong in the Republic of Armenia, many people
believed it had caused the recent earthquake as a means to punish the
Armenian nationalist movement.

*Ubiquitous.*    The West encircles Muslims and squeezes them. "On the
west coast of Africa, on the southern coast of Africa, on the eastern coast
of Africa, on the southern coast of India, on the coast of the Pacific Ocean,
and there in Spain and there in Japan, they have surrounded [us] here in
Egypt and in North Africa and . . . in central Asia."[53]

The West can reach right into the forbidden cities of Mecca and Medina. When Juhayman al-'Utaybi and his exteme fundamentalist followers seized the Great Mosque of Mecca in November 1979, Muslims around the world suspected Western powers of commissioning them to stage a revolt (unwilling, perhaps, to believe that Muslims could commit such an outrage against Islam's holiest sanctuary). It was "not farfetched," Ayatollah Khomeini initially declared, to assume that "criminal American imperialism" had perpetrated the incident.[54] Within a few days, he became more certain: the United States "and its corrupt colony, Israel," stood behind the attempted takeover.[55] A decade later, President Khamene'i accused the United States and Israel of setting off bombs in Mecca. There's no escaping the West's hidden hand.

*Exerts central control.*     As a political scientist notes, it is common to see the puppeteer pulling the strings of many puppets: "A common misperception is to see the behavior of others as more centralized, planned, and coordinated than it is."[56] Western governments completely control their media, which in turn transmit messages to spies and "lackeys all over the world."[57] Similarly, when the Iranians heard that some British police officers at a London airport used a picture of Ayatollah Khomeini for target practice, they assumed a decision handed down from on high. Arguing that the police "could not do something so inhuman and spiteful without having received orders from the hierarchy," one newspaper even pinpointed the home secretary as the one who gave the order.[58]

Indeed, the enemy—even a democratic one—controls his people far better than one can do oneself. Against all evidence, Gamal Abdel Nasser explained that Egypt is "a tourist country and we consider tourism an important economic resource since it provides us with nearly 100 million dollars in hard currency annually. On the other hand, Israel is a closed country from the security and information point of view. Furthermore the Jews hold their tongues while the Arabs always let their tongues run away with them. This is why they have a great deal more information about us than we have about them."[59]

Related to this, the conspiracy theorist disbelieves in individual volition. Personal decisions count for nothing in light of state needs. Jerusalem and Washington strenuously denounced the Hebron massacre of February 1994, in which an Israeli gunned down over two dozen Arabs in a mosque. Still, the event prompted this telling comment from an Egyptian: "the real criminals in this crime, as in other crimes, are the U.S.

and Israeli governments."[60] He was not about to be deceived by a show
put on by the authorities.

*Farsighted.*    The enemy plans for the distant future. The Zionist conspiracy "chooses its agents, puppets and pawns well in advance and
motivates and moulds them by many methods."[61] Not for an instant does
the conspiracy theorist believe that the British occupation of Egypt in 1882
happened in a fit of absentmindedness or due to an ambitious personality
or to momentary considerations; decades of planning preceded the event.
Yasir 'Arafat sometimes tells of a 1907 conference of European states that
decided to create a "hostile, alien nation" (i.e., Israel) to keep the Middle
East "disunited and backward."[62] At other times, he ascribes Israel's
existence to an imperialist decision "following the first discoveries of oil in
the Gulf."[63]

Middle Easterners also engage in such long-term planning. The 1966
'Alawi seizure of power in Syria, a surprising event because 'Alawis had
always been a downtrodden people, inspired many stories of long-term
planning. According to some sources, 'Alawis in 1959 formed the highly
clandestine Military Committee of the Ba'th Party, intending to avenge
the suppression of an 'Alawi rebel movement in the early 1920s. In 1960,
a secret assembly of 'Alawi religious leaders and officers (including Hafiz
al-Asad) met to plan out the route to power; six years later, 'Alawis had
seized power. According to a Pakistani daily, Saddam Husayn began
planning "Operation Kuwait" when the Kuwaiti authorities closed down
the country's parliament in July 1986, fully four years before the invasion
took place.[64]

*Clever.*    Middle Easterners see bureaucrats sitting in Washington, London, and Jerusalem as awesomely skillful. They create dangers to fool
Muslims. To justify a Western military presence in the Persian Gulf, they
came up with "the existence of an imaginary threat" from Iran.[65] Israel and
the West often entrap their adversary. A young, Western-educated
Jordanian businessman tells why Israel expelled 400 Palestinians in December 1992: Israel

> created the Hamas organization in order to foil Palestinian national-
> ism. But Israel's grip on the leadership was slipping. So the Israelis
> selected a new group of leaders and, together with several hundred
> decoys, shipped them off to Lebanon, where they will become heroes
> of the struggle. Eventually the Israelis will allow them to return,

where they will form the new Hamas power structure. Then Israel will once again be fully in control.[66]

When Conoco, an American corporation, announced that it had reached an agreement to develop oil fields in Iran, an outcry was heard in the United States against this help to the mullahs. (The dismay extended even to the board of DuPont, Conoco's parent organization.) The U.S. government responded by scuttling the deal. In Tehran, the incident was seen as stage-managed from the start. "Why did the U.S. administration not prevent Conoco from going ahead and signing it [the deal with Iran]? This indicates a planned scenario for a display of strength." It was a "trap."[67] Conspiracy, clearly, is not an amateur's game.

*Never wins.*    Despite his many fearsome qualities, the conspirator somehow does not fully marshal his resources and close in for the kill. Doom looms but never occurs. Schemers are always about to take over but, strangely, never quite do. The hour is late but time enough seems always available to rally the forces of virtue, heroic action can still prevail.

Jewish and imperialist designs neither succeed nor fail decisively. "The Jews may try, but they will never destroy [the Muslims]."[68] Or, in the words of an editorial from *The Baghdad Observer* at the height of the Kuwait crisis:

> A savage campaign has been conducted by the U.S. inside the Security Council to hurt Iraq, choke its economy and starve its people. Yet, as the first chapters of the conspiracy have failed to weaken Iraq, the final phase of the enemies' scheme is definitely going to meet the same fate. The whole conspiracy is doomed to failure.[69]

The same argument later echoed from the PLO, which saw itself

> subjected since its inception to many conspiracies—military, political, and security. . . .
> Fat'h, however, with its leadership, cadres, and elements, and with the masses rallied around it, has wrecked all these conspiracies one by one on the rock of the movement's unity, foundation, and loyal adherence to principle.[70]

According to the Iranian media, U.S. efforts to bring down the Islamic Republic by lowering the price of oil, embargoing technology, and repressing Islam are but "plots that temporarily disturb our lofty mission."[71] President Khamene'i declared that "there are still conspiracies, but they do not stand a chance."[72] In a sermon broadcast nationally, Ayatollah Mohammad Emami-Kashani emphasized this same theme:

> The enemy is strong, but weak in the face of justice. Satan's conspiracies are weak. No matter who the enemy is, his conspiracies are weak in the face of justice, provided the followers of justice remain alert and pursue the matter. . . . the enemy's plots are strong, the enemy is alert. But history has shown that since the first day the power of Islam and the alertness of Muslims, whenever it comes about, have foiled them all.[73]

This statement implies that the only escape route lies in supporting the conspiracy theorist.

## MOTIVES

Zionist or imperialist conspirators expend great energy to control huge populations; why do they bother? What gains do they achieve by dominating the whole world? Many: wealth in the first place, but also a chance to harm Muslims, tamp down rivals, resurrect imperialism, satisfy hatreds, and divert attention from other nefarious activities.

### Gain Wealth

Most commonly, Middle Easterners suspect imperialists of seeking economic gain. Not being Muslims, Sayyid Qutb explained, they believe "the most fundamental needs of a human being are those which are common with the animals, that is 'food, shelter and sex.'" Indeed, from their point of view, "the whole of human history is nothing but a struggle for food!"[74] Toward this end, the Europeans and Americans exploit the non-Western world for cheap raw materials and inexpensive labor, then find consumers for the resulting (overpriced) manufactured goods. They ascribe special importance to the Middle East, due to its vast oil and gas deposits—and the resulting free-spending consumers.

Westerners have lusted after others' resources for centuries. This explains, for example, why the British Empire came into existence. According to a Turkish tract, British state policy has long been based on "exploiting the natural riches of the world . . . , employing their inhabitants like beasts, and transferring all the resultant revenue to Britain."[75] Gamal Abdel Nasser's radio station announced that the West "wants to remain the master of the world so that it may colonise, enslave, and exploit it."[76] Forty years later, an Egyptian newspaper commentary asserted that the Casablanca economic conference of late 1994, ostensibly to encourage Arab-Israel commerce, was really "designed to seize the Arabs' natural resources."[77]

Despite their mortal differences, the shah, his leftist opposition, and Khomeini all agreed that the West seeks to steal Iranian resources. Mohammad Reza Pahlavi worried that "as Iran continued to grow and prosper, we would become an increasingly attractive prize for foreign predators."[78] Jalal Al-i Ahmad, a leftist writer, held that "all our ruin and disorder spring from . . . the fact that, in global terms, they [the Westerners] have forced us to act for the sake of the economic interest of the makers of the machine."[79] Khomeini asserted that "everything in our treasury has to be emptied into the pockets of America"[80] and his followers suspected "an all-encompassing plot for devouring the rich resources of the Middle East."[81] Iran's politician ayatollahs took this thesis to its logical conclusion. Ahmad Jannati held the British "took the wealth from here [Iran] to create [its] civilization. Western civilization is the result of plundering here."[82] 'Ali Hoseyni Khamene'i, Iran's spiritual leader, drew out the implication of this suspicion: only if his country were to offer its oil reserves gratis to the Western industrial states would it "not have any enemies."[83]

Israel is accused of cheating the Palestinians of their just wages. The PLO says Palestinians working in Israeli factories earn less than Israelis because of a conspiracy to pay them less (nothing here about the Palestinians' lesser skills). At the same time, it says that those same Palestinians earn more than their agricultural brethren because of an Israeli conspiracy to lure laborers off the land (nothing here about their greater skills).

Saddam Husayn has speculated that Americans and Israelis seek to control the Middle East as a means permanently to ensure the flow of oil. Michael Field offers a "remarkable example" of such suspicion, giving the case of the Iraqi ambassador at an elegant private lunch in London in 1988:

> after warming up with some rather suspicious remarks during the meal, over coffee in the reading room the ambassador launched into a tirade which began with the assertion that Britain, and in particular Mrs Thatcher, had never forgiven his country for the nationalization

of the Iraq Petroleum Company (owned partly by BP and Shell) in 1972. He then claimed that the Foreign Office wanted to undermine Iraq because it was the only force that was able to put some resolution into the weak Saudi and Gulf rulers, whom the British and Americans were exploiting to force down the price of oil so that they could rob the Arabs of their only resource. . . . In the long run, the ambassador concluded, Britain would very much like to install a new puppet government (like the monarchy) in Baghdad, get back IPC's concession and control Iraq as it had in the days of the mandate.[84]

This argument became the mainstay of Iraqi propaganda during the Kuwait war; Washington dreamed of "securing complete and total control over the Arabian Gulf oil fields and rearranging the international scene without any obstruction or real crises."[85] This outlook explains, for example, why the allies liberated Kuwaiti from Iraqi rule. It was, Mu'ammar al-Qadhdhafi observed, not "the American flag that liberated Kuwait. It was the Kuwaiti dinar." U.S. troops were but "mercenaries of Arab oil," doing work against their will at the behest of their Kuwaiti masters ("they could not say no").[86] Anis Mansur, an Egyptian editor with vehemently pro-Saddam views, claimed that the U.S. government not only made huge amounts by fighting Iraq on Kuwait's behalf ("more than $90 billion in salaries, social security, and allowances"), but that the president of the United States and his secretary of state personally profited from the Kuwait war: "two large companies owned by the sons of President Bush and his secretary of state, James Baker, have been established . . . . Bush was rewarded with a ton of gold, which he took back with him [from his trip to Kuwait in 1993]. This gold is his own."[87]

## Hate Islam

Fundamentalist Muslims tend to lay stress on Islam as the number-one target of conspiracism. Khomeini held that Israel had "penetrated all the economic, military, and political affairs" of Iran with the intention to "annihilate Islam."[88] Sayyid Qutb traces the Jewish conspiracy against Islam back to the time of the Prophet Muhammad and predicts it will continue until Islam is destroyed. An Egyptian preacher traces the enmity back yet further, announcing anachronistically that "the Torah vilifies the Qur'an and scorns it; sometimes it vilifies the Prophet [Muhammad] and scorns him; sometimes it vilifies Islam and scorns it; and sometimes it vilifies Muslims and scorns them."[89]

As for Western sentiments, nothing has changed over the centuries. Christians may have learned to hide their venomous attitudes toward Islam, but the hostility of past eras still festers below the surface. Sayyid Qutb held that Western "enmity toward Islam is especially pronounced and many times is the result of a well-thought-out scheme" that aims to "demolish the structure of Muslim society."[90] Libyan media revealed a U.S.-Israeli "tenth crusade."[91] Ahmad Khomeini maintained that the U.S. government directs its "all-embracing plots" to undermine Islam.[92] Christian support for Zionism reveals that deep hatred of Islam.

This enmity extends also to Muslims who live in the West. On hearing that the American police had arrested three persons of Middle Eastern origin in connection with the Oklahoma City bombing, an Iranian newspaper deemed this "part of the propagandistic plots that are usually hatched by the U.S. hierarchy."[93]

Such anti-Islamic sentiments are sometimes portrayed as an end in themselves—the result of inherited bigotry. At other times, they are seen to have an ulterior purpose: the protection of Western wealth. Were true Muslims to come to power, goes the argument, then the Western world would have to pay for the true value of Middle Eastern labor and resources, and that would lead to severe economic depression in the West.

Looking at the West as deeply anti-Islamic has two important implications. First, it suggests that fundamentalists see tensions with the West not as conflicts between states but between religions. They believe in a "clash of civilizations" fought over deep cultural issues, not fleeting political differences. Consequently, the usual mechanisms of international diplomacy—peace treaties, conventions, and the like—have no role. Put differently, short of converting to Islam, Israelis and Americans and Britons cannot satisfy the fundamentalist rulers in Tehran.

Second, Muslims worry that Jewish and Christian hatred of Islam implies an effort actually to eliminate their own religion. Ayatollah Khomeini feared Jews plan to take over the whole world, then promote their religion. "The Jews and their foreign backers are opposed to the very foundations of Islam and wish to establish Jewish domination throughout the world. Since they are a cunning and resourceful group of people, I fear—God forbid!—they may one day achieve their goal."[94] As for Christians, they retain the aggressiveness of medieval knights. Husayn al-Musawi, leader of Islamic Amal in Lebanon, reminded his listeners of "the French crusader mentality" that had caused earlier disasters and placed the United States squarely in this tradition.[95] 'Adil Husayn, the Egyptian fundamentalist, explained that the pharaohs and tyrants "are plotting to annihilate mankind on our continents, with the Islamic nation heading their targets, of course."[96] Thinking they face an enemy who wishes to destroy Islam, fundamentalist Muslims naturally respond with deep hatred.

## Harm an Ally

*Western.* Washington and its allies are often portrayed as seeking to harm one another's interests. A U.S.-British battle for control of the Middle East explains key events through decades of Middle Eastern history, including: the collapse of the Iraqi monarchy in 1958, the Iranian revolution of 1979 (a British plot to oust the Americans from the Persian Gulf), and the seizure of the U.S. embassy later in 1979 (a British means to humiliate Washington and regain supremacy in Iran). Muhammad Husayn Fadlallah, the Hizbullah thinker, discerns Western rivalry for influence over Lebanon: "The U.S. plan is this: to eliminate the French influence which is active to a great extent within the Maronite and Christian ranks and possibly within some Islamic ranks that are appendages to political Maronism.[97]

Washington's acute interest in Persian Gulf oil is thought to have little to do with its own energy needs but rather "to control Germany, Japan, and the Russia of the future."[98] El Mahdi Abas Allalu, chairman of the People's Association for Unity and Action in Algeria, found a similar reason to explain why the U.S. government had so soft a policy toward the fundamentalist Islamic Salvation Front (FIS): Washington "is supporting the fundamentalists because it wants Europe to have a time-bomb near its borders to as to prevent it from becoming a serious competitor."[99]

*Muslim.* Princess Ashraf of Iran mused on the question why the U.S. government brought down her dynasty in 1979 and concluded, in idiosyncratic English, that they envied what her brother was building in Iran:

> I am sure that it couldn't be only the mullahs. . . . It was a concerted effort from the foreigners also. It happened the same thing with my father. It happened the same thing with my brother. There are foreigners who saw that Iran was becoming very important . . . and Iran in ten years' time would be another Japan. They couldn't afford another Japan in Asia.[100]

## Reestablish Imperialism

Fond memories of imperial domination and the hope to regain the glories of old are thought to motivate Europeans, especially the British and French. The Americans may not have fond memories, but they have present-day ambitions. A Jordanian newspaper reports from an alleged National Security Council Document (No. 2,000) that the U.S. government has plans to turn "Arabs and Muslims into the new Red Indians under the hegemony of the New World Order."[101]

The imperialist theme comes most often from Iraq and Libya. Saddam Husayn accused Westerners of clinging to the illusions of colonialism, while his foreign minister declared that "the new imperialist schemes aim at returning the old colonialism to the region."[102] The speaker of the National Assembly saw London wanting to treat Iraq again as a protectorate that "can be led in whatever way Britain likes."[103] The Libyans worked up a whole imperialistic schema centered on the United States and premised on the notion that one "not rule out that history repeats itself."[104] They say the Central Intelligence Agency has put together "a world dictatorial police system under the control of the United States where freedom, justice, and democracy have no worth and where colonialism will be restored."[105] The U.S. government uses the North Atlantic Treaty Organization (NATO) to further its colonial ends. No one should cooperate with the United States, for that means either finding one's economy destroyed or becoming "an American colony."[106]

This effort is first taking place in various parts of Africa. In sub-Saharan Africa, said Qadhdhafi, "so-called democracy" is the chosen vehicle to return the continent to tribalism. In Egypt, the goal is geographic division: "They [the Americans] want to wipe [the state of] Egypt off the map. . . . Egypt must be divided in the interest of Israel into a Coptic state, an Islamic state, a Nubian state and an Arab state." In Algeria, he noted, civil war is the weapon of choice:

> French and American intelligence have been working together against Algeria. They have been distributing money and weapons to see Algerians killing Algerians. . . . Colonialism, which wants to return once again to Algeria, because there is oil and gas in Algeria, is behind this massacre in Algeria. . . . America has an oil crisis and consequently wants to occupy the regions of the world where there is oil.[107]

Thus do many Middle Easterners believe, against all evidence, that Europeans and Americans seek to reassert colonialism.

Imperialists require very strict obedience and punish their agents who get out of order. An Arab Jerusalemite interpreted events along these lines to an Israeli journalist just after the 1973 war: "The Americans arrange everything. In '56 they sent the British and the French to wallop Egypt, and in '67 they helped you beat the Egyptians and the Syrians. Today you have a very big country, and the Americans felt you should be cut down to size. So they decided to help the Egyptians beat you."[108] The shah of Iran sometimes explained the apparent illogic of blaming his patrons (the oil companies, the CIA) for supporting his enemies on this basis. As he put it in 1980:

> I suspected that Big Oil financed the demonstrations and that the CIA helped organize them. I know this sounds contradictory since both of these powerful interests had also supported my rule. But I do believe now that the West created an organized front against me to use whenever my policies diverged from theirs.[109]

The Khomeini regime used exactly the same reasoning to explain why Washington allowed its agent Saddam to invade Kuwait and then went to war against him. By similar logic, many Arabs held Washington responsible for the civil war in Yemen in 1994, seeing it as the way to punish Yemenis for supporting Iraq during the Kuwait war.

## Indulge Malice

In two odd codas to these enormous claims, conspiracy theorists see Satans small and great engaging in plots either to indulge their own spite or to distract the world from their own malfeasance.

On the first matter, Middle Easterners widely believe the West remembers medieval history as acutely and they do. It is thought still to resent the two principal waves of *jihad*, an Arabian campaign in the west from the eighth to the tenth centuries and a Turkish campaign in the east from the fourteenth to the seventeenth centuries. The first took Arab warriors to Poitiers, 200 miles southwest of Paris; the second brought Ottoman soldiers to the outskirts of Vienna.

In addition, Britain and France are assumed yet to suffer from the loss of empire and hoping to win them back. In the case of Britain, Sa'di Mahdi Salih, speaker of Iraq's National Assembly, credits "the old malice of British colonialism" as a motivating force in London's trying to control his country.[110] Oddly, most of the Iranians who suspected London of engineering the shah's fall stressed not British national interests but pique. Perhaps London smarted yet over the nationalization of the Anglo-Iranian Oil Company in 1951; perhaps it envied the Americans' favored presence in Iran; or perhaps it recalled the press conference some years earlier when the shah had insulted British workers, saying they were inferior to Iranian ones. One former high official, Mohammed Behbehanian, went so far as to suggest that if the shah apologized for his rashness, the British might let him regain his throne.[111]

Conspiracy theorists charge the West with not forgiving Muslims for the end of empire. Anger remains particularly acute concerning Algeria, the Middle Eastern country where colonizer and colonized both lost the most lives. According to a Lebanese newspaper published in London, recent troubles in that country result from the Mossad, French intelligence, and the CIA being "involved in the murder, financing, training, and armament operations, so that Algeria would pay the price for its independence and rebellion against France."[112]

## Divert Attention

The final pattern consists of the conspirator who plots as a way to divert attention. Sometimes he does so to hide his own malfeasance, sometimes to keep attention away from an enemy's achievements.

Israel hides its evil acts this way. *Al-Ahram*, Egypt's most serious newspaper, speculated in May 1983 about Israeli agents having concocted the Hitler diaries hoax. Why? Because the episode reminded everyone of the Jews' past sufferings and thus diverted "the world's attention from the tragedy that Israel is inflicting on the Arabs."[113] Radio Tehran claimed that a 1990 clash between Israel's Labor and Likud parties served to distract attention from the oppression of Palestinians. Iraq's Tariq 'Aziz asserted that the Iranians released Western hostages from Lebanon to distract attention from the "ugly crimes" committed by the Israelis against the Palestinians.[114] Hizbullah blamed the November 1991 bombing of the American University of Beirut on Israel, reasoning that this violence diverted attention from Israeli attacks in the Bekaa Valley. Using the exact same reasoning, Syrian politicians accused Israel of setting off a bomb in a Maronite church in March 1994, thereby diverting attention from a Jewish settler's massacre of Muslims in Hebron two days earlier.

Imperialists rely on the same trick. The Iranians saw Baghdad's plummeting relations with the West during the months before its invasion of Kuwait as a ploy arranged with the Soviets and Israelis to divert world attention from "the treacherous plot for the transport of Soviet Jews to occupied Palestine."[115] The British arrest of several Iraqis for the illegal export of materiél prompted the Iranian Foreign Ministry to portray the incident as "a means for covering up the migration of Eastern European and Soviet Jews to Israel."[116] American efforts in Somalia diverted attention from the lack of similar resolve in Bosnia. The U.S. government contrived a crisis over Iranian control over some islands in the Persian Gulf so as to slip through various gambits in the Arab-Israeli peace process.

Arab leaders also try to divert attention in this way. In February 1981, a Jordanian diplomat in Lebanon disappeared in a part of Beirut under Syrian control. Denying complicity, Damascus accused the Jordanian government of being "the party behind the kidnapping." Why would Amman abduct its own employee? Because it "has an interest in exploiting the incident to deceive public opinion and divert the attention of the Jordanian people from what is taking place in Jordan."[117]

Less commonly, plots turn attention away from some event the conspiracy theorist takes pride in. Syrian Foreign Minister Shar' accused "fanatic Muslim Turks" of undertaking the September 1986 massacre of 23 Jews in Istanbul's Neve Shalom Synagogue to divert attention from positive developments in Syria.[118] Iranians sometimes interpret events outside the Middle East as a way to detract from the Iranian revolution. News from Romania about the collapse of the Ceausescu regime was first received as a Western tactic to divert attention from the Romanian leader's visit to Tehran: "The West has launched an extensive adverse propaganda campaign to overshadow the visit and the important agreements between Iran and Romania."[119] Astonishingly, Iranians even saw the Bush administration's campaign against South American drug traffickers as a devious way to harm Iranian interests. An official of Iran's Drug Enforcement Headquarters explained that the joint U.S.-Colombian antidrug efforts was a sham: "U.S. and Colombian leaders are all, in one way or another, the main elements of the Mafia that distributes drugs in the world." The real purpose was "to distract attention from Iran and turn it to Colombia so that the world would not notice that a war against smugglers is being carried out in Iran." In short, all the noise coming from Colombia "was a plot against our country."[120] Once a conspiracy theorist goes into action, anything can result!

## NOTES TO CHAPTER 9

1. Jedidiah Morse, *A Sermon . . . Delivered at Charlestown, April 25, 1799, the day of the National Fast* (Charlestown, 1799). Quoted in Vernon Stauffer, *New England and the Bavarian Illuminati* (New York: Columbia University Press, 1918), p. 300.

2. *Protocols of the Meetings of the Learned Elders of Zion,* trans. Victor E. Marsden (London: The Britons, 1923), p. 60.

3. *Ar-Ra'y* (Amman), 23 October 1993.

4. *Al-Hadath* (Amman), 9 August 1995.

5. *Ash-Sha'b,* 13 January 1995.

6. Samir al-Khalil [pseud. of Kanan Makiya], *Republic of Fear: The Politics of Modern Iraq* (Berkeley: University of California Press, 1989), p. 48.

7. As reported by Husni Mubarak, Radio Cairo, 4 October 1990.

8. Leaflet by Khomeini distributed on (the Iranian date) 21/7/1341. Quoted in Sayyed Hamid Ruhani, *Barrasii va Tahlili az Nahzat-e Imam Khomeini* (Qom: n.p., n.d.), p. 178.

9. Sayyid Qutb, *Ma'rakatna ma'a'l-Yuhud,* edited by Zayn ad-Din ar-Rakkabi. Text translated in Ronald L. Nettler, *Past Trials and Present Tribulations: A Muslim Fundamentalist's View of the Jews* (Oxford: Pergamon, 1987), p. 77.

10. Ibid., pp. 76-77.

11. Paraphrased by Ethan Bronner, "Psycho-Semitic," *The New Republic,* 24 May 1993.

12. Quoted in Sylvia G. Haim, "Sayyid Qutb," *Asian and African Studies* 16 (1982), p. 156. For a firsthand account of a deportation (from Egypt in 1965) on account of suspicious activities, see Frederick H. Gerlach, "Student or Spy? Reflections on the Perils of Field Research," in Reeva S. Simon, ed., *The Middle East and North Africa: Essays in Honor of J. C. Hurewitz* (New York: Columbia University Press, 1990), pp. 230-37.

13. Sayyid Qutb, *Ma'alim fi't-Tariq,* trans. as *Milestones* (Kuwait: International Islamic Federation of Student Organizations, 1398/1978), p. 213.

14. Neil Asher Silberman, *Between Past and Present: Archeology, Ideology, and Nationalism in the Modern Middle East* (New York: Henry Holt, 1989), pp. 187, 197.

15. Lila Abu-Lughod, "Anthropology's Orient: The Boundaries of Theory on the Arab World," in Hisham Sharabi, ed., *Theory, Politics and the Arab World: Critical Responses* (New York: Routledge, 1990), p. 81.

16. Ruhollah Khomeini, *Hukumet-e Islami* (Najaf, 1391/1971). Translated by Hamid Algar in *Islam and Revolution: Writings and Declarations of Imam Khomeini* (Berkeley, Calif.: Mizan, 1981), pp. 139-40.

17. CDLR Monitor, Bulletin No. 51, 9 June 1995, on the Internet.

18. Shabbir Akhtar, *Be Careful with Muhammad! The Salman Rushdie Affair* (London: Bellew Publishing, 1989), p. 9.

19. Ibid., pp. 139, 28, 136, 128. The depth of this fear prompts the observer to wonder why Muslim leaders did not sponsor "Occidental" studies as a precursor to taking power in Europe and America.

20. New York: Pantheon, 1978.

21. *Ar-Ra'y al-'Amm*, 17 July 1990. This passage occurred in an anti-American screed that appeared, curiously, the very day Saddam Husayn began his campaign which culminated two weeks later with the Iraqi occupation of Kuwait.

22. Michael Field, *Inside the Arab World* (Cambridge, Mass.: Harvard University Press, 1994), p.165.

23. *Politiken* (Copenhagen), 26 February 1994.

24. Robert Fisk, *Pity the Nation: Lebanon at War* (London: Oxford University Press, 1991), p. 603.

25. Quoted in Abdel Magid Farid, *Nasser: The Final Years* (Reading, Eng.: Ithaca Press, 1994), p. 13.

26. *Ash-Shams* (Tripoli), 12 May 1994.

27. Leaflet No. 74 of Hamas. Text in Shaul Mishal and Reuben Aharoni, *Speaking Stones: Communiqués from the Intifada Underground* (Syracuse, N.Y.: Syracuse University Press, 1994), pp. 282-83.

28. *Al-Akhbar* (Cairo), 5 October 1992.

29. Muhammad at-Tawil, *Mu'amarat al-Qarn 21* (Cairo: Az-Zahra' li-l-A'lam al-'Arabi, 1990).

30. Libyan Television, 6 April 1995.

31. *Al-Ahali* (Cairo), 6 April 1994.

32. *Al-Majalla*, 5 December 1993.

33. Great Jamahiriya Radio, 13 March 1994.

34. Tripoli Television, 7 April 1990.

35. Shah: Khomeini, *Islam and Revolution*, p. 258. Sheikhs: *Jahan-e Islam*, 22 April 1993.

36. Voice of the Islamic Republic of Iran, 4 May 1994.

37. *Al-Majalla*, 9-15 January 1991; *Al-Akhbar al-Yawm*, 26 January 1991.

38. *Ar-Ra'y*, 5 November 1991.

39. Quoted in Kamal Salibi, *The Modern History of Jordan* (New York: I. B. Tauris, 1993), p. 224.

40. *Resalat*, 14 July 1992.

41. Khalil Mustafa, *Suqut al-Jawlan!?* (Amman: Dar al-Yaqin, 1969), pp. 97-315.

42. *Al-Jumhuriya* (Baghdad) 24 January 1995; *An-Nida'* (Kuwait), 16 September 1990. Also, Iraqi News Agency, 8 August 1988.

43. *Protocols of the Meetings of the Learned Elders of Zion*, trans. Victor E. Marsden (London: The Britons, 1923), p. 41.

44. Radio Tehran, 25 July 1990.

45. Radio Baghdad, 11 April 1991.

46. Ayatollah Mohammad Yazdi, chief of the Iranian judiciary, Voice of the Islamic Republic of Iran, 26 August 1994.

47. *The Pakistan Times*, 4 February 1991.

48. Quoted in Farid, *Nasser*, p. 141.

49. Quoted in Benjamin N. Schiff, *Refugees unto the Third Generation: UN Aid to Palestinians* (Syracuse, N.Y: Syracuse University Press, 1995) p.111.

50. Ibid., p. 12.

51. Sattareh Farman Farmaian, with Dona Munker, *Daughter of Persia: A Woman's Journey from Her Father's Harem Through the Islamic Revolution* (New York: Crown, 1992), p. 84.

52. Republic of Iraq Radio, 17 October 1992. An American writer, Dave Emory, looked up, not down: noting the incidence of earth tremors when the U.S. space shuttle was in the air, he theorized that the American military had developed capabilities to engage in "seismic manipulation." See Jonathan Vankin, *Conspiracies, Cover-Ups, and Crimes: Political Manipulation and Mind Control in America* (New York: Paragon House, 1991), p. 99.

53. An Egyptian preacher, quoted in Patrick D. Gaffney, *The Prophet's Pulpit: Islamic Preaching in Contemporary Egypt* (Berkeley: University of California Press, 1994), p. 148.

54. Radio Tehran, 21 November 1979.

55. *The New York Times,* 24 November 1979.

56. Robert Jervis, *Perception and Misperception in International Politics* (Princeton, N.J.: Princeton University Press, 1976), p. 319.

57. *Jomhuri-ye Islami,* 21 June 1990. This statement refers to the BBC.

58. *Abrar,* 5 December 1990.

59. Quoted in Farid, *Nasser,* p. 13.

60. *Al-Ahram,* 28 February 1994.

61. *The Pakistan Times,* 4 February 1991.

62. *Al-Usbu' al'Arabi* (Beirut), 22 January 1968. Text in *International Documents on Palestine 1968* (Beirut: Institute for Palestine Studies, 1971), p. 299.

63. *An-Nahar,* 31 December 1974. Quoted in Danny Rubinstein, *The Mystery of Arafat,* trans. from Hebrew by Dan Leon (South Royalton, Ver.: Steerforth Press, 1995), p. 36.

64. *Jang,* 4 August 1990. American intelligence reportedly concluded that the invasion was planned as early as 1985 (*The Philadelphia Inquirer,* 21 September 1990).

65. Editorial, *Jahan-e Islam,* 22 April 1993.

66. Bronner, "Psycho-Semitic."

67. *Resalat,* 6 April 1995.

68. Qutb, *Ma'rakatna ma'a'l-Yuhud,* in Nettler, *Past Trials and Present Tribulations,* p. 85.

69. *The Baghdad Observer,* 28 November 1990.

70. Sawt Filastin (Algiers), 2 August 1992.

71. *Kayhan International,* 10 February 1994.

72. Radio Tehran, 19 April 1995.

73. Voice of the Islamic Republic, 19 February 1993.

74. Qutb, *Ma'alim fi't-Tariq,* p. 91.

75. M. Sıddık Gümüş, *Confessions of a British Spy,* 3d ed. (Istanbul: Hakikat Kitabevi, 1993), p. 4.

76. 4 June 1954. Quoted in Patrick Seale, *The Struggle for Syria: A Study of Post-War Arab Politics, 1945-1958* (London: Oxford University Press, 1965), p. 197.

77. Mahjub 'Umar, quoted in *Ash-Sha'b*, 8 November 1994.

78. Mohammad Reza Pahlavi, *Answer to History* (New York: Stein and Day, 1980), p. 141.

79. Jalal Al-i Ahmad, *Gharbzadagi*, trans. R. Campbell as *Occidentosis: A Plague From the West* (Berkeley, Calif.: Mizan, 1984), p. 83.

80. "In Commemoration of the First Martyrs of the Revolution," 19 February 1978. Text in Hamid Algar, trans. and ed., *Islam and Revolution: Writings and Declarations of Imam Khomeini* (Berkeley, Calif.: Mizan, 1981), p. 221.

81. *Jomhuri-ye Islami,* 20 July 1991.

82. Voice of the Islamic Republic of Iran, 5 March 1993.

83. Voice of the Islamic Republic of Iran, 25 March 1993.

84. Michael Field, *Inside the Arab World* (Cambridge, Mass.: Harvard University Press, 1994), p.166.

85. *Al-Jumhuriya* (Baghdad), 2 August 1994.

86. Jamahiriya Arab News Agency, 3 March 1991.

87. *Al-Ahram,* 21 May 1993. Mansur's accusation neatly summarizes what a Middle Eastern potentate would have done in President Bush's place.

88. Message to Pilgrims," 6 February 1971. Text in Algar, *Islam and Revolution,* p. 197.

89. Quoted in Gaffney, *The Prophet's Pulpit,* p. 149.

90. Qutb, *Ma'alim fi't-Tariq,* p. 217.

91. Jamahiriya Arab News Agency, 26 April 1990.

92. Voice of the Islamic Republic, 6 August 1991.

93. *Jomhuri-ye Islami,* 22 April 1995.

94. Khomeini, *Hukumet-e Islami* in Algar, *Islam and Revolution,* p. 127. The phrase "and their foreign backers" deserves notice, for it points to a joint Zionist-imperialist effort even in the realm of religion.

95. Sawt al-Mustad'afin (Lebanon), 3 December 1989.

96. *Ash-Sha'b,* 22 April 1994.

97. *Ash-Sha'b* (Cairo), 3 June 1994.

98. Sawt Filastin (Algiers), 22 August 1992.

99. *ABC* (Madrid), 17 October 1994.

100. BBC Radio, 16 and 23 March 1982. Quoted in Gary Sick, *All Fall Down: America's Tragic Encounter with Iran* (New York: Random House, 1985), p. 165-66.

101. *Ad-Dustur* (Amman), 1 September 1994.

102. Muhammad Sa'id as-Sahhaf, quoted in Republic of Iraq Radio, 31 August 1992.

103. Sa'di Mahdi Salih, Iraqi News Agency, 18 April 1990.

104. Libyan Television, 6 April 1995.

105. Jamahiriya Arab News Agency, 18 May 1994.

106. Libyan Television, 16 April 1995.

107. Libyan Television, 6 April 1995.

108. Quoted in Rafik Halabi, *The West Bank Story,* trans. Ina Friedman (New York: Harcourt Brace Jovanovich, 1982), p. 97.

109. Pahlavi, *Answer to History,* p. 22.

110. Iraqi News Agency, 18 April 1990.
111. William Shawcross, *The Shah's Last Ride: The Fate of an Ally* (New York: Simon and Schuster, 1988), p. 71.
112. *Al-Hayat* (London), 25 May 1994.
113. *Al-Ahram*, 11 May 1983.
114. Iraqi News Agency, 3 May 1990.
115. *Jomhuri-ye Islami*, 8 April 1990.
116. 'Ali Mohammed Besharati, *Kayhan* [London], 17 May 1990.
117. Radio Damascus, 13 February 1981.
118. Quoted in Suha Bölükbaşı, "Turkey Challenges Iraq and Syria: The Euphrates Dispute," *Journal of South Asian and Middle Eastern Studies*, Summer 1993, p. 21.
119. *Abrar*, 20 December 1989.
120. Tehran Television, 14 October 1989.

# 10.

# The Conspirator's Methods

> . . . could you and I with Him conspire
> To grasp this sorry Scheme of Things entire,
> Would not we shatter it to bits—and then
> Re-mould it nearer to the Heart's Desire!
> —*Edward FitzGerald*,
> The Rubáiyát of Omar Khayyám

To effect his terrible goals, the conspirator deploys every means available, including armies, fundamentalist Islam, and "wine, women and gold."[1] The plotters' capacious bag of tricks includes many instruments of power. One author, writing in *The Pakistan Times*, fills a single long sentence with a catalogue of Zionist crimes. These include

expanding the geographical boundaries of Israel, breaking up all other countries into mini-states or cantons on ethnic, linguistic or sectarian lines, disintegrating and diluting their military assets, including nuclear power, and economic resources, privatising all essential services, communications, media, transportation, banks, financial institutions and development projects in all the cantons and giving their control to multinational companies and the World Bank, IMF, all of which are in the hands of Jews, secularising the educational systems and political institutions, eliminating religious customs and practices including the institutions of formal marriage and home-life and enforcing Zionist culture of obscenity, promiscuity, total freedom for women and even children and freedom for all forms of entertainment and pleasure.[2]

Of these many accusations, we concentrate here on those that come up with the greatest frequency, starting with the most destructive and ending with the most trivial.

## DEATH AND DESTRUCTION

### Genocide

Israel occasionally stands accused of genocide: a Palestine National Council meeting in March 1971 resolved that Jordanian and Israeli steps against the Palestinians constituted an effort to achieve "the actual liquidation of the Palestinian people itself."[3] Egypt's parliament concluded (an Iraqi newspaper reported) that Israel stole Egyptian groundwater in northern Sinai and planned to build, jointly with the Ethiopian government, six dams at the Nile River's fountainheads, thereby depriving Egypt of its life waters.[4]

Mostly, it's the West that kills off whole peoples. In 1990, fundamentalist Muslims gave a figure of 12 million Muslims in the Middle East who had died at American hands.[5] Saddam Husayn accused the Europeans of "keeping Arab territories with oil deposits sparsely populated wherever possible so they would remain too weak to resist colonial greed."[6]

Imperialists murder Muslims through various means, starting with raw violence. Shortly after Operation Desert Storm, reports came out of Kuwait of "special execution squads" dedicated to "pursuing and hunting Palestinians throughout Kuwait."[7] Western military power allows them to conquer territory and then debilitate, starve, and execute Middle Easterners. This thesis was often heard in 1992, when strife engulfed Muslim peoples all over the world (in Liberia, Sudan, Eritrea, Somalia, Bosnia, Azerbaijan, Lebanon, Iraq, Tajikistan, Afghanistan, Kashmir, and Burma). "They are slaughtering children," went out the cry. Necmeddin Erbakan, the Turkish fundamentalist leader, espied "international alliances" seeking to annihilate Muslims.[8]

Bosnia-Herzegovina aroused special alarm. Bosnia's ambassador to Iran announced that the fall of the city of Gorazde was "a pre-planned Western plot" and Western states were "directly responsible for the massacres of Gorazde Muslims."[9] Lebanese fundamentalists saw the war in Bosnia as a concerted Western effort "to drive Islam from Europe" as well as "a war against Islamic identity that is likely to spread to the Islamic world itself."[10] Similarly, Qadhdhafi perceived an intent to make Europe purely Christian by ridding the continent of Muslim Bosnians.[11] Iranian media posed the problem in yet more apocalyptic terms, as the enemy girding his loins "to annihilate Islam."[12]

Killing may be necessary, but, the Egyptian lawyer 'Abd al-Halim Manzur notes, weapons need not crush people: "An explosion has to be engineered from within."[13] Disease serves better. Western colonialism stands accused of causing all "diseases rampant in the Arab lands."[14] Specifically, the British imported cholera and malaria to Egypt after World War II. A British midwife who trained in the Kabylia province of Algeria got accused by his angry Algerian supervisor of working in league with the "white-coated saboteurs passing their hands from vagina to vagina, infecting my heroic people with syphilis!"[15] An unnamed enemy—presumably American—infiltrated deadly diseases into Iraq via maggot-ridden cigarettes. Israel transmitted cancer to Palestinians by getting them to take dangerous factory jobs or subjecting them to phosphorous searches. It also smuggled irradiated fruit into Egypt to cause cancer.

AIDS, combining sex and disease, prompts recurring nightmares. Jerusalem hires young Jewish women infected with AIDS to spread the affliction in Egypt. One article in the Egyptian press focuses on an Israeli named Sarah who cavorted in luxurious apartments and infected the young and the prominent, while other versions count between 20 and 327 infected Israeli agents. The most imaginative account conjures up a "special formula" of the AIDS virus that infected sexual partners without in any way affecting the Israeli female carriers.[16]

The West also uses more indirect mechanisms to kill, such as drought and even poor housing materials. Na'im Haddad, a member of Iraq's Regional Command, accused "U.S. imperialism" in 1975 of "pushing certain regimes, particularly the Syrian regime, to cut off water from our masses."[17] When tremors from a June 1990 earthquake in Iran killed more than 30,000 persons, one Iranian writer blamed shoddily constructed buildings on "the United States and its filthy hands." The connection? Americans plundered Iran's wealth, and so prevented Iranians from putting up strong housing.[18] Likewise, Israel was responsible for the deterioration of Egypt's infrastructure and so for the deaths caused by collapsed buildings.

The best genocidal method of all, however, is contraception. Not only does it require no violence, but Muslims cheerfully do this to themselves. It is a way to kill Muslims "without shedding blood."[19] In an astonishing (but quite typical) statement, a leading Egyptian religious figure announced that Western efforts to spread birth control are "prompted solely by the growing vitality of Muslims. Should Muslims disappear from the surface of the earth, this debate would come to an end and all people will be left to propagate at will."[20]

## Eliminate Enemies

The great powers overthrow regimes not to their taste. In Iran alone, they disposed of the Qajars, the Pahlavis, and have persistently tried to get rid of the Islamic Republic. They ended the Ottoman Empire, the monarchy in Egypt, and almost toppled Abdel Nasser: "Washington, losing hope that any of Nasser's policies would change, then decided to resume its plots to overthrow the regime,"[21] writes an aide to Abdel Nasser. In a colorful example of this thinking, Kamal Junbalat, Lebanon's interior minister, blamed a failed coup d'état by the Syrian Social Nationalist Party in December 1961 on the British; he even claimed personally to have witnessed Her Majesty's ambassador on the roof of the British Embassy signalling a British warship at sea. (That the closest British naval unit at that time was in Gibraltar hardly diminished the enthusiastic reception for Junbalat's story.)

Imperialists kill leading fundamentalist figures, such as Hasan al-Banna, founder of the Muslim Brethren, fearing their influence. More often, they murder rulers, and with great cleverness. British elements arranged for the traffic accident that killed King Ghazi of Iraq in 1939 and helped murder King 'Abdallah of Jordan in 1951. The CIA tried to assassinate 'Abd al-Karim Qasim of Iraq soon after he took power in 1958 by sending him a poisoned handkerchief. Gamal Abdel Nasser died at the hands of an American doctor who injected him with poison hidden in a fountain pen. King Faysal of Saudi Arabia offended both Israel (because of his staunch views on Jerusalem) and the Western powers (because he organized the oil boycott against the West in 1973-74), so he had to die; a nephew recruited by Washington carried out the assassination. The Phalangists of Lebanon, sometime allies of Israel, accused Jerusalem of killing the Phalangist leader Bashir Gemayel because he resisted its demands for a peace treaty. The United States and Israel stood "behind the vile attempt" on Mubarak's life at Addis Ababa in June 1995, according to Farid Zakariya, deputy leader of Egypt's Liberal Party.[22]

Most suspicions concern Muslim rulers, but not all: When Rajiv Gandhi was assassinated, *Jomhuri-ye Islami* instinctively picked out the CIA as the "most probable" force behind the killing.

## Divide and Rule

"Whenever any Muslim state anywhere in the world has tried to stand independently, or tried to be economically strong, or has attempted to get political stability, immediately the leaders of the international Jewish-Christian force—the United States, Britain, and France—engaged in a conspiracy to destroy them." According to this writer, a Bangladeshi, the main weapons in this conspiracy are the United Nations, World Bank, International Monetary Fund, and NATO. Recent successes have included conflicts between Iraq and Iran, Iraq and Kuwait, and Saudi Arabia and Yemen.[23] To this, a Pakistan writer adds that "The United States wants to start a war between Pakistan and India by making noise about the danger of nuclear war between the two countries."[24] An Egyptian suspects that an international conspiracy keeps his government in "perpetual hostility" with the Sudan.[25] And so forth.

In the Middle East, the imperialist powers created a host of small states to keep the Arabs divided and weak; why else does a polity so unlikely as the United Arab Emirates exist? Israel and the West staged the near assassination of Gamal Abdel Nasser and made the Muslim Brethren appear responsible, thereby turning these two allies against each other. Other joint efforts by the two lead conspirators included: sparking Lebanon's civil war, setting Sunnis against Shi'is in Pakistan, and spurring Saddam Husayn to make war on God's experiment in Iran. Qadhdhafi accused Americans of generally making "Arabs fight among themselves."[26]

The Phalangists claimed Jerusalem dressed up its Lebanese allies as Phalangists in 1982 and had them massacre Palestinians in Shatila, thereby weakening the position of the Phalangist leader, Amin Gemayel, and boosting the electoral prospects of Israel's favored candidate, Camille Chamoun. 'Abd al-Halim Khaddam of Syria portrayed the Western media as an important source of dissension: "At a time when they [Westerners] are depriving us of the technology we need, they are exporting to us through the media whatever distorts ethics, culture, and affiliation. . . . Quarreling Arabs make easier targets."[27]

Conspirators also resort to highly imaginative methods to stir up trouble, undermining morale and giving away secrets. The Syrian military magazine, *Army of the People,* published an article in late April 1967 ridiculing Islam and condemning God and religion as "mummies that should be transferred to the museums of historical remains,"[28] prompting a vociferous response (which the Saudi government stood accused of funding) and a political crisis so severe, it threatened to bring down the regime. To deflect responsibility for the offending article, the governor of Damascus announced that it was the handiwork of a CIA agent who had "squalidly infiltrated the army to create confusion among the citizens."[29]

When Muslim girls of Upper Egypt discovered marks on their veils in 1987 resembling crosses, alarm spread through their villages. Who was responsible, how was this outrage caused, and to what purpose? A Cairo newspaper reported two principal theories making the rounds, one concerning Christians and the other Jews:

> some people said that Christians had sprayed a chemical on the veiled women's clothes and this material assumed the form of a small cross no larger than an ant; as soon as the clothing was moistened, the size of the cross would increase and come to about 3 centimeters. Some people reiterated another interpretation, which held that the cloth of the head covering had been imported from Israel and that it was scientifically treated to form crosses with the purpose of stirring up dissension between Muslims and Christians.[30]

Israel often stands accused of creating dissension among the Arabs. The Palestinian rebellion against Israeli rule (the *intifada*) inspired some imaginative scenarios. An affluent West Bank lawyer calls the *intifada* "An American-Israeli plot . . . to turn us against each other." To which a woman agrees, but gives a different explanation: "Yes, yes, yes, I am telling you: It was meant to ruin us [economically]."[31] Yusuf Abu Sunayna, preacher at the Al-Aqsa Mosque, charged Israel's security forces with spreading arms among Palestinians. "They want to turn the West Bank and Gaza Strip into a second Lebanon."[32] Asked about a clash between PLO and Hamas elements in late 1994, the PLO's "foreign minister," Faruq Qaddumi replied: "it was a Zionist plan."[33]

Enemies of the Arabs sometimes coordinate their efforts. In one notable case, the Arab League accused Israel, Turkey, and other "foreign parties" of "fomenting a struggle for water in the Arab world."[34] More generally, a U.S.-Israeli conspiracy to liquidate the PLO rears its ugly head whenever "a Palestinian fighter raises arms against another Palestinian fighter."[35]

A recessive view also exists, portraying the Arab-Israeli conflict as a Western means to keep Arabs and Israelis weak. The notion of the West setting Arabs and Israelis against each other has won surprisingly wide backing; even Ismail Fahmy, the foreign minister of Egypt, has played with it. 'Adnan Kashoggi, the prominent Saudi businessman, carried this view to its eccentric conclusion, divulging to a British journalist in the high-flying 1970s: "It is obvious. Oil is power. Cash is power. I say God help America and Europe when we unite with the Jews. Then we can really run the show. You could wake up one morning and find yourself occupied by an Arab-Israeli nation."[36] This interesting plot casts Israel in the unusual role of being not the source of evil but a fellow victim of imperialism.

## POLITICS, ECONOMICS, AND RELIGION

### Political Domination

Whenever possible, the conspirator takes over all aspects of decision making. The notion that Americans run every aspect of life in Saudi Arabia has particular resonance. It was actually the U.S. Senate that wrote an agreement between Aramco and the Saudi government. On the eve of hostilities in January 1991, Baghdad spread word that Washington intended to dump the Saudi crown prince and foreign minister.[37] Such domination has obvious attraction to the conspirator, permitting him to skip elaborate mechanisms; but for the same reason, it seems not to attract conspiracy theorists, who would seem to find it too dull to capture their imagination. Hence, political control does not feature much in Middle Eastern conspiracism.

### Economic Exploitation

Western manufactured goods attract Muslims; therefore, using the logic of the conspiracy theorist, these must have been developed with an eye to insinuating them in the Middle East and to leading Muslims astray. And it's not just the West; Ayatollah Khomeini worried about tiny Israel flooding the entire Middle East with its goods. Israel and the West get two main benefits from selling to the Middle East: they get rich and powerful even as Muslims get poor and weak.

In their hearts, Westerners want nothing more than to wreck Arab and Iranian economies. The editor-in-chief of a Baghdad newspaper explained this, referring to the situation before the invasion of Kuwait: "the United States had planned to destroy Iraq completely and return it to the pre-industrial age, as both former U.S. Secretary of State James Baker and President George Bush had promised."[38] When such drastic means are not available, the West foments inflation and unemployment to achieve its aims.

The West has two mechanisms of economic exploitation, employing Arabs and Iranians or selling to them. The first gives the conspirator direct control over the lives of Middle Easterners. Ibrahim Ghawsha of Hamas offers a dire warning of the consequences should Muslims work for Israelis:

> Israel will dominate the region like Japan dominates Southeast Asia. The Arabs will all become employees of the Jews. . . . [Israel] plans to destroy all the resources and powers of the Muslim nations. The Zionist regime will attack Iran, Pakistan, and all Islamic countries. It is not too far-fetched to say that it will harm the resources of these countries by disrupting their industry and technology.[39]

Selling—or making sure that "the people in power" develop a consumer economy—gives the West several sorts of influence over Middle Easterners. It incapacitates the Arabs militarily: "After all, the West keeps them in power because they buy their perfume and fancy cars and arms which they can't use or will not harm Israel."[40] To make sure it keeps this power, the West keeps the Persian Gulf sheikhs in office—and keeps going their ridiculous purchases of luxury and military items. Western businessmen induce naïve Middle Eastern rulers to enter into contracts which eventually bankrupt the treasury and render the state ineffectual. Some draw frightening conclusions from this situation. Should the abundance of glossy Western goods remain in Iranian stores, a newspaper warned, "we will have to sound the knell of Islam."[41]

To make sure Iran is not party to this process, Tehran tries to prohibit trade relations with the United States. In response, Americans seek trade relations, seeing these as a form of warfare by other means. For Mohtashemi, the Iranian hardliner, they constitute a fallback position for Washington: "The Americans have tried by negative political, intelligence, and military means to do this [destroy the Islamic Republic of Iran] but failed, so now they wish to enter by means of commercial relations."[42]

## Undermine Islam

Seeing Islam as the ultimate bulwark against foreign encroachment, fundamentalists understand the modern West's deep impact on the Middle East not as the inexorable influence of a leading civilization over a more backward one but a plot cooked up in London and Paris. Rafsanjani claims that a British foreign secretary told Parliament, "So long as the Qur'an is revered by Muslims, we will not be able to consolidate a foothold among the Muslims."[43] Ayatollah Mohammad Yazdi, chief of the Iranian judiciary, says that the enemies of Islam use "every possible method" to destroy Islam.[44] Westerners sometimes stand accused of trying to eradicate Islam (as in Bosnia), but more often are suspected of alienating Muslims from their faith through one of four main stratagems.

*Seduce Muslims from the Islamic law.*    Hatred of Islam and greed for Muslim resources inspired a two-century effort to weaken Muslims by luring them away from the Shari'a and their ancestral way of life. The West's false but irresistible civilization seduces Muslims away from the Shari'a, thereby undermining "the people's genuine Islamic morals." Many customs innocuous in their homelands become weapons in the Middle East because they draw Muslims away from their own customs. Wearing elegant clothing, listening to classical music, and studying philosophy are all pernicious. Ideals such as humanism, liberty, and freedom of thought are ways to lure impressionable Arab youth.[45] Worse yet, Muslims now drink alcohol, charge interest on loans, and abandon the rituals of prayer, fasting, and pilgrimage. In time, Westernized Muslims no longer even care that they are violating God's commands.

Most threatening of all, however, are women unconstrained by Muslim custom. No less than Zionists and imperialists, women can devastate the fabric of society: "The Muslim order faces two threats: the infidel without and the woman within."[46] Traditional Muslims saw women almost as an internal conspirator. In premodern times, authors tended to avoid the subject of women, but when they took it up, they often warned about the danger of women because of their promiscuous desires; to combat this evil, it was thought best to keep women as uneducated as possible. Advice on the subject of women from the second caliph gets often cited: "Consult them, and do the contrary of what they advise."[47] Women threaten to create an anarchy (*fitna*) that would undermine the entire social order, possibly ending with the destruction of Islam itself.[48] In this spirit, it is not hard to see why fundamentalists tend to see feminism as a plot to destroy the fabric of Muslim society.

In addition, fundamentalists worry enormously about relaxed relations between the sexes—men and women attending mixed-sex schools, interacting socially, working side by side, exerting in sports (especially swimming). The easy availability of pornography, contraception, and abortion is a particular problem. Worse yet, female Muslims now wear blue jeans and bikinis, listen to pop music, watch movies, and attend nightclubs; Ayatollah Musavi-Tabrizi, Iran's prosecutor general, explains that "girls and women who do not fully observe Islamic dress are part of a much wider plot against Islamic values. Watching indecent videos or imitating Western practices are also part of the same process."[49] Very worst of all is the tolerance of non-marital sex.[50]

*Exclude Islam from politics.*    Fundamentalist Muslims see secularism, the ideology of removing religion from public life, as an anti-Islamic conspiracy. "The separating of religion from politics . . . is an age-old enemy plot," Khamene'i once explained.[51] Colonial administrators encouraged pietistic practice and repressed any expression of Muslim-based politics. Of Muslims, Atatürk fell most deeply into this trap. Progovernment preachers carry on this conspiracy; even the modern-day Wahhabis of Saudi Arabia are seen as sponsoring an Islam in which meaningless external manifestations replace a vibrant faith. Outside Iran, Muslim governments purvey what Khomeini called ceremonial Islam or "American-style Islam," a creed brewed up in the White House to subvert the "pure Islam of Muhammad"[52] and spread with considerable success.

*Encourage apostasy from Islam.*    Fundamentalist Muslims worry about Zionists and imperialists converting fellow believers to other religions; in their eyes, this offers a sure way to subordinate Muslims to the West. Christian missionaries seek apostasy through direct methods, as do the prophets bringing such post-Islamic movements as the Baha'i and Ahmadi faiths. Teachers and rock stars who promote Western ways seek the same end through more subtle means. More subtle yet are those economists and development specialists who portray Islam as an impediment to progress, insisting that Muslim advancement requires leaving behind such practices as the five daily prayers, the Ramadan fast, and the separation of men and women.

Jews rely primarily on another method: distorting scriptures. To understand the resonance of this accusation, it is important to recall that, in the Islamic vision, God sent down His message on many occasions, but until Muhammad's perfect transmission, every one of the prophets (including Moses and Jesus) had introduced errors into the text. The perfection of the Qur'an stands as the basic premise of Islam; it also explains why Islam is superior to all other faiths.[53] Accusations of tampering with texts therefore have deep significance for a Muslim audience.

Traditional Muslims see the distortion of texts resulting from human foibles; in contrast, fundamentalists discern a conspiracy. Ayatollah Mohammad Emami-Kashani explains how

> since early times the arrogant powers, especially the Zionists, were engaged in drawing up plans against the groups standing up to them. . . . a person by the name of Paul raised the issue of the Holy Trinity in the Gospel. Father, Son, and the Holy Ghost are put forward by a Zionist.[54] Thus, he brought about the downfall of the Gospel.

In other words, Emami-Kashani portrays Paul as a Jewish agent who adulterated the Gospel, thereby rendering Christianity an imperfect faith. Zionists then tried the same ploy with Islam to keep it from achieving perfection. "They intended to raise accusations that the Qur'an had been altered, but they were prevented from doing so."[55] The Jews failed, but had they succeeded, Islam, too, would have been imperfect.

Even today, Jews are trying to sabotage the Word of God; Khomeini accused Israelis of printing millions of faulty Qur'ans to distribute in Iran, while an Egyptian newspaper charged that Israel "prints Qur'ans falsified through her poison and distributes them in Asian and African countries in their native languages in order to cause Muslims there to abandon Islam."[56] Were these distorted texts to be accepted, they would undermine Islam.

*Assault the dignity of Islam.* Non-Muslim intelligence agencies have produced a range of texts designed to denigrate Islam in the eyes of its faithful. In 1925, the British embassy directed 'Ali 'Abd ar-Raziq to write *Islam and the Bases of Political Power,*[57] a renowned study which argued that Islam is a spiritual quest with no political implications.[58] In 1981, the well-known Egyptian author Fat'hi Ghanim noted a proliferation of printed materials "suggesting strange thoughts and interpretations of Qur'anic passages and Hadiths" and declared "[t]here is proof that . . . international Zionist forces" had financed these.[59] In 1989, British and American intelligence agencies convened leading specialists on Islam to confer among themselves and draw up "a comprehensive way to confront Islam" through "a collective and extensive effort to instigate a cultural confrontation with Islam,"[60] they came up with *The Satanic Verses,* a sustained assault on the sanctities of Islam. A commentary on Radio Tehran declared that this magical realist novel would "weaken the Islamic faith among Muslims, thereby secularizing Muslim societies."[61]

## Foist Fundamentalist Islam

Antifundamentalists approach the subject with exactly the opposite premise, especially in Egypt: they see fundamentalist Islam as a clever concoction brewed up by enemies intent on returning Muslims to the dark ages. The Wahhabis and the Muslim Brethren came into existence to serve Zionist and imperialist ends. A conspiracy-minded journalist writes that the U.S. government "is supporting armed violence in Egypt," while Israel hired mercenaries "to carry out terrorist operations."[62] That a prominent Egyptian fundamentalist, Sheikh 'Umar 'Abd ar-Rahman, took up residence in the United States, prompted one Egyptian commentator to argue that, with the Soviet Union gone, "The West is working to explode Islam from inside by attracting people like 'Umar 'Abd ar-Rahman."[63] A biographer of the sheikh claimed that he received U.S. funds to promote terrorism in the Middle East.[64] The Cairo media states as a fact that 'Abd ar-Rahman, even as he sits in a Manhattan jail, "is a CIA agent."[65]

Muhammad Sa'id al-Ashmawi, a leading Egyptian antifundamentalist, sees Israel as "one of the most important causes behind the spread of extremism in Egypt and the Arab world." In one flight of fancy, he accused the Saudis not just of having joined forces with the Americans and Israelis but of borrowing their methods:

> Saudi Arabia, in the Arab and Islamic countries, follows the same method that Zionism used to control the economy, media, and press of the United States and Europe. With this, Saudi Arabia seeks to control the minds, eyes, and ears of the Arab nation, with particular interest in Egypt. So it buys people to use against Egypt, whether directly or indirectly. . . . there is covert cooperation among Saudi Arabia, U.S. intelligence, and Israeli intelligence . . . to finance terrorism in Egypt and throughout the region.[66]

Libyan media holds that the fundamentalist phenomena "are produced by America and fuelled constantly with the aim of destabilising some countries."[67] Qadhdhafi himself goes further, saying of violent fundamentalists that "there are foreign forces that are directing this naïvete and exploiting it," with the intent "to eliminate the Arab nation."[68]

More surprisingly, fundamentalists themselves sometimes raise the specter of foreign patronage for their movement. Hasan Nasrallah, the secretary general of Hizbullah, tells of his organization's strong suspicion that many Islamic movements have been established and equipped with weapons by the great Satan, America. . . . individuals have joined together who call themselves Islamists or Islamic fighters but are, in reality, manipulated by the United States. . . . The West is pleased by the atrocities in Algeria, because they provide it with the opportunity generally to condemn Islam.[69]

But the most detailed and interesting claim that a Western power sponsored fundamentalist Islam is the elaborate plot devised by Turkish Sunni Muslims to explain how the British government in the early 1700s planted a spy named Hempher who conceived of and spread the Wahhabi doctrine.[70] To make a long story short, Hempher's instructions called on him to disguise himself as a Muslim and to weaken the Ottoman Empire by whatever means he could. While he did resort to such aides as "alcohol and fornication," his main instrument was political: the sowing of dissension. "When the unity of Muslims is broken and the common sympathy among them is impaired, their forces will be dissolved and thus we shall easily destroy them." If he could manage this, Britain's ascendance would then be assured, and its citizens could expect lives of "welfare and luxury."

Hempher's first mission to divide the Muslims was also his most successful. He began by locating a capable but impressionable young man named Muhammad ibn 'Abd al-Wahhab of Najd. "Muhammad of Najd was the sort I had been looking for. . . . I established a very intimate friendship with [him]. I launched a campaign of praising him everywhere." Together, these two began reinterpreting the Qur'an in a way very much at odds with traditional Islam.

Hempher proceeded to bring Muhammad more fully under his control by setting him up with one of the Christian women specifically sent out from London to seduce Muslim youth. Together the two pseudo-Muslims "began to pull the shawl of belief slowly off the shoulders of Muhammad of Najd." Hempher "never left him alone" but insisted on keeping a close eye on his ward. They discussed theological and political subjects, and Muhammad fell ever more under the Briton's influence. As Hempher reports with satisfaction, he "was following the path I had drawn for him." Finally, "this ignorant and morally depraved man" fulfilled his puppeteer's wishes and decided the time had come to found a new sect, the tenets of which had been set out in London. In short order, Muhammad founded the Wahhabi doctrine that still today prevails in Saudi Arabia.

Hempher exulted in the moment, secure in his knowledge that Muhammad would thereby "demolish Islam from within."

This success achieved, London sent Hempher orders to move on, now to make trouble among the Shi'a. Although the Ottoman sultan had been "kind and generous" to the Shi'a of Iraq, Hempher managed to turn them against the sultan by joining their circles of religious instruction. Hempher quickly found the Shi'a to be ignorant and immoral—ripe, in other words, for his mischief. But he also found them "sound asleep" and unwilling to revolt against the authorities in Istanbul.

Having not succeeded on this second mission, Hempher was duly recalled to London. There he studied a fascinating book titled *How Can We Demolish Islam*. Hempher also learned that he was only one of 5,000 British agents assigned with the same mission of weakening the Muslims, and that the government planned to increase the number of agents to 100,000 by the end of the eighteenth century: "When we reach this number we shall have brought all Muslims under our sway." At that happy moment, Islam will be rendered "into a miserable state from which it will never recover again."

Armed with this new knowledge, Hempher returned to the field, where he again connected with Muhammad ibn 'Abd al-Wahhab, instructing him in the distinctive doctrines of Wahhabism (such as the rejection of mausoleums). Hempher stayed two years more with Muhammad, under the guise of being his slave. In 1730, Hempher orchestrated Muhammad's revolt against the Ottomans. To help the cause, 11 other Arabic-speaking British officers turned up, and they, too, paraded themselves as Muhammad's slaves. Thus did the Wahhabi variant of fundamentalist Islam come to dominate most of the Arabian peninsula through an elaborate conspiracy.

## CULTURE, MEDIA, AND DIRTY TRICKS

### Keep Muslims Backward

Conspiracy theorists agree that Western decadence saps Muslims of strength and integrity. But they contradict themselves on the method. One school of thought argues that the West imposes its own civilization to dupe Muslims into accepting "false gods"; the opposite one holds that the West purposefully withholds the best of its civilization.

*The West imposes.* In 1958, a Muslim author wrote that a glut of Western cultural influences aiming "to cut off the Oriental peoples from their past . . . is the single cause of ignorance, poverty, and sickness."[71] This view gained strength in succeeding decades, eventually becoming the ideology of revolutionary Tehran. Thus did an Iranian editorial hold that for decades, "interfering British, American, and Russian hands prevented the natural growth of the old tree of knowledge and culture in the Islamic countries."[72] In the eyes of an Egyptian fundamentalist preacher, the role of imported ideas is "to disgrace women, to destroy the decency of men, and to lead the nation to ruin and the people to destruction."[73]

Educational materials deemphasize Arabic contents so that students remain ignorant of their heritage. A school teacher living on the West Bank points to the curriculum: "there's very little about our tradition and more about the West; the rulers decree this to please their Western masters."[74] Muhammad Anis, professor of modern history at Cairo University, held that every history of nationalist movements in the Arab world was (as paraphrased by Nissim Rejwan) "a collection of lies perpetrated by the imperialists and their agents."[75]

*The West withholds.*     Adherents of the opposite view believe the West keeps back the knowledge that makes it so powerful. But which knowledge is that? Some Muslims point to the intellectual output, others to values or technological know-how. 'Ali Akbar Mohtashemi holds that "the United States and the West will never give us the technology" to pursue what he quaintly calls "the science of industrialization."[76] Sa'di Mahdi Salih of Iraq's National Assembly explains that Westerners "look at the Arabs in a derogatory manner—as a nation incapable of developing and success-fully coping with the challenges of modern technology and science." Not only that, but they do everything to deprive the Arabs "of all the methods of progress and development from which they and Israel benefit."[77] In a particularly ironic twist, some Muslims conjecture that Western praise for the East's "spirituality" serves as a mechanism to discourage the spread of science and technology.[78]

## Media Distortions

Grand conspiracy theorists concur on Jewish and imperialist domination of the press. "The media is controlled by the infidels," declares As'ad Bayyud at-Tamimi, a leader of Palestinian Islamic Jihad.[79] King Fahd of Saudi Arabia once mused on this problem: "It is regrettable that corre-spondents for the international press are in Saudi Arabia and from time to time send reports to their newspapers and magazines contrary to the truth.

Of course, we know why this happens and we know that there are certain plots and designs against this country."[80] The media use a variety of means to forward plots.

*Suppress Muslim arguments.*   Jewish influence sometimes closes the door on Muslims. Nuri as-Sa'id, the perpetual Iraqi politician, told an American ambassador in 1957 of the "New York Zionists" who suppressed an article he wrote for *Life* magazine.[81] At other times, imperialists interfere. Mu'ammar al-Qadhdhafi recounted: "A correspondent of the British *Times* asked me for an article they would print. When I sent it to them, they did not print it, and when I asked their correspondent about it, he told me that the government did not allow it."[82] 'Ali Hoseyni Khamene'i told how Ahmad Khomeini (son of the ayatollah) offered a sizable fee to a major Western newspaper for it to publish one of his father's pilgrimage messages, but the editors refused. Why should "the slaves of money" do that? Because "their intelligence service realized that the imam's message would explode there like a bomb."[83]

*Ignore news.*   A paucity of reporting amounts to what one Maronite calls a "conspiracy of silence."[84] Media neglect of the Palestinian movement proves a plot. For example, to protect Israel from negative publicity, the U.S. government in 1991 ordered media inattention to the Arab-Israeli negotiations taking place in Washington.[85] Likewise, Iranians see the little attention given to Hindu rioting against Muslims in India as part of a plot. To solve this problem, Hamas resolved "to break the barrier of media blackout imposed by the enemy's apparatus."[86]

*Distort facts.*   A PLO spokesman in 1991 denounced *The New York Times*'s version of an interview with Yasir 'Arafat, claiming that its "deliberate distortions" revealed a "U.S.-Zionist attempt to undermine and deform Arab steadfastness."[87] Reports of a crushing Allied victory over Iraq prompted the Iraqi ambassador to France to protest that "Western media are exaggerating their imaginary victories, which have no truth to them at all. At the same time, they play down the importance of Iraqi and Arab steadfastness. We see they are following a planned scheme."[88] Foreign Minister Faruq ash-Shar', on the occasion of the very widely noted first-ever Syrian interview to Israeli television, said that Israeli media had fabricated the notion of Syrian attacks on Israel. "[T]he Israelis were very influential in the international media, especially the Western and American media. They turned the facts [of the 1948-67 confrontation] upside down."[89]

*Use biased terminology.*    The very term "Middle East" is sometimes thought to cover "some very subtle and sinister aims"[90] (because it portrays the region as auxiliary to Europe). References to what Arabs call the Haram ash-Sharif as the Temple Mount strikes the PLO as a "constant conspiracy against our sanctities in Palestine."[91] When, in an attempt to please Arabs, the media refer to the Persian Gulf as the Arabian Gulf, Iranians discern not just a Western "plot of arrogance . . . damaging the historical and natural rights of Iran" but even insidious attempts to alter the area's political geography.[92]

## Sex, Drugs, Coca-Cola, and Rock'n'Roll

The West and Israel rely on seductive means to debilitate Muslims and render them incapable of resisting foreign encroachments.

Sexual corruption is a favorite method, though conspiracy theorists disagree whether it makes Muslim youth more or less likely to take up arms. On the one hand, Israeli secret services are said to use female vamps to incite vulnerable Muslim boys to violence. Faysal ibn Musa'id, King Faysal's assassin, for example, "had been latched on to by an Israeli girl" who convinced him to murder his uncle.[93]

More often, sex debilitates. A Pakistani author dated the start of his country's decline to 1971, when "secret agents" began to flood the country with "blue films," "foreign sensational sex literature," and "cheap sex magazines." He primarily blamed Jews for this "very well-organized and secret cultural attack," and he trembled at the effect: "The slow poisoning of the Islamic world is so effective that it will not be necessary to resort to armed force in order to, God forbid, conquer the Muslims."[94] One leading Egyptian weekly reports that Israel distributes pornographic movies and drugs into Egypt to "lure away the youth and deplete them of all moral principles," and so to render them militarily ineffectual, while another portrays telephone-sex lines as an Israel ploy.[95]

Or was it drugs? Some Saudis believe Faysal ibn Musa'id had been unwittingly given hallucinogenic drugs by the CIA while living in California. Along similar lines, the Iraqi media spread stories about Mossad recruiting members of the Arabian ruling families, then getting them to import drugs through legitimate-appearing companies. Baghdad also accuses Americans, Britons, and Israelis of having "turned vast areas in Kurdistan into fields for growing hashish and opium."[96] From Pakistan comes an account that Zionists mould their agents through "special drugs" administered through food and drink. These mind-controlling, psychochemical drugs were "originally developed by an all-Jewish team of CIA researchers through testing on German POWs after World War II. In the mid-1960s the project was shifted from the United States to Israel."[97] The editor of a Cairo newspaper tells a colorful story about Israel cultivating drugs in southern Lebanon with Egyptian consumers in mind. Why? Because Egyptian drug addicts are "prone to having regular [diplomatic] relations with Israel."[98]

Coca-Cola may look like a mere soft drink, but for Middle Eastern[99] conspiracy theorists it serves as a potent symbol of America. During one frenzy of paranoia in 1968, Iraqi officials decided that drinking Coke amounted to an imperialist act, so they executed the president and general manager of Coke's Iraqi affiliate, two Muslim Iraqis. Without going to quite this extreme, Khomeini's supporters made a similar argument. In 1978, before the Islamic revolution, Ayatollah Yahya Nuri issued pamphlets that portrayed the drinking of Coca-Cola as a "multilateral contribution to evil" and accused Washington of helping the Zionist cause through its sale. He demanded that Iranians boycott the potion.[100] The Islamic Republic indeed banned Coca-Cola, but as revolutionary fervor wore off, the drink returned to Iran. A bottling plant began operations in February 1993, leading to anguished reactions from radicals. Competitors losing business to Coke's "clean bottles" used any means to undermine the drink, including complaints that its secret formula was laced with alcohol, making it not just contrary to the Shari'a but a force for undermining Islam itself.

Western tunes also threaten. Ayatollah Khomeini told a Western journalist that "Music dulls the mind, because it involves pleasure and ecstasy, similar to drugs. Your music I mean. Usually your music has not exalted the spirit, it puts it to sleep. And it destructs [sic] our youth who become poisoned by it, and then they no longer care about their country."[101] Of all Western music, the popular kind coming from the United States is the worst; indeed, it epitomizes what some Muslims hate about Western culture. This accounts for a Pakistani fundamentalist group, Hizbullah, singling out Michael Jackson and Madonna as cultural terrorists trying to destroy Islamic civilization. A spokesman for Hizbullah explained: "Michael Jackson and Madonna are the torchbearers of American society, their cultural and social values . . . that are destroying humanity. They are ruining the lives of thousands of Muslims and leading them to destruction, away from their religion, ethics and morality." Accordingly, Hizbullah called for the two Americans to be brought to trial in Pakistan.[102]

## Dirty Tricks

If conspiracy theorists begin with genocide and revolution, they end with subterfuges of the most derisory kind, including laziness, rumors, and mice. The enemy, it would seem, will stoop to anything to debilitate Muslim countries.

"The rumors are endless," observes Egypt's President Mubarak,[103] and no one in the Middle East seems to disagree. Some see a hidden hand here. Ayatollah Mohammad Emami-Kashani of Iran sees rumors as "the work of the usurping Zionist regime, the White House, and the hypocrites [People's Mojahedin]."[104] His colleague Ayatollah Ahmad Jannati concurs that the West "is spreading rumors" and explains how:

> Four people sit in Tehran on the telephone; they can fill the country with rumors very quickly. . . . They pick up the telephone and call their friends here and there, in this city and that city, for a few hours. They say: This has happened, this issue should be said, this issue should be publicized. And their friends start talking to their friends and family. Suddenly, after twenty-four hours or so, the country is filled with rumors.[105]

As is so often the case, Baghdad agrees with Tehran. Soon after the gassing of Iraqi Kurds in Halabja, killing thousands, the Iraqi ambassador to Great Britain accused the British government of trying to discredit Iraq by spreading false rumors about the use of poison gas.

The conspirator infiltrates dysfunctional practices among his opponents. Imperialists do what they can to aggravate everyday problems, hoping that this will cause an eruption of violence. They have a hand in traffic jams, crop failures, even squabbles between spouses. President Hafiz al-Asad told a national audience that the Syrian habit of wasting time results from "the suffering and the policies of obscurantism and injustice that had been practiced against us during the dark colonial ages."[106]

Even more imaginatively, a Beirut intellectual journal informed its readership in 1986 that foreign-made pills caused the civil war in Lebanon (without explaining how they could do this). Manufactured in the West, these dissentious pills were smuggled across the Arabian desert by "camels, trucks, donkeys, bicycles, and even sheep."[107] Speaking of sheep, in a colorful example dating from 1994, Iraq's Interior Ministry claimed that "some Arab and foreign quarters" were "smuggling sheep and certain items of state property out of Iraq." Elaborating, the ministry's senior undersecretary explained that the goal of this international plot was to reduce Iraq's already limited supply of meat.[108]

Ever since Israel opened an embassy in Cairo, the Jewish state has been persistently accused of using it as a headquarters for plotting. From it come many of the material problems, large or small, bothering Egypt. Israel stands accused of bringing into Egypt a wide range of defective products that, with the exception of a shampoo that causes baldness, are mostly agricultural (and so, reminiscent of the biblical plagues): powdered milk with unacceptable radiation levels, a plague of mice afflicting Egyptian towns and fields, seeds causing cancer and kidney failure, hoof and mouth disease, and a virus called the "red devil" that caused a 40 percent drop in cotton production. Imperialists, in contrast, tend to make trouble in Egypt through their technological prowess:

> The American Reliance Company, which helped set up the unified telephone network in greater Cairo and Alexandria, established an information line between the Egyptian Telephone Exchange network and the central computer in the United States. The line could be used to tap the telephone communications of various ministries, parties, trade unions, and different subscribers.

And it was: Mubarak's phone was supposedly tapped during the *Achille Lauro* crisis of 1985 (when a Palestinian group hijacked an Italian cruise ship) and 'Arafat's phone was then tapped during the peace process.[109]

In a word, Zionists and imperialists are accused of aiming to keep Muslims poor or dumb or powerless or dead.

### NOTES TO CHAPTER 10

1. Sayed Abdul Wadud, *Conspiracies Against the Quran* (Lahore: Khalid Publications, 1976), pp. 68, 82.
2. *The Pakistan Times*, 4 February 1991.
3. *Al-Anwar*, 5 March 1971. Quoted in Y. Harkabi, *Palestinians and Israel* (New York: John Wiley & Sons, 1974), p. 132.
4. *Al-'Iraq*, 9 September 1991.
5. *Ash-Sha'b*, 4 September 1990.
6. Radio Baghdad, 23 August 1990. Saddam's career in Kuwait makes him vulnerable to precisely this accusation.
7. *Sawt ash-Sha'b* (Amman), 5 April 1991.

8. Türkiye Radyoları, 29 August 1992.

9. Voice of the Islamic Republic of Iran, 22 April 1994.

10. Sawt al-Mustad'afin (Lebanon), 16 September 1992.

11. Tripoli Television, 16 October 1993.

12. Voice of the Islamic Republic of Iran, 9 December 1992.

13. *Al-Ahram Weekly*, 25-31 August 1994.

14. Unnamed author quoted in G. E. von Grunebaum, *Modern Islam: The Search for Cultural Identity* (New York: Vintage, 1964), p. 235.

15. Ian Young, *The Private Life of Islam* (New York: Liveright, 1974), p. 121.

16. *Ash-Sha'b*, 26 July 1988, 13 March 1990; *Ash-Shira'*, 29 August 1988; *The Washington Times*, 21 May 1991, quoting *Ash-Sha'b*.

17. Radio Baghdad, 4 April 1975. Quoted in Eberhard Kienle, *Ba'th v. Ba'th: The Conflict between Syria and Iraq, 1968-1989* (London: I. B. Tauris, 1990), p. 103.

18. *Jomhuri-ye Islami*, 24 June 1990.

19. 'Adil Husayn, *Ash-Sha'b*, 12 August 1995.

20. Muhammad al-Ghazali, quoted in *Ash-Sha'b* (Cairo), 23 August 1994. In light of these statements, it is interesting to note that in the premodern Muslim world, "contraception was viewed as an ordinary part of life" and was widely practiced. See B. F. Musallam, *Sex and Society in Islam: Birth Control Before the Nineteenth Century* (Cambridge, Eng.: Cambridge University Press, 1983), pp. vii and passim.

21. Abdel Magid Farid, *Nasser: The Final Years* (Reading, Eng.: Ithaca Press, 1994), p. 92.

22. *Al-Ahrar* (Cairo), 28 June 1995.

23. *Inqilab* (Dhaka), 4 May 1995.

24. *Nida-e Khilafat* (Lahore), 5 July 1995.

25. *Ash-Sha'b*, 22 October 1995.

26. Libyan Television Network, 6 October 1994.

27. Syrian Arab Television, 8 March 1995.

28. Ibrahim Khalas, *Jaysh ash-Sha'b*, April 25, 1967. Quoted in Jabir Rizq, *Al-Ikhwan al-Muslimun w'al-Mu'amara 'ala Suriya* (Cairo: Dar al-I'tisam, 1980), p. 111.

29. Quoted in Walter Laqueur, *The Road to Jerusalem: The Origins of the Arab-Israeli Conflict, 1967* (New York: Macmillan, 1968), p. 79.

30. *Al-Wafd*, 5 March 1987. I am grateful to Barry Rubin for pointing out this reference.

31. *The Forward*, 11 August 1995.

32. *The Jerusalem Report*, 23 March 1995.

33. *Ha'aretz*, 16 December 1994.

34. *Al-Ahram al-Masa'i*, 10 March 1993.

35. *Ad-Dustur*, 23 June 1983.

36. Quoted in Andrew Duncan, *Money Rush* (Garden City, N.Y.: Doubleday, 1979), p. 15.

37. Sawt al-Jamahir (Baghdad), 15 January 1991.

38. Salah al-Mukhtar, *Al-Jumhuriya* (Baghdad), 2 August 1994.

39. *Kayhan* (Tehran), 31 October 1992.

40. A West Bank resident, quoted in Saïd K. Aburish, *Cry Palestine: Inside the West Bank* (Boulder, Col.: Westview, 1993), p. 162.

41. *Pasdar-e Islami* (Tehran), Azor 1371.

42. *Salam* (Tehran), 27 July 1994.

43. Radio Tehran, 24 February 1989. This author has been unable to find anything resembling such a statement.

44. Voice of the Islamic Republic of Iran, 26 August 1994.

45. Nissim Rejwan, *Nasserist Ideology: Its Exponents and Critics* (New York: John Wiley & Sons, 1974), p. 138.

46. Fatima Mernissi, *Beyond the Veil: Male-Female Dynamics in a Modern Muslim Society* (Cambridge, Mass.: Schenkman Publishing, 1975), p. 12.

47. Quoted in Edward William Lane, *Arabian Society in the Middle Ages: Studies from* The Thousand and One Nights, ed. Stanley Lane-Poole (London: Chatto & Windus, 1883), p. 220.

48. Mernissi, *Beyond the Veil*, pp. 4-5, 11-14 explains the fear of *fitna* (which, significantly, also means *femme fatale*).

49. Paraphrased on Islamic Republic of Iran Broadcasting, 2 August 1993.

50. Curiously, this reverses the pattern of the premodern era, when Christians saw Islam as a shockingly permissive religion because it sanctioned nonmonogamous, non-marital, nonprocreative sex, it permitted divorce, and it tolerated contraception.

51. Radio Tehran, 28 June 1990.

52. *Resalat*, 22 June 1991,

53. Wilfred Cantwell Smith, *Islam in Modern History* (Princeton, N.J.: Princeton University Press, 1957), pp. 10-15.

54. Muslims see the Christian Trinity as a denial of pure monotheism and so a distortion of God's message to Jesus.

55. Iran's main sermon, broadcast on Voice of the Islamic Republic, 19 February 1993.

56. *Ash-Sha'b* (Cairo), 3 March 1981. Quoted in Rivka Yadlin, *An Arrogant Oppressive Spirit: Anti-Zionism as Anti-Judaism in Egypt* (Oxford, Eng.: Pergamon, 1989), p. 25. "In their native languages" refers to the Qur'an being untranslatable from Arabic; to make it available in vernaculars, therefore, is to undermine Islam.

57. 'Ali 'Abd ar-Raziq, *Islam wa Usul al-Hukm: Bahth fi'l-Khilafa wa'l-Hukuma fi'l-Islam* (Cairo: Matba'at Misr, 1925).

58. Radio Tehran, 1 March 1983.

59. *Al-Masa'* (Cairo), 10 February 1981. Quoted in Yadlin, *An Arrogant Oppressive Spirit*, p. 25.

60. Radio Tehran, 23 February 1989.

61. Radio Tehran, 15 February 1989.

62. Mahmud Bakri reporting from Egypt, *Al-Muharrir*, 15 May 1995.

63. *Al-Musawwar* (Cairo), 4 December 1992.

64. Anwar Muhammad, *Khumayni Misr: 'Umar 'Abd ar-Rahman* (Cairo: Dar Aya, 1993), pp. 21-22.

65. *Al-Jumhuriya*, 8 July 1993.

66. *Al-Ahali* (Cairo), 6 April 1994. For Western responsibility for the Iranian revolution, see chapter 4, "Who Overthrew the Shah?"

67. Jamahiriya News Agency, 7 February 1995.

68. Libyan Television, 29 July 1995.

69. *Der Spiegel*, 17 July 1995.

70. This account derives from M. Sıddık Gümüş, *Confessions of a British Spy*, 3d ed. (Istanbul: Hakikat Kitabevi, 1993).

71. Unnamed author quoted in G. E. von Grunebaum, *Modern Islam: The Search for Cultural Identity* (New York: Vintage, 1964), p. 235.

72. *Ettela'at*, 5 July 1990.

73. Quoted in Patrick D. Gaffney, *The Prophet's Pulpit: Islamic Preaching in Contemporary Egypt* (Berkeley: University of California Press, 1994), p. 309.

74. Quoted in Aburish, *Cry Palestine*, p. 162. Samir Sam'an, *Al-Mu'amarat as-Sahyuniya wa'l-Isti'mariya li-Tajhil 'Arab Filastin mundhu al-Qarn at-Tasi' Ashar* (Amman: Dar al-Bayraq, 1407/1987) makes this point at great length.

75. Rejwan, *Nasserist Ideology*, p. 13.

76. *Shahid*, Farvardin 1369/1990.

77. Iraqi News Agency, 18 April 1990.

78. Raphael Patai, *The Arab Mind* (New York: Charles Scribner's Sons, 1976), pp. 290-95.

79. *Al-Watan al-'Arabi* (Paris), 2 December 1994.

80. Riyadh Television, 1 June 1983.

81. Waldemar J. Gallman, *Iraq Under General Nuri: My Recollections of Nuri al-said, 1954-1958* (Baltimore: Johns Hopkins Press, 1964), p. 168.

82. *Al-Majalla*, 5 December 1993.

83. Radio Tehran, 19 April 1995.

84. Joseph Abu Halka, quoted in Barbara Newman, with Barbara Rogan, *The Covenant: Love and Death in Beirut* (New York: Crown, 1989), p. 50.

85. *Ar-Ra'y*, 7 December 1991.

86. Leaflet No. 39 of Hamas. Text in Shaul Mishal and Reuben Aharoni, *Speaking Stones: Communiqués from the Intifada Underground* (Syracuse, N.Y.: Syracuse University Press, 1994), p. 260.

87. Sawt Filastin (Algiers), 7 January 1991.

88. Radio Amman, 6 February 1991.

89. Israel Television Channel One, 7 October 1994.

90. Rejwan, *Nasserist Ideology*, p. 130.

91. WAFA, 25 October 1990.

92. *Abrar*, 6 September 1990; Islamic Revolution News Agency, 22 January 1991.

93. *The Pakistan Times*, 4 February 1991.

94. Ghulman Rasul Tanvir writing in *Nawa-i-Waqt*, 29 April 1983.

95. Movies and drugs: *Mayu*, 4 November 1985, quoted in Yadlin, *An Arrogant Oppressive Spirit*, p. 24. Telephone sex: *Ruz al-Yusuf*, cited in *The New York Times*, 10 October 1995.

96. *Al-Jumhuriya* (Baghdad), 10 August 1993.

97. *The Pakistan Times,* 4 February 1991.

98. Muhammad al-Hayawan, writing in *Al-Jumhuriya* (Cairo), 14 April 1985. Quoted in David Lamb, *The Arabs: Journeys Beyond the Mirage* (New York: Random House, 1989), p. 129.

99. And others too. An unlikely debate took place in France from 1948 to 1950, when the parliament came close to banning the potion; only the need for continued Marshall Plan credits turned the tide in Atlanta's favor. See Richard F. Kuisel, *Seducing the French: The Dilemma of Americanization* (Berkeley: University of California Press, 1993), ch. 3. American Muslims condemn "Coka-Cola" as un-Islamic and rue the fact that "Things go better with Coke" gets said more often than "Glory be to God." See Mohammed Abdullah Locks, "Swimming in Coka-Cola," *New Trends* (Kingsville, Md.), May 1994.

100. Quoted in John R. Stempel, *Inside the Iranian Revolution* (Bloomington, Ind.: Indiana University Press, 1981), p. 110.

101. Oriana Fallaci, "An Interview with Khomeini," *The New York Times Magazine,* 7 October 1979.

102. Ne'matullah Khan, *The Philadelphia Inquirer,* 13 February 1995.

103. ESC Television, 28 November 1995.

104. Radio Tehran, 14 April 1995.

105. Voice of the Islamic Republic of Iran, 21 April 1995.

106. Syrian Arab Republic Radio, 12 March 1992.

107. *Al-Fikr al-Islami,* March 1986, p. 106.

108. *Al-Jumhuriya* (Baghdad), 13 February 1994.

109. *Al-Ahali* (Cairo), 23 March 1994.

## Part III

# THE PARANOID STYLE

At first glance, the conspiracy mentality appears to be a jumble of fearful and aggressive impulses; but a systematic survey shows predictable and distinctive patterns emerging. We consider several aspects of the paranoid style in the pages ahead, starting with an inquiry into the question, Who believes, who exploits? Are conspiracy theorists genuine in their accusations, or do these merely serve as a ploy? We then look at the logic of the grand conspiracy theory as imagined in the Middle East. What approaches and which assumptions do conspiracy theorists regularly rely on? We pay special attention to one particular assumption, that of an opaque relationship between appearance and reality.

# 11.

# The Conspiracy Theorist: Manipulative or Sincere?

Falsehood of the tongue leads to that of the heart.
— *Thomas Jefferson*[1]

You can reach the point where there is no longer any difference between developing the habit of pretending to believe and developing the habit of believing.
— *Umberto Eco*[2]

Are those who claim to find conspirators under every bed as scared as they would have us think? Our goal here is not to decide whether a conspiracy theory is true or not, but to assess what Middle Easterners think. Do they believe what they say?

Every indication suggests that the public in the Muslim Middle East unrehearsedly and sincerely believes in conspiracy theories, and that repetition works. Observers widely concur on the deep credulity of Middle Easterners in conspiracism. Here are three testimonies, from an American diplomat, a British journalist, and a Palestinian historian. William R. Brown writes that "innumerable suspicions are voiced and avidly believed whenever politics are discussed in the Middle East."[3] In Pakistan, Emma Duncan writes, "everybody is an amateur conspiracy theorist, and nothing is taken at face value."[4] Hisham Sharabi writes that "the ordinary man sees a plot behind every shift in every policy, every decision or development, whether within the army, by a foreign power, or by a political group."[5]

But what about the rulers and the elite? They are different and their views more nuanced. We begin by considering the characteristics of a typical Middle Eastern conspiracy theorist, follow with a review of the evidence indicating either manipulation or sincerity, and conclude with an assessment.

## PERSONALITY

The archetypical conspiracy theorist's personality is not a pretty picture. The conspiracy theories he espouses points to his being obsessed with his own importance, adhering to fringe political beliefs, illogical, and showing a dour, suspicious, and pessimistic disposition.

*Self-centered.*    Conspiracy theorists make themselves more important than the facts warrant. Iranians in particular manage to insinuate themselves as chief victims of plots, no matter how farfetched; Marvin Zonis notes that Iranians believe that "the rest of the world is somehow so taken with Iran's significance that it cannot let go."[6] They saw their country as the imperialists' biggest prize throughout the modern era, when it was nothing of the sort. (A century ago, India came first; Saudi Arabia does today.) When Saddam Husayn threatened that "if Israel were to attempt any aggression against Iraq, then, by God, our fire shall devour one half of Israel,"[7] the Iranian media reported this as a threat to Tehran. Yes, Saddam specified Israel by name, but *Kayhan International* nonetheless insisted that "Iran, and not Israel was in Saddam's mind."[8] When Washington staged joint antidrug efforts with Colombia, Iranians saw in this a move against themselves (because it took the shine off Iranian antidrug efforts launched about the same time).

Although George Bush's "new world order" dealt with all parts of the globe, Iranians understood it as an American effort to stop "the growing Islamic sentiments in the world."[9] Closer to home, they saw the new world order implying "domination and, ultimately, the exploitation of the Middle East."[10] Libyan leaders agreed, insisting that Arabs served as "the cornerstone" of American plans for world hegemony.[11] The Jihad group in Egypt saw U.S. policies in Vietnam, Grenada, and Cuba as inspired by a hatred of Islam and a need to protect American interests in Muslim countries. Yasir 'Arafat, of course, placed Palestine at the heart of the matter: "The objective is to build Greater Israel, based on territorial annexations as a premise of the 'New Order.'"[12] General Mirza Aslam Beg, Pakistan's top military officer, fell into this mindset, too, predicting that the United States would follow victory over Iraq with the destruction of Pakistan's nuclear program.

Twisting every action into a plot against oneself often distorts understanding of the opponent's intentions. Oil price declines in the early 1980s prompted Middle Eastern speculation about a Western plot; but to what end? The obvious motive—Western economic gain through lower energy costs—received little attention. Instead, mired in self-absorption, Arabs and Iranians imagined the West sought to harm the Muslims by blocking "the possibility of an Arab awakening or cultural revival." This in turn would enable Washington to "implement its plans to expand from the [Persian] Gulf to the [Atlantic] Ocean."[13] Even U.S. efforts to end the Arab-Israeli conflict are a "vast conspiracy" against Iran, according to Mohsen Reza'i, commander general of Iran's Guard Corps. After solving this problem, the United States will organize an alliance between the Arab states and Israel directed against Iran. The first Oslo accord brought the conspiracy against the Islamic Republic of Iran to a "new phase."[14]

*Politically extremist.* Heavy reliance on conspiracism points to an unhealthy environment of political extremism, in both individuals and societies. A world starkly divided between forces of good and evil leaves no room for neutrality. Things are either supremely good (the American way of life, socialism, Arab unity) or supremely evil (the American way of life, socialism, Zionism). That Saddam Husayn's accusation against Kuwait of trying to destroy the Iraqi economy "seemed credible" to many Arabs[15] points to the depths of political extremism among Arabic-speaking peoples. Looking to the Muslim world as a whole, perhaps one third of this huge body interpreted the Iraqi invasion of Kuwait in a conspiratorial fashion.

In general, relying on conspiracy theories points to unsettled politics. That the Kuwait war saw conspiracy theories becoming scarce in Syria and blossoming in official Tunisia provided an indication that the Syrian leadership was moderating and the Tunisian one not. Contrarily, its relative absence provides an important (but not infallible)[16] sign of wholesome politics (e.g., in Turkey).

*Nonanalytical.* Conspiracism is rife with contradictions, some blatant, others quite subtle. Wrought up by his own emotions, the conspiracy theorist hardly notices them; nor, when pointed out, does he much care. Rarely does he engage in introspection or ponder his inconsistencies. In one speech, Western civilization has a terrible influence on Muslims; in that one, all good things in the West derive from the Muslim world. On one occasion, the West is permeated by atheism; on the next, it is engaged in a Crusader war against the Muslims. United States uses Israel; Israel runs the United States. Unsystematic to the end, conspiracy theorists seem not to notice these contradictions. For them, context is all. When Israel as spearhead of colonialism fits their purposes, they say that; they accept the idea of Israel as the real power in the United States when that suits better.

Conspiracy theorists also have no trouble accounting for opposite results. Like vulgar Freudianism, the conspiracy mentality lends itself to explain any phenomenon—or its reverse. When Washington and Baghdad get along, Tehran sees a conspiracy; when they go to war, it's another conspiracy. The same goes for U.S.-Israel, Israeli-Syrian relations, and so on.

*Humorless.* Conspiracy theorists have precious little sense of humor. They denounce as "a cultural plot" a political cartoon that shows Ayatollah Khomeini kicking a soccer ball.[17] They actually establish organizations with earnest names such as (this one in Libya) the "Center for Resistance Against Zionism, Imperialism and Reactionary Plots."

This dour outlook renders Arabs and Iranians gullible to pranks and hoaxes. In May 1992, Fahmi Huwaydi, an Egyptian columnist, wrote a satirical piece how a clandestine group of fundamentalist Arabs called the Bilalis planned and directed the riots in Los Angeles following the Rodney King verdict, in which several Los Angeles policemen were acquitted of using unnecessary violence against King, a black motorist. In Huwaydi's account, King was a member of the Bilalis, as was the bystander who videotaped the incident and passed it on to a television station. Huwaydi expected his account to be understood as a spoof; but it was taken literally and since has entered into the mythology of radical fundamentalism.[18]

*Seeks order.* Conspiracy theories reduce complexities to seductive patterns of orderliness. "Political life had to be simplified. Conspiracy ordered this uncertain and vastly confusing world and gave it shape."[19] It defines dangers and brings a welcome rational order to unpleasant and erratic events. They bring blessedly logical rules to the entwined, motley, and unpredictable historical record. A composite of errors and ambiguities turns into a rational whole. What would otherwise be a unwieldy welter of events and peoples take shape in a sensible way. Conspiracy theorists ignore accidents, bureaucratic in-fighting, and muddling through, for their obsessively neat minds cannot countenance errors or the haphazard. They offer relief to someone who feels he lacks control over his own destiny. Ultra-rationalists, who find chaos intellectually unsatisfying and who seek a single, coherent explanation, often turn to conspiracism. The easy reductionism of the hidden hand brings offers comfort in a messy, hostile environment. "It is imperative," Graham Fuller observes, "to recognize the existence of powerful external forces that dominate or control events; it is essential to bring some analytic order to a chain of events to demonstrate the deeper meaning, the plan, or even the plot that exist behind them."[20] Thomas Friedman tells how deeply felt was this need in Lebanon during the civil war:

> During the entire time I was in Beirut [most of the period from 1979 to 1984] I don't remember more than one or two cases where the perpetrators of a car bomb, an assassination, or a major killing were ever identified, caught, and punished. . . . In an attempt to make the anxiety this produced more controllable, the Lebanese would simply invent explanations for the unnatural phenomena happening around them; they would impose an order on the chaos.[21]

Myriad troublemakers become a single hostile force. In Qadhdhafi's words: "All these things everywhere are a conspiracy. This is one single plan."[22] Streamlining of this sort concentrates enmity and rouses the spirit. Faced with anarchy, the conspiracy theorist prefers someone to be in charge, even if he is hostile, rather than some large, undefined force. Alarmed at the pervasiveness of intrigue, as Jean Said Makdisi notes, also in reference to Lebanon, "a certain perverse comfort is taken from the assurance that someone, at least, knows what is going on and why."[23]

*Content with complexity.*     At the same time, conspiracy theorists find solace in complexity. Tangled and baroque explanations hold no terror for them. In the conspiratorial universe, the rule of logic known as Occam's Razor ("no more things should be presumed to exist than are absolutely necessary") is suspended. Quite the contrary, a long and unlikely sequence of events seems to enhance a scenario and make it more credible. Drawing on years of experience, Fuller notes that "Many Iranians will regularly choose the most complex explanation of political events as the most likely, particularly in gauging the intention of foreign powers. . . . Events never have simple explanations but rather reflect the existence of unseen political forces at work behind the scenes manipulating reality."[24]

Examples abound. What prompted the Jordanian authorities to suppress the PLO in September 1970, that "Black September" of Palestinian lore? The simple reason, King Husayn's real fear for throne and life, typically gets ignored. Instead, conspiracy theorists forward a range of imaginative reasons. Jerusalem had manipulated its Palestinian agents to provoke Jordanian hatred of the PLO; the Americans wanted to get rid of the PLO (some believe the CIA planned the operation with Husayn from the start); or American and Israeli agents jointly did "their bit to guarantee . . . a catastrophe for the Palestinian people."[25] Why accept a simple explanation when a fanciful one will do?

The American role in the Arab-Israeli conflict provides two examples of this pattern. The unwashed may believe that Israeli forces invaded Lebanon in 1982 to eliminate the PLO, but an Iranian Revolutionary Guard in Lebanon explained it otherwise: "The Israeli war against Lebanon" in 1982, he said, "was a conspiracy aimed at getting Iran to send its troops to Lebanon and to forget the war with Iraq."[26] B. J. Odeh, a Palestinian teaching political economy in the United States, offers an even more elaborate Israeli goal: to provoke the Arabs, thereby sabotaging their relations with Washington.

> The Israeli invasion of Lebanon was a major attempt, the last of a series, to disrupt the US-Arab rapprochement. Israel had bet on the likelihood that the Arab states would take to war against her thus bringing the US to Israel's side, which, in turn, so Israel thought, would arouse Arab outrage against the US.[27]

In other words, the Israelis' real purpose was not what it seemed (to win on the battlefield) but something much more complex (to change public opinion in the United States).

A confrontation at Jerusalem's Temple Mount led to 19 Palestinian deaths at Israeli hands in October 1990. The U.S. government, hoping to keep Egypt and Syria in the American-led coalition against Iraq, responded by placing all blame on the Israeli police, then joining in two United Nations resolutions condemning Israel. But, in Arab eyes, Washington had also instructed the Israeli police to kill Palestinians, hoping to use the incident as a means to prove its anti-Israeli credentials. Here, too, the real purpose was not what it seemed (Americans making the best of a tense situation) but something much more complex and clever (Americans plotting out the whole scenario for their own benefit).

## MANIPULATIVE . . .

Focusing on rulers and the elite, it is clear that the head of government, foreign minister, or editorial writer shares some of the public's fears even as he manipulates a gullible public for his own ends. Statements from the top show a mixture of fear and nihilism; while spinning grand conspiracy theories, the leader sometimes appears to believe what he is saying and at other times displays obvious cynicism. The same individual will alternately be sensible and indulge in conspiracism. An outsider has difficulty explaining the switch from one approach to the other; and finds it even harder to say which view better represents a leader's innermost thinking. How does one distinguish sincerity from opportunism, gullibility from skepticism? And what is the ratio of one to the other?

We begin by marshaling evidence suggesting that leaders use conspiracy theories; then follow that with materials explaining that, to the contrary, they are sincere it what they say; and conclude with some observations.

Inner logic and circumstantial evidence sometimes make government manipulation obvious. The ruler who rails against Israeli plots in speeches while whispering on the side that no one should take these seriously is obviously engaged in pretence; and such contradictions are common (on these, chapter 17, "Public-Private Discrepancies"). When the Syrian defense minister accuses Abu Nidal of working for the CIA and he in fact lives in Damascus and acts with the Syrian regime's blessing, the insincerity is transparent. When Abu Nidal responds to Algerian efforts to control his group by accusing the Algerian security services of conspiring against the Palestinian people, he is obviously not sincere.

Authorities sometimes exploit grass-roots conspiracy theories for their own Machiavellian purposes. The campaign against Salman Rushdie began on the streets of Great Britain and Pakistan; only later did the Saudi and Iranian governments adopt it and turn it into an international incident. On a lesser scale, rumors about a five-year old Muslim girl being raped by a Copt led to a riot in the town of Sinnuris, Egypt, in April 1990, leading to Coptic property being set on fire and street violence. Prime Minister 'Atif Sidqi unhelpfully and implausibly blamed the unrest on "international organizations" intent on disrupting stability and diverting "young people's attention from productive work."[28]

And while Muslim-Christian strife in Egypt obviously results primarily from local causes, all sides (the authorities, opposition parties, fundamentalist Muslim groups, and the Coptic Church) fall back on the comfortable crutch of a foreign enemy. Who the culprit is depends on the enemy of the moment. In 1972, American imperialists and Zionists made trouble to weaken the country vis-à-vis Israel. Eight years later, the new Iranian regime got blamed. By way of proof, an Iranian "spy" was turned up who, very cooperatively and in fluent Arabic, confessed on television to burning down a church with an intent to exacerbate religious tensions and so to weaken the Egyptian government.[29] The same goes for acts of terror in Egypt. While the deputy prime minister declared that "Arab and foreign states supplied weapons to terrorists [i.e., fundamentalist Muslims] in the governorate [of Asyut] within a plot aimed at playing Egyptian citizens against one another,"[30] Egyptian newspapers a little later blamed Mossad for violence in Cairo.[31]

Abdel Nasser's accusations of a joint U.S.-Israel plot against Egypt in 1967 rang so hollow that American diplomats saw them only in terms of political utility, as a cable reported in telegraphic style:

> We found it hard in circumstances to conclude Egyptians seriously believed story of Israel-American plot or that they would be taking present actions without promises Soviet support. Goal appeared be elimination US influence from Middle East as much as it did to strike a blow against Israel.[32]

Preposterous stories also give the game away, as when the Iranian government uncovered a plot against itself in December 1970, arresting hundreds; trouble was, the alleged mastermind of the plot, General Teimur Bakhtiar, had died four months earlier. Could the Beirut journalist have been serious when he claimed that Ethiopian Jews arriving in Israel were deployed as sandbags at the Litani River?[33]

Iraqi media made claims that stretch the imagination, announcing that "Turkey is providing the Zionist entity with its water needs by tankers via Iskanderun"[34] and that U.S. planes set fire to wheat and barley fields near Mosul to starve Iraqis.[35] Radio Baghdad reported over 165,000 American soldiers killed or wounded in the war for Kuwait.[36] From Algeria came further details: to hide the vast numbers of dead from the American public, the U.S. authorities embalmed the corpses in Saudi Arabia, evacuated them to (of all places) Djibouti for storage, and then transported them to Crete for secret burials.[37]

Leaders' actions — turning the conspiracy theory spigot on and off — also point to manipulation. Saddam Husayn had grounded his policies in conspiracy theories about the United States in 1980 (when he attacked Iran) and ten years later (when he attacked Kuwait), but between those times, especially in the period from 1985 to 1987, he dropped the conspiracy theory references and improved relations with Washington. Did he change his behavior for reasons of expediency (fear of an Iranian invasion) or due to a change of heart? Circumstantial evidence points to Saddam's underlying beliefs remaining intact throughout and his deciding to keep his own counsel during the mid-1980s.

Other factors point to politicians merely pretending to believe in the wild theories they espouse. It's one thing for those unfamiliar with policy-making to take conspiracy theories seriously, but how can someone with first-hand experience working for the state? Sure, peasants believe in the stupendous powers ascribed to American and Israeli governments, but the politician's own career contradicts hidden-hand explanations. He knows that restrictions of all sorts (legal, political, personal, customary) hem in even the most powerful officeholder, to which one has to add the confusion of the moment. Policy planners admit the oxymoronic quality of their task; action drives planning, not the other way around. If the outsider finds the idea of fine-tuning the actions of adversaries in distant countries plausible, the politician who knows the difficulty prevailing over institutions under his direct authority has to laugh at the idea.

Also, where the uninitiated see the grand sweep of history, bureaucrats know the role of personality and accident—an undersecretary's absence permits his rival to clear the president's speech; a friendship across the ideological spectrum mutes a bill; a backroom compromise causes policy inconsistencies. The Iranian insistence on conspiracies deeply misunderstands the capabilities of a modern state. As Richard Cottam writes, "No large bureaucracy is capable of orchestrating a conspiracy so elaborate as that the Iranians attributed to the British."[38] If conspiracism implies little understanding of government life, Middle East leaders would seem to be feigning.

### . . . OR SINCERE?

But politicians do not always manipulate when raising the conspiracy bogey. Several patterns point to at least occasional sincerity: their sharing many attitudes with their publics, fear and ignorance of the West, their being surrounded by lies, the confluence of beliefs and interests, and personal behavior.

## Mirror of Society

Leaders echo the notions common to their societies and these, we have seen, are replete with conspiracy theories. This pattern has two elements.

First, government officials enter office carrying the prejudices of their political milieu, sharing much with the citizenry, including fears of violence and resentments of the West. When the political culture features real and imaginary plots, politicians are swayed no less than peers outside the government.

Second, seeing the world as does the public may be important if a leader is to be successful. Gamal Abdel Nasser's remarkable popularity and huge influence owed much to his ability to identify with and respond to the deep fears of his Egyptian and Arab audience. His biographer, P. J. Vatikiotis, ties this to Abdel Nasser's conspiracy mentality, holding that "in his suspicious and limited perception of the world about him, Abdel Nasser personified the view of the vast majority of his fellow-countrymen, especially the poor and miserable of Egypt."[39] The same observation applies to such figures as Shah Mohammed Reza Pahlavi and Ayatollah Khomeini.

## Awe of Israel and the West

Humans seem to universally to overestimate an adversary's competence, farsightedness, and willfullness, a habit shared by politicians. They tend to suspect their foreign counterparts enjoy awesome strengths they themselves lack:

> the tendency to see the other side as centralized and Machiavellian is widespread. . . . decision-makers generally overestimate the degree to which their opposite numbers have the information and power to impose their desires on all parts of their own governments. The state's behavior is usually seen as centrally controlled rather than as the independent actions of actors trying to further their own interests and their partial and biased conceptions of the national interest.[40]

In addition, politicians tend to read malevolence in others: "Decision-makers often spontaneously perceive an evil plan rather than make a calculated decision to act on the assumption that it lies behind the disparate events."[41] Such expectations make conspiracism the more plausible.

The First World-Third World divide exacerbates this tendency. Someone sitting in Cairo or Baghdad finds it easy to imagine that things are done differently in Washington or Jerusalem. His own policy planning staff does not function as it is supposed to, but surely those in the West do. Political stability allows for long-range strategy; democracy means less internal bickering; modern communications facilitate an international outlook; a well-educated populace permits sophisticated institutions; and financial power assures everyone's loyalty.

(Of course, these suppositions are dead wrong. In fact, Washington—with its unending bureaucratic battles, its leaks, and the provincialism of Americans—is particularly unsuited to the cunning manipulation of foreigners. The American political system is both the most open and the most chaotic. Many more institutions play a role in policymaking than elsewhere: not just the head of the executive branch and his foreign policy specialists, but also the military, the legislative branch, the lobbyists, the media, and academic specialists. Rivalries may be less driven, but in other ways policymaking becomes more difficult as a society opens up.)

Interestingly, conspiracism derives more from a sense of weakness than from actual powerlessness. Arab and Iranian politicians feel excluded from the centers of power; even absolute despots like Qadhdhafi feel disenfranchised. A Libyan newspaper expresses this sense of inferiority: "The Arabs always represent the weaker party in the equation of international relations. When Congressman Tom Lantos asked Hafiz al-Asad his thoughts on the peace process, Asad replied with disarming frankness: "I have no doubt you know everything anyway. America is the engine that drives things, and your ambassador knows everything."[42] Arab impotence is crystal clear in the issue of the Arab-Zionist conflict."[43] To the extent that conspiracy theories express the frustrations of outsiders, they suit even the most powerful Arabs and Iranians.

## Ignorant of the West

Middle Easterners often appear to be more familiar with the West than actually is the case. Arabs

> may be well informed on currency movements and the latest chat on the prospects of the Western economies but know surprisingly little about how Western societies and governments operate. Even those who live in the West or visit it frequently on holiday do not have much understanding of it because, in most cases, when they are there they mix with

other Arabs, principally their own relations, and take no interest in the
culture, history or institutions of the countries they are in.[44]

As an example of this pattern, Middle Easterners commonly believe that
Europeans hope to regain their empires of old, although this is something
extremely few Europeans aspire to. Just as mistakenly, Middle Easterners
dismiss human rights activism as a hypocrisy, whereas it is in fact deeply
felt. This sort of ignorance goes far to explain conspiracism among even
the most sophisticated Arabs and Iranians.

### Surrounded by Lies

Leaders tend to be especially susceptible to conspiracy theories. Like
everyone else living in the Middle East, they feel the ubiquity of conspiracism in rumors, sermons, and news reports. The very banality of these
notions has an erosive effect, making the conspiracy mentality more
plausible, causing leaders automatically to think in conspiratorial ways.
Routinized repetition has a cumulative impact, prompting leaders unthinkingly to shift problems on to a hidden hand, thereby enhancing the
credibility of conspiracy theories.

Also, a leader consumes more of his own propaganda than does most
of his audience, and at closer range. "Tell a lie long enough and often enough,"
a Western diplomat in Saddam's Baghdad notes, "and inevitably you start
believing it."[45] Kanan Makiya, a native of that same city, agrees: "Eventually
many ended up genuinely believing the lie they had at first only pretended to
believe in."[46] Mouthing words doubles the need to believe them.

Surrounded by yes-men who pander to their egotism, leaders often
find it impossible to maintain their critical faculties. As their partial author
and frequent propagandist, the politician has more invested in conspiracy
theories than does ordinary citizens, and so he becomes especially susceptible to their charms. He needs to believe his own statements; not to do so
would mean living a lie. Also, rulers inculcate their families with the same
conspiracy theories the rest of the country hears. Hafiz al-Asad recounted
in 1974 that his eight-year-old son, Bashshar, asked him how he could
shake hands with Richard Nixon, "an evil man who is completely in control
of the Zionists and our enemies."[47]

Supreme rulers seek new realms to dominate — and what establishes
power more conclusively than an ability to create reality? "The litmus test
of absolute authority is this capability of turning lies into truth." The more
the ruler fancies himself godlike, the more he is seduced by this vision. It

is in this sense that Saddam Husayn "does not think of himself as a liar, but as a theorist whose current reality is always 'proof' of any assertion he chooses to make."[48]

And suppose the conspiracy theory turns out to be true? No one else has as much to lose as the ruler. If Americans had helped Israel destroy the Egyptian air force in 1967, was it not incumbent on an Egyptian leader to prepare for the worst? Abdel Nasser could plausibly argue that, lacking firm information, he owed it to his constituents to deal with all eventualities. He happened to have been wrong, but he had genuine concerns.

## Behavior

That leaders forward conspiracy theories in private, when they have no reason to engage in pretense, suggests sincere belief; as does their occasional hesitancy about conspiracism and their willingness to risk ridicule to put forward their theories.

Even in moments of acute stress, leaders resort to the conspiratorial explanation. As he was being overthrown by a military coup d'état, President Husni Za'im of Syria tried desperately but unsuccessfully to escape execution by bribing his guard. When Za'im realized he was done for, he reportedly muttered, "This is a plot by the British to destroy the independence of the country."[49] At such a moment, one presumes, Za'im vented true feelings.

Private conversations confirm conspiracy theories uttered in public. Gamal Abdel Nasser told his closest associates that Washington "believes that the time is ideal for getting rid of our political system and thereby achieving victory for itself and for Israel."[50] During a closed-door meeting in 1979, Yasir 'Arafat explained to Soviet foreign minister Andrei Gromyko how a whole range of events—including poor Syrian-Iraqi relations and an uprising in Syria—resulted from an American plot.[51] Westerners meeting in private with the shah and his officials at the time of the Islamic Revolution all became convinced of their sincerity of their conspiratorial ideas. In particular, the U.S. ambassador wrote that the conspiracy mentality extends "from the lowliest peasant all the way up to the shah himself," a conclusion seconded by his British counterpart.[52] A few weeks before his appointment in 1991 as Jordan's foreign minister, Jabir Abu Kamil portrayed Saddam Husayn in a private conversation as falling into a trap laid by the U.S. government.

Hesitancy on the part of rulers to reveal their thinking about conspiracy theories also suggests genuine belief. Consider the following speculation by Iran's President 'Ali Akbar Hashemi-Rafsanjani on the subject of dissension among Iran's foreign enemies:

> I am just guessing here, I am not sure, but it could be that all the clashes and the hue and cry raised between Iraq, Israel, the U.S., Britain, and their likes in the world, and inside Israel when the Labor and Likud parties fight each other in the parliament, are all for show to distract public opinion away from the tragedy they are perpetuating.[53]

The musing, almost hesitant quality of this presentation argues for the speaker's sincerity; even as he considers the possibility that the whole world of politics is but a theatrical production to fool him, he indicates his uncertainty. Similarly, King Husayn of Jordan expressed considerable uneasiness when interviewed about Saddam Husayn's invasion of Kuwait, garbling his answer: "I can't justify or condone [the invasion], but the reason must have been pretty substantial to have had it happen. Both sides, I fear, gradually succumbed to a conspiracy theory about the other."[54] The stunning illogic of this statement points to candor.

Although Middle Eastern leaders know their conspiracy theories meet a cool reception in the West, still they forge ahead, both in private and in public. Shah Mohammad Reza Pahlavi offered an unexpurgated version of his conspiratorial fears in his 1980 memoir *Answer to History,* knowing full well the skepticism these would arouse in the West.[55] Educated at Harvard and Oxford, Benazir Bhutto recounted her version of 1977's tumult in Pakistan with some shyness: "Asians have always been prone to conspiracy theories. But in this case my father [Prime Minister Zulfikar Ali Bhutto] and other members of the PPP [his political party] were convinced that the unrest was due to American involvement." She added that she "didn't want to believe" that Washington was engaged in destabilizing the democratic government in Pakistan—but she did nonetheless.[56] That Yasir 'Arafat used his moment at the United Nations in May 1990 to tell how a 10-agorot coin from Israel foreshadowed its plans for conquest showed either that he truly believed in this thesis, or that he was such a bad politician that he failed to understand it would be counterproductive. The first explanation makes more sense.

## Operational

Middle Eastern leaders act as if truly worried about conspiracies against themselves, confirming that at least some of the time they believe their theories. For the most consequential examples, see chapter 1; here we look at smaller, perhaps more revealing instances.

Politicians seem to expect at any moment to be the victims of a conspiracy. They live stealthily, surround themselves with tasters, and build up vast security apparatuses. The more total the autocracy, the more fearful the atmosphere and the more redolent with conspiracy theories. Abdülhamit II, the Ottoman sultan, rarely left his palace, reportedly insisted on having documents disinfected before he would touch them, smoked only cigarettes prepared in his presence, and maintained a kitchen that prepared food for himself alone. Gamal Abdel Nasser "was always alert. Anxiety gnawed continually at his heart, as he regarded everybody with suspicion."[57] After 1967, he "had to sleep with one eye open and the other only half closed."[58] Fearing treachery in his own ranks, 'Arafat famously did not inform companions on his private plane where they are headed until the aircraft took off. Before the 1992 flying ban on Libya, Qadhdhafi reportedly took four planes when traveling abroad: one for himself, aides, and family; one for bodyguards; one for the families of those who might try to take power in his absence; and one with a large portion of the national treasury.

Rulers fret about covert messages being sent through the media and spies sent from abroad. Here is a first-hand account from Sadat's Egypt: "The reports of each [intelligence] service go to the President. If two report a rumor, while the third does not, it is at once suspected that there is a conspiracy in the third to suppress it. That's Egypt, a land where the leadership does not trust the people."[59] Similarly, Abdel Nasser is said to have trusted no more than one out of five reports his aides brought him, while Saddam Husayn publicly declared that "Out of every three rumors I take only one seriously," suggesting a similar set of assumptions at work in Iraq.[60] Also in Iraq, security personnel must sign a pledge disassociating themselves with conspiracies: "none of my relatives has any relation with the traitors and conspirators [involved] in the last conspiracy [or with] the sectarian events, enemy parties, [or is of] Iranian origin."[61] Supreme autocrats seem to spend many of their waking hours worrying about conspiracies against themselves.

## Paranoia

Leaders talk in a paranoid manner that points to their true belief in conspiracy theories. Mustafa Barzani, the longtime Kurdish leader, on meeting someone new, would ask: "For whom are you spying?" Writing about the

Syrian people, a Damascus newspaper held in 1950 that "we are looked upon as prey by Turkey, Iraq, Transjordan, and even by the Jewish gangsters. All these people are encouraged by the Russians, the British, the Americans and the French."[62] A generation later, Hafiz al-Asad saw his brother Rif'at as the tool of an American, Saudi, and Moroccan plot to stage a coup d'état against himself. A clandestine Palestinian radio station broadcasting out of Damascus declared that "King Husayn is conspiring against Syria, Yasir 'Arafat is conspiring against Syria, Yitzhak Rabin is conspiring against Syria," and the U.S. government stands behind them all.[63]

During his time in power, General Michel 'Awn of Lebanon sounded like a paranoid (admittedly, with some reason): "The whole world is against me. The whole world seeks to foment trouble in Lebanon. . . . Let them dispatch the Sixth Fleet, Syrian tanks, NATO, or the Warsaw Pact to topple me."[64] In the aftermath of the Iraq-Iran war, Taha Yasin Ramadan, Iraq's first deputy prime minister, explained that

> imperialist circles had not bargained on Iraq's success [against Iran]. They did not want the war scenario to turn out the way it did. They had hoped that Iran would end up being in control of Iraqi territory, just as Israel's wars with the Arabs had ended. They would have liked Iran to capture Iraqi territory the way Israel conquered other Arab lands, to humiliate the Arab nation.[65]

Ayatollah Khomeini declared that "The world is against us."[66] A Cairene newspaper holds that "The West is determined to humiliate us; to trample our pride, honor, and dignity; and to destroy our military and economic power, for no other reason except that we are Arabs, Muslims, and orientals."[67] These plaintive fears have ring of sincerity.

When a lone Syrian pilot, Bassam al-'Adl, defected to Israel in October 1989, Minister of Defense Mustafa Tallas characterized his action as the result of a vast conspiracy by the Israelis.

> They worked in the pitch dark, like blind bats, to find an agent and traitor willing to sell his conscience at the cheapest of prices. They found their lost soul in the traitor Bassam al-'Adl. . . . Their aim is, of course, to influence and affect our people and armed forces psychologically and morally.[68]

The effect of such suspicion is to spawn an atmosphere of the deepest mistrust in one's own ranks: if the enemy is everywhere, how can he be resisted? Defeatism and despair are the natural responses, as is anger against the regime for so poorly protecting the country's interests. Tallas's statement would seem to come from heartfelt fear, not calculation. Leaders who confess to seeing conspiracies all around them approach the clinical definition of paranoia ("pervasive and unwarranted suspiciousness and mistrust"), a condition that bears the hallmarks of sincerity. Indeed, "Conspiracy thinking is in fact isomorphic with paranoia."[69]

## ASSESSMENT

"It is especially difficult to know how much of their own mumbo jumbo charlatans believe."[70] Indeed, rulers act with inconsistency, sometimes suggesting that they use conspiracy theories for ulterior purposes, at other times appearing sincere. What explains this contradictory behavior? Personal character, personal confusion, and personal interests.

### Fanatics, Cynics, and Enigmatics

A politician's personal character can answer the question of manipulation or sincerity. Norman Cohn records noteworthy cases of three European anti-Semites who knew *The Protocols of the Elders of Zion* to be bogus. The man who actually compiled *The Protocols*, Sergey Nilus, acknowledged its spurious nature; but he so totally believed that Jews planned to take over the globe that he considered his own creation as good as true. Count Ernst zu Reventlow, a leading propagandist of Jewish conspiracy theories in interwar Germany, privately admitted not believing in the *Protocols*-inspired literature he so avidly forwarded. (He called it a "clumsy hoax.") Publicly, however, he called it genuine, "because this seemed to me to answer the purpose best at that time. . . . Heil Hitler!"[71] As for Hitler himself, the ex-Nazi Hermann Rauschning quotes him as indifferent to the issue of whether *The Protocols* was historically true; if it was not, he said, "its intrinsic truth was all the more convincing."[72] Cohn writes of Hitler:

> It has sometimes been argued that Hitler was simply a super-Machiavellian, a man without convictions or loyalties, an utter cynic for whom the whole aim and value of life consisted in power and more power. There certainly was such a Hitler—but the other Hitler, the haunted man obsessed by fantasies about the Jewish world-conspiracy, was just as real. What one would like to know is just how far the near-lunatic was active even in the calculating opportunist.[73]

Nilus is the fanatic whose absolute conviction renders facts irrelevant. Reventlow personifies the cynic who knows full well the falseness of his claims but makes them anyway because he in some fashion gains from them. Among Nazi leaders, Josef Goebbels and Alfred Rosenberg represent these two types. While manipulation and credulity do exist in their pure forms, politicians more often exhibit a complex compound of these two elements. Hitler—part fanatic, part cynic—stands somewhere between these two and presents an enigmatic mix.

The third category, enigmatics, presents the most problems for an analyst, for these politicians appear capable of sincerity and manipulation at the same time. Friedrich Nietzsche's observation that "In all great deceivers, a remarkable process is at work" helps understand them: the act of deception becomes "overcome by their belief in themselves," rendering the deception at least partially genuine. Ron Rosenbaum comments that this mental process

> begins with what seems like a cynical calculation that what is important is not to believe but *to be seen to believe*—that the counterfeiting of belief counts for more than the sincerity of belief. But if there is calculation initially, what follows is the "remarkable process" whereby the actor-deceiver becomes carried away, becomes a believer in his own deception—possessed by himself.[74]

In principle, the enigmatic believes in international plots against his rule; but he then decides each case on its merits. He neither has thought through his own convictions nor clearly distinguishes his own views from those of his constituency. He accepts some elements of a plot even as he rejects others. He retains complete freedom to pick and choose.

Arab and Iranian leaders also divide into these three archetypes. Khomeini falls into the fanatic category, Saddam Husayn into the cynical one, and Yasir 'Arafat into the enigmatic. The last, because of its complex nature, requires more analysis.

## Confusion and Contradiction

Enigmatics wear their confusion on their sleeves. On some occasions, they proclaim dire conspiracies against themselves; on others, they denounce the conspiracy mentality. Examples are easy to find; here are Palestinian, Syrian, Pakistani, and Iranian (both monarchical and revolutionary) leaders.

Salah Khalaf of the PLO revealed his susceptibility to conspiracism when he said this about Abu Nidal: "He had an inclination to dismiss most of humanity as spies and traitors. I rather liked that."[75] But Khalaf also decried the fact that "whenever some marginal conflict distracts us from our principal objective—Zionism or, more generally colonialism—we Arabs are quick to cry out about an imperialist plot."[76]

Hafiz al-Asad often laced his statements with conspiracy theories, but cut these out in 1990 as Iraqi aggressiveness became increasingly evident. In May of that year, he observed that "sometimes we Arabs exceed our bounds or our rights by blaming others or having them shoulder more than they should."[77] Following the Iraqi invasion of Kuwait, he explicitly denied the existence of a conspiracy against Iraq.

Zulfikar Ali Bhutto, the leader of Pakistan from December 1971 to July 1977, both suspected those in his entourage of plots against himself and promoted an archconspiracist vision of world politics. On one occasion in April 1977, for example, he blamed his troubles on both American efforts to weaken Pakistan and Soviet ones to dismember it, and accused the Indians of aiding their efforts. At the same time, Bhutto understood the bankruptcy of conspiracy theories: "we in the Third World should not be swayed by conspiratorial theories and forget the fact that the fault lies on the ground and within ourselves. To quote [George] Meredith, we are betrayed by what is false within."[78]

'Abdolkarim Musavi-Ardebili, one of revolutionary Iran's leading firebrands and an archconspiracist (he explained the Kuwait crisis as Washington's way of solving "the problem of a united Europe"), also remarked that his country was "still at a stage that we are trying to blame others for our sins. We have to go through this stage and if we don't, it will bring catastrophe."[79]

But Shah Mohammad Reza Pahlavi offers the most startling contrast. He saw conspiracies everywhere; chapter 4 details how, as he fell from power, he blamed his problems on anyone but the Iranians and himself. He pointed a finger at the Western media and oil companies, plus a host of foreign governments—the Iraqi, Soviet, British, and Israeli. Most of all, however, he blamed Washington. After losing power, Pahlavi wrote in his memoirs, "the Americans wanted me out."[80] Elsewhere in the very same book, however, he showed second thoughts:

> I find it hard to believe that the Iranian disaster [i.e., his own overthrow] was simply the result of short-sighted or non-existent policy and unresolved conflicts within the American government. Yet

analysis of both the past and of events since the seizure of the hostages does not allow any other conclusion.[81]

Even more remarkably, the shah rejected highly specific warnings about American plots against him from Alexandre de Marenches, the head of French intelligence. Marenches recounts telling the shah "Beware of the Carter administration" and going on to explain that President Carter had decided to replace him:

> The shah did not want to believe me. "I believe in everything you tell me, except this point."
>
> "But Your Majesty, why don't you believe me here too?"
>
> "Because it would be stupid to replace me. I am the best protector of the West in this part of the world. I have the best army. I have the greatest power." He added: "This is so absurd that I cannot believe it."
>
> And, after a silence, during which I thought about what I would say, I said to him, "And what if the Americans make a mistake?"[82]

These examples of startling contradiction suggest that most conspiracy-oriented politicians are neither fanatics nor skeptics. Rather, they respond intuitively to immediate circumstances. At times, these raise the specter of conspiracies, at times not.

## Beliefs Follow Interests

The argument for manipulation rests in large part on the advantages that conspiracy theories bring. They help rulers rewrite history, they justify any policy, salvage reputations, shore up a weak government, build cohesion, and justify aggression. They hobble the enemy by delegitimating him and invalidating his arguments. In addition, finding themselves beholden to conspiracy-minded governments, many Middle Easterners find they must toe the party line, and that means purveying conspiracy theories. Michael Field comments, with good sense, after hearing an Iraqi ambassador hold forth about alleged British aims to take control of Iraq: "Most likely the ambassador would have acknowledged to himself that half of what he was saying was just the Baghdad party line, but the other half he probably believed. And he must have thought his ideas were at least intelligent enough to be worth telling to a Western journalist."[83]

These benefits do exist; at the same time, beliefs follow interests. The record shows that the utility of conspiracy theories makes them that much more credible. Self-interest and circumstance sometimes propel the sober politician toward conspiracy theories. To cite an American example, "Gentile businessmen in Utah merged anti-Mormonism with plans for exploiting mines and lands."[84] Pondering King Faysal's thesis about a joint Zionist-Communist conspiracy, Henry Kissinger observed how the opportunist and the fanatic can coexist comfortably. However bizarre the king's vision, it "was clearly deeply felt. At the same time," Kissinger correctly noted,

> it reflected precisely the tactical necessities of the Kingdom. The strident anti-Communism helped reassure America and established a claim on protection from outside threats (which were all, in fact, armed by the Soviet Union). The virulent opposition to Zionism reassured radicals and the PLO and thus reduced their incentive to follow any temptation to undermine the monarchy domestically.[85]

Because interests tend to make themselves felt over time, politicians tend to succumb slowly to the conspiratorial approach. Gamal Abdel Nasser's ruse about American and British attacks on Israel during the Six-Day War (detailed in chapter 2) happens to be well documented and neatly illustrates this point. Although Abdel Nasser began by rejecting accusations against the Western powers in a "firm and unyielding," way,[86] he soon changed his tune, and not very convincingly. His first accusations about the Americans and British taking out his air force were clearly fabricated; the telephone conversation with Husayn bears all the hallmarks of an overt lie. But then — and this is the subtle part — the lie seems to have turned into earnest belief. In their moment of supreme defeat, Abdel Nasser, 'Amr, and King Husayn cooked up a conspiracy theory to shuck responsibility for the disaster they had caused. Just four days later, when Abdel Nasser offered his resignation on 9 June, his confidant Mohamed Heikal deemed this "not propaganda but what he genuinely believed."[87] Heikal later explained one reason why: just as Israel had been joined by two Western powers (Great Britain and France) in the 1956 conflict, so Nasser believed it was joined by two of them (Great Britain, the United States) in the 1967 one, too.[88] Presumably, Abdel Nasser's admission in March 1968 that he had been mistaken was also sincere.

This behavior points to several stages in the evolution of a conspiracy theory: initial skepticism, the adoption of a conspiracy accusation because of its utility in a moment of need, eventual conviction, and slow retreat. Judging from information about other leaders (again, Goebbels comes to mind), this inconsistent pattern seems more typical than surprising.

This discussion points to three rules of thumb. First, leaders should be viewed as sincere when they postulate conspiracy theories unless specific reasons exist to think otherwise. Despite the many factors pointing to manipulation, real fears seem more prevalent. Second, the larger and more pervasive an alleged conspiracy, the more likely it is put forward sincerely. In part, this has to do with the big lie being more compelling than the little one; in part, a lack of specificity calls on emotions but is more difficult to contradict. Third, politicians increasingly believe their own games over time. Duplicity eventually turns into conviction.

In conclusion, politicians generally believe what they say; and if not every word, then the basic thrust.

## NOTES TO CHAPTER 11

1. Letter to Peter Carr, 19 August 1785. Text in Adrienne Koch and William Peden, ed., *The Life and Selected Writings of Thomas Jefferson* (New York: Modern Library, 1944), p. 374.
2. Umberto Eco, *Foucault's Pendulum* (London: Picador, 1990), p. 467.
3. William R. Brown, *The Last Crusade: A Negotiator's Middle East Handbook* (Chicago: Nelson-Hall, 1980), p. 67.
4. Emma Duncan, *Breaking the Curfew* (London: Michael Joseph, 1989), p. 33.
5. Hisham Sharabi, *Nationalism and Revolution in the Arab World* (Princeton, N.J.: Van Nostrand, 1966), p. 101.
6. Marvin Zonis, *Majestic Failure: The Fall of the Shah* (Chicago: University of Chicago Press, 1991), p. 260.
7. "*Statement* made by President Saddam Hussein," Baghdad, 2 April 1990.
8. *Kayhan International,* 14 April 1990.
9. Radio Tehran International (Arabic service), 7 August 1990; Radio Tehran, March 1, 1989.
10. *Jomhuri-ye Islami,* 20 July 1991.
11. *Al-Jamahiriya,* 19 July 1991.
12. *Folha de São Paulo* (São Paulo), 18 February 1991.
13. *Al-Khalij* (U.A.E.), 29 January 1983.
14. *Kayhan* (London), 7 October 1993.
15. Ann Mosely Lesch, "Contrasting Reactions to the Persian Gulf Crisis: Egypt, Syria, Jordan, and the Palestinians," *The Middle East Journal,* 45 (1991): 34.

16. When pressed to the wall by Iranian forces in the mid-1980s, Saddam Husayn suppressed his usual conspiracism, only to revive it after the end of the war with Iran. In this case, crisis seems to have brought out the pragmatist in him and confidence made him more self-indulgent.

17. Agence France Presse, 17 September 1992.

18. Ehud Ya'ari, "Pederasty in Paradise, Despair on Earth," *The Jerusalem Report*, 30 July 1992.

19. *The New York Times*, 16 September 1990.

20. Graham E. Fuller, *The "Center of the Universe": The Geopolitics of Iran* (Boulder, Col.: Westview, 1991), p. 22.

21. Thomas L. Friedman, *From Beirut to Jerusalem* (New York: Farrar Straus Giroux, 1989), p. 36.

22. Libyan Television, 15 January 1992.

23. Jean Said Makdisi, *Beirut Fragments: A War Memoir* (New York: Persea Books, 1990), p. 61.

24. Fuller, *"Center of the Universe,"* pp. 22, 8-9.

25. Alan Hart, *Arafat: A Political Biography* (Bloomington: Indiana University Press, 1989), p. 284.

26. Quoted in Robert Fisk, *Pity the Nation: Lebanon at War* (London: Oxford University Press, 1991), p. 470.

27. B. J. Odeh, *Lebanon: Dynamics of Conflict* (London: Zed, 1985), p. 197.

28. *Al-Jumhuriya* (Cairo), 20 April 1990.

29. Nadia Ramsis Farah, *Religious Strife in Egypt: Crisis and Ideological Conflict in the Seventies* (New York: Gordon and Breach, 1986), chap. 1.

30. Middle East News Agency, 14 July 1992.

31. *As-Safir*, 25 May 1993; *Al-Ahali*, 2 June 1993.

32. Telegram 7973, 25 May 1967 from Cairo to Department of State, describing Richard Parker's account of a conversation with an Egyptian official (whose name was deleted for declassification). Text in Robert Hopkins Miller, *Inside an Embassy: The Political Role of Diplomats Abroad* (Washington, D.C.: Congressional Quarterly, 1992), p. 122.

33. *Al-Afkar*, 3 June 1991.

34. *Al-'Iraq*, 9 September 1991.

35. Republic of Iraq Radio, 18 June 1992.

36. Radio Baghdad, 26 February 1991.

37. Algérie Presse Service, 29 January 1991; Sawt Filastin (Algiers), 17 February 1991.

38. Richard W. Cottam, *Iran and the United States: A Cold War Case Study* (Pittsburgh: University of Pittsburgh Press, 1988), pp. 41-42, 59.

39. P. J. Vatikiotis, *Nasser and His Generation* (New York: St. Martin's Press, 1978), p. 322.

40. Robert Jervis, *Perception and Misperception in International Politics* (Princeton, N.J.: Princeton University Press, 1976), pp. 327, 324.

41. Ibid., p. 321.

42. *Yedi'ot Ahronot,* 15 January 1995. This passage is back-translated from Hebrew.

43. *Az-Zahf al-Akhdar,* 25 February 1993.

44. Michael Field, *Inside the Arab World* (Cambridge, Mass.: Harvard University Press, 1994), p. 165.

45. *Newsweek,* 8 October 1990.

46. Samir al-Khalil [pseud. of Kanan Makiya], *The Monument: Art, Vulgarity, and Responsibility in Iraq* (Berkeley: University of California Press, 1991), p. 17.

47. Richard Nixon, *Memoirs* (New York: Grosset & Dunlap, 1978), p. 1013.

48. Khalil, *The Monument,* pp. 17-18.

49. Fadlallah Abu Mansur, *A'asir Dimashq* (Beirut: n.p., 1959). Quoted in Elie Kedourie, *Arabic Political Memoirs and Other Studies* (London: Frank Cass, 1974), p. 183.

50. Quoted in Abdel Magid Farid, *Nasser: The Final Years* (Reading, Eng.: Ithaca Press, 1994), p. 137.

51. Text in Raphael Israeli, ed., *PLO in Lebanon: Selected Documents* (New York: St. Martin's Press, 1983), pp. 39, 49. Archival evidence points to an equally fervid Soviet belief in conspiracy theories, especially those of a Zionist nature. "Many KGB officers believed that the US 'military-industrial complex,' which they saw as the Soviet bloc's most dangerous opponent, was manipulated by the 'Jewish lobby.'" See Christopher Andrew and Oleg Gordievsky, eds., *More "Instructions from the Centre": Top Secret Files on KGB Global Operations, 1975-1985* (London: Frank Cass, 1992), pp. 90f.

52. William H. Sullivan, *Mission to Iran* (New York: W. W. Norton, 1981), p. 47; Anthony Parsons, *The Pride and the Fall: Iran 1974-1979* (London: Jonathan Cape, 1984), p. x.

53. Radio Tehran, 6 April 1990.

54. *The New York Times,* 16 October 1990.

55. Mohammad Reza Pahlavi, *Answer to History* (New York: Stein and Day, 1980). In contrast, his twin sister Ashraf Pahlavi censored virtually all hers in *Faces in a Mirror: Memoirs from Exile* (Englewood Cliffs, N.J.: Prentice-Hall, 1980).

56. Benazir Bhutto, *Daughter of Destiny: An Autobiography* (New York: Simon and Schuster, 1989), p. 94.

57. Anwar el-Sadat, *In Search of Identity: An Autobiography* (New York: Harper & Row, 1977), pp. 78-79. See also pp. 90-91, 123, 183, 196, 209.

58. Farid, *Nasser,* p. 133.

59. Saad El-Shazly, *The Crossing of the Suez* (San Francisco: American Mideast Research, 1980), p. 121.

60. Republic of Iraq Radio, 25 September 1991.

61. Isam Khafaji, "State Terror and the Degradation of Politics," in Fran Hazelton, ed., *Iraq Since the Gulf War: Prospects for Democracy* (London: Zed, 1994), p. 23.

62. *Al-Fayha,* 1 May 1950. Quoted in Patrick Seale, *The Struggle for Syria: A Study of Post-War Arab Politics, 1945-1958* (London: Oxford University Press, 1965), p. 95.

63. Al-Quds Radio (Damascus), 31 August 1995.

64. *Al-Qabas ad-Duwali,* 15 May 1990.

65. *Al-Ahali* [Cairo], 16 May 1990.

66. *Kayhan-e Hava'i*, 5 September 1984. Quoted in Ervand Abrahamian, *Khomeinism: Essays on the Islamic Republic* (Berkeley: University of California Press, 1993), p.122.

67. *Al-Wafd*, 7 February 1991.

68. Damascus Television, 16 October 1989.

69. Marvin Zonis and Craig M. Joseph, "Conspiracy Thinking in the Middle East" (unpublished paper, 1991), pp. 5-6.

70. Ibn Warraq [pseud.], *Why I Am Not a Muslim* (Amherst, N.Y.: Prometheus, 1995), p. 22.

71. Norman Cohn, *Warrant for Genocide: The Myth of the Jewish World Conspiracy and the Protocols of the Elders of Zion* (New York: Harper & Row, 1969), pp. 93, 140.

72. Hermann Rauschning, *Gespräche mit Hitler* (New York: Europa, 1940), pp. 224-25.

73. Cohn, *Warrant for Genocide*, p. 192.

74. Ron Rosenbaum, "Explaining Hitler," *The New Yorker*, 1 May 1995, p. 67.

75. Quoted in Patrick Seale, *Abu Nidal: A Gun for Hire* (New York: Random House, 1992), p. 69.

76. Abou Iyad, *Palestinien sans Patrie* (Paris: Fayolle, 1978), p. 334.

77. Radio Damascus, 7 May 1990.

78. Address to the United Nations General Assembly, 20 September 1973. Quoted in Stanley Wolpert, *Zulfi Bhutto of Pakistan: His Life and Times* (New York: Oxford University Press, 1993), p. 222.

79. Radio Tehran, 17 August 1990; Islamic Republican News Agency, 8 February 1989.

80. Pahlavi, *Answer to History*, p. 165.

81. Ibid., 24.

82. Christine Ockrent and Comte de Marenches, *Dans le secret des Princes* (Paris: Stock, 1986), pp. 248-49.

83. Field, *Inside the Arab World*, p.166.

84. David Brion Davis, "Some Themes of Counter-Subversion: An Analysis of Anti-Masonic, Anti-Catholic, and Anti-Mormon Literature," *Mississippi Valley Historical Review* 47 (1960): 224. "Gentile" here means non-Mormon.

85. Henry Kissinger, *Years of Upheaval* (Boston: Little, Brown, 1982), p. 662.

86. Sadat, *In Search of Identity*, p. 175.

87. Mohamed Heikal, *The Sphinx and the Commissar: The Rise and Fall of Soviet Influence in the Middle East* (New York: Harper & Row, 1978), p. 181.

88. Muhammad Hasanayn Haykal, *1967, Al-Infijar: Harb ath-Thalathin Sana* (Cairo: Markaz al-Ahram, 1411/1990), p. 715.

# 12.

# The Conspiracy Theory

> What distinguishes the paranoid style is not, then, the
> absence of verifiable facts . . . but rather the curious
> leap in imagination that is always made at some
> critical point in the recital of events.
> —*Richard Hofstadter*[1]

The "curious leap" identified by Richard Hofstadter in the epigraph above has two main qualities: deductive reasoning unconstrained by facts and unconventional notions about causation. Each plays a key role in building an alternative reality.

## THE PERILS OF DEDUCTION

Conventional thinking starts with data and then builds theories (a process known as induction). Conspiracy theorists reverse the order, starting instead with a paradigm and arranging the information to prove it (the process of deduction). Seeking knowledge in this peculiar manner has a great number of implications. What elsewhere would indicate weakness — obscure evidence, farfetched schemas, and imprecise language — seem not to harm a conspiracy theory.

*Unbound by mere facts.*    In inductive reasoning, facts determine views; a change in facts leads to a change in views. Not so with deduction, where convictions precede and override facts. Elevating beliefs into a faith implies a closed-mindedness that broaches no contradiction. Focusing on what fits his thesis, the conspiracy theorist ignores everything else. A ferocious war took place in Afghanistan that lasted a decade and pitted the U.S.-backed *mujahidin* forces against the Soviets and their allies. The Khomeini regime somehow disregarded this major conflict on its border and insisted on U.S.-Soviet collusion in Afghanistan. In its fantastical interpretation, the great powers had joined together in a plot "to sow discord among the *mujahidin*," with the ultimate aim of breaking Muslim solidarity.[2]

In a similar spirit, the conspiracy theorist shows great talent at finding ways to get around new evidence that shows him to be wrong; rather than reconsider, he redoubles his allegations of conspiracy. Iranian leaders proclaimed Saddam Husayn a stooge of the United States through the 1980s and made this claim a centerpiece of their foreign policy. When the United States went to war against Iraq in 1991, the Iranians stuck resolutely to this thesis.

*Implausible.*     The conspiracy theorist pays no heed to the restrictions of probability: implausibility is not a word in his lexicon. His predisposition to believe renders such considerations unimportant. In the words of a novelist: "Quite absurd! Which suggests that there had to be a plan. A sublime plan."[3]

Internal consistency alone matters, causing the distinction between credible and farfetched to disappear. Eye-popping evidence, elaborate ruses, and bizarre implications follow. The conspiracy theorist makes a speciality of listing a sequence of events unfavorable to his side—illness, deaths, award prizes, even earthquakes—then points to the freakishly small chance of these events occurring on their own. His conclusion: a hidden hand must be at work, any chain of events must be deliberately planned. Iranians summarily rejected the notion that the U.S. government miscalculated in letting the shah fall in 1978-79; Washington just does not make such mistakes. They dismissed as untruthful or naïve anyone who held differently. Why then did Carter not save the shah? Why did he oust a reliable ally of 38 years' standing? Inexplicable motives imply deviousness of purpose. Conventional accountings of U.S. interests cannot answer this question, so (rather than reconsider his premise), the conspiracy theorist turns to the unconventional and the subterranean.

License to explore outlandish hypotheses means that conjectures no longer need be sensible. The shah and his supporters concluded that the U.S. and Soviet governments had carved up the globe (including Iran) and sought a weak Iranian leadership; or, contrarily, that Americans saw

Khomeini as a stronger bulwark against Communism; or that they envied Iranian progress under the shah's leadership.

To justify their explanation of events, conspiracy theorists often key in on some minor matter and make it central. Never mind the millions of Jews who died at Nazi hands; they instead focus on the benefits accrued by Zionism from the Holocaust. Minor areas of agreement between Syria and Israel loom larger than the Asad government's massive military buildup directed at Israel. Layers of sophisticated gloss render straightforward events counterintuitive and tangled.

*Vague enemies.*      Conspiracy theorists seem content not to know much about their enemies. They resort to imprecise language, attributing acts to unknown individuals, using imprecise words, or resorting to the mysterious "they." "Informed sources" provide cover for making any outlandish piece of speculation sound authoritative. When Iran's radio network wanted to blame the World Trade Center bombing on Israel, it ignored the conviction of a Muslim gang for this atrocity and reported that "Informed sources say that Mossad and Israeli fingerprints can clearly be seen in the New York bomb explosion."[4] When a Cairo newspaper wanted to blame Israel for making 'Umar 'Abd ar-Rahman a media star, it reported that "Some believe the Zionists played an influential role in exaggerating the importance of the man."[5] The audience never learns who these "sources" or those "some" are. "There is evidence to suggest that" and "apparently" similarly permit the writer unbridled license.

As for the mysterious "they," Saïd K. Aburish concludes from a series of conversations on the West Bank that

> outside forces are always "they" and "them." When talking about such forces, the average West Banker is loath to identify them by name even when that is simpler, because the constant use of personal pronouns adds to the sinister nature of the supposedly evil powers in question. . . . Occasionally I had difficulty determining who "they" were, only to discover that this is a deliberate vagueness by people who are happy to use this very inclusive term to describe all those whom they accuse of being responsible for their problems.
>
> It took me a while to discover the extent to which the use of "they" represented an abdication from responsibility for Palestinian and Arab failure: a clear statement that the speaker, and people like him or her, are totally blameless.

Aburish draws a harsh but accurate conclusion:

> The "they" my interviewees talked about are people who in one way or another contribute towards Arab weakness, which harms the attainment of the rights of the Palestinian people, and they themselves are guilty of this crime. The use of "they" . . . is a symptom of a culture unable to cope with its own problems because the most basic requirement, the will of the people to change their condition, is absent. There is no "they": the critic and the person criticized are one and the same.[6]

"In the absence of any supporting evidence," Kanan Makiya concludes, vague words "evoke the smell of great conspiracies while making a disingenuous claim to innocence. . . . the caveats and the qualifiers . . . are sometimes all that it takes to be irresponsible."[7]

*No real research.*    Because the conclusion is known ahead of time, conspiracy theorists engage in research only as a way to convince others. Faith not needing verification, the dispassionate evaluation of evidence does not take place. Documentation serves not to discover truth but to build a case. They follow a highly subjective approach to evidence, achieving "consistency through omission and embellishment."[8] Typically, this means permissive standards for materials supporting their case and restrictive standards for rebutting it.

*Esoteric information.*    The conspiracy theorist assumes that the less well known a piece of information, the greater its validity. Any information explicit and visible must be a cunning deceit to fool the gullible; real knowledge is hidden. Truth does not parade itself but hides below layer after layer of subterfuge. Concealed information usually falls into one of three categories: an esoteric reading of public sources, such as interpreting the real intent behind George Bush's "new world order"; clandestine information, ideally a memo from the heart of an intelligence service; or exotic knowledge, such as translations from the language of a remote land.

*Any evidence acceptable.*    When conjecture does the work of proof, evidence can take any form. Coincidence or outlandish fact will do; should even this be missing, the merest hint or allusion serves as evidence. When it's convenient, the conspiracy theorist applies a most undemanding standard of proof. Any piece of confirming information serves as evidence. What supports his paradigm readily becomes established fact. The conspiracy theorist bends the rules of evidence and logic to prove his point to others, liberating him from all constraints. Fantastical minutiae and specious documents take on a life of their own. A few facts and hunches spin a full and detailed fabric. Things that never happened are as important as those that did. The conspiracy theorist adapts to reality to inventing new twists and turns in his theories. Low probabilities pose no problem. Relying on "blind, obsessive ingenuity," he weaves "jumbles of the most diverse scraps of information, libels, and half-baked inferences" into "satisfying and insane patterns."[9]

Khomeinists often make arguments without proof. They suspect any Iranian who holds an American Express card of working for the CIA. When Austrian security forces surrounded Iran's embassy in Vienna in 1989, Tehran blamed Washington: "the evidence offered by the Austrian Justice Ministry," wrote the Iranian news agency, is "so baseless that it leaves no doubt the U.S. is involved in the new plot."[10] Fittingly perhaps, Iranians find the identical methods used against them. Thus, an Egyptian opponent of the Islamic Republic draws an alarming, and completely unwarranted, conclusion from the fact that 'Ali Hoseyni Khamene'i issued a *fatwa* banning neckties:

> I have noticed that Israelis, both citizens and leaders, do not wear ties except on very rare occasions. . . . If we realize that relations between Iran and Israel were, and still are, strong, why should we rule out that President [*sic*] Khamene'i is, with this decision, trying to imitate the Israelis in their dress, just as he imitates their goals and expansion at the expense of Arab land?[11]

Yasir 'Arafat held that the Western powers were less interested in defending Kuwait in 1991 than in profiting from the country's reconstruction. To illustrate this point, he told an anecdote about the wartime visit of Britain's Prime Minister John Major to Saudi Arabia, where he conferred with the exiled emir of Kuwait. According to 'Arafat, business executives accompanied Major in the hopes of winning major contracts from the Kuwaiti authorities, including representatives of a firm that specializes in building power stations. When Major inquired about an agreement to rebuild Kuwait's power station, the emir replied, "The Kuwaiti power station is intact." To this, Major replied, "No, we will hit it." On 24 February 1991, 'Arafat claimed, the British forces did just that, destroying the station in an intent to lift "the last petro-dollar from these Arab pockets."[12]

***Proof from silence.***    In an extreme example of this tendency to accept any evidence, conspiracy theorists often interpret silence or lack of activity as proof positive of guilt. In the mirrored world of conspiracism, the absence of proof is a proof in itself, for it confirms the conspirator's success at hiding his tracks. That very few investors had put money in his country prompted the Lebanese information minister "truly" to conclude in 1992 that a conspiracy was under way to harm Lebanon economically.[13] Lebanon's having gone through 15 of war and being virtually annexed by Syria seemed not to matter; the minister read malign intent into a simple lack of confidence. Innocence is a clever ruse—the most subtle cover for scheming.

For the most fervid conspiracy theorists, the very appearance of normality signals danger; quiet serves as a mask to lull the unsuspecting prey. A radical Iranian newspaper noted in 1992 that older Iranians see the Islamic Revolution as a British plot; when asked for proof, they reply, "the proof is, there's no trace" of the British hand.[14] The same goes for the United States: Richard Cottam points out that the Iranian leadership in 1980 unanimously agreed that Washington stood behind the Iraqi attack on Iran. "The fact (and it is a fact) that there is no overtly available evidence confirming this inference is of no interest to those who accept the conclusion";[15] they interpret this to mean that the Americans expertly covered their tracks. Everything-as-usual carries sinister implications. Graham Fuller observes that "the CIA's apparent failure to observe the deterioration of Iran and to "save the shah" in the end can only be evidence, therefore, of a deeper unspoken U.S. political agenda—all the more worrying because the immediate goals of that agenda are not fully evident." "The less clear the foreign hand," he concludes, "the more convincing the case for its existence and ability to work in unseen ways."[16]

If an enemy's goals are not apparent, they must be concealed. If not logical within the conspiracy theorist's terms (philanthropy, for example, is mystifying), they must be malign. "Otherwise inexplicable behavior is seen as part of a devious plan, usually a hostile one."[17] Indeed, the more benign an activity appears, the more suspect it becomes.

***Denying reality.***    Evidence that does not fit a preconceived thesis gets a very different treatment. At minimum, it gets ignored, for mere facts cannot be allowed to get in the way. In one stunning example, in February 1954, the residents of Damascus initially dismissed the declaration by the military leaders of a coup d'état when they announced over the radio that they had taken power. They did so in the belief that the declaration was an Israeli effort to provoke troubles in Syria.

When confronted with news of the Iraqi loss in Kuwait, Saddam's partisans found reasons, ever more spurious, to maintain their fantasy of an Iraqi victory. Some claimed that the ground war never took place and that Iraqi troops withdrew from Kuwait of their own accord. Others found even more slender threads on which to hang their hopes. Sami Jundi, a taxi driver, ignored Radio Baghdad's own report of an Iraqi retreat: "The announcement just said 'This is Radio Baghdad,'" he noted, "while all previous official announcements were always made in the name of the Revolutionary Command Council, so this is an allied trick."[18] Saddam Husayn did not hide the fact that his forces mined the Kuwaiti oil fields and blew them up just before leaving the country in February 1991. But Mu'ammar al-Qadhdhafi could not accept this reality. Asking "Who set fire to one hundred oil wells?" he replied, "It was not Iraq. It was the West and America, which [did so] for imperialist reasons."[19] Thus do conspiracy theorists rely on an indiscriminate mix of strong and weak data. Thus do they dispute established truths and proffer preposterous ones in their stead.

## BASIC ASSUMPTIONS

Conspiracism creates a world complete in itself, a shadow reality that parallels normal existence, displaying its own rules of logic, imaginative flourishes, and psychological vulnerabilities. Five broad assumptions stand behind conspiracist patterns of logic in the Middle East conspiracism. In combination, these define the conspiratorial outlook.

### Conspiracies Drive History

Mainstream historians portray conspiracies as a minor force, but conspiracy theorists portray them as the driving force of history. An Iranian newspaper noted that historians tend to belong to the great-man or the common-man school of history, but that in reality conspirators have been the true force behind events, and especially Freemasons, Jews, or the two combined.[20] Politics consists not of open processes but of surreptitious machinations. Clandestine cliques cause change to occur. Hidden forces undermined the Arab nation, overthrew the king, bankrupted the cotton industry, and are even now plotting terrible deeds. On a personal level, "they" caused my business to fail or insects to eat my harvest.

The conspiracy theorist ignores historical context. He has no use for comparative analysis or the larger picture. He ignores other motor forces of history, including supernatural agents (God, the Devil, fate, or the occult), natural agents (human nature, heredity, the environment, culture, probability), and the self.[21] The complexities of historical causation disappear; a single factor accounts for an infinity of events. What others see as an episode or an aspect, the conspiracy theorist turns into an all-embracing explanation. Reductionism goes no further.

In what may be the ultimate conspiracy theory, some see a conspiracy in the very proliferation of conspiracy theories. Lebanese playwright Ziyad Rahbani included a character in his play *Long American Film* who reduced every explanation to the "Zionist-imperialist conspiracy." Finally, another character stands up, index finger pointing in the air, and announces: "The conspiracy itself is a conspiracy!"[22] As ever, life imitates art. "The real conspiracy lies in the fabrication of the plot theory," wrote Fouad Ayoub, press secretary to King Husayn of Jordan.[23] A Turkish daily agrees: "to create confusion, theories are drawn up about plots and conspiracies in suspicious and dark rooms."[24]

## Power Is the Goal

What does the conspirator want? Many things, but in the end it boils down to power. In the conspiracy theorist's schema, power is an end in itself and it leads to the other good things in life: material well-being, high status, and sexual satisfaction. Each person ceaselessly seeks to promote his own interests at the expense of others.

If power is the only goal, then altruism, goodwill, and philanthropy are illusory. Indeed, they are deceits. Middle Eastern conspiracy theorists find the professed concern for human rights a particularly transparent mechanism to justify Western mischief. Projecting their own lack of concern about distant people's welfare, they find it unbelievable that Westerners could really care, much less make sacrifices for perfect strangers. A Pakistani editorial captures this suspicion: noting a report that the U.S. government might restrict the import of Pakistani products made by child labor, it replies: "It is clear that the United States has no other goal but to sabotage Pakistan's economy or seriously harm it. . . . It means that the United States has a solid plan to destroy Pakistan." (The editorial then goes on, deliciously, to wish Pakistan were strong enough to retaliate by banning all products from the United States until that country stops "all extra-marital relations.")[25]

Western attempts to build the Middle East's economy, whether through foreign aid or investment, are but a cover for stealing resources. Thus, the Casablanca economic summit of late 1994, ostensibly intended to spur investment and trade in the Middle East, was really a clever effort to seize the Arab's natural resources.

Christian remorse for past transgressions meet with a similarly skeptical response. Sayyid Qutb notes that Christians today "try to deceive us by distorting history and saying that the Crusades were a form of imperialism. The truth of the matter is that the latter-day imperialism is but a mask for the crusading spirit."[26] For conspiracy theorists, the drive for power ultimately explains all, from the distasteful to the seemingly noble.

## Benefit Indicates Control

"If we want to find the criminal," Sheikh Muhammad Fadlallah of Hizbullah says, "we must find who benefits from the issue." In the case of the World Trade Center bombing in February 1993, Israel was the "only party to benefit," leading Fadlallah to conclude that Israelis most likely caused that bombing.[27] *Cui bono* ("who benefits?") is the key question for conspiracy theorists.

Noting that the assassination in Paris of Shahpour Bakhtiar, the shah's last prime minister, spoiled Franco-Iranian relations and thereby served American interests, the Iranian media blamed the killing on U.S. agents. Accused of plotting the February 1993 assassination of Uğur Mumcu, a prominent Turkish journalist, the Iranians retorted by bringing in the U.S. and Israeli governments, using *cui bono* logic: "Who stands to benefit most from this murder?" Washington, of course; from its viewpoint, the murder "kills several birds with one stone."[28] Or maybe Israel killed the journalist to "upset the tranquil and friendly atmosphere between Iran and its neighbors" and to "accuse Iran of terrorist activities."[29] Or maybe both countries did it together and then (according to Islamic Amal's leader in Lebanon, Husayn al-Musawi) "used their influence over the newspapers . . . to blame us for Mumcu's murder" in an effort to weaken Hizbullah.[30]

When Arabs take steps which hurt themselves, you can be sure Jerusalem commissioned the event. According to some Palestinians, the Israel Defense Forces launched the Scuds that fell on Tel Aviv in 1991 to make Saddam Husayn look bad. As for violence in the Occupied Territories, "Israel is facilitating the delivery of various types of weapons, including explosives and bombs, to the Gaza Strip and some areas of the West Bank to ignite the fires of a Palestinian civil war."[31] The Palestine Liberation Front under Abu'l-'Abbas launched a sea-borne operation in May 1990 to massacre swimmers and beachcombers on the Israeli shore, only to be foiled before reaching the intended victims. Not only did the operation fail, but Yasir 'Arafat's unwillingness to denounce the PLF prompted President George Bush to call off the U.S. dialogue with the PLO. In brief, the raid harmed the PLO and helped Israeli interests, so Middle East conspiracy theorists concluded that Israel had to have plotted the raid. But how? According to Ahmad Hamrush, an Egyptian writer, "elements of Mossad sneaked into the decisionmaking body of the PLF." This made the beach operation "an act of the Mossad" that "victimized" those innocent Palestinians who carried it out and lost their lives or ended up in Israeli prison.[32]

The conspiracy theorist has a special weakness for *post hoc ergo propter hoc* (after something, therefore caused by it), an elemental fallacy of historical reasoning. If General Valiullah Qarani received a light sentence of three years' jail for plotting against the Iranian government in 1958, he must have had American connections. On hearing that some 1,500 Muslim pilgrims died in an overcrowded pedestrian tunnel outside Mecca, Iranian leaders discerned "not an accident but a pogrom"[33] by the Saudi authorities. An Iranian newspaper even accused the Saudis of intentionally designing the facilities to trap pilgrims.

### Nothing Is Accidental or Foolish

"Untoward events . . . do not simply happen, nor do events happen in isolation."[34] Conspiracy theorists exclude the possibility of accident or coincidence; instead, "they suspect that well-laid plans give events a coherence they would otherwise lack."[35] The theorist's overly logical mindset compels him to find deeper, more structured explanations behind history.

Coincidence implies a hidden hand. The conjuncture of three events in 1979—the siege of the Great Mosque in Mecca, the seizure of the American embassy in Tehran, and the crash of a plane carrying Pakistani pilgrims—prompted many Pakistanis to surmise a worldwide plot against Islam.

Mistakes don't happen. If it appears that the enemy is ignorant or mistaken, that's proof of a ruse, for "the fervid, conspiracy-mad world of the Middle East . . . gives Washington the conspiratorial benefit of the doubt."[36] Thus, Saddam Husayn's launching of two wars with disastrous consequences for Iraq proved not his stupidity but his agentry for a foreign power. More generally, the prominent Egyptian fundamentalist Muhammad al-Ghazali holds that the British never blunder:

There is not a single Englishman who commits a mistake on purpose, for he does everything on principle . . . making war against you on the principle of nationalism, robbing you on the principle of commerce, enslaving you on the principle of imperialism, threatening you on the principle of pride.[37]

Conspirators sometimes dissemble to hide their omnipotence. The Oslo agreement was negotiated without American participation? Impossible. A Beirut newspaper analyst explained this apparent lapse: "Washington pretended—in front of the other Arab parties and the Russian 'partner'— not to know, to avoid embarrassment to itself and to others."[38] Iranian officials brushed aside the U.S. figures of 300,000 to 400,000 troops in the Persian Gulf region in late December 1990, claiming the accurate figure was 1 million. Graham Fuller generalizes about this phenomenon:

The greater the foreign power, the more incomprehensible and naive it would seem to assume that a particular series of developments might be unrelated. Even when one assures such an Iranian that one is personally aware of the role of, for example, American ignorance, lack of attention, inconsistency, bureaucratic oversight, or lack of interests as key factors lying behind a given series of actions (or inactions) of the U.S. government, an Iranian will assume the speaker is either naive or himself dissembling: It is impossible that the mighty U.S. government would be capable of error, oversight, or uncoordinated action. . . . And the CIA itself is attributed with a ubiquity, omniscience, and omnipotence that is virtually superhuman. . . . Legal, cultural, or operational limits to the CIA's power are not recognized.[39]

Washington claimed that 'Umar 'Abd ar-Rahman slipped through the regulations and got a visa for the United States, but Egyptians did not fall for this ploy. The U.S. government cannot "deceive people into believing" it made a mistake, remarked a Cairene newspaper.[40] Egyptian columnist Ihsan Bakr used similar logic to prove that Palestinians could not have bombed the World Trade Center in February 1993, because they lost the most from this episode. "No Palestinian party . . . would have undertaken such an operation because it would harm all of them." Rather, the Israelis must have done it.[41] Referring to the fact that Muhammad Salama gave the detectives their big break by returning for a $400 rental car deposit, a Lebanese radio commentary took this logic even further: "Is it reasonable for the person who is supposed to be the main clue in the case to return and jeopardize himself . . . simply to get a refund on a small sum of money?"[42] (This logic neglects the key fact that the perpetrators never expected to get caught.)

Traffic accidents — if they involve the mighty — must be planned. On 4 April 1939, King Ghazi of Iraq drove his own car at high speed, smashed into an utility pole, killing both his companions immediately, and himself died about an hour later. Ignoring the king's predilection for alcohol and fast cars, Iraqis tended only to see a politically motivated murder, one that allowed the British to control Iraq more effectively. Rumors along these lines spread rapidly through the whole country and aroused such anger that an Iraqi the next day murdered the British consul in Mosul with a pickax. In the same spirit, Khomeini interpreted his son's 1977 death in a traffic accident near Baghdad as an incident planned by SAVAK, the shah's secret police. Official reports had it that Syrian president Hafiz al-Asad's son Basil died in a Mercedes 600 he was driving at a high speed near the Damascus airport on 21 January 1994. Many doubted this version, instead seeing the 31-year-old as a victim of his or his father's enemies.

Even a mudslide must have human causes. In the winter of 1992, massive rains in Jerusalem caused the wall of an Arab cemetery to collapse onto the roof of an Arab café, killing 23 and injuring 20. Israeli Jews turned out in numbers to pick through the rubble and bring out victims; still, conspiracy theories quickly spread. When an unknown and anonymous Jewish organization calling itself Mehatz Pa'atey Mo'av claimed responsibility for the incident, many Arabs readily accepted its boast.

Freed to overinterpret, the theorist devotes immense effort to fathoming below the surface for the connections behind seemingly unconnected events. Where the ignorant sees fortuity, the cognoscente find patterns of surreptitious association, malice aforethought, and grand ambition. Conspiracy theorists transform accident into plan, coincidence into schema, inadvertency into machination, randomness into sequence, and chaos into plot. They also turn aimlessness into strategy, stupidity into intention, and foolishness into volition.

## Appearances Deceive

This assumption has so many ramifications, its explanation requires a whole chapter.

## NOTES TO CHAPTER 12

1. Richard Hofstadter, "The Paranoid Style in American Politics," in Richard Hofstadter, *The Paranoid Style in American Politics and Other Essays* (New York: Vintage, 1967), p. 37.
2. Islamic Revolution News Agency, 3 May 1990.
3. Umberto Eco, *Foucault's Pendulum* (London: Picador, 1990), p. 121.
4. Voice of the Islamic Republic, 7 March 1993.
5. *Al-Akhbar,* 9 July 1993.
6. Saïd K. Aburish, *Cry Palestine: Inside the West Bank* (Boulder, Col.: Westview, 1993), pp. 151, 164.
7. Kanan Makiya, *Cruelty and Silence: War, Tyranny, Uprising, and the Arab World* (New York: W. W. Norton, 1993), p. 255.
8. Martin Kramer, *Hezbollah's Vision of the West* (Washington, D.C.: Washington Institute for Near East Policy, 1989), p. 7.
9. J. M. Roberts, *The Mythology of the Secret Societies* (New York: Charles Scribner's Sons, 1972), pp. 182, 58, 181.
10. Islamic Revolution News Agency, 3 December 1989.
11. Ibrahim Sa'da, *Akhbar al-Yawm* (Cairo), 9 July 1994.
12. Radio Monte Carlo, 25 February 1991.
13. Radio Lebanon, 8 March 1992.
14. Quoted in Michael Field, *Inside the Arab World* (Cambridge, Mass.: Harvard University Press, 1994), p. 168.
15. Richard W. Cottam, *Iran and the United States: A Cold War Case Study* (Pittsburgh: University of Pittsburgh Press, 1988), p. 224.
16. Graham E. Fuller, *The "Center of the Universe": The Geopolitics of Iran* (Boulder, Col.: Westview, 1991), pp. 22, 20.
17. Robert Jervis, *Perception and Misperception in International Politics* (Princeton, N.J.: Princeton University Press, 1976), p. 323.
18. *Jordan Times,* 27 February 1991.
19. Libyan Television, 16 February 1994. The actual number of oil wells on fire was well over 600.
20. *Kayhan-e Hava'i,* 30 December 1987-16 November 1988 [sic], quoted in Ervand Abrahamian, *Khomeinism: Essays on the Islamic Republic* (Berkeley: University of California Press, 1993), p.125.
21. These categories derive from Charles Y. Glock, "The Way the World Works," *Sociological Analysis* 49 (1988): 93-103.
22. Umberto Eco put it similarly: "There exists a secret society with branches throughout the world, and its plot is to spread the rumor that a universal plot exists." *Foucault's Pendulum,* p. 317.
23. Letter to *The Washington Post,* 18 December 1990, responding to the alleged Iraqi-Jordanian-Yemeni plan to seize Saudi Arabia (described above on pp. 21, 23).
24. *Cumhuriyet,* 13 February 1993.

25. *Jasarat* (Karachi), 28 May 1995.
26. Sayyid Qutb, *Ma'alim fi't-Tariq*, trans. as *Milestones* (Kuwait: International Islamic Federation of Student Organizations, 1398/1978), p. 303.
27. *Al-Anwar*, 16 March 1993.
28. *2000 Ikibin'e Doğru*, 31 January 1993.
29. *Resalat* (Tehran), 30 January 1993; idem., 30 January 1993.
30. *Sabah* (Istanbul), 17 February 1993.
31. *Ash-Sharq al-Awsat*, 4 October 1992.
32. Ahmad Hamrush, "Hadith az-Zawraq . . . Muhzin wa-Mustafizz," *Ruz al-Yusuf*, 11 June 1990, pp. 36-37.
33. *Kayhan International*, 9 July 1990.
34. Fuller, *"Center of the Universe,"* p. 22.
35. Jervis, *Perception and Misperception*, p. 321.
36. Edward G. Shirley, "Is Iran's Present Algeria's Future?" *Foreign Affairs*, May/June 1995, p. 32.
37. Muhammad al-Ghazali, *Min Huna Na'lam*, 5th ed. (Cairo: Matba'at as-Sa'ada, 1965), p. 95.
38. *Al-Anwar* (Beirut), 29 September 1993.
39. Fuller, *"Center of the Universe,"* p. 22.
40. *Al-Wafd*, 28 March 1993.
41. *Al-Ahram*, 14 March 1993.
42. Sawt al-Mustad'afin, 7 March 1993.

# 13.

# Appearances Deceive

Things are not always what they seem.
— *Phaedrus*[1]

Things are seldom what they seem
Skim milk masquerades as cream.
— *William Gilbert*, H.M.S. Pinafore, act II

Things are not always what they seem,
but sometimes they are.
— *Dean Acheson*

Nothing is as it seems and nothing
can be taken for granted.
— *Kanan Makiya*[2]

Because the enemy excels at duplicity, the conspiracy theorist disbe-lieves the obvious. "There is more to all this than meets the eye," one Soviet leader mused after the failed 1991 coup attempt.[3] The forces of evil spin conspiracies so thick, even the suspicious have difficulty following the trail. When opponents appear to lose, they are actually hiding victory: the United States benefited from the oil shocks of the 1970s. Killers are victims and victims are perpetrators: Israelis massacred by PLO terrorists were murdered by their own government as part of a ruse to discredit Palestinians — the real victims. Enemies are really allies: Qadhdhafi and Khomeini toil for the U.S. government, while Zionists cooperate with anti-Semites worldwide. Allies really are pawns, to be discarded when no longer useful: the British and Israeli governments are controlled by Washington. Hunted and hunter blend, as do enemies and allies, leading to doubts about reality itself.

## GAINS ARE LOSSES, LOSSES ARE GAINS

Apparent gains are really setbacks, while apparent losses are really gains.

### No Good News

Good news challenges the conspiracy theorist's dour personality, so he fights back by turning it into trouble. Usually this means finding an angle that shows success to be illusory. Oil exporters explain away a rise in the price of oil as the West's cunning way to increase their own dependence on the West. Fundamentalists argue that the shah's patrons let him fall from power in the clever belief that Khomeini's poor leadership would discredit their cause. Many Arab armies took part in the victory over Iraq in the Kuwait war, but Westerners are said to "think that the Arabs, without exception, were defeated in this war."[4] An increase in trade between Iran and the United States got turned into an American attempt to "undermine the Islamic Republic."[5]

Western governments allow immigration with an eye to worsening Muslim divisions. Germany lets in fundamentalist Muslims from Turkey to organize against their government. Washington lets Yemenis immigrate into the United States as a way of weakening Yemen in its conflicts with Saudi Arabia. By "handing out fliers in Jerusalem promoting [Palestinian] emigration to the United States and promising facilities to help," the U.S. government prevents a Palestinian state from coming into existence, according to a PLO radio station. By removing Palestinians from their homeland, the conspiracy theory goes, the Americans empty it for Jewish settlement.[6] In Yasir 'Arafat's words, "While America closed its doors to the Jews, it is trying to open them to the Palestinians. The issue amounts to a wide-scale conspiracy; the aim is to vacate Palestine of Palestinians."[7]

Similar reasoning convinced the Arabs that the effort to integrate Palestinian refugees into their new homelands was a conspiracy. Arthur Geaney, UNRWA's field director in Syria in 1964, reported that there had been growth in the belief among the refugees generally, which seems to be shared by the Government, that the Agency is engaged upon a "plot" to solve or liquidate the refugee problem through the absorption of the refugees into the economy and the society [of the Arab countries where they live].[8]

Even the most benign-appearing move by Israel turns out to be a plot; fundamentalist Muslims see Israel's withdrawal from Arab territory as a trick intended to win the Jewish state more power. Revolutionary Iran denounced a unilateral Israeli withdrawal from Gaza as a "calculated plot" to "spread discord among Palestinians."[9] Rashid al-Ghannushi, Tunisia's leading fundamentalist, deemed the Oslo accords "a Jewish-American plan encompassing the entire region, which would cleanse it of all resistance and open it to Jewish economic and cultural activity, culminating in complete Jewish hegemony from Marrakesh to Kazakhstan." Ibrahim Ghawsha of Hamas saw in Israeli willingness to give territories under its control to the Arab states and the Palestinians a ruse, lulling the Arabs to relax their guard:

> God forbid, if by means of signing the peace accords the Arabs and Israelis reach a compromise and they implement their plan for autonomy, Arab economies will collapse because they will not be able to compete with the Israelis' modern industries. Thus, Israel will dominate the region as Japan dominates Southeast Asia, and the Arabs will all become employees of the Jews.[10]

Conspiracy theorists habitually increase the ranks of their enemies. On the premise that "the Jews prefer Communism" to Islam, the fundamentalist Sayyid Qutb portrayed Marxism-Leninism as a "virtual branch" of Zionism.[11] Leftists purvey the opposite view—that Israel is a leading anti-Communist force. Khalid Baqdash, leader of the Syrian Communist Party for over a half century, held that "world Jewry is ranged against the Soviet Union."[12] These examples, which can be multiplied many times, show an inclination to read events as negatively as possible.

One might expect Libya's Qadhdhafi, a man who volubly discusses the plight of Muslims worldwide, to applaud the 1995 American military effort in Bosnia; by bombing the Serbs, it defended the Muslims and forced the Serbs to sign a peace agreement. Not so. Only "the naive and the simple-minded" believed this was Washington's goal, he said; in fact, it really sought "revenge on Yugoslavia, the leader of neutrality and the Non-Aligned Movement."[13] On another occasion, he explained the American effort as a way for NATO to test its weapons in preparation for an attack on Muslims.[14]

## The Conspirator Always Gains

Conversely, apparent defeats suffered by conspirators mask what are really victories. Not distinguishing between central and peripheral issues, the conspiracy theorist switches them around to suit his own convenience. Moscow's establishment of diplomatic relations with several Persian Gulf states in 1985 looked like a setback for American interests, but Iranian officials knew better:

> Washington is doubtlessly in the picture and background of these developments, since the U.S. monopoly of influence, in any case, leaves no room for Soviet infiltration. . . . [Perhaps] there is a tacit agreement between Washington and Moscow to defend the region vis-à-vis a third party [i.e. Iran] that threatens the interests of both sides.[15]

In a deft slight of hand, Iranians discern an American gain in the expansion of Moscow's influence! This heads-I-lose-tails-you-win quality insists on benefits to the conspirator, no matter how trivial or speculative.

In a complex situation all parties have some small gains, making every one of them a potential conspirator. While nearly every country suffered from the Iraqi invasion of Kuwait, a narrow enough reading could select out advantages. "All the states that participated in the war [against Iraq] also gained something," theorized Anis Mansur, an Egyptian with very pronounced pro-Iraqi views. Saudi Arabia got increased oil prices, Syria won a free hand in Lebanon, Egypt had its American debt cancelled, the United States placed forces in the Persian Gulf. Israel gained got paid handsomely, as Mansur explains: "Israel alone received $11 billion, $1 billion for every missile that landed in Israel. Most of these missiles were packed with sand and pebbles and fell in the cities' Iraqi neighborhoods."[16] Emphasizing such gains enabled pro-Iraqi elements to blame the crisis on all parties other than Baghdad.

The ups and downs of oil pricing illustrate the notion of the conspirator always winning. As Arabs and Iranians came to recognize the devastation that oil wealth had left behind they came to see the oil boom as a vast conspiracy. Naturally, the West got credit for seeing that high oil prices would hinder the Middle East's progress. It understood that too much money for the Arabs would mean, in Mohamed Heikal's words, "still more swollen incomes, which they could either use up on expensive and unnecessary gadgets, like elaborate defence systems against unspecified enemies, or plough back into the American economy by investing it there. Either way it was the USA which scored."[17]

Others took a different tack, seeing increases in the price of oil as a direct gain for the United States. This is not easy to do, for the 1970s price rises caused major dislocations, including high inflation and low growth, and cost the U.S. economy about $1.5 trillion. To prove that the United States nonetheless gained from higher prices, conspiracy theorists dwelt on those small areas where Americans benefited from high prices: oil company profits, a boom in Texas, a strengthened dollar, and petrodollars (those Middle Eastern profits that went right back to the West's banks). It also hurt America's allies:

> The skyrocketing oil prices that helped push the United States into an economic recession are the result of a plot by its own Central Intelligence Agency. . . . The C.I.A. realized the Western European countries were forging ahead of the United States in economic growth and contrived the jump in oil prices to punish the Europeans.[18]

Even more implausibly, Jews are sometimes held to be the main beneficiary of the rise in oil prices: "Who takes the interest from the billions from the price of oil which belongs to the Arabs? The Jews!"[19]

When oil prices went down, this, too, of course resulted from a Western plot. The price of oil plummeted in 1985-86, prompting 'Ali Akbar Hashemi-Rafsanjani to suspect an American effort to bankrupt the Islamic Republic of Iran. The earlier vision of inner Western rivalry vanished, replaced by one of total Western solidarity; now Iran's parliament condemned "the big powers' conspiracy to drive down oil prices."[20] To counter this alleged plot, Tehran actually met with the Libyans and Algerians in 1986. Saddam Husayn portrayed the price decline as "a conspiracy against the region's economy."[21] Nothing the U.S. government did could change this mindset. The Iranian media brushed aside Vice President George Bush's surprising call in 1986 for a higher price of oil as nothing but "an attempt to hide responsibility for the oil price collapse conspiracy."[22]

When the opponent meets an unexpected setback, conspiracy buffs get to work to incorporate and figure out how he actually gained. Who planned it and what were his motives? When the shah died, Iranians across the political spectrum asked, "Who did it, and why?" Some went so far as to ask: "Why did he do it?" Which brings us to the next topic: how the conspirator gains from his own injury and death.

## BLAME THE VICTIM, PITY THE PERPETRATOR

Conspiracy theorists give new meaning to the phrase "blame the victim." In case after case, they shift the onus of responsibility from the aggressor to the injured party.

### Actual Events

Events get turned into their opposite. According to the PLO, Washington "planned" the Soviet shooting down of a Korean airliner in 1983.[23] When Libyan aircraft bombed Sudan's main radio station in 1984, conspiracy theorists (including Edward Mortimer of *The Times*)[24] suspected a Sudanese government plot. Just three months before American air force jets strafed Mu'ammar al-Qadhdhafi in April 1986, Baghdad's Voice of the Masses deemed the Libyan strongman "subservient" to the United States and Israel.[25] A Bahraini paper called the bombing of a TWA airliner in 1986 "the most clear example of the West's enmity to the Arabs."[26] The Yemeni press widely portrayed the seizure of the Saudi ambassador in their country as a Saudi ploy to make Yemenis look bad.

The politician unlucky enough to be assassinated not only loses his life but might be blamed for his own murder. President Zia ul-Haq's demise in an August 1988 airplane crash prompted the thesis in his native Pakistan, "advanced without any evidence whatsoever, that he may have tried to fake a plane accident in order to impose martial law or at least cancel the [November 1988] elections, but that this plan went tragically wrong."[27] Who but his own Islamic Republican Party blew up Mohammed Beheshti and many others in June 1981? Who but members of his own Jewish Defense League killed Meir Kahane in November 1990? And so on.

Unlike Americans, who took Sheikh 'Umar 'Abd ar-Rahman and his virulently anti-Western followers at face value—as fundamentalist Muslims who hate the United States—Middle Easterners saw a more elaborate pattern. Many thought the purpose of the World Trade Center explosion was to discredit Palestinians, Egyptians, Arabs, or all Muslims. Egyptian columnist Ihsan Bakr argues the first: "No Palestinian party . . . would have undertaken such an operation because it would harm all of them."[28] The editor of a Cairene newspaper suggested that the World Trade Center bombing revealed how Americans "want to attack Egypt as part of their frantic campaign against Islam."[29] Bakr saw an even larger purpose: the explosion was intended "to tarnish the Arabs' image, undermine Arab-American relations, and undermine the Arab and Islamic communities in Europe and America."[30] The Muslim Brethren in Jordan agreed, portraying the explosion as an Israeli scheme for "distorting the international image of Islam and Muslims."[31]

Iranians worried less about image and more practical matters; for them, the bombing mainly diverted attention from Muslims in trouble. But even here they disagreed. While Deputy Foreign Minister 'Ali Mohammed Besharati saw it as "a ploy to mask the bloodthirsty face of the despotic regime in Palestine and an effort to divert public opinion from the Palestinian deportees' troubles," a radio commentary pointed to the need "to play down reports on the tragedy in Bosnia-Hercegovina."[32]

In what Richard Nixon once dubbed "the ultimate conspiratorialist notion,"[33] Arabs and Iranians routinely blame the Israeli government for the deaths of its own citizens. An early example comes from October 1937, when King 'Abd al-'Aziz ibn Sa'ud of Saudi Arabia responded to the news of the Arab rebellion in Palestine (the murder of a senior British official, his police escort, and two constables, then arson at the unfinished airport at Lod) by telling the British that it was "as clear as daylight" to him what had happened: "Godless Arab gunmen," hired abroad, engaged in these vile deeds on behalf of the Zionists.[34] In a similar spirit, the king's son, Faysal, later held that "Zionists were behind the Palestinian terrorists."[35]

Israelis and Germans together murdered the Israeli athletes at the Munich Olympics in 1972. Leon Klinghoffer was killed aboard the hijacked ship *Achille Lauro* by his wife to make the PLO look bad (according to Faruq Qaddumi of the PLO). When a London court convicted Nizar al-Hindawi, a Syrian agent, of trying to blow up an El Al passenger plane, Damascus accused the Israeli authorities of planting the lethal device on their own airplane. When a Jewish woman and her three children were killed in Jericho by the bombing of a bus, the PLO accused Prime Minister Yitzhak Shamir of Israel of the murder. Similarly, when nine Israelis lost their lives in an assault on their bus in Egypt, a Jordanian paper accused Mossad "of planning and carrying out this operation."[36] Cairo's leading newspaper merely speculated that "it is possible that there was an Israeli hand behind the incident," while another daily published a lengthy account with details on the origins of the Israeli plan, the location of Palestinian agents to execute it, and the expected benefits.[37] The specificity of this account did much to enhance its authenticity.

Khomeinists make a specialty of blaming their victims. In July 1989, when bombs went off by Islam's holiest shrine in Mecca and all the world suspected the Saudis' main rivals in Iran, then Speaker of the Parliament Rafsanjani suggested that "maybe the Saudis themselves did it."[38] When one faction seized the American embassy in Tehran in November 1980 to ferret out the "den of espionage" masterminding conspiracies against the Islamic Revolution, another faction portrayed the takeover as Washington's ploy to isolate Iran internationally or to justify its freeze of $10 billion in Iranian assets. Khomeini's one-time ally and Iran's first president, Abol Hassan Bani Sadr interpreted the continued holding of the Americans as a plot by Ronald Reagan against Jimmy Carter. According to this scenario, Candidate Reagan secretly reached an agreement with the mullahs in Paris on 19 October 1980, making sure the Americans would be held until after the American elections. Participants at the Paris meeting supposedly included George Bush and the CIA director, William Casey. To hide this agreement's existence, the crafty mullahs engaged in mock negotiations with President Carter over the next three months.[39]

Iraqi authorities had their own gloss on the embassy takeover, which they presented as a pretext for the U.S. imperialists to invade the Persian Gulf region. This conveniently permitted Baghdad to portray the Iranian regime as party to an American conspiracy versus the Arabs.

Western hostages in Lebanon prompted similar flights of logic. President Rafsanjani contended that the U.S. government wanted American hostages to remain in captivity.[40] In this spirit, an Iranian editorial called these men "victims of imperialist policies of the West."[41] A headline in *Al-Musawwar*, a highly respectable Egyptian weekly, paraphrased Reagan administration officials telling Tehran, "Do not release the hostages."[42]

### Anticipated Events

Middle Easterners sometimes anticipate when a victim will act against himself. The Iranian foreign ministry warned on 23 February 1989 that "global arrogance was planning to unleash a new wave of terrorism and blame it on the Islamic Republic."[43] Sure enough, two weeks later, a bomb went off in San Diego, destroying the family car belonging to the captain of the *Vincennes*, the U.S. Navy ship that seven months earlier had brought down an Iran Air jet. Pre-preempting blame made it easier for Tehran's media to point to the Federal Bureau of Investigation as the culprit. The FBI's goal? To blacken Khomeini's name.

The same impulse will someday lead to Salman Rushdie's death, according to an editorial in *Kayhan International*:

> The only thing left in completing the circle being woven around the *fatwa* [edict] will be to kill the man. This however, will not be the work of any Muslim hands, but of Western intelligence services. Rushdie is now like unto a goose being fattened for slaughter. . . . the death of Rushdie goes much further than the taking of his life. The idea is to turn up the decibel level of the anti-Iran, anti-Islam campaign that seems to be the lifeblood of American and British-led foreign policy regarding the Muslim world.[44]

Just before the second anniversary of the July 1990 stampede in Mecca that left 1,400 dead, the Iraqi media predicted a repetition.

Not every preemption proves necessary. A newspaper in Abu Dhabi reported the following scoop in February 1990:

> *Al-Ittihad* has learned that Palestinian security organs have obtained serious information that elements collaborating with the internal Israel intelligence service, known as Shin Bet, are planning to fabricate a terrorist operation. They will hijack an Israeli El Al airliner with the aim of aborting the Middle East peace process.[45]

No such airplane hijacking occurred; but had one taken place, this news leak would have set the stage plausibly to transfer responsibility from the Palestinians actually undertaking it to the Israelis suffering the consequences. There are few limits to the utility of conspiracy theories.

## ALLIES FEIGN ENMITY, ENEMIES FEIGN ALLIANCE

A hostile confrontation between two parties covers their clandestine alliance. Indeed, the more extreme the enmity, the better the subterfuge; and actual war provides conspirators with the ultimate mechanism to fool their enemies. At other times, quite the contrary, apparent friendship masks true enmity. In this case, alliance in war confirms the depth of hostility. Accusing someone of supporting his adversaries does much to discredit him. In the confusing world of conspiracism, seeming friends are secret enemies, while seeming enemies are secret friends.

We have already seen (chapter 7, "Communist Assistants") how the Soviet Union and Communist parties served imperialist interests. Other monumental false enmities number five—two concerning Israel (the PLO, Syria) and three concerning the U.S. government (Hafiz al-Asad, Saddam Husayn, and Ruhollah Khomeini).

## Phony Enmity with Israel

Israel's enemies are really its agents, starting with Saddam Husayn and Ayatollah Khomeini. Antun Sa'ada, founder of the aggressively anti-Zionist Syrian Social Nationalist Party, was widely accused of enjoying Zionist support. According to Hasan, an Iraqi businessman, Saddam's connection to Israel goes back to his three years in Egypt, 1960 to 1963: "For one of those years, no one knows exactly where he was. That's probably when he got his Mossad training."[46] It was widely thought in mid-1982 that the Israelis were ready to attack the PLO in Lebanon but needed an excuse to do so; when the Iraqis obligingly had an agent shoot the Israeli ambassador in London (hoping this would divert Syrian attention and maybe even win a cease-fire with Iran), and Jerusalem followed two days later with Operation Peace for Galilee, a large military operation in Lebanon, Middle Easterns saw the Iraqi-Israeli ties confirmed.

Iraq's enemies made much of this alleged connection during the Kuwait crisis. Husni Mubarak accused Saddam Husayn of secretly plotting with Israeli leaders how their two states might avoid withdrawing from the territories they had occupied.[47] While Saddam portrayed his conflict with the West as an effort to forward the Palestinian cause, the Saudi ambassador to Indonesia portrayed Saddam as an "Israeli agent planted in the Ba'th Party to stab the Arab world in the back." Even as the Allied ground war against Iraq was in full pitch, the official Kuwaiti newspaper reported the defection of an Iraqi diplomat carrying "a file on secret contacts" with Israeli officials.[48]

Nor did Khomeini's extreme anti-Israel rhetoric protect him from being perceived as a covert Zionist. For example, a Saudi newspaper reported in 1989 that 16 Iranians regularly attended courses arranged by Mossad.[49] But Israel's main two phony enemies are the Palestinians and the Asad regime.

*Al-Fat'h and the PLO.*     Yasir 'Arafat's Al-Fat'h organization is often portrayed as an Israeli ally. Unhappy about the creation in 1964 of the rival PLO, the old-guard Arab Higher Council sought to undermine the new institution by calling it "a colonialist, Zionist conspiracy aiming at the liquidation of the Palestinian cause."[50] In a neat parallel, Gamal Abdel Nasser initially ascribed Fat'h to Muslim Brethren allies of the imperialists, while the Saudis saw it as an agent of international Communism. These misgivings increased as Fat'h purposefully provoked Israeli retaliation in the mid-1960s (to gain attention for itself), prompting suspicions of its working for some hidden power—the pan-Arab nationalists, the CIA, or even Israel. Syrian defense minister Mustafa Tallas discerned "an Israeli plan which involved Fatah" as the cause of the Six-Day War's outbreak in 1967.[51]

The Palestinian movement's record of failure against Israel opened its leadership to Syrian charges of secretly working for Israel. Damascus called Yasir 'Arafat "a U.S. tool against Palestine and Palestinian rights."[52] Tallas accused 'Arafat of collaborating with the Egyptian secret services when he was at the University of Cairo (in the late 1940s), and through them with the CIA;[53] this connection paid off for the CIA when 'Arafat killed Communists in Lebanon. Sulayman Faranjiya, president of Lebanon from 1970 to 1976 and a Syrian protégé, accused 'Arafat of being an Israeli agent on the grounds that "he's done more harm to the Palestinians than anyone else."[54] Similarly, Iranian in 1991 media reported 'Arafat boasting of having prevented over 200 Palestinian operations against Israel and the United States.[55]

The PLO in turn accused Abu Nidal, the extremist Palestinian leader who gunned down 'Arafat's men and mounted operations to foil 'Arafat's diplomacy, of working for the enemy. According to Salah Khalaf, "Every Palestinian who works in intelligence is convinced that Israel has a big hand in Abu Nidal's affairs."[56] For good measure, Yasir 'Arafat added that the U.S. government encouraged the Persian Gulf states and Iran to fund Hamas, his main rival.

*Syria.*     The Syrian relationship with Israel, the subject of a decades-long debate, deserves close attention. One camp, made up of those sympathetic either to the Syrian regime in Damascus or to Israel, sees President Hafiz al-Asad as deeply hostile to Israel. The other, made up of Arab opponents of both Asad and Israel (primarily leftists, pro-PLO types, and fundamentalist Muslims), sees the Syrian ruler as an agent of the Jewish state.

For group one, the real gauge of the two states' relations is their record of war, their hostile statements, the tension along their mutual border, and their ever-growing military forces. Minor areas of common interest that do exist—the quiet along the Golan Heights since 1975, a limit on hostilities in Lebanon, and for many years a shared antipathy toward 'Arafat—result from an incidental convergence of interests.

Group two, the enemies of Syria and Israel (including Israeli Leftists), ignore the fact that Asad's government has long been the Arab state almost single-handedly keeping the conflict with Israel alive. Instead, they point to the two states' essential harmony of interests. The quiet of the Syrian-Israeli border convinces this school that the two states are not even in conflict. (Similar reasoning, incidentally, applied to the Soviet Union and the United States, the two never having fought each other.)

Adherents of this logic point to the fact that Hafiz al-Asad commanded the air force in 1967 when the Golan Heights fell to Israel almost without a fight. Still in the same post, they noted, he refused to supply air cover for a Syrian expedition to help the PLO against the Jordanian government in 1970. Asad subsequently never permitted the PLO to stage operations from Syria. Asad's enemies accuse him of much else, such as

> sabotaging an Iraqi offensive against Israel in 1973, permitting the massacre of Palestinians at Tel Za'tar in 1976, cutting up the Lebanese National Front and attempting to divide the Palestinian resistance, playing partition games with the Israelis in Lebanon, [and] stabbing Arab Iraq in the back when it was attacked by Khomeini's Iran.[57]

To top things off, Asad expelled the PLO from Lebanon in late 1983. The fundamentalist Muslim Brethren discerned "an international Jewish-'Alawi conspiracy" against Sunni Muslims in general and Palestinians in particular.[58] Indeed, it saw "collusion between the Asad regime and the Zionist enemy" underpinning the whole of Syrian foreign policy.[59] The National Alliance for the Liberation of Syria went further, arguing that "a burning hostility to Arabs and Islam" motivated Asad's actions and that "all his crimes are in the interest of the Zionist enemy."[60] Alliance with Israel also implies close relations with its friends; the Syrian opposition accuses Asad of allying with "Maronite Crusaders"[61] as well as the United States.

Group one is correct in its analysis, but group two has real political importance. However preposterous, the barrage of criticism that characterizes Asad as an agent of Israel wears down the president and his entourage, provides Syrians with a powerful alternative to the state-sponsored message, and justifies extremist acts against the regime.

## Phony Enmity with the United States

The more fervently a politician attacks the United States, the more likely he will be seen as an agent of the U.S. government. Accordingly, Hafiz al-Asad, Saddam Husayn, and Ayatollah Khomeini all come under special suspicion.

*Hafiz al-Asad.* Asad has served as an American agent at least since 1977, when he took a $12 million bribe to improve relations with the U.S. government. In the words of an Iraqi columnist, "Hafiz al-Asad always coordinates with the U.S. administration on serious issues, especially those related to the struggle against imperialism."[62] A Palestinian casually asserts that "the Syrian regime, like all Arab regimes, is a lackey of American imperialism."[63] When Syrian and American troops jointly defended Saudi Arabia in 1991, these conspiracy theorists found all their suspicions confirmed.

*Saddam Husayn.* He began working for the CIA while living in Cairo during 1960 to 1963; Egyptian intelligence has pictures of him at the U.S. embassy in Cairo. The vehemently anti-American Ba'th Party came to power in Iraq in February 1963 "on an American train."[64] As evidence, King Husayn of Jordan points to secret meetings with Americans and clandestine American broadcasts to Baghdad on the day of the coup.[65] When Saddam's forces killed the wife of his rival, Hirdan at-Takriti, the latter got even by going public with details about CIA support for Saddam during the second Ba'th coup of 1968. In the years following 1968, Saddam was "routinely identified by Baghdad's academic community as 'the CIA's man in the Ba'th party.'" Evidence? He had taken part in an assassination attempt on the archleftist 'Abd al-Karim Qasim; he killed Communists on reaching power; and his speedy rise through the ranks hinted at a powerful patron.[66] According to Syria's mercurial defense minister, Mustafa Tallas, Gamal Abdel Nasser was "the first person to discover the truth" about Saddam's work for the United States; Tallas tells of Abdel Nasser meeting with Saddam in 1969, then telling Tallas his conclusion that Saddam is "America's man in the region."[67]

After simmering for years, these accusations took off with the Iraqi-U.S. confrontation of 1990-91. Iraqi opposition forces claimed they would "long ago" have overthrown Saddam Husayn had the West not aided him.[68] Mustafa Tallas spun the most elaborate conspiracy theories. Calling Saddam an American "stooge," he accused the Iraqi leader of dreaming to become "the U.S. policeman in the Gulf." Toward this end, Saddam invaded Iran in 1980, intending to conquer Tehran, free the American hostages, and "present them as a Christmas gift to President Carter." Eleven years later, Saddam invaded Kuwait to divert Arab attention from Israel. But he erred in swallowing Kuwait whole, a brazen aggression that forced the U.S. government to go through the motions of pushing Iraqi forces out of Kuwait.[69]

Things got worse for Saddam after he lost, when even his most ardent supporters started to see him as a traitor to the Arabs and an agent of the U.S. government. Lamis K. Andoni, a reporter in Jordan, reported that "What torments many in Baghdad is that the leadership, including President Saddam, has not said a word to explain the decision to withdraw [from Kuwait], giving rise to speculation and rumours about treachery among the president's aides and other similar stories."[70] Reviewing his strategy, some saw an intent to lose: the Scud missile attack on Israel, for example, did little damage but won wide sympathy for the Jewish state. That Saddam managed to stay in power prompted further speculations some about his being an American agent. A resident of Nablus explained: "I wouldn't be surprised if it comes out that Saddam was a CIA agent aiming to destroy Iraq's military machine and Arab resources."[71] A Palestinian clerk in Jordan concurred: "If the U.S. leaves Saddam Husayn alone, it means there was some kind of deal beforehand."[72]

*Ayatollah Khomeini.*     Being the most vitriolic of all anti-Americans, fundamentalist Muslims are particularly susceptible to accusations of working for Washington. Usually they are seen serving American purposes by posing as a barrier to Communism or to modernity.

Take the Islamic Republic of Iran. On the left, a Soviet-backed radio stated that Khomeini's regime, despite its "outward clamor" of anti-Americanism, "is exerting all its efforts in order to pull Iran once more into the orbit of dependence on imperialism headed by world-devouring America."[73] Toward this end, another source noted, the regime allowed American and British agents to infiltrate key government departments. Bani Sadr accused Khomeini of working hand-in-glove with Ronald Reagan. Iranian leftists portrayed Khomeini as the chosen American instrument to steal the revolution from them. Iranians of a Maoist persuasion went further yet, seeing Khomeini as the "trusted agent" of both the American and Soviet intelligence services.[74]

On the right, Khomeini's fundamentalist Muslim opponents accused him of collusion with the West. In his book, an Egyptian Muslim Brethren exposed American and sometimes Soviet support for Khomeini and nearly all the early revolutionary figures — Bazargan, Qotbzadeh, Yazdi, et al.[75] The Saudi government refused to accept at face value his edict against Salman Rushdie and the publishers of *The Satanic Verses*, preferring to interpret it as an elaborate ruse to discredit Islam. Arguing (rightly) for the edict's illegality according the laws of Islam, the Saudis noted the harm it did to Islam's international standing, then concluded that Khomeini issued the edict to discredit Islam. More generously, radical groups in Egypt merely saw the Iranians as dupes of the West. In their view, the Rushdie affair was a plot "into which the Iranians, in their haste, have fallen."[76]

A virtuoso conspiracy theorist turns black into white and white into black. When Rafsanjani of Iran publicly called on the Palestinians to execute five Americans, Britons, or Frenchman for every Palestinian killed,[77] his extremism inadvertently discredited the Palestinian cause. Enemies of Tehran seized on this threat and turned it around, claiming that it proved "that the regime of Iranian leader Ayatollah Khomeini is working for Israel and rendering it the greatest service."[78]

Of course, the Iranians find such collusion insulting and preposterous. If the headline of a Beirut newspaper in late 1987 read "Washington encourages Tehran to strive for an 'Islamic revolution' in the Soviet Union,"[79] the authorities in Tehran saw themselves in competition with the Americans. For example, when Secretary of State James Baker visited Alma Ata, the capital of Kazakhstan, in September 1991, they presented this as an American attempt to dominate the Muslim republics, both directly and through Saudi, Turkish, and Israeli proxies.[80]

In turn, Tehran accuses fundamentalist Muslim groups not under its control of being Western agents. For example, as the *mujahidin* captured Kabul, the Iranian-backed faction accused archfundamentalist Gulbeddin Hikmatyar of serving as "an operative of the United States."[81]

### Phony Alliance

Conspiracism can also turn ostensible friends into enemies, cooperation into scheming. In the pithy words of a Middle Eastern proverb: "Beware of your enemy; but beware even more of your friends." Most allies-are-really-enemies schemas involve the U.S. government, the epicenter of world conspiracy, and while the pattern applies especially to the U.S.-Israel tie, it obtains among Arabs and Westerners alike.

Arabs sometimes portray American allies as supinely doing Washington's bidding. Abdel Nasser dismissed Britain as "an American colony" that "cannot express an opinion on any international issue without first . . . clearing it with Washington."[82] His acolyte Mu'ammar al-Qadhdhafi likewise called Britain "subordinate" to the U.S. government.[83] Yasir 'Arafat went further, deeming all Europe subject to "U.S. blackmail" and therefore unable to act independently.[84] When France's newly elected president, Jacques Chirac, decided to resume nuclear testing in the Pacific, Mu'ammar al-Qadhdhafi hailed this event as "an indication that a European country has regained its independence from the U.S. occupation." He even called the pro-American Chirac "a hero of European independence from the hated U.S. colonialism."[85] Picking up on this same theme, the Iranian media shortly afterwards ascribed a series of bombings in Paris to the CIA. Agreement on Europe's subordination comes from all parts of the Middle East, including Iraq ("those who are called U.S. allies are, in reality, not allies but satellites")[86] and Sudan ("All that is called the traditional West has become part of America").”[87]

Palestinians say that their so-called Arab allies betrayed them, which accounts for the long string of military losses. "Treacherous conspiracies on the part of Arab regimes"[88] is how al-Fat'h explains the defeat of 1948-49, while the PLO's Khalil al-Wazir sees a deep deception: "the Arab regimes of the day put on a show to pretend they supported our cause. But really their intention was to neutralize us."[89] According to Hamas, "the intervention of Arab rulers prevented the holy war from advancing."[90] (Palestinians are not alone in this suspicion: the defeat of 1948-49 also prompted wide suspicion in the Egyptian and Iraqi militaries of a betrayal by politicians.)

Subsequent wars saw similar treachery. In 1967, the Jordanian king play-acted at fighting Israel, issuing blank ammunition to his forces, while the Saudi king paid Israel handsomely to defeat Abdel Nasser. The Jordanian High Command then sponsored an extremist Palestinian organization, the Victory Legions, to undercut Fat'h. In 1982, the Arab states deserted the Palestinians because, 'Arafat says, "We did better than all the Arabs in this war. They therefore couldn't let us win."[91] During the *intifada*, Hamas claimed, "Arab rulers . . . pretend to support the uprising but in fact are immersed in a deep sleep."[92]

Arab regimes throw the blame right back to the Palestinians, accusing them of collusion with Zionism. Through the 1980s, Syrian politicians and journalists routinely made this argument against 'Arafat, whom they deemed an agent of Israel.

If enemies are really allies, how can allies also be enemies? At a deeper psychological level, these contradictory impulses contain a kernel of consistency. In the conspiracy mentality, balanced relations never exist, for everyone is either exploiter or exploited—or both at once. The interplay of interests, the give-and-take of daily life, and normal reciprocal bonds disappear in a haze of duplicity. Conspiracy replaces all other relations, especially friendship but also enmity. Such terms mean nothing to conspirators, who know only opportunism. For this reason, as Hannah Arendt, the political philosopher, writes, "reality—real enmity or real friendship—is no longer experienced and understood in its own terms but is automatically assumed to signal something else."[93]

## A STAGED REALITY

Some conspiracy theorists draw the logical conclusion from these many deceptions: All what you see around you, they say, is a sham. Leading institutions are fraudulent creations intended to deceive. Law courts are rigged. Labor unions exist to fool gullible workers. Voluntary organizations are government fronts. Schools and universities purvey false learning. Scholarly and artistic competitions are fixed. Even quiz shows and sporting matches, especially when they have commercial or political consequence, get fixed. Economic conditions lose importance, social forces become irrelevant, and intellectual debates are meaningless. Ideas count for nothing, mobilizing ideologies (such as nationalism and socialism) serve as a mechanism to fool the unwashed into thinking they have a role to play. In this nihilistic world, moral principles are fraudulent and altruism signals greed.

Society consists of a few conspirators and many dupes. Any process that involves the multitudes is a charade; everything is manipulated. Conspiracy theorists dismiss the notion that the competing interests of thousands or millions of people could produce something worthy. The masses, ever gullible, count for nothing. Elections are a pantomime carried out by Tweedledee and Tweedledum parties; real power is held by the police, the bureaucracy, the rich, and special interests. "Politics," says 'Abd al-Majid az-Zindani, a member of Yemen's Presidential Council, "always goes on behind closed doors."[94] A Libyan political editor rips the veil off the fraud of American elections: "We have in our possession documents, information, and recordings which concern the rigging of elections in the United States and the money and bribes paid during it. We are also aware of the way by which the U.S. president [i.e., Clinton] was able to win the presidential election."[95]

The free market is in fact controlled by an oligopoly, prices of commodities are fixed, stock markets are an immense sham. Bankers plot out panics and crashes. The millions of small shareholders who buy and sell may think they are establishing prices, but a small group of insiders in fact controls these. 'Arif Dalila of the Economics and Commerce Faculty at Damascus University explains that "money markets everywhere are subject to abuse because they become transformed into casinos where a few speculators who control money from behind the scenes gamble with the savings of thousands of stockholders."[96]

Military battles are planned out in advance. Yusuf Idris, an Egyptian author, described the October 1973 war as a conspiracy in which the Egyptian, Israeli, and American governments all colluded. In Taghi Modarressi's novel, *The Pilgrim's Rules of Etiquette*, an Iranian intellectual tells a friend of his intention to write about the Iraq-Iran war's historical roots. The friend, a general, "looked at the ceiling with a desperate expression" and replied: "You're wasting your time. All wars are a sham. They've struck a deal. All the strategies are decided on the other side of the world. They want to cheat this poor nation. With so much education, how can you be so gullible?"[97]

Diplomacy and negotiations, of course, are staged. The parties pretend to disagree at the table; in fact, they privately determine the results in advance. The Egyptian-Israeli peace process that began in 1973 and ended nine years later played itself out mostly in public; any interested observer knew that the two governments, with American assistance, sought to end their state of war. Still, many Arab observers insisted on dubbing this a plot. In a typical formulation, the fourteenth session of the Palestine National Council, meeting in January 1979, declared the Camp David agreements "a conspiracy which should be rejected and resisted by all means."[98] This accusation conveniently discredited the negotiations: instead of Egyptians and Israelis contending for their interests, they become agents of Washington.

The same applied, of course, to the Cold War. Overt Soviet-American ideological conflict hid covert cooperation for mastery of the Third World. A Soviet-American summit in November 1985 prompted President Khamene'i of Iran to explain that the great powers, having already divided up the globe, were meeting to iron out minor disagreements. The dramatic lessening of Soviet-American tensions in the late 1980s intensified these suspicions. The calm atmosphere, one Iranian commentary noted, made it possible "to loot the Third World without provoking international conflict."[99]

When simplicity is a form of duplicity and denial a form of confirmation, conspiracism makes it very hard to see facts plain and true. Which raises the question: How is it that conspiracy theories have become so numerous and influential in the Middle East?

## NOTES TO CHAPTER 13

1. *Fables*, Book 4, Fable 2. Many writers have repeated this observation, some strengthening it. For example, James Fenimore Cooper held that "Things *in fact*, are very different from things *as they seem to be*" (italics in the original). See Thomas Philbrick and Constance Ayers Denne, eds., *Gleanings in Europe: France* (Albany: State University of New York Press, 1983), p. 177.

2. Samir al-Khalil [pseud. of Kanan Makiya], *Republic of Fear: The Politics of Modern Iraq* (Berkeley: University of California Press, 1989), p. 63.

3. *The New York Times*, 28 August 1991.

4. Radio Monte Carlo, 23 April 1993.

5. *Salam*, 10 April 1993.

6. Voice of the PLO (Baghdad), 5 February 1990.

7. Sawt Filastin (Sanaa), 9 April 1990.

8. Quoted in Benjamin N. Schiff, *Refugees unto the Third Generation: UN Aid to Palestinians* (Syracuse, N.Y.: Syracuse University Press, 1995) p.91.

9. Voice of the Islamic Republic of Iran, 13 April 1993.

10. Both quoted in Martin Kramer, "The Jihad against the Jews," *Commentary*, October 1994, p. 40.

11. Sayyid Qutb, *Ma'rakatna ma'a'l-Yuhud*, edited by Zayn ad-Din ar-Rakkabi. Text translated in Ronald L. Nettler, *Past Trials and Present Tribulations: A Muslim Fundamentalist's View of the Jews* (Oxford, Eng.: Pergamon, 1987). Quoted on pp. 80, 84.

12. Mohamed Heikal, *The Sphinx and the Commissar: The Rise and Fall of Soviet Influence in the Middle East* (New York: Harper & Row, 1978), p. 196.

13. Libyan Television, 4 October 1995.

14. Jamahiriya Arab News Agency, 18 September 1995.

15. Tehran International Service, 16 November 1985.

16. *Al-Ahram*, 21 May 1993. Actually, 40 missiles fell on Israel and the country received $650 million from the U.S. government for damages suffered, coming to a little over $16 million per missile. None of them, it hardly needs adding, were "packed with sand and pebbles."

17. Mohamed Heikal, *The Road to Ramadan* (New York: Quadrangle/The New York Times Book Co., 1975), p. 274.

18. *The New York Times*, 6 January 1980.

19. Quoted in Patrick D. Gaffney, *The Prophet's Pulpit: Islamic Preaching in Contemporary Egypt* (Berkeley: University of California Press, 1994), p. 306.
20. Islamic Republic News Agency, 29 January 1986.
21. Iraqi News Agency, 1 July 1990.
22. Islamic Republic News Agency, 2 April 1986.
23. Voice of the PLO (Baghdad), 6 September 1983.
24. *The Times*, 21 March 1984.
25. Sawt al-Jamahir (Baghdad), 8, 11 January 1986.
26. *Akhbar al-Khalij*, 6 April 1986.
27. *The New York Times*, 30 August 1988.
28. *Al-Ahram*, 14 March 1993.
29. *Al-Akhbar*, 21 March 1993.
30. *Al-Ahram*, 14 March 1993.
31. *Jordan Times*, 7 March 1993.
32. *Jomhuri-ye Islami*, 13 March 1993; Voice of the Islamic Republic of Iran, 6 March 1993.
33. Richard Nixon, *Memoirs* (New York: Grosset & Dunlap, 1978), p. 1012. In this author's view, the real "ultimate conspiratorialist notion" is thinking that the hidden hand mentality is itself a conspiracy.
34. Conversation on 25 October 1937 with H. R. P. Dickson, Foreign Office 371/20822 E7201/22/31. Text in Elie Kedourie, *Islam in the Modern World* (New York: Holt Rinehart and Winston, 1980), p. 73. This argument foreshadows the Iranian one against Salman Rushdie half a century later.
35. Nixon, *Memoirs*, p. 1012.
36. *Sawt ash-Sha'b*, 14 February 1990.
37. *Al-Ahram*, 14 February 1990; *Ash-Sha'b*, 20 February 1990, p. 4.
38. *The Washington Times*, 12 July 1989.
39. Abol Hassan Bani Sadr, with Jean-Charles Deniau, *Le Complot des ayatollahs* (Paris: Éditions la Découverte, 1989), pp. 48, 57.
40. *Tehran Times*, 12 June 1991.
41. *Tehran Times International Weekly*, 22 February 1990.
42. *Al-Musawwar*, 3 May 1991.
43. Islamic Revolution News Agency, 23 February 1989.
44. *Kayhan International*, 20 May 1993.
45. *Al-Ittihad*, 11 February 1990.
46. Quoted in Ethan Bronner, "Psycho-Semitic," *The New Republic*, 24 May 1993.
47. Middle East News Agency, 1 October 1990. Mubarak was replying to Iraqi accusations of agentry for Israel.
48. *Sawt al-Kuwait*, 26 February 1991.
49. *Al-Madina*, 28 September 1989.
50. *Al-Kitab as-Sanawi li'l-Qadiya al-Filastiniya, 1964*, p. 102. Quoted in Helena Cobban, *The Palestinian Liberation Organization: People, Power and Politics* (Cambridge, Eng.: Cambridge University Press, 1984), p. 31.

51. Quoted in Janet Wallach and John Wallach, *Arafat: In the Eyes of the Beholder* (New York: Lyle Stuart, 1990), p. 197.

52. Radio Damascus, 18 June 1985.

53. *Il Messaggero*, 25 September 1989.

54. Quoted in Charles Glass, *Tribes with Flags: A Dangerous Passage Through the Chaos of the Middle East* (New York: Atlantic Monthly Press, 1990), p. 324.

55. *Jomhuri-ye Islami*, 5 August 1991. Such a statement made sense after September 1993 but not before then.

56. Quoted in Patrick Seale, *Abu Nidal: A Gun for Hire* (New York: Random House, 1992), p. 43.

57. Charles Saint-Prot, *Les Mystères syriens: La Politique au Proche-Orient de 1970 à 1984* (Paris: Albin Michel, 1984), pp. 22-23.

58. Anon., *Al-Muslimun fi Suriya wa'l-Irhab an-Nusayri, 1964-1979* (Cairo: n.p., n.d.), p. 72. President Hafiz al-Asad adheres to the 'Alawi religion.

59. Anon., *As-Siyasa al-Kharijiya li-Nizam Hafiz al-Asad* (Beirut: Dar Bardi, n.d.), p. 46.

60. *Ad-Dustur*, 24 January 1983.

61. Jabir Rizq, *Al-Ikhwan al-Muslimun w'al-Mu'amara 'ala Suriya* (Cairo: Dar al-I'tisam, 1980), p. 97.

62. *Ath-Thawra* (Baghdad), 7 October 1989.

63. Quoted in Fawaz Turki, *Exile's Return: The Making of a Palestinian American* (New York: Free Press, 1994), p. 76.

64. 'Ali Salih as-Sa'di, a former secretary-general of the Ba'th Party in Iraq, quoted in Sami Yousef, "The Iraqi-US War: A Conspiracy Theory," in Haim Bresheeth and Nira Yuval-Davis, eds., *The Gulf War and the New World Order* (London: Zed, 1991), p. 58.

65. *Al-Ahram*, 27 September 1963. Cited in Hanna Batatu, *The Old Social Classes and the Revolutionary Movements of Iraq: A Study of Iraq's Old Landed and Commercial Classes and of Its Communists, Ba'thists, and Free Officers* (Princeton, N.J.: Princeton University Press, 1978), pp. 985-86.

66. Joyce N. Wiley, *The Islamic Movement of Iraqi Shi'as* (Boulder, Col.: Lynne Rienner, 1992), p. 66, fn. 2.

67. *Ruz al-Yusuf*, 25 December 1995.

68. *Le Monde*, 14-15 October 1990.

69. *Al-Majalla*, 9-15 January 1991.

70. *Jordan Times*, 23 March 1991.

71. *The Jerusalem Report*, 14 March 1991.

72. Islamic Revolution News Agency, 26 February 1991.

73. National Voice of Iran, 24 June 1983.

74. Free Voice of Iran, 27 October 1982.

75. 'Abdallah Muhammad al-Gharib, *Wa-Ja' Dawr al-Majus: Al-Ab'ad at-Ta'rikhiya wa'l-'Aqa'idiya wa's-Siyasiya li'th-Thawra al-Iraniya* (Cairo: Dar al-Jil, 1983), pp. 260-96.

76. *The Guardian*, 3 March 1989.

77. Islamic Revolution News Agency, 5 May 1989.

78. *Al-Akhbar* (Cairo), 7 May 1989.

79. *Al-Liwa'*, 8 December 1987.

80. *Jomhuri-ye Islami*, 17 September 1991.

81. Islamic Revolution News Agency, 26 April 1992.

82. Statement of 22 July 1966. Quoted in P. J. Vatikiotis, *Nasser and His Generation* (New York: St. Martin's Press, 1978), p. 282.

83. *Al-Hawadith*, 25 October 1991.

84. Sawt Filastin (Sanaa), 10 July 1990.

85. Great Jamahiriya Radio, 28 June 1995.

86. Salah al-Mukhtar, writing in *Babil*, 16 February 1994.

87. Minister of State 'Ali al-Hajj, quoted in *Ar-Ra'y* (Amman), 30 June 1995.

88. May 1980 Al-Fat'h conference, text in Raphael Israeli, ed., *PLO in Lebanon: Selected Documents* (New York: St. Martin's Press, 1983), p. 12.

89. Quoted in Alan Hart, *Arafat: A Political Biography* (Bloomington: Indiana University Press, 1989), p. 79.

90. Leaflet No. 28 of Hamas. Text in Shaul Mishal and Reuben Aharoni, *Speaking Stones: Communiqués from the Intifada Underground* (Syracuse, N.Y.: Syracuse University Press, 1994), p. 237.

91. Quoted in Rashid Khalidi, *Under Siege: P.L.O. Decisionmaking During the 1982 War* (New York: Columbia University Press, 1986), p. 148.

92. Leaflet No. 2 of Hamas. Text in Mishal and Aharoni, *Speaking Stones*, p. 206.

93. Hannah Arendt, *The Origins of Totalitarianism*, 2d ed. (Cleveland: Meridian Books, World Publishing, 1958), p. 471.

94. *As-Safir*, 16 July 1994.

95. Jamahiriya Arab News Agency, 23 November 1993.

96. *The Middle East*, August 1992.

97. Taghi Modarressi, *The Pilgrim's Rules of Etiquette* (New York: Doubleday, 1989), p. 171.

98. *International Documents on Palestine, 1979*, p. 26.

99. Tehran International Service, 7 August 1990.

Part IV

# WHY SO MANY
# CONSPIRACY THEORIES?

Tariq 'Aziz, the foreign minister of Iraq, mused shortly after the Kuwait war on the question why conspiracy theories "exist more in our part of the world than elsewhere." Because, he suggested, the Middle East has oil, a strategic position, and Israel.[1]

This observation contains two points of interest. First, 'Aziz assumes that the Middle East hosts more conspiracy theories than other regions, an impression that may well be accurate. Though parallel fears of conspiracy are found in many other regions, rarely do they have quite the same pervasive and consequential qualities as in the Middle East. 'Aziz then offers three sensible explanations for the profusion of conspiracy theories in the Middle East. Oil points to the maneuvering for commercial advantage. Strategic location suggests great power interests in sea lanes, bases, and allies. Israel raises the Arab-Israeli conflict and its many implications.

Part IV takes up these issues. Why do not just the cranks and the fringe in the Middle East subscribe to terrible and unverifiable conspiracy theories, but also leading figures? Has this always been the case there? Will it always be?

# 14.

# The Trauma of Modern Islam

A Westerner takes the credit for his own successes and
blames himself for his failures. An Arabian thanks
God for the good things and blames the bad on evil
influences beyond his control.
—*Robert Lacey*[1]

Our forefathers gave praise to God for their successes,
and laid the blame for their failures on their sins and
shortcomings. . . . We thank ourselves for our
successes, and lay the blame for our failures on others.
—*M. Plessner*[2]

The two Western authors cited in the epigraphs above, Lacey and
Plessner, argue contrary hypotheses. Lacey points to a dividing line
along religious lines, while Plessner sees the real division having to do with
chronology. Is one of them right? Is the Muslim by nature different from
the Westerner? Or has he, with the rest of the world, changed over time?

## COMMONLY CITED FACTORS

Analysts have postulated several reasons to explain widespread conspiracism in the Middle East: the region's history of domination, Iranian child-
rearing practices, the religions of Iran, and the nature of Islam.

## History of Domination

The geographic centrality of the Middle East within the Eurasian and African landmass, plus its permeability by sea, have made the region particularly susceptible to foreign conquest. Virtually all would-be world conquerors (Alexander, Caesar, Tamerlane, Napoleon) made their way to the region or (Chinggis Khan, Wilhelm II, Hitler, Brezhnev) sent troops there. The result is very striking: for centuries, aliens dominated the Middle East. In Egypt, not a single son of the Nile ruled the country between 525 B.C. and A.D. 1952; for 2,500 years rulers came from areas as diverse as Iran and Great Britain, Ethiopia, and Albania. A similar pattern of foreign domination obtained in other Middle East states, too, especially Syria, Iraq, and Iran. This pattern persisted into modern times, when Western powers controlled most of the region.

The legacy of foreign rule fueled nationalist anger and nativist suspicion, sentiments that may have foreshadowed conspiracism. Already in the mid-nineteenth century, Egyptians harked back to Pharaonic splendors and blamed foreigners for causing Egypt to lose its ancient greatness. In the twentieth, Gamal Abdel Nasser (the son of the Nile who seized power in 1952) had a personal sense of the harm done Egypt by centuries of foreign rule and aroused his listeners with frequent references to foreign sabotage. In other countries, too, foreign conquest continues to be blamed for a range of ills, creating a mood conducive to conspiracism. Looking at Iran, Ervand Abrahamian holds that the paranoid style "can be explained by history, especially Iran's experience of imperial domination."[3] "Bombarded from early childhood with stories of foreign intrigue, machinations, intervention, and nefarious practices," Jahangir Amuzegar finds it only natural that most Iranians, even the most sophisticated ones, "harbor a nagging suspicion in the darkest recesses of their minds that nothing significant ever happens in their country without some foreign interest and involvement."[4]

## Iranian Child-Rearing Practices

Picking up on Amuzegar's emphasis on childhood, some analysts see conspiracism as a habit of mind inculcated into children, especially in Iran. Sattareh Farman Farmaian, an American-educated Persian, points to this. "Taught from childhood to be quick-witted and alert to others' moods that they might know better who was a friend and who an enemy, many Persians learned to admire those who were wily and good at dissembling, since cleverness and disguising one's true feelings often seemed the only way to survive against a stronger force."[5] Anne Sinclair Mehdevi, an American woman living in Iran and married to an Iranian, noted the approprobation given such behavior. She "was constantly regaled with stories of rascality and guile, stories told with pretenses of censure but which really gave all kudos to the trespasser . . . almost every day some member of our family came home with a tale of how he had been shamelessly but cleverly fleeced."[6] Marvin Zonis and Craig M. Joseph develop this observation into a systematic argument: the "intense or chronic psychosocial stressors" of Arab-Iranian-Muslim culture — secrecy, early childhood experience, and sexuality in particular — prompts "paranoid or paranoid-like ideation." This in turn creates a propensity to rely on conspiracy theories.[7]

## Iranian Religions

The religions of ancient Iran — Zoroastrianism, Manicheanism, and Mazdakism — contained notions of a perpetual battle between good and evil that may have started the tradition of Middle East conspiracism.

Zarathustra (in Greek, Zoroaster) founded the religion named after him in about 600 B.C. in Iran. In his theology, the one God, Ahura Mazda, had two sons. Zarathustra associated one of them with light, good, truth, justice, and life, the other with the opposite attributes. The combat of these two sons and the forces they represent determines the course of human history. Through this dualistic cosmology of good and evil, Zarathustra in effect took evil out of the hands of humans and ascribed it to larger forces.

Mani built on these ideas, founding the religion named after him in Iran during the mid-third century A.D. Manicheanism featured a complex theology about the forces of Light and Darkness engaged in a cosmic battle. The religion's dualism, which sets the forces of evil on a perpetual mission to overwhelm the forces of goodness, makes it particularly hospitable to the conspiracy mentality. Manicheanism spread as far as Spain in the west and China in the east, but it had the most impact in the Middle East, where it flourished for about 600 years before dying out in about the fourteenth century. Still, its influence remains vigorous, intermediated through Iranian culture and Christian and Islamic doctrines.

Mazdakism developed from Manicheanism. It holds that the principles of Good and Evil coexist, and that man releases Good through moral and ascetic activities — or Evil through bad behavior.

All three Iranian religions postulate the existence of an evil force so strong that it causes the concept of sin to shrink in importance. Evil no longer results from human weakness but derives from a universal force. This approach reifies the devil, enhancing his role and diminishing that of humans. If evil becomes a force in its own right, the global conspirator exists. Derivative conspiracies are easy to imagine. Those in the know believe that Good is fated to defeat Evil; therefore, they pursue a triumphalist eschatology; they are even ready to destroy the world to eradicate the evil in it.

Dualistic thinking still holds Middle Easterners in thrall. Here is Saddam Husayn, delivering his 1990 Christmas message: "The evildoers stand on one side, led by Satan, and the good people stand on another side, governed by lofty values dictated by God Almighty."[8] Accordingly, current Middle Eastern fears of conspiracy might connect back to Zoroastrian, Manichean, and Mazdak sources.

## The Nature of Islam

Islam may also play a role, especially in its concepts of political order and fatalism; and in the Shi'i traditions of esotericism, dissimulation, and martyrdom.

The adage "better a 100 years of repression than a day of anarchy" sums of the dread of anarchy (*fitna*) that lies deep in Islamic civilization. This alarm at the prospect of disorder might incubate conspiracy theories. Musawi of Islamic Amal raised the prospect that "one spy could cause widespread sedition that could destroy a sect and a community, Sedition is the work of polytheist forces hostile to God and against the interests of Islam and the Muslims."[9] If one spy can destroy the social order, what can a single conspirator do?

Others point to the fatalism inculcated by Islam. Kanan Makiya sees the "extreme fatalism . . . that may be a characteristic of Islamic culture generally" as a key explanation for conspiracy theories. In his view, this outlook undermines the notion of man as responsible to himself.[10] Likewise, Homa Katouzian traces conspiracy theories to an "unimaginable fatalism"; and Jahangir Amuzegar ascribes them to a "fatalistic streak."[11]

Three aspects of Shi'i Islam may have a role here: hidden meaning, dissimulation, and martyrdom. Religious authority derives in part from an ability to locate hidden meanings: "To be regarded as a [holy] sheikh in the fullest sense means that the individual has to establish [a] personal reputation for knowledge and insight into what the ordinary, lay eye does not see."[12] Shi'i esotericism holds that the Qur'an has two or more meanings: an external (*zahir*) one directed to the hoi polloi and internal (*batin*) ones addressed to the elect. The latter can become so arcane that, in the end, they lose any connection to the overt text. Shi'a imbue a great many phrases of the Qur'an with references to Imam 'Ali or the later imams, thereby constructing a mental world of no fixed points. Such emphasis on the hidden may conduce to conspiracism.

*Taqiya,* the Shi'i practice of dissimulating for self-protection and the preserve of faith, appears to create an environment of suspicion and intrigue that lends itself to the conspiracism.

*Taqiya* distinguishes between external appearance and internal faith; it usually takes the form of hiding one's Shi'i identity and pretending to be a Sunni Muslim. Its spirit is captured in a saying of the Syrian 'Alawis (also known as Nusayris), a breakaway Shi'i sect: "We are the body and other sects are but clothing. However a man dresses does not change him. So we remain always Nusayris, even though we externally adopt the practices of our neighbors. Whoever does not dissimulate is a fool, for no intelligent person goes naked in the market."[13] *Taqiya* permits a Shi'i to pray with Sunnis, even while silently cursing the Sunni caliphs, and to raise children falsely to tell strangers they are Sunnis. Only Shi'i Islam formally incorporates the doctrine of *taqiya,* but the practice has echoes among Sunnis, especially fundamentalists. For example, Muhammad 'Abd as-Salam Faraj, the intellectual behind the group that assassinated Anwar as-Sadat in 1981, quoted the medieval writer an-Nawawi to the effect that "lying is essentially permitted, but it is better to limit oneself to speaking ambiguously."[14]

Finally, the Shi'i tradition of martyrdom *(shihada)*, writes anthropologist William O. Beeman, causes Iranians to externalize evil. Corruption occurs when individuals lack the strength to resist these forces from without. "As internal conditions become more and more difficult, the tendency is to search for external conspiracy."[15]

Before considering further how the concepts of *fitna, batin, taqiya,* and *shihada* might induce conspiracism in the Middle East, we take up a quite different subject, the question of conspiracy theories in premodern Islam. The connection will become readily apparent.

## FEW CONSPIRACY THEORIES IN PREMODERN ISLAM

Is the paranoid style an endemic feature of the Middle East and an unchanging feature of Islamic life? Some writers think so. John Stempel of the State Department points to "Iran's traditional xenophobia" to account for the Persian tendency to blame their troubles "on outside invaders such as the Mongols or the Arabs."[16] Peter Hopkirk, a historian, says that the intrigues widespread in Istanbul during World War I "had always been part of the natural order of things."[17] Walid Mahmoud Abdelnasser, an Egyptian diplomat and writer, notes a "tradition of Muslim intellectuals since the time of the Crusades and the tatar [i.e., Mongol] invasion to blame all the ills of Muslim countries on foreign threats and incursions."[18]

## A Legacy of Success

But Stempel, Hopkirk, and Abdelnasser are wrong to maintain that Muslims have for centuries resorted to conspiracy theories; in fact, through the great sweep of premodern Muslim history, A.D. 600 to 1800, Muslims rarely depended on the hidden hand to understand the world around them. To the contrary, they displayed a vaulting confidence very much at odds with the fearful mood of conspiracism.

Islam's exceptionally successful earthly career imbued premodern Muslims with high self-esteem. The Prophet Muhammad went from outcast to powerful ruler in the course of a mere eight years, 622 to 630. It took his community less than 100 years to gain an empire reaching from Spain to India. For centuries hence, Muslims were stronger, richer, and more civilized than any of their neighbors. The conjunction of Islam and high worldly standing quickly became seen as a matter of right; the well-being of Muslims implicitly confirmed the truth of Muhammad's prophecy. Muslims came to assume that God rewarded the faithful with bounty on earth, and found justification for this in the well-known Qur'anic assertion that "You [Muslims] are the best of peoples" (3:110). The connection of Islam to power seemed natural and inevitable; it even acquired a theological cast. As the French orientalist Louis Gardet writes, Muslims "had an innate respect for the force that triumphs, for there is no success other than what is wished for and blessed by God."[19]

Of course, individuals here and there resorted to petty conspiracy theories during the millennium of Muslim leadership. The absence of an accepted pattern of dynastic succession in Muslim dynasties, for example, caused much infighting and more than a few plots. But the record shows hardly any grand conspiracy theories (belief that an enemy seeks universal power) or the conspiracy mentality (the paranoid fear of a far-ranging plot directed against oneself).[20]

Assaults by European Christians on the Muslim patrimony hardly dented these superior feelings. Muslims made no serious effort to understand the reasons behind the Crusades, a series of unprovoked invasions from Europe that began in 1097 and lasted three and a half centuries. While the Franks acquitted themselves creditably—signaling troubles to come—Muslims hardly bestirred themselves to learn about these aliens living in their midst. A Syrian aristocrat, Usama ibn Munqidh (1095-1188), articulated the casual arrogance of the Muslims toward the uncouth hordes from Europe when he noted that "those who have recently arrived from the land of the Franks are coarser in manners than those who have acclimatized and lived longer among Muslims."[21] This scornful attitude, already outdated by Usama ibn Munqidh's time, was even more inaccurate in 1400 when Ibn Khaldun (1332-1406), the great North African historian, offered a nonchalant appraisal of the Europeans:

> We are told that philosophical learning is flourishing in the land of the Franks of Ruma [in this context, Italy] and what lies beyond it along the northern shore [of the Mediterranean]. Philosophical thought is said to be revived, its instruction widespread, its books comprehensive, its scholars numerous, and its students many. But God alone knows what goes on over there![22]

Over the centuries, then, Muslims dismissed European Christians as barbarians deserving little attention.

## Falling Behind

The connection between Islam and power began to fray in the sixteenth and seventeenth centuries, as the northern savages made great advances in science and technology, as their standard of living began to rise markedly, and as their projection of power far outpaced that of the Muslims. Before Muslims quite understood what hit them, Europeans had engaged in global explorations, trade, and conquests that directly challenged Muslims.

Muslims initially responded to their traditional antagonists' surge of power and wealth without resort to conspiracy theories. Instead, they continued to indulge in a traditional superciliousness toward Franks. Certain of their civilization's superiority, they presumed that Muslim problems resulted from inadequacies in their own faith and slippage from earlier standards of behavior. As borders shrunk and economic decline set in, thinkers and politicians looked into their own culture and behavior to ascertain the causes for their misfortune. Intense Muslim introspection produced a wealth of analyses seeking to locate the inner sources of weakness—quite the opposite of conspiracism.

Even as they fell behind, Muslims most in contact with developments in Europe (Ottomans principally) shared these scornful attitudes toward the Franks. Far from succumbing to conspiracy theories, smug Muslim analysts slighted developments in Christendom that very much deserved their attention. Although compelled to take some notice of Europe, they did so grudgingly, with an intent to absorb no more than the necessary information from the Christian West. "The Ottomans," writes historian Lewis V. Thomas, "as leaders of the Muslim world and Muslim civilization, had grown to be so self-contained, so sure that they themselves embodied the good and the true, that they failed to pay the indispensable minimum of attention to the 'heathen.'"[23] To their later regret, immutably superior feelings led the Ottoman Turks to ignore the earth-shaking developments taking place in their vicinity.

Although this bias began to erode in the eighteenth century, Muslims still found it exceedingly difficult to get themselves to make use of Europe's powerful new inventions. For example, Jews had set up the first printing press in Istanbul as early as 1488, but Muslims chose to continue to rely on manuscripts for almost another 250 years; only in 1729 did they avail themselves of publishing (and even then only under the influence of a Hungarian convert and only for 13 years). The Turks ignored other industrial and mechanical advances in similar fashion. When they did avail themselves of European products (guns, ships, watches, spectacles) and techniques (for shipbuilding, mining minerals, medicine), they did so in a vacuum, without understanding the philosophical and scientific breakthroughs behind these innovations. As Bernard Lewis writes, "the discoveries of Parcelsus and Copernicus, of Kepler and of Galileo, were as alien and as irrelevant to the Ottomans as were the arguments of Luther and Calvin."[24]

Ottoman Muslims persisted in looking inward to understand their decline from grace. Reviewing the many inquiries into the floundering state of the Ottoman Empire that were commissioned around 1800, historian Stanford Shaw notes that "inevitably their solutions followed the same pattern—follow the old laws, restore the old ways, eliminate the abuses."[25] Roderic Davison notes that this "backward-looking reform" continued well into the nineteenth century, long after the European powers had proven their overwhelming power.[26] For example, the Hatt-i Sherif of

Gülhane, promulgated in 1839 as one of the key westernizing documents of its age, begins this way:

> All the world knows that since the first days of the Ottoman State, the lofty principles of the Qur'an and the rules of the Shari'a were always perfectly observed. Our mighty Sultanate reached the highest degree of strength and power, and all its subjects [the highest degree] of ease and prosperity.
>
> But in the last one hundred and fifty years, because of a succession of difficulties and diverse causes, the sacred Shari'a was not obeyed nor were the beneficent regulations followed; consequently, the former strength and prosperity have changed into weakness and poverty.[27]

This tradition of taking responsibility for one's circumstances continued until World War I. Abdullah Cevdet, a radical Westernizer, rejected the growing Middle Eastern predisposition to conspiracism, arguing in 1913 that "To believe that the entire world is our enemy and the world of Christianity is working against us is a symptom of persecution mania."[28] Writing a year later, the Pan-Turkic nationalist Ahmet Ağaoğlu blamed Muslim decline on rulers, ulema (religious leaders), and bureaucrats, all of whom had neglected their duties. Rulers were despots, while ulema and bureaucrats appeased the rulers rather than stand up for Islamic principles.

Even later, an ambivalence existed as Middle Easterners wrestled between conspiracism and Realpolitik. Richard Cottam observes that, until the early 1950s, "Iranians simultaneously believed that (a) all of Iran's ills could be ascribed to foreign interference and hence foreign interference per se was an evil, and that (b) foreign interference was inevitable and Iran needed a disinterested foreign power which would support Iranian independence against the avarice of the British and the Russians."[29]

Linguistic evidence confirms the paucity of conspiracy theories before 1800; remarkably, Middle Eastern languages even lacked a word for "conspiracy." Turkish lacking an indigenous term, the modern language uses the word *komplo,* a transliteration of the French *complot.* To conspire is rendered *komplo kurmak* (to prepare a plot). Until the twentieth century, the Arabic word for conspiracy, *mu'amara,* meant consultation. In Persian, too, *tawti'a* and *dasisa* came to mean conspiracy only in the modern era.

How could Muslims so firmly believe their problems resulted from Muslim weakness and not foreign strength? Mostly this resulted from a deep sense of superiority. It also had to do with two other factors, one geographic and the other historical. First, Muslim trade and travel routes hardly touched European ones, so that adherents of the two religions rarely encountered each other; this permitted Muslims to continue delude themselves that their civilization remained preeminent.

Second, Muslims first became aware of Europe during the eighth to tenth centuries A.D., exactly the low ebb in European history. The disdain for Europe formed then remained a long-lived prejudice for the next millennium. When Europe surged ahead, Muslims kept their old attitudes, too self-absorbed to notice. As Muslims fell in arrears, attitudes from an entirely different era remained in place. Nothing short of a cataclysm could wake them; and when that cataclysm came, they were wholly unprepared.

In short, Muslims did not resort on conspiracy theories or other facile explanations to account for their failings until sometime after the year 1800. Whereas seventeenth-century Ottomans located failings within themselves, Arabs and Iranians today blame others for everything from a poor tomato crop to a military defeat. Conspiracy theories are a phenomenon of the past century or two.

## Implications

That Muslims did not indulge in conspiracism before 1800 has a highly important implication for understanding their causation: explanations have to account for its appearance in modern times. Something happened in the nineteenth century. Because static phenomena cannot account for change, permanent features (such as the region's geography or its religious practices) cannot account for conspiracism, just as a mountain range does not cause a war, a river cannot cause a revolution. Long-established faiths such as Zoroastrianism and Islam change too little to explain the burst of conspiracism in modern times.

Change causes change; the main factors behind conspiracy theories, then, are historical in nature. Islam can be a factor, but only in so far as it changed. That is, the Qur'an's verities matter here less than its modern evolution.

Two questions need to be answered: What happened to the Middle East over the past century plus that caused conspiracy theories to flourish? What caused those changes to stay in place? This chapter addresses the first question, pointing to the trauma of European dominion. The remainder of part IV takes up the second question: conspiracy theories then proliferated due to the impact of European thought, the incidence of real intrigue, and the region's political structures.

## TWO CENTURIES OF FRUSTRATION

The Muslims' anachronistic sense of superiority contained within it the seeds of the paranoid style; the arrogance of one age turned into the conspiracy mentality of the next. After 1800, the Middle East hosted ideal conditions for a florescence of conspiracism.

### A Triumphalist Legacy

Napoleon's conquest of Egypt in 1798 marked the symbolic moment when Muslims no longer could delude themselves about the irrelevance of Europe; as such it opened a new era in the Middle East. Foreign invasion drove home to Muslims a wide range of problems — cultural backwardness, poverty, psychological humiliation — thereby sundering the link between Islam and worldly success. As historian Elie Kedourie notes, "military defeat was defeat not only in a worldly sense; it also brought into doubt the truth of the Muslim revelation itself."[30]

Even two centuries later, the West's success continues to pose many dilemmas, few of which receive satisfactory answers. Muslims have to account for the terrible gap between a millennium of history and the realities of contemporary life, between past triumphs and current disappointments. What happened to leave Muslims defeated and poor? Had Muslim devotions become inadequate, did their faith lose validity, or did the Europeans subscribe to a faith more favored in God's eyes?

Muslims have found it very difficult to answer these questions, in part because memories of past glories invoked a disdain for the West at time when respect would be more appropriate. "As a community, Muslims are burdened with the triumphalist legacy of an imperialist past."[31] Wilfred Cantwell Smith explains Muslim outrage at the modern predicament with great insight:

> The Islamic tradition was formed on the principle that destiny is in the hands of God. It is Allah who controls events. The Mu'tazilah [a group that flourished in the early Islamic period] and others argued the point: some Muslims have felt that, under God, destiny was in their own hands. The recent bitterness was that it seemed to be neither God nor the Muslims who controlled events but the British or Americans — the domineering, discourteous, brash infidels who suddenly pushed themselves noisily on the scene.[32]

Cultural crisis followed, as the Muslims' traditional sense of superiority vis-à-vis Christian Europeans rapidly turned into pervasive insecurity. An official at the Dome of the Rock in Jerusalem captured the plaintive quality of this situation: "Before, we were masters of the world, and now, we're not even masters of our own mosques!"[33]

The sense that history has gone wrong leads many Muslims to see their fall from grace resulting not from the West's achievements but from its treachery and conspiracy. Muslims expected the area of their sovereign rule (Dar al-Islam) to expand without limit, but instead it almost vanished, prompting dire suspicions. Fundamentalist Muslims tend especially to see modern history as one gigantic trick by the West. In a typical observation, Khamene'i of Iran blames the Muslims' predicament on the "materialist, arrogant, powerful, unbridled, selfish, haughty, and bullying hands of the arrogant powers."[34] Similarly, Saddam Husayn held that "If only God Almighty spared the peoples of the Middle East the evil intentions of other powers, then they would never have lived with war, destruction, and problems. The wars in the Middle East are brought from overseas, not from the Middle East."[35] Confronted with failures, Muslim conspiracy theorists chose see themselves as victims rather than accept their own responsibility.

By thus blaming their problems on Western evil, weakened Muslim peoples find solace and the means to cope with crisis. Conspiracism permits them to escape responsibility for weakness and poverty; were it not for Western intrigues against Islam, they tell themselves, Muhammad's people would still enjoy their former superiority over Europe. Conspiracism allows Middle Easterners to see themselves as powerful but naïve, as enervated and exploited by conniving Western agents. An unlikely turn of speech dating from 1891 captures this sentiment: "Mussulman lambs are being devoured by European foxes."[36]

Blaming so much on outside powers implies a harking back to a time in the past when things were better. Plots go far to explain how past glories degenerated into today's tribulations. Young Egypt (Misr al-Fat'h), a fascistic group with much influence on the young Gamal Abdel Nasser, held that Egypt had been a great center of power and civilization until ruined by Great Britain. "Were it not for English policy, intervening and inciting against us, we would be over all today."[37] Specifically, London sabotaged Egyptian unity after 1919 by sponsoring competing political parties; Ahmad Husayn, founder of Young Egypt, held that parties undercut political will and corrupted the country's virtues by introducing usury, prostitution, and gambling.

## Special Muslim Difficulties

Problematic aspects of the Christian-Muslim relationship further explain the great appeal of conspiracy theories in the modern Middle East.

First, the West historically had far worse relations with the Muslim world than with any other major civilization, making it more difficult for Muslims to accept Europe's ascension. This pattern began at the very dawn of Islam: in a sermon on Christmas Eve in 634, for example, the patriarch of Jerusalem referred to the Muslims as "the slime of the godless Saracens [that] threatens slaughter and destruction."[38] Such antagonism predominated on the Christian side for centuries. And not wholly without reason: with just one exception (the Mongols), Muslims launched every serious military threat against Christendom after the tenth century. In all, the Muslim danger continued to preoccupy Christians of Europe for more than a millennium, until some years after the second siege of Vienna in 1683.

European hostility persisted even longer, well into the modern era. It is hard in this era to conjure up the outspoken hostility that intellectual and political leaders showed to Islam. By way of example, here are three typical British writers discussing the Prophet Muhammad. Richard Chenevix (1774-1830), an important chemist and mineralogist, held that "Mahomet was, perhaps the most dexterous, as well as the most enthusiastic imposter whom the world has beheld."[39] William Muir (1819-1905), the prominent Scottish administrator in India and scholar of Islam, evoked this sentiment in his biography of the Islamic prophet: "the sword of Mohammad, and the Kor'an, are the most stubborn enemies of Civilisation, Liberty, and Truth which the world has yet known."[40] Charles Doughty (1843-1926), the English poet and traveler through Arabia, termed Islam a "thin-witted religion" and said this of Muhammad: "the household and sheykhly virtues that were in him—mildness and comity and simplicity and good faith, in things indifferent of the daily life—cannot amend our opinion of the Arabian man's barbaric ignorance, his sleight and murderous cruelty in the institution of his religious faction; or sweeten our contempt of an hysterical prophetism and polygamous living."[41] Vilification of the Prophet Muhammad represents just the most visible tip of Europe's deep antagonism to Islam. Such attitudes did much to obstruct the Muslim ability to emulate Europe.

While this animus has faded, Westerners remain fearful of Islam even today. Terrorism, rogue states, unconventional weapons, and protracted warfare combine to create intense worry. When asked in March 1994, "Which country today do you think poses the biggest threat to world peace?" 26 percent of Americans fingered Middle Eastern states, 17 percent pointed to the ex-Soviet bloc, 16 percent to East Asia, 1 percent to Western Europe, and 3 percent to other regions.[42]

Second, Muslims harbored negative feelings of their own toward the Christian West. Christianity has always been Islam's main spiritual rival. For centuries, Crusaders landed in Muslim lands, unpredictable except in their readiness to kill Muslims. Between 1757 and 1919, European imperialists conquered nearly the whole of the Muslim world; only those regions either contested among European powers (Turkey, Iran, Afghanistan) or very remote from them (Arabia, Yemen) escaped the humiliation of colonial rule. With their religious imperative for independence, Muslims found colonialism even more degrading than did other peoples. Faced with Europeans' might, military heroes emerged in all parts of the Muslim world to fend them off. Names such 'Abd al-Qadir in Algeria, 'Umar al-Mukhtar in Libya, the Mahdi Muhammad Ahmad in Sudan, the "Mad Mullah" in Somalia, Muhammad 'Urabi in Egypt, Sultan al-Atrash in Syria, Kemal Atatürk in Turkey, and Shamil in the Caucasus remain revered today.

These problems going back centuries translate into a vituperation on the part of some Muslims, extreme leftists in previous decades and extreme fundamentalist Muslims these days. Muslim hostility remains very much alive in recent years. While only a minority in the Muslim world, fundamentalist Muslims have a powerful voice that very much affects the tenor of relations with the West.

Fundamentalists hate the West and harp on its evil nature. Take the case of Iran. The leader of the Islamic revolution, 'Ali Hoseyni Khamene'i, considers the United States "the mother of corruption of the century."[43] Naturally, Iranian schoolchildren get indoctrinated with this outlook: a 14-year-old Iranian reports learning from her teacher that "Everything in the West is bad; everyone in America is going to hell when they die."[44]

Third, Muslim civilization contained many elements that rendered it a poor fit with the culture and customs of nineteenth-century Europe. As the French diplomat Louis de Corancez observed in 1810 about life in Syria and Egypt, "After scouring the whole world, we shall nowhere find such peculiar usages, such diverse customs, observances so different from ours."[45] Whatever it was that Muslims held dear—political ties based on religious solidarity, a legal system deriving from divine revelation, a daily life bound by religious precepts, social disabilities for religious minorities, or keeping men and women apart—Westerners almost invariably scorned as wrong or backward. These differences raised the hurdles Muslims had to leap over and encumbered their adoption of Western ways.

Finally, Muslims faced not just the imperialist enemy but also Zionism, a frightening and humiliating secondary foe. The West, with its huge population and vast geographic expanse, at least represents Islam's millennial nemesis; but Jews were long a powerless and despised people who even today number less than 15 million and control a tiny piece of land. That Jews have consistently defeated Muslims through this century deeply challenged Muslim self-perceptions and inspired reckless attempts to find an explanation. Conspiracy theories fit the bill.

## Avoid Unpleasant Facts

When a person comes upon information at odds with his beliefs, what psychologists call "cognitive dissonance" results.[46] This situation presents him with two unhappy alternatives: adopt new beliefs to fit the new facts, or find ways justifying the old beliefs. The first response is tantamount to an admission of error and so is difficult to do; as a rational step, it does not concern us here. The second response, which entails an insistence on the validity of one's original belief, is highly tempting, for no one likes to admit error. Conspiracy thinking, Marvin Zonis notes, "can be seen as a means for individuals in the throes of a sense-making crisis to construct a meaningful world after a profound disturbance in self—self-object relationships."[47]

This course entails the adoption of explanations to shore up that belief. These may be irrational, but that is acceptable so long as they help bridge the gap between old beliefs and new evidence. Conspiracy theories (along with propaganda and rumors) serve as one of the most powerful mechanisms for reducing dissonance, especially when the matter cuts close to home. "The more important the subject and the greater the number of beliefs that would have to be changed if the causes of an event were seen as deep-seated, the greater the acceptance of conspiracy theories."[48]

What applies personal level holds on the even more to groups. The larger the number of persons involved, the easier it becomes to deny the evidence of one's own eyes and to ignore the discrepancy between beliefs and reality; and the easier it is to make conspiracy theories operational. When an entire society experiences dissonance, the temptation becomes very great to resort to the irrational. Accordingly, conspiracy theories tend to flourish especially among those buffeted by circumstances, including those inhabiting the fringes of political life and those heavily weighed down by problems. Almost any sort of severe dislocation—natural disaster, social upheaval, political instability, or foreign invasion—creates the need for an answer to the question: Why has this happened to me, who is basically a good person—or to my society, which is virtuous? Stress inspires a need for culprits; this often means rooting out evildoers intent on conspiracy.

This approach greatly appeals to Middle Easterners, who review their modern history and find a record incommensurate with their own sense of destiny. To "avoid the shame of having to admit that the event was their own societies' fault,"[49] they turned to the hidden hand. In about 1905, the Druze leader Shakib al-Arslan said that "the evils under which we suffer are due to the foreign nations who refuse to allow the Turkish empire to move in any direction.[50] Soon after, the Committee of Union and Progress (the "Young Turks") promoted a conspiracy mentality that had wide influence on the Ottoman successor states.

Over time, conspiracism filled a growing need. The frustration of the Mosaddeq episode of 1951-53 prompted Iranians to find "an explanation of Anglo-American cleverness more comforting than an explanation that would force them to examine their own vulnerability."[51] When the magnitude of the Iraqi defeat in 1991 had become undeniable, Saddam's enthusiasts avoided the terrible reality by taking recourse to conspiracy theories. Iraqis tended to blame double-crossing by Saddam's subordinates. Jordanians faulted the Arab regimes for deceiving their Iraqi brethren: "We are betrayed . . . it was an Arab treachery"; "They left us alone to confront twenty-eight countries"; "I put the blame on all Arab regimes." Others blamed the West for trickery: "Misinformation has succeeded in affecting Arab people psychologically. It was aimed at destroying and weakening the Arab spirit through its poisonous means and devious methods."[52]

Another case along these lines occurred in December 1994, when fundamentalist Muslims captured an Air France jet on Algerian soil and killed three foreign passengers before flying to Marseilles. There, French commandos attacked the plane, fatally injuring all four hijackers but none of the passengers. Humiliated by the French success and their own failure to deal with the hijacking, Algerian authorities resorted to hints about French collusion with the hijackers. The Algerian interior minister noted French unwillingness to have all the passengers released while the plane was still in Algiers; along similar lines, one newspaper, *L'Authentique,* wondered if the French "manipulated" the hijackers to get them to France and cast a suspicious eye on the fact that all four of the captors were in the cockpit of the plane when it was assaulted.[53]

Conspiracy theories reveal more about the speaker's unwillingness to take responsibility for himself than about the actual behavior of others.

Like many other peoples who find events too painful to be faced rationally, modern Muslims have found solace in conspiracy theories.

The appeal of conspiracy theories lies largely in their utility: they help a people unhappy with current circumstances to explain their predicament while avoiding responsibility for it. These factors go far to explain why conspiracism flourishes in the modern Middle East.

Returning to the question posed at the beginning of this chapter: Plessner is right. The Middle Easterner has changed through contact with the West. Western ideas also had a role in this transformation, as did actual Western conspiracies.

## NOTES TO PART IV INTRODUCTION

1. Quoted in Milton Viorst, *Sandcastles: The Arabs in Search of the Modern World* (New York: Alfred A. Knopf, 1994), p. 345.

## NOTES TO CHAPTER 14

1. Robert Lacey, *The Kingdom* (London: Hutchinson, 1981), p. 386.
2. M. Plessner, "Ist der Zionismus gescheitert?" in Weiner Library, London, *Mitteilungsblatt*, 24 October 1952, no. 42. Quoted in Bernard Lewis, *The Middle East and the West* (London: Weidenfeld and Nicolson, 1963), p. 96.
3. Ervand Abrahamian, *Khomeinism: Essays on the Islamic Republic* (Berkeley: University of California Press, 1993), p.116.
4. Jahangir Amuzegar, *The Dynamics of the Iranian Revolution: The Pahlavis Triumph and Tragedy* (Albany: State University of New York Press, 1991), p. 91.
5. Sattareh Farman Farmaian, with Dona Munker, *Daughter of Persia: A Woman's Journey from Her Father's Harem Through the Islamic Revolution* (New York: Crown, 1992), p. 28.
6. Anne Sinclair Mehdevi, *Persian Adventure* (New York: Alfred A. Knopf, 1953). Quoted in Marvin Zonis, *The Political Elite of Iran* (Princeton, N.J.: Princeton University Press, 1971), pp. 13-14.
7. Marvin Zonis and Craig M. Joseph, "Conspiracy Thinking in the Middle East" (unpublished paper, 1991), pp. 6, 29.
8. Iraqi News Agency, 31 December 1990.
9. Sawt al-Mustad'afin, 3 December 1989.
10. Samir al-Khalil [pseud. of Kanan Makiya], *Republic of Fear: The Politics of Modern Iraq* (Berkeley: University of California Press, 1989), p. 100.

11. Homa Katouzian, *The Political Economy of Modern Iran: Despotism and Pseudo-Modernism, 1926-1979* (New York: New York University Press, 1981), p. 65; Amuzegar, *Dynamics of the Iranian Revolution*, p. 91.

12. M. Gilsenan, *Recognizing Islam: Religion and Society in the Modern Arab World* (New York: Pantheon, 1982), p. 116.

13. Sulayman Efendi al-Adhani, *Kitab al-Bakura as-Sulaymaniya fi Kashf Asrar ad-Diyana an-Nusayriya.* Summary and Arabic extracts in Edward E. Salisbury, "The Book of Sulaiman's First Ripe Fruit: Disclosing the Mysteries of the Nusairian Religion," *Journal of the American Oriental Society* 8 (1866): 298. The third sentence in this quote comes from Henri Lammens, *L'Islam, croyances et institutions*, 2d ed. (Beirut: Imprimerie Catholique, 1941), p. 228.

14. An-Nawawi, *Sahih Muslim bi-Sharh an-Nawawi* (Cairo: Muhammad Tawfiq, Matba'at Hijazi). Quoted in Muhammad 'Abd as-Salam Faraj, *Al-Farida al-Gha'iba.* Trans. Johannes J. G. Jansen, as *The Neglected Duty: The Creed of Sadat's Assassins and Islamic Resurgence in the Middle East* (New York: Macmillan, 1986), pp. 210-211.

15. William O. Beeman, "Images of the Great Satan: Representations of the United States in the Iranian Revolution," in Nikki R. Keddie, ed., *Religion and Politics in Iran: Shi'ism from Quietism to Revolution* (New Haven, Conn.: Yale University Press, 1983), p. 197.

16. John D. Stempel, *Inside the Iranian Revolution* (Bloomington: Indiana University Press, 1981), p. 42.

17. Peter Hopkirk, *Like Hidden Fire: The Plot to Bring Down the British Empire* (New York: Kodansha International, 1994), p.129.

18. Walid Mahmoud Abdelnasser, *The Islamic Movement in Egypt: Perceptions of International Relations, 1967-81* (London: Kegan Paul International, 1994), pp. 220-21.

19. Louis Gardet, *La Cité musulmane: vie sociale et politique* (Paris: Librairie Philosophique J. Vrin, 1954), p. 37.

20. It is not easy to prove a negative. Letters to the author from several leading medievalists (Franz Rosenthal, 28 May 1990, C.E. Bosworth, 1 June 1990, Bernard Lewis, 25 June 1990) confirm this view, as does this author's own research.

21. Usama b. Munqidh, *Kitab al-I'tibar*, ed. P. K. Hitti (Princeton, N.J.: Princeton University Press, 1930), p. 134.

22. Ibn Khaldun, *Al-Muqaddima*, ed. E. Quatremère (Paris: Académie des Inscriptions et Belles-Lettres, 1858), vol. 3, p. 93.

23. Lewis V. Thomas, *A Study of Naima*, ed. Norman Itzkowitz (New York: New York University Press, 1972), pp. 82-83.

24. Bernard Lewis, *The Muslim Discovery of Europe* (New York: W. W. Norton, 1982), pp. 237-38.

25. Stanford J. Shaw, *Between Old and New: The Ottoman Empire Under Sultan Selim III, 1789-1807* (Cambridge, Mass.: Harvard University Press, 1971), p. 110.

26. Roderic H. Davison, *Reform in the Ottoman Empire, 1856-1876* (Princeton, N.J.: Princeton University Press, 1963), p. 19.

27. 3 November 1839. Text in J. C. Hurewitz, *The Middle East and North Africa in World Politics: A Documentary Record*, 2d ed. (New Haven, Conn.: Yale University Press, 1975-79), volume 1, p. 269.

28. Abdullah Cevdet, "Şime-i Muhabbet," *Içtihad*, no. 89 (1913). Quoted in Niyazi Berkes, *The Development of Secularism in Turkey* (Montreal: McGill University Press, 1964), p. 357.

29. Richard Cottam, *Nationalism in Iran* (Pittsburgh: University of Pittsburgh Press, 1964), p. 212.

30. Elie Kedourie, *Islam in the Modern World* (New York: Holt, Rinehart and Winston, 1981), p. 3.

31. Khalid Durán, "Muslims and Non-Muslims," in Leonard Swidler and Paul Mojzes, eds., *Attitudes of Religions and Ideologies Toward the Outsider* (Lewiston: Edwin Mellen Press, 1990), p. 85.

32. Wilfred Cantwell Smith, *Islam in Modern History* (Princeton, N.J.: Princeton University Press, 1957), p. 111.

33. Quoted in Abbas and Magnum Photos, *Allah O Akbar: A Journey Through Militant Islam* (London: Phaidon, 1994), p. 288.

34. Voice of the Islamic Republic of Iran, 3 September 1993.

35. Interview with John Town Albert, Iraqi News Agency, 4 March 1993.

36. Foreign Office 60/522, no. 116, 29 April 1891. Quoted in Nikki R. Keddie, *Sayyid Jamal ad-Din "al-Afghani": A Political Biography* (Berkeley: University of California Press, 1972), p. 339.

37. Ahmad Husayn, *Murafa'at ar-Ra'is: Misr al-Fat'h wa'l-Hukuma amana al-Qada* (Cairo, 1937), p. 31. Quoted in James P. Jankowski, *Egypt's Young Rebels, "Young Egypt": 1933-1952* (Stanford, Calif.: Hoover Institution Press, 1975), p. 47.

38. Sophronius, "Weihnachtspredigt des Sophronos," ed. H. Usener, *Rheinisches Museum für Philologie* N. F. 41 (1886): 506-07

39. Richard Chevenix, *An Essay upon National Character* (London: James Duncan, 1832), vol. 1, p. 96.

40. William Muir, *The Life of Mohammed from Original Sources*, a new and revised edition by T. H. Weir (Edinburgh: John Grant, 1912), p. 522.

41. Charles M. Doughty, *Travels in Arabia Deserta* (New York: Random House, 1937), vol. 1, p. 141; vol. 2, p. 405.

42. "Polls in Four Nations, 1994," unpublished survey conducted by *The New York Times* in the United States and dated 24 March 1994. The survey shows that Britons share American fears of the Middle East, while Germans and Japanese most fear the ex-Soviet bloc.

    A December 1994 poll focused on foreign policy issues rather than foreign countries: it found 16 percent of Americans most worried about Arab-Israeli relations, making this the third most serious concern after Bosnia (25 percent) and instability in the former Soviet Union (17 percent). See *National Journal*, 14 January 1995, p. 130.

43. Voice of the Islamic Republic of Iran, 7 June 1995.

44. *The New York Times Magazine*, 30 April 1995.

45. Louis Alexandre Olivier de Corancez, *Histoire des wahabis; depuis leur origine jusqu'a la fin de 1809* (Paris: Chez Crapart, 1810); trans. by Eric Taber as *The History of the Wahabis from Their Origin until the End of 1809*, (Reading, Eng.: Garnet, 1995), p. 115.

46. The following two paragraphs draw primarily on Leon Festinger, *A Theory of Cognitive Dissonance* (Stanford, Calif.: Stanford University Press, 1957), especially chapters 8-10 on "the role of social support."

47. Marvin Zonis, "Leaders and Publics in the Middle East: Shattering the Organizing Myths of Arab Society," in Stanley A. Renshon, *The Political Psychology of the Gulf War: Leaders, Publics, and the Process of Conflict* (Pittsburgh: University of Pittsburgh Press, 1993), p. 287.

48. Robert Jervis, *Perception and Misperception in International Politics* (Princeton, N.J.: Princeton University Press, 1976), p. 301.

49. Michael Field, *Inside the Arab World* (Cambridge, Mass.: Harvard University Press, 1994), p.167.

50. Gertrude Bell, *The Desert and the Sown* (London: William Heinemann, 1907), p. 152.

51. Richard W. Cottam, *Iran and the United States: A Cold War Case Study* (Pittsburgh: University of Pittsburgh Press, 1988), p. 109.

52. *Jordan Times*, 1 March 1991.

53. *L'Authentique*, 28 December 1994, quoted in *The Philadelphia Inquirer*, 29 December 1994.

# 15.

# The Impact of Western Thought

If intrigue were to depart this life in Europe she would
be born again at Beyrout, and send her offspring to
Damascus to "increase and multiply."
*—Isabel Burton*[1]

The Western imprimatur has great weight in the Middle East, and this applies as to much to conspiracy theories as more conventional exports. When politicians, scholars, and journalists of stature propagate conspiracy theories about their own and allied governments, Middle Easterners listen closely and are predisposed to believe these. In particular, they take seriously remarks about Jews and imperialists coming from the great powers. If Jewish capabilities impress such powerful peoples as the Russians,[2] Americans, French, British, and Germans, who are the Arabs and Iranians to disagree?

## HISTORICAL

### Christian Anti-Semitism

Jews are few in number and vulnerable, so why do they appear to Muslims as one of the two grand conspirators? This question takes on additional force when one remembers that the themes of Christian anti-Semitism, which so magnify the role of Jews, hardly existed in Islam. Islam traditionally had little to parallel the Christian tradition of exaggerating Jewish power.[3] Quite the contrary, Muslim stereotypes stressed Jewish feebleness. Rather than see them as archconspirators plotting to gain world domination, Muslims dismissed them as a people of little consequence, the remnant of an outdated religion. In the Muslim world, Jews were more despised than feared. Bernard Lewis writes that, in the eyes of premodern Muslims, the outstanding characteristic of the Jews was their "unimportance."[4]

How then did Jews get turned into one of the most dangerous forces in the world? Because some very pronounced Christian fears reached the Middle East and changed the way Muslims perceived Jews. Europeans and local Christians brought anti-Semitism to the attention of Muslims. When a Capuchin monk and his servant disappeared from Damascus in February 1840, the local Christians and the French consul joined forces to raise accusations of blood libel. Though alien to Muslims, this accusation resonated so widely that over the next 70 years a significant blood-libel incident took place about once every two years in the Levant. With a rich and ancient Western heritage to draw from, Middle Easterners could hardly resist seeing a Jewish conspiracy against their interests. Such Christian stereotypes as the usurious Jew, the blood libel, a separate Jewish race, and a Jewish plan for world domination became common coin.

Then, in the early twentieth century, *The Protocols of the Elders of Zion*, a book that portrays Jews as a distinct people who pose a danger to the whole world, gave anti-Semitism its global underpinnings. Although forged by the tsarist secret police, it came widely to be seen as authentic and had a profound influence in Europe. In the Middle East, the book became a political force even before World War I had ended. In May 1918, the effective mayor of Jerusalem, Musa Kazim al-Husayni, reportedly mentioned to Chaim Weizmann that he had received a copy of *The Protocols* from a British officer of the military administration in Palestine. Innocently enough, he asked Weizmann whether the Zionist leaders were also "the Elders of Zion," and whether they shared the same program.[5]

Christian Palestinians first translated the forgery into Arabic and published it perhaps as early as 1921 and certainly by 1926, followed by many others in subsequent years.[6] Indeed, more translations and editions of *The Protocols* have appeared in Arabic than in any other language. Leading figures lent their names to editions, including the distinguished Egyptian writer 'Abbas Mahmud al-'Aqqad. The volume entered into popular discourse, becoming the top nonfiction best-seller in Lebanon during 1970. *The Protocols* had a slower start in the Persian language, with the first translation only in 1948 and the book not becoming a significant factor until Khomeini's revolution, but the Islamic Republic has caught up for lost time. Pakistani media made special advances in reifying *The Protocols*. In a feature film, Salman Rushdie was shown meeting with Elders of Zion. Newspaper articles elaborated specific facts about the Elders—for example, that this group, which numbers 12 men, "controls and directs the affairs of all the world's Jewish individuals and institutions including the State of Israel. It keeps its identity and business absolutely secret and operates through a front organisation, the World Zionist Organization."[7]

*The Protocols* sometimes serve as a tool of state. In Egypt, Gamal Abdel Nasser handed out copies to foreign journalists and his brother Shawqi wrote the introduction to one edition. Jordanian schools included it in the curriculum. The Saudi government distributed the book gratis to visitors and at embassies abroad. In 1985, an agency of the Iranian government published the book in English, complete with a laudatory introduction.[8] The fundamentalist Palestinian group Hamas cites *The Protocols* by name in its charter (article 32) and its message pervades that document. In all, *The Protocols* serves as the most important single vehicle for transmitting Christian anti-Semitism to the Muslim world. To make matters worse, no refutation appears to have been published in any language of the Middle East. However discredited in the West, the rank old forgery remains "indisputably accepted in the Arab world and viewed as the cornerstone of Zionism."[9]

If *The Protocols* and other books (August Rohling's *Der Talmudjude*, Henry Ford's *International Jew*, and Hitler's *Mein Kampf*) provided the theory of Christian-based anti-Semitism, specific incidents brought the phobia to life. Perhaps the outstanding example of Westerners perceiving a Jewish conspiracy, and thereby influencing Middle Eastern opinion, concerned the Young Turks (or, more formally, the Committee of Union and Progress, CUP), a group that in 1908 forced the Ottoman sultan, Abdülhamit II, to restore the Constitution of 1876. One year later, it deposed the sultan and in 1913 a triumvirate of Young Turks had acquired dictatorial powers. While all evidence points to the Young Turks being primarily made up of Turkish-speaking, Muslim military officers, the British ambassador in Istanbul, Gerard Lowther, insisted that the movement was inspired and led by Jews, Jewish pseudo-Muslims (*dönmes*), and Freemasons. In his view, the Jew:

seems to have entangled the pre-economic-minded Turk in his toils, and as Turkey [i.e., the Ottoman Empire] happens to contain the places sacred to Israel, it is but natural that the Jew should strive to maintain a position of exclusive influence and utilize it for the furtherance of his ideals, viz. the ultimate creation of an autonomous Jewish state in Palestine or Babylonia.

Ambassador Lowther concluded that Jews already "hold or control all the pivotal points in the machinery of the Young Turkey Government."[10] He dubbed the CUP the "Jew Committee of Union and Progress."

Lowther's peculiar interpretation of the Young Turk revolution spread widely in the West, thanks in large part to its promulgation by Philip Graves, Istanbul correspondent for *The Times*.[11] As a result, for many years, both reputable[12] and not so reputable writers[13] portrayed the events of 1908 to 1913 as a Jewish, *dönme*, and Masonic conspiracy. Middle Eastern Christians first picked up these European notions, then passed them along to Muslims. By May 1909, the Syrian Central Committee, a Paris-based Christian group favoring French rule in the Levant, wrote about Jewish and Masonic leadership of the Young Turks; the committee postulated Zionist efforts to destroy the Ottoman Empire in pursuit of a Jewish state in Palestine. As the Young Turk's rule turned despotic after 1912, Muslim Arabs increasingly resorted to seeing them as Jews, and this became a common view of modern Middle East history. Even today, fundamentalists hark back to the Jewish overthrow of Sultan Abdülhamit II as one of the key events in the decline of Islam in modern times and frequently cite it as a leading act of Jewish perfidy.[14] They return to Lowther's original analysis and interpret the Young Turks' deposing the sultan in 1909 as a Zionist act; they portray the Ottoman king as a staunch Muslim whom the Jews had to sideline if they were to take over in Palestine. What began as a British official's mistake turned into a widely accepted conspiracy theory.

With the emergence of Israel, European-like fear of Jews showed up on the diplomatic level, with surprisingly few changes. At times, Middle Easterners made the connection explicit, as when a Saudi newspaper editorialized that "Israel is behaving like the well-known usurer, the merchant of Venice."[15] More generally, the New York intellectual Norman Podhoretz notes, that "all the supposedly characteristic vices of Jews were now translated into the language of international politics and applied to Israel."[16] One of those vices, of course, was the goal to rule the world, an ambition that became slightly less notional when a Jewish state came into existence.

## Perfidious Anglo-Saxons

Just as Muslims traditionally saw Jews as a weak and vestigial people, so did they disdain northern Europeans. Were Eskimos to emerge in the next few years as leading scholars and artists, were factories in Greenland to outproduce those of Japan, and were invaders from the north to conquer the United States and Russia, we would hardly be more astonished than were the Muslims of the Middle East 200 years ago as they fell under European control. For over a millennium, northern Europeans appeared to them as primitive peoples of the extreme north, "more like beast than like men," in the words of an eleventh-century document, affected by a cold climate that made their temperaments "frigid, their humors raw, their bellies gross, their color pale, their hair long and lank. Thus they lack keenness of understanding and clarity of intelligence."[17]

In large part, Muslim attitudes toward Europe changed due to the latter's enormous power. In part, too, they changed as a result of exposure to elaborate conspiracy theories of the European far right and left connecting Anglo-Americans with imperialism, as well as similar theories among the mainstream politicians of Britain's geopolitical rivals (French and German ones especially). Indeed, a substantial literature, going back to the eighteenth century, sees Great Britain as "Perfidious Albion," an aggressive power that depends on cunning to extend its rule; similarly, the American adversary culture tends to reduce U.S. policy in the Middle East to a thirst for oil. In addition, Europeans increasingly saw Britons or Americans on one side and Jews on the other as two elements of a single universal conspiracy.

Various Arab and Iranian elements—returning students, radio stations, publications—transported these fears of British and American trickery to the Middle East, where they found a ready audience and flourished after World War I. The widespread Middle Eastern fear of a joint Zionist-imperialist conspiracy derived from these sources. The Nazi and Soviet governments then did much to forward such ideas, so that by the 1950s conspiracy theories about Great Britain and the United States had became common currency, familiar to all.

As leaders in modernization, Westerners cannot imagine mortal danger coming anywhere but from within the West, and so they look almost exclusively for conspirators in Europe and America. To the extent that Middle Easterners follow the Western example, they, too, look exclusively to the West for archconspirators. Conversely, the fact that Middle Easterners see only Jews and imperialists as conspirators points to the European origin of their conspiracy theories.

## CONTEMPORARY

Even today, Westerners (mostly government officials and journalists, but also scholars) continue to develop conspiracy theories about Jews and imperialists in the Middle East; and even today, Arabs and Iranians adopt them. But modern times have also brought an important change: rather than flow only from the West to the East, conspiracy theories now travel back and forth between civilizations. That is, the Middle East also influences the West.

### Western Influence

So long as they are in official positions, government employees in Israel and the West keep their views largely to themselves. But on leaving the service and regaining their freedom of public speech, they sometimes come out with startling statements that replicate and validate the worst of Middle Eastern fears.

Victor Ostrovsky's *By Way of Deception*, an exposé of the Mossad, his alleged former employer, confirmed many Arab nightmares about Israeli intelligence. Mossad, he said, placed bombs into the construction of bridges in Arab countries, preparing them to explode in time of war; it kept the Iraq-Iran war going by keeping each side informed of the other's ships; it used bullets that incriminated the PLO; and it killed Palestinians (such as Na'im Khadir) willing to talk to Israel. Israeli forces helped Christians massacre Palestinians at Sabra and Shatila; and Israeli intelligence was "fully aware" of Syrian plans to kill Bashir Gemayel, Israel's ally in Lebanon, yet made no effort to save him. Had Mossad been more forthcoming with information about U.S. hostages in Beirut, the whole Iran/*contra* affair would have been avoided. Most sensationally, Ostrovsky alleged that Israeli agents knew in advance about the truck bomb that killed 241 U.S. Marines in October 1983 — they even watched the truck carry out its mission — but chose to give their American counterparts only the vaguest information about it. He quotes the director of Mossad: "We're not there to protect the Americans. They're a big country."[18]

(*By Way of Deception* itself became the subject of an American conspiracy theory. The Israeli government's failed attempt to have the book censored in Canada and the United States caused it to rocket to the top of the best-seller charts. A reviewer in *The Nation* suggested this was not the public relations disaster it appeared to be, but a cunning Mossad operation to win wide attention for an account emphasizing its prowess and ferocity.)[19]

The CIA is also a fertile source of conspiracy theories. An exposé of the CIA quotes an agent in 1961 describing the just-appointed prime minister of Iran, 'Ali Amini, as "all right . . . one of our boys."[20] Roger Morris, an ex-CIA agent, writes of a "special Israeli bureau of the CIA" that engaged in "a gruesome intervention" in Lebanon.[21] Miles Copeland, a former American intelligence official, wrote in a famous set of revelations that during the 1940s the xenophobic Muslim Brethren of Egypt "had been thoroughly penetrated, at the top, by the British, American, French and Soviet intelligence services, any one of which could either make active use of it or blow it up, whichever best suited its purposes."[22] More spectacular yet, Copeland claimed that CIA officials met three times with some of the Free Officers who plotted the 1952 coup d'état,[23] and over the next decade provided them with confidential advice. Although Copeland's claims prompted a number of denials (Wilbur Crane Eveland, also of the CIA: "The July 1952 coup caught the CIA completely by surprise");[24] they became accepted truth in the Middle East,[25] complete with embellishments (for example, that some of Nasser's closest associates worked for the CIA). Only a few holdouts remained skeptical, such as a Lebanese journalist who found Copeland's "so-called memoirs . . . deliberately filled with misleading information."[26]

When John Stempel, a U.S. diplomat formerly stationed in Tehran, wrote that "surprisingly, the revolutionary victory in February 1979 created a situation not wholly unfavorable to U.S. interests,"[27] he provided Iranians with just the proof they need to establish that Washington had all along supported Khomeini. The head of French intelligence, Alexandre de Marenches, recounts his efforts to convince Shah Mohammad Reza Pahlavi that Washington was plotting to remove him from power. He provided a host of details about "the name of those who, in the United States, had been charged with overseeing his departure and his replacement. I had even taken part in a meeting where we discussed how to make the shah leave and with whom he would be replaced."[28]

Ex-officials sometimes really let their imaginations roam. Articles in *The Washington Report on Middle East Affairs* have raised the possibility of Mossad killing two American presidents (ex-congressman Paul Findley had it assassinating John F. Kennedy; ex-ambassador Andrew I. Kilgore claimed the organization was in 1992 considering the assassination of George Bush) and overthrowing a third (Richard H. Curtiss sees it behind the fall of Richard Nixon). In the first two cases, Israeli leaders hoped to replace the American president with a supposedly more friendly and pliant vice president; in the latter, they made sure Nixon would not force them to make peace with the

Arabs.[29] Kilgore also used current Middle East politics to validate *The Protocols of the Elders of Zion,* something one might think beyond the pale of civilized discourse. "Israeli reality gives 20th-century credence to the 19th-century Czarist Russian fabrication called 'The Protocols of the Elders of Zion,'" he writes. "That was a forgery alleging that Jews had a plan to rule the world. Now Shamir seeks to demonstrate that Jews *do* rule—through Washington. Countries seeking favors from the one remaining superpower must go through Israel to get them."[30]

Western journalists often assert collusion between Washington and its professed enemies. John Cooley reports that Mu'ammar al-Qadhdhafi enjoyed American protection upon seizing power in 1969. "In the first three years after Qaddafi's revolution," he writes, "the United States had regarded the Libyan colonel, a certified Libyan patriot and definitely an anti-Communist, with fairly benign approval." At least until 1974, Cooley continues, "the United States and Western European intelligence services protected Qaddafi from his enemies, and most assuredly helped him to remain in power."[31] A Toronto newspaper reported[32] that Munzir Qassar, a Syrian businessman close to Rif'at al-Asad, helped win the release of American hostages in Lebanon; in return, he received CIA help to get drugs into the United States.

If Libya and Syria, why not the Palestinians? Journalist Jonathan Vankin claims that CIA employees (and ex-Nazis at that) trained the first Palestinian terrorist groups during the 1950s.[33] Patrick Seale wrote a full-length biography of Abu Nidal, the Palestinian murderer, centered on the conceit that Abu Nidal worked for Israel.[34] Janet and John Wallach, other journalists, wrote how two PLO mischief-makers, a drug-runner and an informer, ever-so-conveniently turned out to be enemy plants (one Libyan, the other Israeli).[35] Several writers hold that 'Ali Hasan Salama, the head of PLO security and of Black September's European operations, cooperated with the CIA in the early 1970s. The Wallachs write that the Agency was so impressed with "his ability to maintain order and protect American interests," it offered him $3 million to work for the U.S. government. David A. Korn (a former government official) adds a relaxing note: the CIA paid for Salama's vacations in Louisiana and Hawaii. So intimate was Salama's bond with the Americans, the Israelis dared not assassinate him until they received clearance from the CIA.[36]

Discussing President Bush's dispatch of U.S. troops to the Persian Gulf in 1990, the left-wing columnist Alexander Cockburn surmised a U.S.-Iraqi collusion to raise oil prices. His proof? "I might remind you that the president's official legal address . . . is in Texas."[37] The war against Iraq stimulated similar insights in France. On the left, Didier Motchaneof of the Socialist Party held that "France has accepted to help the U.S. restore a world domination that its economic situation no longer assured." On the right, Jacques Chirac, the future president of France, spoke of George Bush's worry about Japanese and European economic might and his effort to control the world's oil so has to make the U.S. their economic equal.[38] In a similar argument, Vankin claimed that George Bush had American forces invade Panama in 1989 to destroy records linking the CIA, and perhaps him personally, to the American destruction of Pan Am 103 a year earlier.[39]

Scholarly influence from the West tends to be limited to just one area: showing just how bad the West really is. Indictments of American policy in the Middle East written by figures such as Noam Chomsky, the linguist and far-left commentator, and Edward Said echo in the Middle East. The most interesting of these ideas may be *dependencia* theory, a Marxist outlook dating from the 1960s that substitutes geography for the class structure. The heroes of this scheme no longer are the poor of the rich countries but the whole of the poor countries (dubbed the "periphery"). "Economic development and underdevelopment are the opposite face of the same coin. Both are the necessary result and contemporary manifestations of internal contradictions in the world capitalist system."[40] Treating non-Western countries as the geographic equivalent of the working class found an immediate reception in the Middle East, where a millennial religious suspicion of the Christian foe easily transmuted into economic terms.[41] In this spirit, 'Ali Akbar Mohtashemi, a leading Iranian hard-liner, argues that Westerners try

> to inject into the Third World . . . the assembly-line type of industry which depends entirely on them. In this way, they assure themselves two functions: First, they will wrest agricultural self-sufficiency from the Third World, so as to make the Third World dependent on them for foodstuffs. Second, whatever replaces agriculture will be designed to create greater dependency on the United States.[42]

True to the *dependencia* mold, Mohtashemi discerns a systematic effort by industrial states to exploit the economies of weaker countries, thereby making them incapable of establishing their own industrial base. *Dependencia* theory probably flourishes in the Middle East because it systematizes and articulates what many there intuitively suspect.

These Western conspiracy theories tend to win a much more favorable reception in the Middle East than in their homelands. (No leading Western politicians, for example, have incorporated *dependencia* theory into their public utterances.) Arab and Iranian opinion leaders sometimes make the connection explicit, by citing Westerners as their authority. President 'Abd ar-Rahman 'Arif of Iraq quoted his French counterpart by name as a source of information about the Jews: "General de Gaulle complained about the control of the French news media by international Zionist forces."[43] Even more revealingly, Yasir 'Arafat repeatedly cited an obscure professor in England as an authoritative source to prove his claims about the existence of a Zionist plan for a Greater Israel extending across the Middle East.[44] At other times, even though Middle Easterners do not credit their Western sources, a connection can be discerned. In 1954, the distinguished French orientalist Robert Montagne wrote that "young Arab patriots . . . ponder the example of Israel. The Israeli terrorists capable of carrying off the most audacious actions . . . have served as a kind of school for Muslims."[45] Four decades later, the Syrian government still regularly claimed that "it was the Zionist gangs that brought terrorism to this part of the world."[46]

The Middle Eastern predilection for conspiracy theories guarantees that Western notions get emphasized and amplified. Existing worries get confirmed, non-conspiracy-minded holdouts find it difficult to hold out, and Middle Easterners reach new heights of paranoia.

### Back and Forth

Conspiracy theories tie the Middle East and the West in complex and sometimes paradoxical ways. Arabs and Iranians draw their anti-Semititic and anti-imperialist ideas from the West, yet they also export these same constructs back to the West. This ping-pong of mutual influence leads to a situation in which some conspiracy theories reverberate between the West and the Middle East, losing plausibility but gaining significance as they ricochet, magnifying and colliding as they move back and forth.

Travel to the Middle East familiarized Paul Findley, an Illinois congressman, with Arab conspiracy theories about Israel. He became convinced of their truth and eventually packaged them in a book, *They Dare to Speak Out.* In it, he held that the American Israel Public Affairs Committee, the pro-Israel lobby in Washington, seeks to restrict free speech in an effort to muzzle Israel's opponents. The 1989 edition ends with a call for Americans to liberate themselves "from the heavy hand Israel's lobby lays on our cherished political institutions." Action is needed sooner rather than later, "for the opportunity may be fleeting."[47] Back in the Muslim world, conspiracy theorists cited Findley's book as proof of their own beliefs. Along the way, they exaggerated his conclusions; a Pakistani summary of the book, for instance, reported that it "reveals, along with evidence, that in the United States, the White House, the Congress, the Administration all are controlled by organised American Jewry."[48]

Lyndon LaRouche, the crank figure who sought the U.S. presidency in 1988 but ended up in jail for credit-card fraud, gained a significant following in the Middle East, for his plot-mongering substantiated fears there. Some of LaRouche's theses, such as his blaming the war against Saddam Husayn on "Israeli-controlled Moslem fundamentalist groups," were too strong medicine even for Middle Easterners. But many liked his way of blaming everything untoward on the great powers. When King Husayn of Jordan renounced Jordanian claims to the West Bank in July 1988, LaRouche's media explained this as a Moscow-Washington deal recognizing Jerusalem as Israel's capital.[49] LaRouche won a following at the highest levels in Iran. Thus, Mehdi Bazargan, the generally sensible former prime minister of Iran, repeated LaRouche's notion of a "Bernard Lewis plan" for dividing the Middle East into small, ethnically homogeneous and weak states.[50]

But by the far most significant of LaRouche's theories concerned the "October Surprise" theory, the notion that presidential candidate Ronald Reagan colluded in 1980 with Iranian mullahs to keep American hostages in Iran, thereby stealing the election from Jimmy Carter. A LaRouche magazine first laid out this conspiracy theory in late 1980, then another one repeated it in 1983.[51] The plot attracted little attention until the Iran/*contra* scandal imbued U.S.-Iranian ties with a greater complexity. Abol Hassan Bani Sadr, the former president of Iran, tentatively picked up this theory in April 1987.[52] When commentators in the United States (Christopher Hitchens of *The Nation* in particular)[53] echoed back the idea, Bani Sadr felt emboldened to make larger and more elaborate claims.[54]

About this time, an international cast of sources jumped in with stories confirming and elaborating Bani Sadr's outline. They included Israelis (Ari Ben-Menashe, Ahran Moshell, Will Northrop), Frenchmen (Robert Benes, Nicholas Ignatiew), Iranians (Jamshid Hashemi, Ahmed Heidari, Houshang Lavi, Hamid Naqashan), Americans (Richard Babayan, Richard Brenneke, William Herrmann, Oswald LeWinter,[55] Heinrich Rupp, Gunther Russbacher), and even a South African (Dirk Stoffberg). Several individuals in the United States (Barbara Honegger,

Martin Kilian, David Marks, Robert Parry, Jurgen Roth, Craig Unger) actively spread these stories from one source to another, egging them on to larger and larger claims. Brenneke's allegations at a 1988 trial in Denver became the official documentation in Bani Sadr's eyes and prompted the former Iranian president to hypothesize a full-blown and long-lasting conspiracy between Khomeini and Reagan.[56]

Still, this conspiracy theory remained at the fringes of American public life. It only became a major story when Gary Sick, a former National Security Council staffer and Ford Federation program officer, alleged in *The New York Times* in April 1991 that "individuals associated with the Reagan-Bush campaign of 1980 met secretly with Iranian officials to delay the release of the American hostages until after the American election. For this favor, Iran was rewarded with a substantial supply of arms from Israel." Sick also raised the possibility that George Bush was one of those Americans.[57] Sick subsequently published a very detailed book on this subject, replete with precise information about events that never took place; for example, in reference to a phantom meeting in Madrid on 27 July 1980, he wrote that "The conversation was interrupted twice, when hotel waiters arrived to serve coffee."[58]

With this, the October Surprise become a serious issue in the United States. Leading television shows devoted hours to the subject, national weeklies made it the subject of cover stories, and Jimmy Carter called for an investigation. A January 1992 poll showed 55 percent of Americans believing these allegations to be true and just 34 percent finding them false.[59] As part of his preparations to run for the presidency, H. Ross Perot sent some associates to talk with Gunther Russbacher in his Missouri jail cell. In February 1992, the House of Representatives voted in favor of an investigation of the charges and the Senate followed suit.

But conspiracy theories flourish in the dark; so much attention meant the theorists' claims got checked in detail, and they could not bear such scrutiny. Several journalistic investigations[60] established beyond any doubt that the conspiracy claimants were hoaxers. The two congressional inquiries then confirmed these conclusions,[61] but only after damage had been done—the legitimacy of the two Reagan administrations had been brought gratuitously into question. At the same time, a convinced conspiracy theorist sticks to his guns; despite all the proof to the contrary, Sick still maintained[62] that he had been right. Middle Easterners tended to follow his lead, clinging to the idea of a Reagan-Khomeini deal.

The October Surprise shows how a conspiracy theory, ricocheting between the West and the Middle East, can grow to have an international reach.

An enduring conspiratorial tie thus links the Middle East and Europe. Although the Middle East was at the receiving end of European conspiracy theories during the period from 1750 to 1950, before[63] and after that period it influenced Europe. Indeed, the hidden hand has proven one of the deepest and most enduring connections between these two regions. An enduring conspiratorial tie thus links the Middle East and Europe.

## NOTES TO CHAPTER 15

1. Isabel Burton, *The Inner Life of Syria, Palestine, and the Holy Land* (London: Henry S. King, 1875), vol. 1, p. 114.

2. As autocratic regimes, the Muslim states had more in common with the Soviet Union than with the capitalist countries and were heavily influenced by Soviet ways, including those in the realm of conspiracy theories.

3. The early Islamic sources do include allegations about Jews killing the Prophet Muhammad, but these had trivial significance compared to their Christian equivalents. The one notable connection between old and new Muslim views concerns the alleged deviousness of Jews.

4. Bernard Lewis, *Semites and Anti-Semites: An Inquiry into Conflict and Prejudice* (New York: W. W. Norton, 1986), p. 126.

5. Papers of 'Arif al-'Arif, as reported by Jon Kimche, *The Second Arab Awakening* (New York: Holt, Rinehart and Winston, 1970), p. 181. This date seems too early, for in 1918 *The Protocols* existed only in the Russian language and were just beginning to be distributed by White Russians.

6. For major editions, see Y. Harkabi, *Arab Attitudes to Israel*, trans. by Misha Louvish (London: Valentine, Mitchell, 1972), p. 518; Pierre-André Taguieff, *Les Protocols des Sages de Sion* (Paris: Berg International, 1992), vol. 1, pp. 378-80; and pp. 372-73 for French-language versions published in the Middle East.

7. *The Pakistan Times*, 4 February 1991.

8. *Jewish Conspiracy: The Protocols of the Learned Elders of Zion* (Tehran: Islamic Propagation Organization, 1405/1985). Bernard Lewis kindly brought this volume to my attention.

9. Rivka Yadlin, *An Arrogant Oppressive Spirit: Anti-Zionism as Anti-Judaism in Egypt* (Oxford: Pergamon, 1989), p. 79.

10. Secret letter to Charles Hardinge, 29 May 1910, Foreign Office 800/193A (Lowther Papers). Text in Elie Kedourie, *Arabic Political Memoirs and Other Studies* (London: Frank Cass, 1974), pp. 256-57.

11. Ironically, a decade later (in 1921), Graves established that *The Protocols of the Elders of Zion* was a forgery.

12. In *The Rise of Nationality in the Balkans* (London: Constable, 1917), pp. 134-35, R. W. Seton-Watson asserted that "the real brains of the movement were Jewish or Judaeo-Moslem [*dönme*]." H. C. Armstrong, *Grey Wolf: Mustafa Kemal, An Intimate*

*Study of a Dictator* (Harmondsworth, Eng.: Penguin, 1937), pp. 27-28, presents the CUP as part of a Masonic conspiracy. Leonard Stein, *The Balfour Declaration* (New York: Simon and Schuster, 1961), p. 35, stresses the Jewish and *dönme* elements in the Young Turk revolution.

13. For references, see Ernest Edmondson Ramsaur, Jr., *The Young Turks: Prelude to the Revolution of 1908* (Beirut: Khayats, 1965), pp. 103-08.

14. For example, Jamal Madi, ed., *Ghazawat Ma'a'l-Yuhud* (Alexandria: Dar ad-Da'wa, 1985), pp. 16-17.

15. *Al-Jazira* (Riyadh), 25 July 1995.

16. "Symposium: Is There a Cure for Anti-Semitism?" *Partisan Review* 61 (1994): 400.

17. Sa'id ibn Ahmad al-Andalusi, *Kitab Tabaqat al-Umam* (Cairo, n.d.), p. 11. Quoted in Bernard Lewis, *The Muslim Discovery of Europe* (New York: W. W. Norton, 1982), p. 68.

18. Victor Ostrovsky and Claire Hoy, *By Way of Deception* (New York: St. Martin's Press, 1990), pp. 119, 124, 146, 253-54, 310-21.

19. Art Winslow, "Mossad's Cover Story," *The Nation*, 22 October 1990.

20. Quoted in Andrew Tully, *CIA: The Inside Story* (New York: William Morrow, 1962), p. 88.

21. Roger Morris, *Uncertain Greatness: Henry Kissinger and American Foreign Policy* (New York: Harper & Row, 1977), p. 261.

22. Miles Copeland, *The Game of Nations: The Amorality of Power Politics* (New York: Simon and Schuster, 1969), p. 184.

23. Ibid., p. 65. For an earlier account see Tully, *CIA*, pp. 102-05.

24. Wilbur Crane Eveland, *Ropes of Sand: America's Failure in the Middle East* (New York: W. W. Norton, 1980), p. 97. In fact, William C. Lakeland, a career foreign service officer, was the first American government representative to make contact with Abdel Nasser.

25. See, for example, 'Abdullah Muhammad al-Gharib, *Wa-Ja' Dawr al-Majus: Al-Ab'ad at-Ta'rikhiya wa'l-'Aqa'idiya wa's-Siyasiya li'th-Thawra al-Iraniya* (Cairo: Dar al-Jil, 1983), p. 240.

26. Saïd K. Aburish, *Beirut Spy: The St George Hotel Bar* (London: Bloomsbury, 1989), p. 49. Joel Gordon authoritatively throws cold water on the whole episode in *Nasser's Blessed Movement: Egypt's Free Officers and the July Revolution* (New York: Oxford University Press, 1992), pp. 163-64.

27. John D. Stempel, *Inside the Iranian Revolution* (Bloomington: Indiana University Press, 1981), p. 306.

28. Christine Ockrent and Comte de Marenches, *Dans le secret des Princes* (Paris: Stock, 1986), pp. 248-49.

29. Kennedy and Bush: *The Washington Report on Middle East Affairs*, March 1992; Nixon: *The Washington Report on Middle East Affairs*, October/November 1995.

30. Andrew I. Kilgore, "Why Shamir is Threatening to Look for a 'New Benefactor,'" *The Washington Report on Middle East Affairs*, March 1992, p. 17.

31. John K. Cooley, *Libyan Sandstorm* (New York: Holt, Rinehart and Winston, 1982), pp. 80, 83.

32. *The Sunday Star* (Toronto), 19 November 1989.

33. Jonathan Vankin, *Conspiracies, Cover-Ups, and Crimes: Political Manipulation and Mind Control in America* (New York: Paragon House, 1991), pp. 177-78, 243.

34. Patrick Seale, *Abu Nidal: A Gun for Hire* (New York: Random House, 1992), pp. 154, 172, 175, 178, 225, 304-05.

35. Janet Wallach and John Wallach, *Arafat: In the Eyes of the Beholder* (New York: Lyle Stuart, 1990), pp. 346-47.

36. Ibid., p. 344; David A. Korn, *Assassination in Khartoum* (Bloomington: Indiana University Press, 1993), p.243; Vankin, *Conspiracies, Cover-Ups, and Crimes*, p. 184. Seale, *Abu Nidal*, p. 168, offers a contrary reading; the Israelis decided to kill Salama only when they learned of his CIA contacts. Michael Bar-Zohar and Eitan Haber say nothing about this episode in their biography of 'Ali Hasan Salama, *The Quest for the Red Prince* (London: Weidenfeld and Nicolson, 1983).

37. Spoken on the *Phil Donahue Show*, 12 October 1990.

38. Flora Lewis, "A Shabby French Sulk," *The New York Times*, 20 February 1991.

39. Vankin, *Conspiracies, Cover-Ups, and Crimes*, p. 187.

40. André Gunder Frank, *Capitalism and Underdevelopment in Latin America* (New York: Monthly Review Press, 1967), p. 9.

41. The most influential Middle Eastern contribution to *dependencia* theory is Samir Amin's *Le Développement du capitalisme en Côte d'Ivoire* (Paris: Éditions de Minuit, 1967).

42. *Shahid*, Farvardin 1369/1990.

43. Quoted in Abdel Magid Farid, *Nasser: The Final Years* (Reading, Eng.: Ithaca Press, 1994), p. 115.

44. On which, see chapter 3, "Proofs: Coin, Flag, Inscription, and Map."

45. Robert Montagne, "Réflexions sur la violence en pays d'Islam," *Preuves* 42 (August 1954): 14.

46. Syrian Arab Republic Radio, 15 October 1994. Another example: Syria's Defense Minister Mustafa Tallas said that terrorism "comes from within Israel" (*Ash-Sharq al-Awsat*, 4 December 1995).

47. Paul Findley, *They Dare to Speak Out: People and Institutions Confront Israel's Lobby*, rev. ed., (Chicago: Lawrence Hill, 1989), p. 360.

48. *The Pakistan Times*, 4 February 1991.

49. "'New Yalta' Plot for Unholy War over Jerusalem Exposed," *Executive Intelligence Review*, 19 August 1988.

50. *Ad-Dustur*, 23 March 1987.

51. *Executive Intelligence Review*, 2 December 1980; *New Solidarity*, 2 September 1983.

52. *The Miami Herald*, 12 April 1987. Mansur Rafizadeh, a former head of the shah's secret police, SAVAK, forwarded an alternate version, what might be called a "November Surprise": after the November 1980 election, CIA agents hostile to Carter convinced the Khomeini government not to release the hostages until Reagan came to power. See *Witness: From the Shah to the Secret Arms Deal* (New York: William Morrow, 1987), p. 347.

53. *The Nation*, 4/11 July 1987.

54.  *The New York Times*, 3 August 1987; *The Miami Herald*, 9 August 1987; August 1987
     interview with Leslie Cockburn, as reported in her book *Out of Control* (New York:
     The Atlantic Monthly Press, 1987), pp. 192-93, 281.

55.  LeWinter had a leading role in another intricate conspiracy theory involving the
     Middle East a few years later: in *The Maltese Double Cross*, a documentary film partially
     funded by Metropole Hotels, a company in which the Libyan government had a large
     interest, he claimed that the Scottish police planted forensic evidence in the case of
     Pan Am 103 to exonerate the Syrian and Iranian governments, the real culprits, and
     instead to implicate the Libyan regime. See *The Sunday Times*, 7 May 1995.

56.  *Playboy*, September 1988; Abol Hassan Bani Sadr, with Jean-Charles Deniau, *Le
     Complot des ayatollahs*, (Paris: Éditions la Découverte, 1989), pp. 48, 57. Deniau notes
     (p. 9) that interviews with Bani Sadr forming the basis for this book took place in
     September and October 1988.

57.  *The New York Times*, 15 April 1991.

58.  Gary Sick, *October Surprise: America's Hostages in Iran and the Election of Ronald Reagan*
     (New York: Times Books, 1991), p. 83.

59.  Unpublished *New York Times*/CBS News poll, 22-25 January 1992; reported in Ted
     Goertzel, "Belief in Conspiracy Theories," *Political Psychology* 15 (1994): 733.

60.  Especially Frank Snepp, "Brenneke Exposed," *The Village Voice*, 10 September 1991;
     John Barry, "Making of a Myth," *Newsweek*, 11 November 1991; Steve Emerson and
     Jesse Furman, "The Conspiracy That Wasn't," *The New Republic*, 18 November 1991;
     and Frank Snepp, "October Surmise," *The Village Voice*, 25 February 1992.

61.  The Senate stated that "by any standard, the credible evidence now known falls far short
     of supporting the allegation of an agreement between the Reagan campaign and Iran to
     delay the release of the hostages." Committee on Foreign Relations, United States Senate,
     *The "October Surprise" Allegations and the Circumstances Surrounding the Release of the American
     Hostages Held in Iran* (Washington, D.C.: U.S. Government Printing Office, 1992), p. 115.
          The House report went further, declaring that "There was no October
     Surprise agreement ever reached." It found "wholly insufficient credible evidence"
     that communication took place between the Reagan campaign and the Iranian
     government and "no credible evidence" of an attempt by the campaign to delay the
     hostages' release. The report also expressed concern that "certain witnesses may
     have committed perjury during sworn testimony." Committee of the Whole House
     on the State of the Union, *Joint Report of the Task Force to Investigate Certain Allegations
     Concerning the Holding of American Hostages by Iran in 1980* (Washington, D.C.: U.S.
     Government Printing Office, 1993), pp. 53, 7-8, 239.

62.  He wrote in *The New York Times* of 24 January 1993 that the House report "does not
     lay . . to rest" his claims of campaign contacts with Iranians and that it "leaves open
     the possibility" of Republican interference with the Carter administration's foreign
     policy negotiations.

63.  Pre-1750 Middle Eastern influences on the West included the dualistic cosmology
     of ancient Iranian religions, supposed Assassin influence on the Knights Templar,
     and the Levantine connection of the Rosicrucians.

# 16.

# Actual Conspiracies

Monstrous fears feed on monstrous realities.
— *William W. Freehling*[1]

It is naive to think that conspiracies do not occur
in history, but it is insane to think that history itself
is a conspiracy.
— *Manochehr Dorraj*[2]

Even paranoids have enemies.
— *Delmore Schwartz*

Conspiracy theories result not just from subjective causes but also from what psychologists term objective anxiety: the Middle East has indeed hosted a great number of actual conspiracies in the past two centuries. Time and again, Western governments relied on covert collusion or devious means to influence Middle East politics; Israelis resorted to unconventional methods; and Arab politicians made use of clandestine means.

Witnessing an overabundance of intrigue, it is entirely rational for Middle Easterners to fear conspiracies. "The perception that others are Machiavellian," the political scientist Robert Jervis notes, "cannot be easily labeled pathological."[3] Looking specifically at the Middle East, Emmanuel Sivan, an Israeli scholar, goes so far as to state that the fear of conspiracy is not a case of the paranoid style in politics; rather, "the dangers they point to are quite real."[4]

## "EUROPEAN DIPLOMACY
## AND ORIENTAL INTRIGUE"[5]

All sides plot regularly—foreign states with ambitions in the Middle East, local politicians extending their power, and locals bending Western powers to their will.

## By Westerners and Israelis

*Europeans.*    The Napoleonic invasion of Egypt in 1798 marked the beginning of sustained European intervention in the Middle East. Since then, the British, French, Russians, and Americans have constantly maneuvered behind the scenes to outflank their rivals. While the whole of the Middle East, from North Africa to India, served as their playing field, they took special interest in the Levant and the Persian Gulf.

London occasionally played with the idea of sponsoring a Jewish Palestine, seeing in this an indirect means to boost British power. As early as 1840, Foreign Minister Lord Palmerston quietly proposed that "The Jewish people, if returning [to Palestine] under the sanction and protection of the [Ottoman] Sultan, would be a check on any future evil designs of Mehemet Ali [the ruler of Egypt] or his successor."[6] In this spirit, Palmerston offered protection to stateless Jews living in Palestine, a practice the British government continued for the next half century.

Zionist leaders reciprocated with veiled efforts to make their movement attractive to the powers. Theodor Herzl lobbied Colonial Secretary Joseph Chamberlain at the turn of the century, persuading him that a Jewish colony in the Sinai Peninsula would help extend British influence to Palestine. In Herzl's words, were the Zionists resident "in El Arish under the Union Jack, then our Palestine would fall in the British sphere of influence."[7] Herzl's successors took up this theme and also pitched it to the French, German, and Russian governments. For example, on 3 October 1917, Chaim Weizmann proposed (in a statement that apparently influenced British decision making to issue the Balfour Declaration a month later) that "a reconstructed Palestine will become a very great asset to the British Empire."[8] The Middle Eastern view of Israel as a Western colony becomes more intelligible against this background.

The characteristically British practice of indirect rule implied a reality at odds with appearance, and so amounted to a form of conspiracy. In Egypt, Lord Cromer held the deceptively modest title of British consul general but ruled the country from 1883 until 1907. Staying behind the scenes, he preferred his power mysterious. "I remained more or less hidden. I pulled the strings,"[9] he boasted in an 1893 letter. Cromer called on his subordinates to do likewise, holding that "the less they are talked about the better."[10] The legacy of indirect rule caused Middle Easterners rightly to fear behind-the-scenes manipulation.

Westerners saw control of economic assets as a way to power. Thus, *The Times* celebrated Disraeli's purchase of nearly half the Suez Canal's shares with this example of editorial triumphalism: "To this country will belong the decision on every question, whether scientific, financial or political; administration and negotiation will be in our hands, and, as we will have the power, so we shall have the responsibility before the world."[11] All this just for buying some stock?

The British often conspired in Iran. After signing a treaty in 1814, the British negotiator privately held that, to assure India's security, "it would be better policy to leave Persia in her present state of weakness and barbarism, than pursue an opposite plan."[12] In 1834, when Fat'h 'Ali Shah died, the British assured his son Muhammad of the throne against his two uncles; and when Muhammad himself died 14 years later, the British and Russians helped his successor, Nasir ad-Din, ascend to power. In 1845, the two powers again intervened, this time to protect a leader of the emerging Baha'i religion because of his importance for international politics.

Also about that time, the British provided a conduit for Indian money to reach Shi'i shrines in Iraq, thus making the mullahs beholden to them. On one occasion, for example, the prayer leader of Tehran wrote the Marquis of Dalhousie, British governor-general of India, asking that he use his influence to protect the Shi'a community in India.[13] British support helped the Constitutional Revolution of 1906; the next year, an Anglo-Russian Agreement divided the country into two spheres of influence. General Edmund Ironside, commander of allied troops in northern Iran, quietly assisted Reza Khan to become commander of the Cossack Division and encouraged him to execute the coup d'état of February 1921, leading to the overthrow of the Qajar dynasty and its replacement by the Pahlavis.

The Russians also connived in Iran, helping to undo the Constitutional Revolution in 1908. In 1912, seeking to show off their might, the Russians dispatched an *agent provocateur* into Iran's holiest site, the shrine of Imam Reza in Mashhad, and then (after getting him out) seized the opportunity to bomb the building.

Nor were the Ottoman territories free from conspiracy in the run up to World War I. When the British sought to conclude a secret treaty with the Emir of Kuwait, their agent used the pretext of a hunting trip to sneak through the Turkish lines. Max von Oppenheim and other German spies used archaeological and anthropological research expeditions in Ottoman territories as a cover for preparing Kaiser Wilhelm's *Drang nach Osten*. The German ambassador to Constantinople knew ten days before the event that Enver, Talat, and Cemal Pashas would overthrow the Ottoman administration in 1913; in fact, he may have helped plot the takeover.

The Sykes-Picot Agreement of May 1916—a secret deal among London, Paris, and Petrograd to divide up the Middle East—remains the archetype of European perfidy. Though long defunct, it still comes up as a principal cause of the Middle East's border problems and is still vividly remembered and resented. For example, a Syrian Ba'th Party official in May 1978 denounced "the false borders established by the Sykes-Picot agreement" and deemed them "no longer acceptable."[14] Likewise, a Damascus newspaper in 1981 declared it intolerable that "the Sykes-Picot logic of 1916 regain the upper hand and redivide the region."[15] Building on Sykes-Picot, T. E. Lawrence, a British agent, had a direct hand in inspiring the Arab Revolt of June 1916, thereby rendering that entire episode suspect in many Middle Eastern eyes.

During the interwar period, the great powers shamelessly manipulated Middle East politics by such furtive tactics as paying off politicians, sponsoring publications and organizations, and propping up minority communities. Leading intellectual figures (including Shakib Arslan and George Antonius) accepted clandestine money from interested parties in Europe.

As World War II approached, the powers became even more assertive in pursuit of their interests. Radio Berlin spread rumors in October 1939 that the British consul in Damascus was distributing swastika armlets and badges, aiming thereby to provoke trouble between the British and French. Nazi Germany won impressive influence in Iraq during 1937 to 1940 under the guidance of the formidable Fritz Grobba, who specialized in fomenting anti-British sentiments.[16]

The exigencies of war prompted Europeans to pull strings more overtly. British troops ringed the royal palace in Cairo, compelling King Faruq to change government. In Iran, the British and Soviets jointly decided that Reza Shah's rule had become inconvenient, so they deposed him in favor of his son, Mohammed Reza Pahlavi. Their influence remained powerful, though nearly invisible. No one could quite tell who controlled what; Marvin Zonis explains that "[t]he British, the Soviets, and the ruling dynasty were involved, in the eyes of many Iranians, in a *folie à trois*, each needing the other, each suspect."[17]

The imperial powers gave up their formal controls over the Middle East in the aftermath of World War II, but not without a fight or without intrigue. The 1953 agreement establishing a consortium of Western oil companies to produce and export Iranian oil included a secret "Clause 28" that permitted the consortium unilaterally to reduce production if it deemed this necessary to maintain high prices. A memo of conversation records Secretary of State John Foster Dulles telling the British foreign secretary in 1955 that "Unpleasant events which we might instigate should have the appearance of happening naturally."[18] The Suez War of 1956 (known in Arabic as the "Tripartite Aggression") saw the British and French governments working secretly with Israel to control Egyptian territory, reinforcing Middle East phobias for years to come. On 24 October 1956, just days before the Suez campaign began, the three governments signed the Sèvres Protocol in which they spelled out in detail the series of steps each of the parties would execute.[19] Of course, all three categorically denied the existence of such an agreement. During the crisis, the British considered assassinating Gamal Abdel Nasser and set up a transmitter in southern France that had the nerve to call him a "minion of Zionism."[20]

The British continued to manipulate Middle East politics from behind the scenes. In 1970, for example, a stringer for the Reuters news agency heard that Sultan Sa'id Bin Taymur of Oman had been deposed, so she took her report to the Cable and Wireless office in Muscat. The Englishman in charge there read the dispatch and, the story goes, handed it back to her, remarking "You're a bit early. Tomorrow, not today." Of course, he was right; a day later the sultan was hustled on to a British plane and taken into exile.[21]

*Americans.*   As for the United States, the two best-remembered actual conspiracies both concerned Iran. Operation Ajax helped overthrow Prime Minister Mohammad Mosaddeq of Iran in 1953 and did much to foster an anti-Americanism that culminated in the 1978-79 revolution. Secret American arms sales to Iran in 1985-86 won the freedom of several American hostages in Lebanon. That President Reagan could overtly pursue one policy (no deals with hostage-takers) and covertly another (deals with hostage-takers) confirmed U.S. government deceptiveness. The Bible, key, and (kosher) cake brought by American emissaries to Tehran all heightened the element of mystery surrounding the transactions.

U.S. intrigue in Iran went well beyond these two major incidents, however. When Arthur Millspaugh, an American, was hired to reorganize the Finance Ministry in 1942, a senior American diplomat privately informed his superiors that this meant "We shall soon be in the position of actually 'running' Iran."[22] In the late 1940s, American intelligence operatives forged the memoirs of Abu'l-Qasem Lahuti, a pro-Soviet Iranian leader, in which he explicitly described Kremlin plans to annex the north of Iran. Shredded documents found in the U.S. embassy in 1979 and pieced together by the Iranian occupiers established that several of Khomeini's aides maintained contact with the U.S. government. Other documents showed that American and Soviet diplomats in Tehran met regularly to discuss developments in Iran and that in October 1978 the Soviet told the American that "the U.S. was not doing enough to help the Shah."[23] Little wonder Khomeinists saw U.S.-Soviet enmity as a ruse.

Iraq was another target. In the early 1970s, the U.S. government joined with Iran and Israel in arming Kurds to weaken the Iraqi regime. Twenty years later, Washington printed false Iraqi dinar notes to undermine Saddam Husayn's regime. The U.S. government reportedly engaged in conspiracies against other states, too, including a feasibility study in 1957 for diverting the Nile River to the Red Sea, thereby leaving Abdel Nasser's Egypt dry,[24] and repeated efforts to oust Qadhdhafi from power in Libya. According to David Lesch, author of a study on U.S.-Syrian relations, Washington "was actively involved in clandestine operations throughout 1957 in an effort to bring down the Syrian regime."[25]

*Israelis.* Israelis have often resorted to clandestine operations.[26] In 1954, they arranged for Egyptian Jews to place bombs in several sensitive locations, including the premises of the U.S. Information Service, to frame Gamal Abdel Nasser's government and disrupt Egyptian relations with the West. Known as the Lavon Affair (after the Israeli defense minister who approved the scheme), this plot created an abiding Arab fear of Israeli agents acting close to home. A year later, Israeli officials acknowledged to American diplomats their intent to overthrow the Abdel Nasser regime. Eli Cohen, the Mossad agent who penetrated the highest reaches of Syrian society in the early 1960s (befriending even the head of intelligence and the president of the republic), helped perpetuate this heritage of paranoia.

Israeli intelligence employed Jonathan Pollard, an American Jew employed by the U.S. Navy, to pass on classified American documents until his arrest in 1985. A year later, Mossad abducted Mordechai Vananu, the renegade nuclear technician who had revealed Israel's bomb-making capacity to *The Sunday Times,* by having a blonde lure him into the arms of its agents.

These were only the most renowned of the Israelis' plots. Others included: paying off King 'Abdallah of Jordan and Husni Za'im of Syria, cooperating with the Maronites of Lebanon, aiding Palestinian fundamentalist Muslims to weaken the PLO, and setting up a very wide web of unacknowledged relations with Arab states. The most important and extensive of these concerned the Hashemite kingdom of Jordan, but others involved Saudi Arabia, the Sudan, and Morocco.

## Among Middle Easterners

Conspiration plays an equally prominent role among Middle Easterners themselves. Secret societies intrigued before World War I, culminating in the overthrow of Sultan Abdülhamit II in 1909. Thereafter, clandestine nationalist groups plotted with and against the foreign rulers. Whether intending to institute democracy or rule despotically, they invariably relied on conspiratorial means. For example, Enver Pasha, the Young Turk leader, came up with the notion of a joint Turkish and German expedition that would clandestinely push Iran and Afghanistan into the war on the Entente side. In the course of the secret expedition, 300 or so Turkish troops donned Iranian clothing.

Military cliques regularly plot to overturn Middle Eastern regimes, with notable success during the 1950s and 1960s. These included Abdel Nasser's "Free Officers" in Egypt and 'Abd al-Karim Qasim's group in Iraq. In Syria, ten military coups d'état took place in the space of 17 years. Jordan from 1951 to 1957 was a "swirl of rumor, intrigue, and conspiracy" where the king prevailed over his opponents because he was a professional conspirator and they but amateurs.[27] Communists and pro-Soviet figures sought to unseat Anwar as-Sadat in Egypt and Ja'far an-Numayri of the Sudan in 1970 and 1971. When Benazir Bhutto won the prime ministership of Pakistan the first time, she never fully controlled her government; eventually the president threw her out of office on dubious charges.

Assassinations are common fare in the Middle East, and virtually every one is part of a real conspiracy. The list of prominent victims is a long one: Kamal Junbalat, Bashir Gemayel, Rashid Karama, René Mu'awwad, King 'Abdallah, Wasfi at-Tall, Anwar as-Sadat, Yitzhak Rabin. Many Palestinian figures lost their lives violently, including Na'im Khadir, 'Isam Sirtawi, Khalil al-Wazir, Salah Khalaf, and Abu Iyad. Musa as-Sadr, leader of the Lebanese Shi'a, vanished in 1978 during an official visit to Libya, probably murdered; and the assassination of Fat'hi ash-Shiqaqi on Malta in October 1995, just after his departure from Libya, prompted Arab press speculations about Qadhdhafi's hand in his death, too. The 1979 assassination in Cannes of Zuhayr Muhsin, head of a

Syrian-backed Palestinian group, was variously ascribed to the Egyptian, Iraqi, Israeli, and even Syrian intelligence agencies. 'Abd ar-Rahman Qasemlu, leader of the Kurdish Democratic Party, agreed to meet with Iranian officials in 1989 in Vienna and was rewarded with an ambush and assassination.

States constantly plot with and against Palestinians. Rightly, the PLO did not believe King Husayn of Jordan when he accepted it as the "sole legitimate representative of the Palestinian people" in 1974 or renounced his claim to the West Bank in 1988. In both cases, he clearly hoped in time to undo both these acts. A Cairo magazine published the purported secret minutes of a 1986 meeting between 'Abd as-Salam Jallud of Libya and the chiefs of the anti-'Arafat Palestinian groups based in Damascus. The transcript quotes Jallud giving instructions to the Palestinians: "play your part in liquidating the 'Arafat group in the camps [of Lebanon] because Syria cannot do that itself. . . . We are prepared to give you all the necessary aid, arms, and ammunition, and so are the brothers in Syria."[28]

On occasion, Arab leaders do in fact ally with Israel against fellow Arabs. In mid-1949, for example, two Arab rivals simultaneously tried to recruit Israelis against the other. Plotting to extend his rule to Syria, King 'Abdallah of Jordan had his emissary inquire of the Israelis whether they would repaint their aircraft "with the colors and markings of Transjordan," and help his effort.[29] At about the same moment, the military dictator of Syria, Husni Za'im, instructed one of his top officers to approach an Israeli counterpart during the two countries' armistice negotiations and offer to assassinate Prime Minister David Ben-Gurion. He hoped thereby to bring the Israeli military to power in Jerusalem so the two military governments could proceed to "obtain control of the Middle East."[30]

The PLO for many years deposited money in Israeli banks for practical reasons (to facilitate the transfer of funds to Palestinians living under Israeli control), but to some it looked like collusion. The PLO itself acknowledged that Israeli intelligence agents had it riddled with agents. Abu Nidal had journalists on his payroll write articles in Lebanese newspapers critical of himself.

Several governments — Tunisian, Egyptian, and Jordanian — encouraged fundamentalist Muslims to gain strength as a way of containing the left, but the most complex such maneuver took place in Algeria, where the fundamentalist Islamic Salvation Front (FIS) replaced the Soviet-oriented National Liberation Front (FLN) as the country's most powerful party. Explaining how this happened, British geographer Hugh Roberts points to the fact that President Chadli Bendjeded and his closest associates "deliberately boosted the FIS's prospects in order to secure the landslide victory of the FIS and the crushing humiliation of the FLN on 12 June 1990. Indeed, evidence indicates that members of the FLN were aware of their leaders' extraordinary conspiracy against their own party."[31] In January 1992, this process came to head when the army deposed Bendjedid, created a *junta*, banned the FIS, and cancelled the elections. Many Algerians read events as does Roberts: Khalida Messaoudi, a leading antifundamentalist, alluded to Bendjeded's conspiracy in noting that "fundamentalism [in Algeria] was born in the presidential dining rooms and in the ministries."[32] Hoçine Aït Ahmed, leader of the Front de Forces Socialistes, saw a FIS victory as "an intentional policy to scare the Algerians, the international public, and to pass as a modern regime."[33]

Arab rulers regularly involved themselves in the internal politics of other countries through terrorism, sabotage, ostracism, propaganda campaigns, military invasions, and outright annexation. Recent decades witnessed many externally sponsored coup attempts; several Arab states had a role in the first military coup d'état of modern times, Iraq's of 1936. When Arab politics were most in flux, during the 1950s, every other military officer seemed to be on a neighbor's payroll. Successful coups often depended on outside aid. The oil boom of the 1970s provided Middle East rulers with resources to lavish on causes abroad. Qadhdhafi of Libya funneled large sums to undermine the shah of Iran, King Husayn of Jordan, and Sadat of Egypt. At times, Middle Eastern money traveled very far from home. Fearing an electoral victory by Jimmy Carter, the shah reportedly made large financial contributions to Gerald Ford's 1976 presidential campaign. As documented by investigative journalist Steven Emerson,[34] the Saudis spawned a whole phalanx of political and corporate hangers-on in Washington prepared to spread Saudi influence.

Middle East authorities alter texts. Not eager for the Western press to know about a hard-line resolution (to the effect that "armed popular revolution" was the "only way" to liberate Palestine) passed at the 1980 congress of Al-Fat'h, Yasir 'Arafat hid the resolutions and blamed reports of them on Israeli propaganda. Hafiz al-Asad joined other Arab leaders in issuing an anti-Iranian resolution in September 1982, then had his media delete mention of the resolution. King Husayn of Jordan took the trouble to deny to an American interviewer rumors to the effect that he had had advance knowledge of the Iraqi invasion of Kuwait. But when Egyptian newspapers reported on this interview the next day, all of them had the king admitting his advance knowledge of the invasion.[35]

## Plots Against Westerners

Middle Easterners also conspire against Westerners. Sa'd Zaghlul, the populist Egyptian leader, reached an agreement with Lord Milner, representing His Majesty's Government, in 1920. Zaghlul pulled a fast one on the British, however, by insisting that the Egyptian people endorse his agreement and promising to urge their support. In fact, he secretly urged Egyptians to demand more than he had won in negotiations, thereby undercutting the agreement.[36] A year later, the ex-Ottoman war leader Enver Pasha agreed to go to Central Asia on behalf of the Bolsheviks and put down a rebellion; once there, he joined the rebellion in an attempt to set up his own Pan-Turkic empire.

Two recent episodes involve Saddam Husayn. The Iraqi attack on the U.S.S. *Stark* in May 1987 appears to have been purposeful. The memoirs of an alleged bodyguard to Saddam ascribes the attack to the Iraqi ruler's desire for vengeance;[37] others interpret the incident as an attempt to have Iran blamed for the deaths, thereby bringing U.S. forces into the war on the Iraqi side.[38] Another incident began in early 1990, when the British authorities arrested Iraqi agents for trying to export nuclear triggers. In response, the Iraqi embassy announced that it had received 28 devices in the mail from an unknown source, in a package marked "nuclear triggers." Portraying this shipment as pretext for an attack on Iraqi territory, the embassy then ostentatiously handed the devices over to the British Foreign Office. Tests showed these to be ordinary electronic components, commonly used in household appliances and widely available in hardware stores.

The Bank of Credit and Commerce International amounted to a gigantic financial conspiracy against the West. As the bank prospered and expanded mightily, its Pakistani leadership conjured up dreams of buying up the West's great commercial institutions even as they plotted to undermine its moral fibre. Taking a step in this direction, it bought the favors of a former American president and a former British prime minister.

## CAUSES OF FOREIGN INTRIGUE

Why so many genuine conspiracies in the Middle East? Those originating outside the region have different explanations from those fomented by locals, so we deal with the two categories separately.

## The Eastern Question System

What L. Carl Brown calls the Eastern Question system[39] accounts for many of the West's plots in the Middle East. This unique and enduring complex requires some explanation.

In the imperial age, India fell to Great Britain, North Africa to France, and Latin America mostly to Spain; but no single power, either external or internal, has dominated the Middle East since 1798. Instead, its territories through two centuries have been the locus of intense competition. Russians, Prussians, Austrians, French, and British all took part in the nineteenth-century tug-of-war over the Ottoman Empire. Both the French and British colonized Egypt. German ambitions in Morocco provoked crises in 1905-06 and 1911. British and Russians faced off in Iran (over control of the country), as did British and Americans (over control of the oil resources). The Italians had aspirations to large stretches of territory, including parts of Anatolia, though they ended up only with Libya. At the same time, proximity to Europe meant that some regions — Ceuta, Melilla, Algeria, the Caucasus, Central Asia — were not just colonized but actually incorporated into the mother country.

World War I changed the tune but not the theme; intense and competitive involvement by outsiders remained the rule. The knottiest questions at the 1919 Paris Peace Conference concerned the Middle East; a peculiar institution called the mandate emerged to regulate relations between European authorities and local residents. As the British gave up control of Palestine in 1948, the United Nations for a brief but important moment bestowed a real voice in Middle Eastern affairs on such distant countries as Guatemala, Peru, and Uruguay; in 1990, Colombia and Malaysia had a critical voice in the U.N. Security Council decision to approve the use of force against Iraq.

## Continuities

Continuities are striking. The Middle East had about as prominent a role in international affairs in the 1830s and 1910s as it does in the 1990s. What the Eastern Question was in the nineteenth century, the Arab-Israeli conflict is in the twentieth — the longest-running and most complex diplomatic issue of the age, and the non-Western issue most likely to cause the Western powers to clash. Nineteenth-century Russophobia foreshadowed twentieth-century anticommunism, while anti-British attitudes turned into anti-American ones. In personal terms, "Muhammad Ali and Nasser,

Palmerston and Dulles, Tsar Nicholas and Brezhnev have been playing the same game."[40] In military terms, the tradition of security missions (German to the Ottoman Empire, French to Egypt) were carried on by Russian and American advisors (to Syria, to Israel). In diplomatic terms, the Vienna Note of 1853 resembles U.N. Resolution 242. What colonial rivalries were in one century, arms sales, foreign aid, and troop commitments were in the next. Understand the one and you understand something about the other too.

Seeing the Middle East as a paramount strategic concern, Western politicians in both centuries embraced it so closely, the rhythms of Western diplomacy came to dominate. The region has been what Brown calls "the most penetrated international relations sub-system," meaning that it has been in the most "continuous confrontation with a dominant outside political system."[41] Looking specifically at Iran, Ervand Abrahamian finds that "foreign powers—first Russia and Britain, later the United States—have, in fact, determined the principal formations in the country's political landscape over the last two hundred years."[42] Politically, the region was turned virtually into an adjunct of Western politics. It was the arena where U.S.-Soviet partnership was seen as most likely, as well as the region which prompted the 1973 nuclear alert and the death-blow to the Nixon-Brezhnev détente.

The powers have acquired such a mystique, they can be blamed even when they are completely absent. British troops were nowhere near the Caucasus in 1826 to 1828 when the Russians won it from Iran; nonetheless, many Iranians held London responsible for this debacle. Similarly, Americans were completely absent from the Caucasus in January 1990, when Soviet troops quelled an Azerbaijani uprising; still, leading Turkish and Iranian voices blamed the West for encouraging the Kremlin "to use force against Azeri Turks" and for "more and more massacres of Muslims."[43] One member of Iran's parliament even saw "America's dirty hands and ugly face" behind the crisis."[44]

For 200 years, Western governments have feared that a rival power was manipulating ostensibly independent Middle Eastern states, thereby becoming puppeteer of the Middle East.[45] In the nineteenth century, each European state perceived its rivals as having more say in the Ottoman capital at Istanbul than was in fact the case. The British (wrongly) saw the Russian-Ottoman Treaty of Hünkâr Iskelesi of 1833 as signifying Russian dominion over the empire. The Russians (wrongly) saw the British ambassador in Istanbul, Stratford de Redcliffe, as the real power behind the Ottoman throne. In the late twentieth century, virtually every American cold war president asserted at one time or another that the Soviets were "meddling," "inflaming," or "inspiring insurrection" in the Middle East. During the Suez crisis, Anthony Eden sent a telegram to Dwight Eisenhower, announcing that "There is no doubt that Nasser, whether he likes it or not, is now effectively in Russian hands, just as Mussolini was in Hitler's."[46] Soviet leaders responded by pointing to arrangements from the Baghdad Pact to "strategic consensus" as proof that American leaders directed Middle East politics. Implicit to this is the notion that Westerners dispose of all power and Middle Easterners are but their playthings.

## How the Eastern Question Spawns Intrigue

The Eastern Question system encourages intrigue in many ways. Rivalry inspires underhanded tricks to gain the smallest advantage. Subterfuge multiplies, while local actors find opportunities to manipulate rivals and powers alike.

First, the Eastern Question system spawned a tradition of the weak getting their way with the strong. What the Ottomans learned about playing off the powers Abdel Nasser applied a century later. Even the weakest players learned the art; in a brilliant move, the Kuwaitis invited both Soviets and Americans in 1987 to protect their oil tankers. Middle Easterners developed or used in novel ways some of the weak state's classic instruments of power, including state-sponsored terrorism, protracted hostage seizures, an oil embargo, and chemical weapons. At times, locals strike a local enemy with an eye to winning help from the powers; thus did Muhammad 'Ali attack Syria in the 1830s and Anwar as-Sadat fight Israel in 1973. Or they can sue the powers for protection from a local enemy, as the Ottoman king responded to Muhammad 'Ali in 1833, Abdel Nasser to Israeli raids in 1970, and the Saudis to Iraqi threats in 1990. The Eastern Question system also encourages preemptive actions to create new circumstances that cannot easily be reversed. What Brown calls "fait-accompli politics" remains the same across two centuries: strike quickly and change facts on the ground before the powers can respond. King 'Abdallah moved into the West Bank, Anglo-French-Israeli forces attacked Suez, the Israelis entered Lebanon, Saddam Husayn invaded Iran and Kuwait, and Hafiz al-Asad seized Beirut.

Second, the system means that the powers ruled most of the Middle East indirectly, at arm's length. Examples include the French in Morocco, the mandatory system in the Levant and Iraq, and Soviet-Syrian ties. Indirect rule spawned competing centers of power and bred scheming.

Ostensibly independent countries experienced more manipulation than those firmly under imperial control. The British could not order about the king of Iraq, but they dearly wanted to, so they did the next best thing and intrigued against him. The French practice of *politique minoritaire*, favoring non-Sunni minorities at the expense of Sunni Muslims (who were expected to be the most antagonistic to French rule), left behind an ugly legacy of suspicion both between ethnic groups and against foreigners. This fear lives on: an unnamed visitor to Secretary of State Cyrus Vance in January 1980 reported that "the Iranians believe the documents found in the [American] embassy [in Tehran] prove that the U.S. is working with minorities and other groups to replace the regime."[47] The ambiguity of power also meant that colonialism began and ended in partial steps; in many cases, no clear date marked the beginning or end of European rule. Historians variously date Egypt's independence to 1922, 1936, 1952, and 1956. The first declaration of a Palestinian state took place in 1948 and a second in 1988; more may yet come. Such ambiguity

> produced a generation of [Middle Eastern] politicians more apt to demand responsibility than to accept it, with a tendency to take refuge from reality that has not entirely died out. This finds expression in an addiction to conspiracy theories: to avoid any serious critical examination of their own societies and even policies and, instead, to place all blame for all evil on former imperial masters and on current enemies, both open and secret.[48]

Third, capitulations (the economic and judicial privileges granted foreign merchants in the Ottoman Empire between the sixteenth and twentieth centuries) contributed to an atmosphere of mistrust. By emphasizing the power of the foreigner and the utility of having foreign protection (better yet: foreign nationality), capitulations spread a mentality of agency throughout the Middle East, a mentality that continues to infect the region's politics long after the disappearance of formal capitulations. Marvin Zonis notes that "Foreign interference has been perceived as so pervasive and so insidious that individual Iranians could best assure their fortune by linking their fates to foreign powers."[49] Peter Avery specifies:

> Foreign patronage was found extremely tempting: it was easy to overcome rivals and to mislead timid compatriots with the air of being "in the know," knowing what the British or the Russians wanted and being able to hint darkly at the consequences of their wants going

unsatisfied. The scope foreign contracts afforded local intriguers was an important feature of Iran's entanglement with the Great Powers.[50]

Not surprisingly, Western diplomats and intelligence agents still receive more offers of assistance than they knew what to do with.

The Eastern Question system permeated deeply into the psyche of the Muslim Middle Easterner, leaving him with fears that shadowy figures in distant capitals make the key decisions affecting his life, that imperial machinations count more than indigenous preferences, and that he is surrounded by conspiracies. If Cromer ruled Egypt as a mere high commissioner, why not suspect the American ambassador of ruling Egypt today?

## CAUSES OF LOCAL INTRIGUE

As for scheming by Arabs and Iranians, they may have learned some practices directly from Europe,[51] but three factors appear to have had the greatest importance: the dream of unity, the personalistic quality of Middle East politics, and the legacy of Jamal ad-Din al-Afghani.

### The Dream of Unity

Reluctant to accept the borders bequeathed them by the colonial powers, Middle Easterners relentlessly pursue expansionist political agendas as they search for larger and more meaningful polities. Their goals include the union of Arabic speakers, Muslims, Turkic speakers, Syrians, and Fertile Crescentians. More than not, politicians have used clandestine means to achieve these larger states.

The drive for Arab unity has spawned the Arab state system, a unique phenomenon. The widely accepted sense that all Arabic-speaking peoples constitute a single nation makes them parts of a larger, mythical whole in which twenty or so governments and the PLO interact as something less than fully sovereign states. Between 1956 and 1967, Gamal Abdel Nasser compiled a stunning record of appealing over the heads of his fellow rulers to inspire Arab populations to agitate for union with Egypt. At the same time, he frequently resorted to clandestine means in pursuing unity ventures with Syria, Iraq, Yemen, the Sudan, and Libya. Mu'ammar al-Qadhdhafi, who provided the farce to Abdel Nasser's tragedy, sought at various times to unify with Mauritania, the Western Sahara, Morocco, Tunisia, Malta, Egypt, Syria, the Sudan, and Chad.

A strange brotherhood at once fraternal and fratricidal drives much of Arab politics. On the one hand, Arab rulers miss no opportunities to lavish fine words of solidarity on their colleagues; on the other, they constantly undermine each other. Thus, six Arab states fought each other in the Lebanese civil war. While almost all the states have pitched in the fight against Israel, they worked at such cross purposes that Israel won every war. In brief, divisions "make the Arab countries prone to manipulation by outsiders."[52]

The dream of unity alternately brings Middle Eastern leaders together and sets them against each other. As rulers look to incorporate their neighbors and fear incorporation by them, they imbue political life with a fluid quality that encourages intrigues and plots. In their more fevered moments, Iraqi pan-Arabists called one minute for the overthrow of the Egyptian and Syrian regimes, the next sought unification with these same polities. 'Abd al-Hamid Zaydani, a fundamentalist Muslim leader in Yemen, neatly summed up these twin tendencies: "Either we unite or we fight."[53]

Harking back to the ancient dream of a single Muslim polity ruled by a single righteous leader, the Muslim Brethren, Ayatollah Khomeini, and radical fundamentalists in Lebanon have sought to create the cooperative basis that might one day lead to the establishment of a latter-day caliphate. They have also plotted across borders in the effort to bring their own kind to power. Afghanistan may be the most prominent victim of this competition.

Pan-Turkic nationalism has had nothing like Pan-Arab nationalism's impact, but here, too, clandestine operations have had a role. Enver Pasha, the Ottoman dictator during World War I, wandered off to Central Asia in 1921 where he tried to carve out an independent anti-Soviet Turcophone state. To attain their goals, Pan-Turkic nationalists took such conspiratorial steps as meeting with Adolf Hitler in late 1941.

Pan-Syrian nationalism, which seeks to create a Greater Syria out of the existing states of Syria, Lebanon, Israel, and Jordan, dominated Levantine politics in the 1930s and 1940s and has been again important since 1974. Its adherents relied mostly on conspiratorial means. Thus, King 'Abdallah of Transjordan furthered his goal of a throne for himself in Damascus by paying Syrians to agitate on his behalf whenever he had adequate funds to spare. Over the years, he gathered these from his royal relations in Iraq, from the Jewish Agency, from smuggling activities, and even from betting on horses in Cairo. The Syrian Social Nationalist Party, founded in 1932, tried to achieve Greater Syria through plots. It had, for example, connections to all three of the Syrian military officers who separately seized power in 1949. It attempted to overthrow the Lebanese government in 1949 and 1961. In recent years, Hafiz al-Asad of Syria has been the key proponent of Greater Syria, and much of his foreign subversion, especially that directed against Lebanese, Palestinians, and Jordanians, seems intended to further this scheme.

Nor should the temptation of the Fertile Crescent be forgotten. This idea, which would add Iraq to a Greater Syria, gets espoused in Baghdad when strong rulers there look to expand westward. It has also inspired plots. Here are two: In 1954, as some Iraqi politicians publicly pursued a federal union with Syria and Jordan, the Iraqi army covertly formulated plans for an invasion of Syria. In 1956, 'Abd al-Illah, the Iraqi regent, contacted the Syrian Social Nationalist Party and established the Free Syrian Movement that planned an invasion of Syria. (Both plots were foiled, however, before they could be put into effect).

## Personality, Not Ideology

Intrigue proliferates when fixed goals are absent and opportunism — the weaving and bobbing for short-term advantage — holds sway.

With rare exceptions, ideologies and ideals matter less to Middle Eastern leaders than the pursuit of power as an end in itself. Arguments are just words and change with circumstance. The politician — Gamal Abdel Nasser and Yasir 'Arafat come to mind — serves as a vessel for others' interests. He avoids taking a clear political position; why make enemies gratuitously? If the prototypical politician in the West takes a stand on the issues and lets the electorate judge him, his Middle East counterpart builds a network of allies, then shifts his stand on the issues as expediency demands.

Political parties represent the interests of a powerful leader, an ethnic community, or a religious gathering — not a group defined by common ideas. (The Syrian Social Nationalist Party is something of an exception.) Parties go through the motions of forwarding causes but really exist to advance interests and ambitions. Coups d'état bring new people to power, not new ideas; in the caustic words of Radio Tehran, Arab coups consist of "moving a handful of tanks at night, changing some faces, and raising new slogans."[54] Even ideologues don't take their own ideas seriously. Samir Qatani, a Jordanian, explains:

> Do you not see [Arab intellectuals] stir us in the mornings with their fiery articles against the alliance countries [versus Iraq] and the

barbarity of the embargo, then appear in the evenings with their happy and joyful faces and perfumed clothes at the parties held by the embassies of the alliance countries where drinks are mixed with women, money, espionage, and buying consciences? Their tongues seem to be saying, "What is said in the morning is wiped out by the night," or, "Hear what we say but do not do what we do!"[55]

Outside observers have frequently noted the insignificance of ideology. A British diplomatic report from Iraq noted in 1933 that politics "had ceased to be a question of parties or policy, and become entirely a matter of personalities."[56] Shmu'el Schnitzer, an Israeli journalist, echoes this view:

In the Middle East, neither the spoken nor the written word has the same meaning it does in the so-called Western, or civilized, or rational world. A man does not say what he thinks, or believes, or intends to do. He says what he deems desirable, right, or worthwhile at any given moment. In two days or two weeks, he will say the very opposite, not because his stand has changed in the meantime, but because his audience, or the public to which he had directed his observations or acts, has changed.[57]

At its most vulgar, this takes the form of selling one's services to the highest bidder; a more refined version is to foreclose no options and stake out no irreversible positions, a mentality summed up by the Arab saying "Kiss the hand you cannot bite."

Two spectacular instances of selling to the highest bidder date from World War I: In December 1915, Cemal Pasha, one of the Young Turk triumvirate running the Ottoman Empire, approached the British and French with the offer that he march on Istanbul, arrest the leadership there, end the campaign against the Armenians, take Turkey out of the war, and cede Istanbul to the Russians. In return, the powers would recognize him as the new head of the Ottoman domains, with his capital in Damascus, and the Armenians would pay him off handsomely.[58] In the other example, Faysal ibn al-Husayn, military leader of the Arab revolt and T. E. Lawrence's partner, proposed to the Turks in late August 1918 that he switch to their side in return for an Ottoman guarantee of Arab independence.[59]

'Abdallah, Transjordan's ruler between 1921 and 1951, simultaneously pursued conflicting activities throughout his long political career. Before World War I, he served as vice-chairman of the Ottoman parliament in Istanbul while conspiring with the British to rebel against the Ottomans. Once ruler of Transjordan, he sought both to attract the backing of his subjects and to make himself useful to his superiors in London. In 1948, he simultaneously cooperated with the Zionists and led the Arab League military campaign to destroy the nascent State of Israel. Such double-dealing is not personal but epitomizes a style found throughout the Muslim Middle East. At 'Abdallah's death, for example, Tawfiq Abu'l-Huda became Jordan's prime minister. A historian says this about him: "His goal was to regain the premiership, and he skillfully maneuvered his way to achieve it. His policy was to take no firm positions on the issues of the day, preferring to make and shed alliances, not commitments."[60]

Gamal Abdel Nasser differed from the Jordanian politicians in many ways, but not this one: he, too, lacked specific principles or goals and was infinitely flexible in his quest for power. Nasserism sounds like an ideology but is neither a system or a movement, much less a coherent body of ideas. It refers, rather, to the charismatic leadership of Abdel Nasser himself. He remained flexible whenever possible, for adopting an ideology would have restricted his freedom of action. What was Abdel Nasser's program of Arab socialism? Lucius Battle, an American ambassador to Egypt, characterizes it as "whatever he wanted to do on any given day."[61] Remarkably, Abdel Nasser held popular adulation without hiding his egoistical purposes. "What is most interesting about him," his biographer P. J. Vatikiotis observes, "is that he was able to retain his mass appeal while openly pursuing a total concentration of personal power."[62]

Musa as-Sadr, the Lebanese Shi'i leader, has been described as being known "to be friend and enemy of the [Lebanese] regime, the rightists, the leftists, and the Syrians, depending on which way the wind was blowing."[63] Hafiz al-Asad and Saddam Husayn were exemplary hard men, ruling on behalf of themselves and their small communities, adopting whatever instruments further their power. Though their speeches brimmed with ideology and principle, these were but a cover for personal ends. While Qadhdhafi went a step further and published his views in books, power for him was not a means to an end but an end in itself. Yasir 'Arafat fit the same mold. He cooperated equally well with fundamentalist Muslims and Marxist-Leninists—without committing himself to either faith; internationally, he wooed conservatives and liberals with the same effectiveness.

As'ad Abu Khalil generalizes: "So desperate are Arab leaders for political legitimacy that they show no consistency in their ideological declarations."[64] But opportunism also infects intellectuals. George Antonius, author of *The Arab Awakening*,[65] spent the final years of his life in a desultory search for power. In the period from 1940 to 1942—that is, during World War II—he sought to work for all of the British, American, German, and Iraqi governments, as well as for Hajj Amin al-Husayni, the mufti of Jerusalem.[66] He was an intellectual for sale, available to the highest bidder (or, in the end, any bidder), with no fixed views or commitments.

Even Ayatollah Khomeini, perhaps the Middle East's outstanding ideologue of the twentieth century, was an opportunist. Early in his political career, he vociferously opposed women or non-Muslims having the right to vote; but when he came to power, both won the franchise. More startling yet, Khomeini disregarded a fundamental Islamic notion and gave the state precedence over Islamic law. Khomeini ruled in January 1988 that "for Islam, the requirements of government supersede every tenet, including even those of prayer, fasting and pilgrimage to Mecca." He also authorized the government to prevent any activity that posed a threat to its interests.[67] This ignores the profoundly important Islamic notion that men bend to God's laws, and not the reverse. In this spirit, his successors helped Christian Armenia in its battle with Muslim Azerbaijan.

In foreign affairs, Arab leaders specialize in abrupt realignments. Damascus backed the PLO in 1975 and fought it in 1976. For 12 years after 1977, Asad relentlessly reviled the Egyptian authorities for making peace with Israel; then one fine day in 1989 he reestablished relations with Cairo and all was sweetness and light. Jordan's King Husayn and 'Arafat made war in 1970; they cooperated in 1982; fell out in 1983; allied in 1985; broke relations in 1986; and made up in 1988. The Kuwait crisis exemplified out this pattern. Saddam Husayn seemingly moderated in the mid-1980s, pleasing his allies of the moment by making the sounds they wanted to hear, only to revert, when the opportunity presented itself, to the most bellicose radicalism. By similar token, he espoused secularism for decades, then adopted Islam at a moment of need. King Husayn of Jordan followed pro-Western policies for 35 years, then abandoned them during the Kuwait Crisis, only to readopt them after the storm passed.

These abrupt changes, astonishing to anyone not conversant with Middle East political mores, constitute an enduring pattern, as Khalid al-Hasan of the PLO explained: "Our Arab history is full of agreements and differences. When we differ and then grow tired of differing, we agree. When we grow tired of agreeing, we differ. . . . This is the Arab nature."[68]

Conspiracies follow from all this pragmatism and opportunism. The typical politician finds plots more congenial than principled stands. "Nobody declares his ambition until certain of success," David Pryce-Jones explains, "because he risks exposure, antagonism, the mobilization of more powerful opponents against him, and perhaps murder. Instead, he intrigues, he influences as best he may, he conspires."[69] In Egypt, for example, conspiracy is much preferred over open political activity. The latter, according to Vatikiotis, "requires a more public commitment to one's convictions," something entirely unwelcome.[70] Conspiracies are a favored, routine means of achieving political goals.

## The Afghani Syndrome

Jamal ad-Din al-Afghani (1839-97), dubbed by his biographer a "confirmed doer, fertile in expedients and stratagems" and an "adroit lifetime conspirator,"[71] served as a model and an inspiration for Muslim activists. Afghani roamed the Muslim world, taking up residence in Tunisia, Egypt, Turkey, Iran, Afghanistan, and India; he also spent periods in England, France, and Russia. In all these places, he propagated his vision of a modernized Islam strong enough to stand up to the rapacious West; he also took money from interested parties, plotted, and (almost everywhere) made himself unwelcome. Afghani joined a Freemason lodge, left it and established his own organization; organized secret societies of thuggish atheists; and was possibly connected to the Babi movement. He planned the assassination of the Khedive Isma'il of Egypt in the late 1870s and he led the Tobacco Boycott that shook the Iranian throne in 1890. In 1896, a disciple of his murdered the shah of Iran, crying out as he pressed the trigger, according to some witnesses, "For Sheikh Jamal ad-Din."[72]

Afghani was personally duplicitous, habitually making up adventures (imaginary trips to Algeria and America) and organizations (the renowned 'Urwa al-Wuthqa apparently existed only in his head). He collected subscriptions for a journal that had suspended publication. Among Shi'a, he presented himself as Shi'i; among Sunnis as a Sunni. When visiting Afghanistan he claimed to be from Istanbul, when in Istanbul he passed as an Afghan; on occasion, he claimed to be Arab; and in London he presented himself as an Iranian (which, in fact, he was). Afghani would spend the day in his library, then disguise himself to roam incognito through the city at night. While posing as the savior of Islam, he espoused some radically antireligious sentiments, at times even doubting the Prophet Muhammad's authenticity. So integral was scheming to Afghani's persona, his life may have ended in a plot: the formal cause of his death was cancer of the mouth, but it came on so quickly many witnesses suspected that the Ottoman authorities, fed up with his conspiring, had poisoned him.

Immersed in the psychology of conspiracy, Afghani reveled in his successes. Writing to his collaborator Muhammad 'Abduh, he explained from Tunis: "Here they believe that we have great wealth and that an unknown force assures our living. What pleases me is these beliefs, more than the wealth itself."[73] Afghani worked with the enemy, taking funds from the Russian imperial government and opportunistically currying favor with the British authorities (praising them on one occasion for "everywhere serving humanity's interests").[74] A maxim revealed both Afghani's deviousness and his intent to undercut religious sensibilities: "Do not cut the head of religion but with the sword of religion."[75] One high Ottoman figure told the Paris police, "This man has never been a Muslim!"[76] and there is reason indeed to believe that his image as a Muslim hid skeptical, not to say atheistic, attitudes. His confusing biography opens him up, not surprisingly, to charges of serving as an agent for the British and other governments.

Afghani also propagated conspiracy theories. To ensure continued rule over India, he held that the British sought to destroy Islam by converting Muslims to Christianity and plotting to undermine Muslim solidarity. This goal allegedly prompted London to place its own candidate in Mecca as caliph and to conquer Egypt in 1882.

Though mainly today remembered as a thinker, Afghani's greater impact may have been in the area of political style. As Bernard Lewis delicately puts it, "The teachings of Jamal al-Din are the expression of a career rather than of an ideology."[77] He created a Middle Eastern prototype much admired and imitated in the century after his death: the conspirator as hero. An idealized image of Afghani's frenetic activities remains a model for all those who would spur change in the Muslim world; and his high personal reputation imbues this with a prestige not attainable in other cultures. Such diverse rulers as Sultan Abdülhamit II, Gamal Abdel Nasser, and Saddam Husayn have all followed his example.

The legacy of nongovernmental activism is even more distinctive. Hajj Amin al-Husayni, Yasir 'Arafat, and other Palestinian leaders worked without the benefit of official power, as did Khomeini before he reached power and Hasan at-Turabi of the Sudan more recently. But Musa as-Sadr, Lebanon's outstanding Shi'i leader in the decade before his death in 1978, most clearly fits Afghani's mold. Like Afghani, Sadr was an ambitious intellectual with (as Fouad Ajami, his biographer, puts it) "the air of conspiracy."[78] On the one hand, Sadr forwarded conspiracy theories; suspecting an Arab-Israeli plot to settle Palestinians in Lebanon, for example, he moved to south Lebanon to help foil this scheme.

Denouncing the shah as an agent of the imperialists, he helped the Khomeini movement.

On the other, he acted conspiratorially. No one knew Sadr's ultimate purpose or the identity of his patron. Pro-shah Iranians painted him as a long-term agent of Ayatollah Khomeini. Anti-shah Iranians claimed that the shah paid as much as $1 million to ensure Sadr's rise to the top of Lebanon's Shi'i hierarchy, or even that he was sent to Lebanon to bring that country under Iranian control. The PLO called him an agent of the CIA or the Lebanese government. The Libyans accused him of building up Shi'a power on Israel's behalf. The Muslim Brethren emphasized Sadr's "deep connections" to Syrian president Hafiz al-Asad.[79] Others tied him to the Iraqi regime. Italian police suspected him of training members of the extreme left-wing organization Prima Linea.

As with Afghani, Sadr's end is a source of enduring mystery. Actually, he went one better than the nineteenth-century figure by not dying but (in the classic Shi'i style) disappearing. Accepting an invitation from Mu'ammar al-Qadhdhafi, he visited Libya in August 1978. The Libyans claimed he then left the country by airplane for Italy, but multiple inquiries make it clear that Sadr never boarded the flight. Why? Many hypotheses have been forwarded; the most likely is that Qadhdhafi accused Sadr of conspiring against Arab unity, Sadr responded with anger, and Qadhdhafi had him executed.[80]

Actual conspiracies spur conspiracy theories by stimulating real fears. And (as we noted in chapter 1, "Spurring Plots"), the reverse holds true, as well: conspiracy theories beget conspiracies. Imaginary plots generate actual ones, actual ones generate imaginary ones, mutually reinforcing each other in an endless, and ever-deepening, cycle of irrationality.

## NOTES TO CHAPTER 16

1. William W. Freehling, "Paranoia and American History," *The New York Review of Books*, 23 September 1971.

2. Manochehr Dorraj, *From Zarathustra to Khomeini: Populism and Dissent in Iran* (Boulder, Col.: Lynne Rienner, 1990), p. 3.

3. Robert Jervis, *Perception and Misperception in International Politics* (Princeton, N.J.: Princeton University Press, 1976), p. 320.

4. Emmanuel Sivan, *Radical Islam: Medieval Theology and Modern Politics* (New Haven, Conn.: Yale University Press, 1985), p. 15.

5. From the title page of W. Morgan Shuster, *The Strangling of Persia: A Personal Narrative* (New York: Century, 1912), which reads: "Story of the European diplomacy and Oriental intrigue that resulted in the denationalization of twelve million Mohammedans." Shuster's memoir is replete with condemnations of European plots.

6. 11 August 1840, Foreign Office 78/392. Quoted in F. S. Rodkey, "Lord Palmerston and the Rejuvenation of Turkey, 1830-41: Part II," *The Journal of Modern History*, 2 (1930): 215.

7. Theodor Herzl, *Zionistisches Tagebücher, 1899-1904*, edited by Johannes Wachten, Chaya Harel, et al. (Berlin: Propyläen, 1985), vol. 3, p. 552.

8. Quoted in Leonard Stein, *The Balfour Declaration* (New York: Simon and Schuster, 1961), p. 519.

9. Letter to Lord Rosebery dated 22 January 1893, quoted in Marquess of Zetland, *Lord Cromer: Being the Authorized Life of Ebelyn Baring, First Earl of Cromer* (London: Hodder and Stoughton, 1932), p. 192.

10. Lord Cromer, "Introduction," in Sidney Low, *Egypt in Transition* (London: Smith, Elder, 1914), p. viii.

11. *The Times* (London), 27 November 1875.

12. Sir Gore Ouseley, letter to Foreign Secretary Castlereagh dated 25 October 1814, Foreign Office 60/9. Quoted in S. F. Shadman, "A Review of Anglo-Persian Relations, 1798-1815," *Proceedings of the Iran Society* 2 (1944): 38. This statement uncannily echoes the pseudotestament of Peter the Great: "Hasten the decadence of Persia, penetrate to the Persian Gulf, re-establish the ancient commerce of the Levant, and advance to the Indies, which are the treasure-house of the world." Quoted in George N. Curzon, *Persia and the Persian Question* (London: Longman Greens, 1892), vol. 2, p. 601. For more on the pseudotestament, see Harry Bresslau, "Das Testament Peter's des Grossen," *Historische Zeitschrift* 41 (1879): 385-409.

13. Juan R. I. Cole, "'Indian Money' and the Shi'i Cities of Iraq, 1786-1850," *Middle Eastern Studies* 22 (1986): 475. In India, the British publicly decried Muslim-Hindu violence but in private they noted the utility of internecine fighting to maintain British rule.

14. Sami al-'Attari on behalf of President Hafiz al-Asad, Radio Damascus, 24 May 1978.

15. *Ath-Thawra*, 14 July 1981. For a conspiracist study on these events, see Yasin Suwayd, *Mu'amarat al-Gharb 'ala'l-'Arab: Muhattat fi Marahil al-Mu'amara wa-Muqawamat'ha* (Beirut: Al-Markaz al-'Arabi, 1992).

16. See Grobba's memoirs, *Männer und Mächte im Orient: 25 Jahre diplomatischer Tätigkiet im Orient* (Göttingen: Musterschmidt, 1967).

17. Marvin Zonis, *Majestic Failure: The Fall of the Shah* (Chicago: University of Chicago Press, 1991), p. 189.

18. Memorandum of a Conversation, 3 October 1955. Text in *Foreign Relations of the United States, 1955-1957*, vol. 14, *Arab-Israeli Dispute 1955* (Washington, D.C.: U.S. Government Printing Office, 1989), p. 543.

19. Keith Kyle reconstructs the protocol's text and related documents in *Suez* (New York: St. Martin's Press, 1991), pp. 565-67.

20. Ibid., pp. 150-51; and also p. 239.

21. John Bulloch, *The Persian Gulf Unveiled* (New York: Congdon & Weed, 1984), p. 26.

22. Wallace Murray quoted in Richard A. Steward, *Sunrise at Abadan: The British and Soviet Invasion of Iran, 1941* (New York: Praeger, 1988), p. 221.

23. Confidential memorandum of conversation written by John D. Stempel, 13 November 1978. Text in Muslim Students Following the Line of the Imam, *Documents from the U.S. Espionage Den (48): U.S.S.R., The Aggressive East*, section 1-2, vol. 48, p. 80.

24. Richard B. Parker, *The Politics of Miscalculation in the Middle East* (Bloomington: Indiana University Press, 1993), p. 102.

25. David W. Lesch, *Syria and the United States: Eisenhower's Cold War in the Middle East* (Boulder, Col.: Westview, 1992), pp. xi-xii.

26. For a cataloguing of these, see Dan Raviv and Yossi Melman, *Every Spy a Prince: The Complete History of Israel's Intelligence Community* (Boston: Houghton Mifflin, 1990).

27. Robert B. Satloff, *From Abdullah to Hussein: Jordan in Transition* (New York: Oxford University Press, 1994), pp. 143, 168.

28. *Ruz al-Yusuf*, 27 October 1986.

29. Quoted in Itamar Rabinovich, *The Road Not Taken: Early Arab-Israeli Negotiations* (New York: Oxford University Press, 1991), p. 105. Jordan was known as Transjordan until June 1949.

30. Quoted in ibid., p. 70; the inquiry is described on p. 102.

31. Hugh Roberts, "From Radical Mission to Equivocal Ambition: The Expansion and Manipulation of the Algerian Islamism, 1979-1992," in Martin E. Marty and R. Scott Appleby, eds., *Accounting for Fundamentalisms: The Dynamic Character of Movements*, vol. 4 of *The Fundamentalism Project* (Chicago: University of Chicago Press, 1994), p. 463. Other analysts dismiss this explanation, saying "[t]here is no non-circumstantial evidence" to support it. See Michael Field, *Inside the Arab World* (Cambridge, Mass.: Harvard University Press, 1994), p.138.

32. *Le Soir* (Brussels), 22 September 1994.

33. *Neues Deutschland* (Berlin), 13 July 1995.

34. Steven Emerson, *The American House of Saud* (New York: Franklin Watts, 1985).

35. *The New York Times*, 16 October 1990; *Al-Ahram, Al-Akhbar*, and *Al-Jumhuriya*, 17 October 1990.

36. For texts of two messages, see 'Abd ar-Rahman ar-Rafi'i, *Thawrat Sannat 1919: Ta'rikh Misr al-Qawmi min Sannat 1914 ila Sannat 1921*, 2d ed. (Cairo: An-Nahda al-Misriya, 1955), vol. 2, pp. 165-69. For an English viewpoint, Lord Lloyd, *Egypt Since Cromer* (London: MacMillan, 1934), vol. 2, pp. 25-32.

37. *Le Nouvel Observateur*, 20-26 December 1990.

38. *The New York Times*, 11 February 1991; Amazia Baram, "Iraq: Between East and West," in Efraim Karsh, ed., *The Iraq-Iran War: Impact and Implications* (New York: St. Martin's, 1989), p. 86.

39. L. Carl Brown, *International Politics and the Middle East: Old Rules, Dangerous Game* (Princeton, N.J.: Princeton University Press, 1984), p. 197. The analysis here derives in large part from Brown's book.

40. Ibid., p. 197.

41. Ibid., pp. 4-5.

42. Ervand Abrahamian, *Khomeinism: Essays on the Islamic Republic* (Berkeley: University of California Press, 1993), p.116.

43. Bulent Ecevit, quoted in *Milliyet*, 6 March 1990; *Jomhuri-ye Islami*, 21 January 1990.

44. Quoted in Tadeusz Swietochowski, *Russia and Azerbaijan: A Borderland in Transition* (New York: Columbia University Press, 1995), p. 208.

45. The ideas and examples in this paragraph derive from Brown, *International Politics and the Middle East*.

46. Quoted in Kyle, *Suez*, p. 272.

47. Warren Christopher et al., *American Hostages in Iran: The Conduct of a Crisis* (New Haven, Conn.: Yale University Press, 1985), p. 103.

48. Bernard Lewis, *The Shaping of the Modern Middle East* (New York: Oxford University Press, 1994), p. 61.

49. Marvin Zonis, *Majestic Failure: The Fall of the Shah* (Chicago: University of Chicago Press, 1991), p. 170.

50. Peter Avery, *Modern Iran* (London: Ernest Benn, 1965), p. 40.

51. Mirza Malkum Khan, a leading Iranian political figure of the nineteenth century, acknowledged sitting at the feet of Westerners to learn about making plots. He told Wilfrid Scawen Blunt, a British admirer: "I went to Europe and studied there the religious, social, and political systems of the West. I learned the spirit of the various sects of Christendom, and the organization of the secret societies and freemasonries." Quoted in Wilfrid Scawen Blunt, *Secret History of the English Occupation of Egypt: Being a Personal Narrative of Events* (New York: Alfred A. Knopf, 1922), p. 63.

   It is hard to tell how true this statement is. Malkum's biographer describes the passage in which it occurs as a "web of distortion, mendacity, and charlantanry." See Hamid Algar, *Mirza Malkum Khan: A Study in the History of Iranian Modernism* (Berkeley: University of California Press, 1973), p. 12. In contrast, Blunt came away from his encounter with Malkum "with the impression that he was the most remarkable man I had ever met" (p. 63).

52. Michael Field, *Inside the Arab World* (Cambridge, Mass.: Harvard University Press, 1994), p.151.

53. Agence France Presse, 15 April 1990.

54. Radio Tehran, quoted in Bruce Maddy-Weitzman, "Islam and Arabism: The Iraq-Iran War," *The Washington Quarterly*, Autumn 1982, p. 185.

55. *Sawt ash-Sha'b*, 30 September 1991.

56. Foreign Office 371/16903, E 1724/105/93, 22 March 1933. Quoted in Mohammad A. Tarbush, *The Role of the Military in Politics: A Case Study of Iraq to 1941* (London: Kegan Paul International, 1982), p. 53.

57. *Ma'ariv*, 4 June 1991.

58. Peter Hopkirk, *Like Hidden Fire: The Plot to Bring Down the British Empire* (New York: Kodansha International, 1994), pp.129-30.

59. Liman von Sanders, *Fünf Jahre Türkei* (Berlin: August Scherl, 1920), pp. 330-31.

60. Satloff, *From Abdullah to Hussein*, p. 28.

61. Quoted in Robert D. Kaplan, *The Arabists: The Romance of an American Elite* (New York: Free Press, 1993), p. 149.

62. P. J. Vatikiotis, *Nasser and His Generation* (New York: St. Martin's Press, 1978), p. 268.

63. Raphael Calis, quoted in Peter Theroux, *The Strange Disappearance of Imam Moussa Sadr* (London: Weidenfeld and Nicolson, 1987), pp. 49-50.

64. As'ad Abu Khalil, "Al-Jabriyyah in the Political Discourse of Jamal 'Abd al-Nasir and Saddam Husayn: The Rationalization of Defeat," *The Muslim World*, July-October 1994, p. 256.

65. George Antonius, *The Arab Awakening: The Story of the Arab National Movement* (Philadelphia: J.B. Lippincott, 1938).

66. Martin Kramer, "Ambition's Discontent: The Demise of George Antonius," in Uriel Dann, ed., *The Great Powers in the Middle East, 1919-1939* (New York: Holmes & Meier, 1988), pp. 409-12.

67. *Kayhan*, January 8, 1988. This edict—and not the one against Salman Rushdie and his publishers—is from an Islamic standpoint likely to be Khomeini's most signficant as well as his most controversial.

68. Radio Monte Carlo, 7 December 1984.

69. David Pryce-Jones, *The Closed Circle: An Interpretation of the Arabs* (New York: Harper & Row, 1989), p. 93.

70. P. J. Vatikiotis, "Egypt's Politics of Conspiracy," *Survey* 18, no. 2 (Spring 1972): 83.

71. Elie Kedourie, *Afghani and 'Abduh: An Essay on Religious Unbelief and Political Activism in Modern Islam* (New York: Humanities Press, 1966), pp. 23, 62.

72. *The Times*, 7 May 1896. Quoted in Homa Pakdaman, *Djamal-ed-Din Assad Abadi, dit Afghani* (Paris: G.-P. Maisonneuve et Larose, 1969), p. 181.

73. Kedourie, *Afghani and 'Abduh*, p. 105.

74. Letter of 19 November 1895 to Sir Philip Larrie, British ambassador in Istanbul, Foreign Office 60/594, folios 173-75. Quoted in Pakdaman, *Djamal-ed-Din Assad Abadi*, p. 177.

75. Asghar Mahdavi and Iraj Afshar, *Majmu'ah-i Asnad u Madarik-i Chap Mashudeh dar Barah-i Sayyid Jamal ad-Din Mashhur bi Afghani* (Tehran: Entesharat-e Daneshgah-e Tehran, 1342/1963), plates 138-39. In this, Afghani may have emulated Mehmed Bey (1843-74), an Ottoman aristocrat with radical ideas and possibly connections to the Carbonari, who occasionally dressed as a Muslim religous official the better to insinuate his ideas.

76. Report dated 28 March 1884, Djemal-Eddin dossier, archives of the Préfecture de Police à Paris. Quoted in Pakdaman, *Djamal-ed-Din Assad Abadi*, p. 83.

77. Lewis, *Shaping of the Modern Middle East*, p. 108.

78.  Fouad Ajami, *The Vanished Imam: Musa al Sadr and the Shia of Lebanon* (Ithaca, N.Y.: Cornell University Press, 1986), p. 159.

79.  'Abdullah Muhammad al-Gharib, *Wa-Ja' Dawr al-Majus: Al-Ab'ad at-Ta'rikhiya wa'l-'Aqa'idiya wa's-Siyasiya li'th-Thawra al-Iraniya* (Cairo: Dar al-Jil, 1983), p. 409.

80.  *Jeune Afrique,* 3 December 1980.

# 17.

# Political Structures

A thousand friends are too few;
a single enemy, too many.
                            —*Persian proverb*

In the East it is safer to treat everyone
as if he might some day be your enemy.
                            —*Isabel Burton*[1]

The failure to establish stable nation-states or democratic political structures in the Muslim Middle East creates a variety of problems, some of which—especially hypocrisy, mirror-imaging, and autocracy—have a direct bearing on the incidence of conspiracism.

## THE ARAB STATE SYSTEM

### Public-Private Discrepancies

The powerful bonds of Islam and the Arabic language have spawned an Arab state system like no other. They require a leader to defer to the Arab consensus, that weighted average of publicly held opinions by the Arab governments, and to keep his true views under wraps. As a result, the kings, presidents, emirs, and their underlings speak one way in public and quite differently in private. The general rule is simple: to the world, profess brotherly feelings for fellow Arabs and hostility toward non-Arabs; in private—or in crisis—let out what you really feel, namely something approximating the reverse.

As long ago as 1925, a British official in Iraq found that Iraqis who agitated for Mosul to be made part not of Turkey but of their country, "when asked in secret for their preferences, replied, not in favour of the Iraq they were so noisily defending, but of Turkey."[2] King 'Abdallah of Jordan was quite prepared to live in peace with a Jewish state but could not let his fellow Arab leaders know this. So he had a crucial role in persuading the Arab League to attack the newly declared Israel in May 1948, and his forces acted with particular vehemence, to the point that they constituted the main danger to Israel's survival. Prime Minister Sulayman an-Nabulsi of Jordan publicly denounced the Eisenhower Doctrine in early 1957; privately, however, he informed the Department of State he found it not a bad idea, and that he was even willing to receive a special American emissary to discuss "mutual problems."[3] The Egyptian government in 1990 publicly condemned General Michel 'Awn of Lebanon for asserting Maronite rights against the Asad regime. In private, Egyptian officials could barely conceal their delight at the trouble 'Awn made for their Syrian nemesis.

Flowery compliments are traded even as preparations are under way for a stab in the back. Yasir 'Arafat perhaps suffers from this syndrome more than anyone else. In 1969, he enjoyed the praise of this Iraqi hosts; but because he didn't sufficiently reciprocate, an army truck purposefully rammed his car, breaking his arm. Saudi publicists celebrated 'Arafat over the decades; but their true feelings came out after the Iraqi invasion of Kuwait. Bandar bin Sultan, the Saudi ambassador to Washington, called 'Arafat "that clown,"[4] and a scathing newspaper article had this to say about the PLO leadership:

> There are vast areas of hatred and degradation between us and them. We are not their kinfolk, nor are they ours. If they howl like hungry wolves, we tell the desert demons to laugh and laugh again, and then let their howls echo like their sirens' echo. From now on we will not show mercy on those who show no mercy on themselves. . . .
>
> They behave as though the world consists of a group of terrorist organizations like the ones they head, which can be swayed very naïvely and stupidly toward their adolescent dreams.[5]

Predictably, Gamal Abdel Nasser exemplified this contradictory pattern, adopting stands as the occasion suited him. Publicly he led the fight in the Arab League against the American idea of a Jordan Valley Authority to allocate Jordan River waters; privately he accepted this plan.[6] Abdel Nasser almost single-handedly made Israel into the central issue of Arab politics early in his presidency, at which time Miles Copeland described him thinking the Palestine issue to be "unimportant."[7] In contrast, at the end of his presidency, Abdel Nasser softened his public position toward Israel, while hardening his position in private. Abdel Nasser even acknowledged his inconsistency. Three days after accepting U.N. Security Council Resolution 242, which set out the terms for a resolution of the conflict with Israel, he instructed the army brass not to "pay any attention to anything I may say in public about a peaceful solution."[8] To President Kennedy he acknowledged that "some Arab politicians were making harsh statements concerning Palestine publicly and then contacting the American Government to alleviate their harshness by saying that their statements were meant for local Arab consumption."[9] Of course, "some Arab politicians" included, preeminently, himself.

To make matters yet more confusing, politicians sometimes break their own patterns. Abdel Nasser on occasion told American officials the same in private as he said publicly: that he was convinced the U.S. government "was trying to keep Egypt weak and that this resulted from Jewish influence" in the United States.[10]

Things can get very complicated, indeed. On some occasions, public utterances about Israel are less bellicose than confidential ones: Yasir 'Arafat publicly renounced terrorism in December 1988 and accepted Israel's right to exist, but he apparently did so with a wink, for reports of his private conversations consistently pointed to a much harder line. At other times, Arabs pretend to have worse relations with fellow Arabs than is the case. Salah Khalaf of the PLO recounts an anecdote from a 1976 meeting with Hafiz al-Asad in which the Syrian dictator thanked Khalaf for warning him that Kamal Junbalat, the Lebanese Druze leader, was an American agent. To this, Khalaf quotes himself replying indignantly, "But it isn't true! I never said that!"[11] To make matters murkier yet, years later Khalaf reported that Walid Junbalat (Kamal's son and political successor) once requested two favors of his Palestinian allies. First, "Insult me so that Syria will be satisfied with me." Second, "Allow me to insult you, so that my relations with Syria will continue to be good."[12] What did Khalaf actually tell Asad? Did Junbalat really make these requests? From the conspiracist point of view, it hardly matters; either way, the anecdotes provide grist for the conspiracy theorist's mill.

Arab leaders praise those they secretely hate and attack those they admire. Brotherly feelings and aggressive intentions coexist in unique proximity, creating a discrepancy between feelings and words, between words and deeds, and between private and public pronouncements. If words do not express genuine feelings, how can the listener know what the speaker really intends? Hypocrisy fosters a mood of mistrust and fears of conspiracy.

## Projection

Individuals often project their own motives and behavior onto others. Overwrought suspicion of imperialism, for example, often signals expansionist ambitions on the part of he who suspects. This important rule of thumb explains some Middle Eastern conspiracy theories.

For example, because pan-Arab nationalist leaders have a history of clandestine support from their putative European opponents, they assume Zionist leaders had the same help and cannot take seriously the idea of Jewish nationalism as a populist movement. Middle East leaders call on their citizens abroad to serve as agents; naturally, they assume foreigners behave in like fashion. Egyptians and Syrians suddenly joined into the United Arab Republic and soon after became enemies; mirror-imaging suggests that Soviets and Americans were not quite the enemies they appear to be. Saddam Husayn killed his own high-ranking Iraqi officials in helicopter crashes, so he suspected something amiss when an Egyptian helicopter crashed in March 1981, killing the commander-in-chief of the army and many top generals. The Saudis bought influence in the United States, so they logically suspected Americans of doing the same in the Middle East. Preoccupied with devising schemes against Great Britain, Ayatollah Khomeini had to believe in a reciprocal British obsession with Iran.

Completely baffled by a free society with independent institutions, the Middle Easterner assumes that discordant opinions in the West are part of a subtle plan to mislead the foreigner. Labor unions in the Middle East are ostensibly independent but actually work for the government; their Western counterparts must fill the same role. Middle Eastern leaders use the media, educational institutions, and preachers to disseminate their own propaganda; they assume Western governments do likewise. Western parliamentarians only make a pretence of disagreeing with the head of government. Judges go through the motions of being independent from the political leadership. Juries strike Middle Easterners as preposterous; allow important decisions to be made by the riffraff? An obvious ploy they would never fall for. And so, a fundamentalist analysis deemed the jury in the World Trade Center case a "bunch of morons" that did precisely "as the establishment wanted it to."[13]

Freedom of the press is a sham; Western governments intervene whenever it pleases them. When a Lebanese reporter saw a colleague from *The New York Times* meeting over drinks in Beirut with a CIA agent, he assumed they were organizing "what the world was going to hear the following day, a doctored version of the US government's point of view."[14] During Desert Storm, two *Wall Street Journal* journalists noted that many Arabs "discount reports in the Western media, assuming that, like so much of their own press, it is in the pay of governments or factions, giving its audience exactly what it wants to hear."[15] For years, Saddam Husayn curried favor with journalists by giving them gifts — sometimes as substantial as luxury cars. Naturally, when his government didn't like news reports from Agence France Presse and Radio Monte Carlo in June 1995 telling about a rebellion of the Dulaym tribe, it asserted that governments had used "petrodollars" to bribe employees at those institutions.[16] Qadhdhafi spoke for many when he asserted that "There is no true democracy in the West, nor freedom of the press, nor freedom of broadcast."[17] When nobody is trustworthy, no information reliable, the environment becomes very favorable to conspiracism.

Intelligence services operate in the Middle East virtually without restraint: so too must the CIA, MI6, and G-2. Sometimes (as in Pakistan) the *mukhabarat* have more power than the head of government, so why not in the United States? The shah of Iran "suspected that a 'hidden force' controlled the United States, assassinating Kennedy and anyone else who got wind of its existence."[18] This outlook helps explain Qadhdhafi's eccentric reading of American politics. "Clinton is a good guy. . . . But the CIA is deceiving him."[19] Qadhdhafi then went further: "Clinton is a victim, just like us. He is a victim of the CIA and imperialism, and we're concerned about him, that he might face the same destiny as JFK."[20]

When faced with the undeniable reality of benign liberal practices, Middle Easterners find some way to explain them malignly. The self-restraint of the Israeli authorities during the *intifada* — no tanks, no massacres — raised suspicions of a conspiracy. One Jordanian explained: "The Likud is interested in the perpetuation of the Intifada, in order to destroy the Jordanian option and afterwords to bring about a population transfer."[21]

Projection extends to conspiracy theories, too. A Libyan writer ascribes to Westerners what Libyans themselves do when they blame everything that goes wrong on outside forces: "should we remain terrified whenever there is a car accident on a road in a Western city because they would accuse us of masterminding the accident by putting sleeping pills in the driver's coffee? . . . we would not be surprised if one day they make us responsible even for the storms which have been hitting the American Mid-West and for the fog in which Britain is shrouded."[22] Such statements betray the way in which conspiracism can overwhelm Middle Easterners.

## AUTOCRATIC REGIMES

By their very nature, autocratic regimes—the type of government that, other than in Turkey and Israel, predominates throughout the Middle East—spawn conspiracy theories. The state not only benefits from them, but it engages in schemes against its own citizenry.

### Benefits

An autocratic ruler finds that conspiracism has many uses to strengthen his government.

*Lay a trap.*    Conspiracy theories spin a web around the enemy and, if practiced with skill, can reduce him to silence. Saddam Husayn once asked an American reporter a provocative question (why the U.S. government helped Israel acquire nuclear weapons), then preempted her response: "I do not want you as an American to answer me, because I know that you cannot answer me out of fear of the Zionist lobby."[23] This canny remark trapped the journalist and permitted her no possible reply.

*Protect the ruler.*    Conspiracy theories isolate the country from foreign influences, build powerful sentiments of unity, and help forge a common identity. Abdel Nasser's constant stress on the imperialist bogeyman united Egyptians against a fearsome enemy. Saddam Husayn insisted that Iraqi children be taught to "beware foreigners, for they are the eyes of their country and some of them seek to destroy the revolution."[24] Accusing foreign short wave radio stations of plotting against the homeland makes it easy to prohibit, even to criminalize, listening to their programs. Conspiracy theories create an atmosphere of suspicion and mistrust, thereby intimidating domestic enemies and enhancing the ruler's power.

*Win support.*    The conspiracy theorist offers a complex brew of despair and hope. Islam and the Muslims are surrounded by enemies, but the day can yet be won—so long as the conspiracy theorist gets your support.

*Burnish a reputation.*    Conspiracy theories exaggerate the enemy threat and so enhance those who stand up to him. The Palestine Liberation Organization long excelled at finding intrigues, especially Israeli assassination attempts, that its heroic fighters just barely managed to defeat. By establishing the organization's prowess, these victories enhanced its political standing.

*Relieve responsibility.*    Conspiracy theories ascribe unpleasant domestic realities to foreign manipulation and so get the authorities off the hook. Thus, Iraqi media referred to the flight of the Kurds in 1991 as the "so-called" refugee problem the Americans and British promoted to make Baghdad look bad and violate its sovereignty.

*Justify misbehavior.*    For those who engage in misdeeds, conspiracy theories have great value, for nothing else will explain away the facts.[25] For example, to get around the simple brutal truth of Saddam Husayn's murderous, unprovoked invasion of Kuwait, every argument in his favor relied on a conspiratorial explanation. These differed one from the other, but all were premised on a hidden hand. Saddam's enthusiasts saw the whole episode as an American ploy to reduce Iraq's oil revenues, destroy the Iraqi arsenal, capture Kuwait, or set up a permanent military presence in the Persian Gulf.

*Explain away awkward situations.*    Conspiracy theories offer great flexibility. In January 1980, when the Iranian government sought to keep United Nations Secretary General Kurt Waldheim out of public view during his visit to Tehran, it conveniently discovered a plot against him and, out of ostensible concern for his safety, kept him under wraps. When Arab states bury the hatchet and reconcile, they often blame Zionist or imperialist manipulation for their prior problems, neatly clearing the slate for improved relations. Thus, Syrian leaders had for ten years viciously assailed Cairo for its peace treaty with Israel; when the moment arrived to renew relations on Egyptian terms, they took refuge in a conspiracy theory, claiming relations between the two states had to be reestablished to combat plots against the Arab nation.

*Impugn a rival.*    Conspiracy theories connect enemies to Zionist or imperialist elements, thereby weakening them. So well did Gamal Abdel

Nasser fabricate evidence about the Egyptian upper classes collaborating with foreigners to topple his regime that he spawned widespread concern about what was in fact a dispossessed and powerless group of people. When Egyptian students demonstrated against new regulations issued by the Ministry of Education in November 1968, the government responded by arresting the leadership and branding at least one of them an Israeli spy. Likewise, the Jordanian authorities muttered about an "imperialist and Zionist design" in 1968, as West Bank notables toyed with the idea of electing one of their own as the area's governor. Saddam Husayn became president of Iraq on 16 July 1979; needing to rid himself of politicians of uncertain loyalty, a mere six days later he convoked a meeting of Ba'th Party stalwarts. There, using the excuse of a Syrian conspiracy against his rule, he picked out 20-plus individuals and promptly had them executed. Revolutionary Iranian leaders accused enemies of "conspiracy against the Imam's line," a very effective line. In 1991, this tactic was used with success against no less a personnage than the deputy speaker of the parliament. In a near parody of this reflex, when two women denounced President Rafsanjani emerging from the elevator of a hotel as a murderer and threw eggs at him, the Iranian press agency dubbed them "Zionist agents."[26]

***Establish a tyranny.***    The conspiracy theorist can make accusations a tool to enhance his own power. Saddam Husayn mastered this mechanism early on in his career and used it often. His biographers say he brought the technique of exposing fabricated plots to "awesome perfection" and describe it as "an excellent tool for eliminating actual and potential opposition, sending pointed signals to external enemies . . . and terrorizing the population into total subservience."[27]

***Find political support.***    Understanding that Palestinian nationalism would gain widespread support only by arousing passions associated with Jerusalem, Mufti Amin al-Husayni accused the Zionists of planning to demolish the Islamic sanctities in Jerusalem and replace them with the Third Temple.

***Justify aggression.***    Conspiracy theories invariably portray the enemy as offensive and so sanction preemptive action. The Arab case against Israel rests on a multitude of conspiracy theories: the global ambitions of the Elders of Zion, Greater Israel, Israel as U.S. agent, and so on. When Saddam Husayn wanted to bully Kuwait into ceding territory and reducing its oil output, he ascribed it an elaborate plot of gobbling up

Iraqi territory in league with the "imperialist-Zionist plan against Iraq."[28] When Saddam invaded Kuwait, he did so in response to an alleged Kuwaiti conspiracy to wreck his country's economy. The patent falsehood of these claims (Iraqi armed forces outnumbered Kuwait's entire citizenry; Saddam received billions of Kuwaiti dollars to prosecute his war against Iran) did not seem to matter.

***Rewrite history.*** Conspiracy theories dispose of awkward news and reduce inconsistencies, permitting the government to control the past. The 1961 Iraqi claim to Kuwait—an event recorded in countless documents, newspapers, and memoirs[29]—was deemed a "phoney story" put forward by British intelligence as "a pretext to wave the flag."[30] News reports from Romania about Arab commandos fighting with the security forces loyal to Nicolae Ceausescu, the deposed dictator, embarrassed the PLO, so it denied their truth and said "Zionist elements" working at Radio Free Europe made them up.[31]

***Attack skeptics.*** Conspiracy theories permit despots to turn the tables on those who question their activities, justifying *ad hominem* and other attacks against their critics. So convinced were Iranian leaders in 1980 that the U.S. government stood behind the Iraqi attack on them that "anyone doubting [this view] runs the risk of being considered part of the conspiracy."[32] Forwarding contrary information points to evil motives; skepticism suggests sympathy for the plot; criticism implies participation in it. Doubt equals complicity, denial confirms that which is denied.

## Media Lies

Authoritarian states do not permit adequate coverage of the outside world, leaving their citizens widely ignorant. The media in the Muslim Middle East reflects the government's (or in Lebanon, the patron's) outlook and makes few efforts to establish the unvarnished truth. This leads in two ways to conspiracism: first, the press constantly harps on conspiratorial themes and sometimes convinces its audience; second, the fog of lies creates an atmosphere conducive to conspiracy theories.

In the perpetual search to mobilize constituents, Arab and Iranian autocrats conjure up a host of enemies via conspiracy theories. "A political opposition that does not exist in reality has to be invented because of the way in which the polity is constructed."[33] Dictators personally instigate major conspiracy theories in speeches and interviews, which their media then repeat *ad nauseam*. Hard news and commentaries alike spew out conspiratorial visions. Scholarship, school materials, novels, dramas, and films then further promote the same themes. The paranoid style eventually becomes ubiquitous.

Do Middle Easterners believe their media? Less well educated citizens seem to take it more seriously than those more knowledgeable about the world. During the Kuwait crisis, for example, when Iraqi and Iranian media alike accused King Fahd of Saudi Arabia of being a covert Jew, a Bedouin on the West Bank believed them. "I didn't believe it when I first heard it," he explained, "but the King of Saudi Arabia, may Allah curse his soul, is a Jew in disguise and that is why he does the Arabs so much harm."[34] Constant repetition makes the palpably false become plausibly true.

Even when audiences respond to disinformation, non-news, and slanted news with wariness, disbelieving much of what the media purveys, still they fall prey to conspiracism. "By intimidating and censoring the press," Sattareh Farman Farmaian writes in her memoir about life in Iran, the shah's government

> kept everyone in a kind of informational fog, a miasma of governmental lies, promises, propaganda, and grandiose claims that no one could disprove even if they wanted to try because the newspapers dared not publish the information. In Iran, no one could ever be quite sure of anything, except that it wasn't what the government said it was.[35]

This may sound like a way to avoid the government's conspiracy theories; in fact, it is not. Not being sure of anything is ideal grounding for conspiracism. Michael Field observes that "among the young belief in conspiracies is partly a product of the incomplete, boring and occasionally distorted information they are fed by their own countries' media. The television and radio is of a low standard everywhere in the Arab world. There are very few news comment programmes and those that are broadcast are uncontroversial."[36]

As the populace seeks alternate sources of news, it most often turns to rumors. Word of mouth (what Americans have dubbed the "souktelegraph") carries the alternate news. Passing along information can take up hours of the day in the authoritarian Middle East. One observer says "it would be no exaggeration to say that gossip mongering is the principal form of amusement in Saudi Arabia for foreigner and native alike."[37] An Iranian newspaper concedes that "if every baseless rumor were to be refuted in the press, there would be no place or time for the actual mission of the media."[38] It's just as well that the official media does not even try, for it would not be believed. "People in Egypt have learned to trust rumor over their Press," observes an Egyptian ex-general.[39] Not only is the whispering campaign "as effective as radio broadcasts," Hisham Sharabi concludes, but its content "is not so much reporting as reading meaning into developments and events."[40]

Rumors typically deal with subjects such as religion, sex, or sports, very often with a conspiratorial content. Sometimes they merely confirm the general fear of conspiracy; at other times, they have specific and weighty consequences. In a striking instance of deep ignorance, many Iranians in the 1970s thought all Westerners to be Americans, increasing their numbers substantially and fueling a widespread belief that Americans were planning to take over Iran. When rumors swirled about a traffic accident in Gaza in December 1987, wrongly alleging that the Israeli driver was the brother of an Israeli murdered two days earlier in Gaza, "the rumor was no rumor but an indisputable fact,"[41] as two Israeli authors put it. This conspiracy theory went on to provoke the *intifada* and years of violence.

## Irregular Procedures

Authoritarian rulers rarely bother to maintain standard operating procedures or hierarchies. Captains give orders to general, errand boys keep an eye on managers, and best friends inform for the secret police. In one striking instance, the head of air force security, one of the key officers in the whole security apparatus, was filled in Asad's Syria by a mere major (who happened to come from Asad's religious community). As Kanan Makiya notes, "things are never what they seem; the janitor may command more real power than the boss."[42] It is reasonable to worry that a person is really someone else.

Further, this twilight world of authoritarianism encourages over-interpretation. Power has a personalized quality; all bends before the Leader. The masters on high are scrutinized for signals, even trivial ones, for clues about the fate of the polity. An apparatchik's presence or absence in a photograph can mean massive changes under way. Such concerns occur even at the highest levels of state. "Asad began [the conversation] by recalling pleasant memories of mutual friends of ours, which clearly indicated to me his determined opposition to the agreement," writes Foreign Minister Elie Salem about his effort to convince the Syrian president not to oppose Lebanon's May 17 withdrawal agreement with

Israel.[43] The citizenry becomes expert at imaginary interpretation — a skill conducive to conspiracism.

Daily life reinforces this susceptibility. To stay out of trouble in an autocracy, citizens must actively avoid and deceive the government. Getting along means breaking laws and routinely engaging in intricate subterfuges. Everyone relies on codes and innuendoes, talks only in certain places, and always stays alert for informers. Fawaz Turki explains that "the Arab confronts revelation by concealment, information by misinformation, and sharing by withholding. Thus, what the Arab leader will say is what he does not mean, the Arab peasant will mean is what he does not say."[44]

Skepticism can lead straight to gullibility. Fevered interpretations promoted by the rulers and their media erode the commonsense ability to weigh evidence within their citizenry. As the fearful bosses create larger and more extravagant lies, truth and falsehood lose their distinctiveness and in some cases nearly merge. A vicious circle sets in, whereby people lose the ability to judge for themselves and become vulnerable to outlandish conspiracy theories. Here's an example of getting carried away, written by Jean Said Makdisi, a sophisticated Beiruti:

> There was a man who lived on the street not far from my home. We had taken him at face value as the lunatic he seemed to be. . . . He had constructed a strange, movable hut of rags and feathers, and he wore a very peculiar, pointed hat over his pointed, bearded face. He would dart out into the street and ring a brass bell at the passing cars. Many are those who, moved by his madness and homelessness, gave him money in charity, and who later beat their fists on their foreheads in anger when they read that in reality he had been a captain in the Israeli army.[45]

That Makdisi could believe the Israelis would deploy an army captain in such a fashion speaks volumes about Middle East credulity.

### NOTES TO CHAPTER 17

1. Isabel Burton, *The Inner Life of Syria, Palestine, and the Holy Land* (London: Henry S. King, 1875).
2. C. J. Edmonds, *Kurds, Turks and Arabs: Politics, Travel and Research in North-Eastern Iraq, 1919-1925* (London: Oxford University Press, 1957), p. 404.

3. Quoted in Robert B. Satloff, *From Abdullah to Hussein: Jordan in Transition* (New York: Oxford University Press, 1994), p. 162.

4. *The New York Times,* 27 February 1991.

5. *'Ukaz,* 12 December 1990.

6. Michael B. Oren, *The Origins of the Second Arab-Israeli War: Egypt, Israel and the Great Powers, 1952-56* (London: Frank Cass, 1992), p. 117. Chapter 5 provides a full account of Abdel Nasser's negotiations with Israel.

7. Miles Copeland, *The Game of Nations: The Amorality of Power Politics* (New York: Simon and Schuster, 1969), pp. 69-70, 113.

8. Quoted in Mohamed Heikal, *The Road to Ramadan* (New York: Quadrangle/The New York Times Book Co., 1975), p. 54.

9. Foreign Broadcast Information Service, *Daily Report,* Near East & South Asia, 21 September 1962, no. 185.

10. Telegram from George V. Allen, 1 October 1955. Text in *Foreign Relations of the United States, 1955-1957,* vol. 14, *Arab-Israeli Dispute 1955* (Washington, D.C.: U.S. Government Printing Office, 1989), p. 539.

11. Abou Iyad, *Palestinien sans Patrie* (Paris: Fayolle, 1978), p. 301.

12. *Al-Watan,* 15 December 1989.

13. Editorial in *Crescent International,* 16-31 March 1994.

14. Saïd K. Aburish, *Beirut Spy: The St George Hotel Bar* (London: Bloomsbury, 1989), p. 17.

15. Geraldine Brooks and Tony Horwitz, "To Hear Jordanians Tell It, U.S. Already Has Lost the War," *The Wall Street Journal,* 22 January 1991.

16. Iraqi News Agency, 14 June 1995.

17. *Al-Majalla,* 5 December 1993.

18. Ervand Abrahamian, *Khomeinism: Essays on the Islamic Republic* (Berkeley: University of California Press, 1993), p.128.

19. *Al-Musawwar,* 11 March 1994.

20. *The Los Angeles Times,* 27 March 1994.

21. Quoted in Meron Benvenisti, *Intimate Enemies: Jews and Arabs in a Shared Land* (Berkeley: University of California Press, 1995), p. 88.

22. *Ash-Shams* (Tripoli), 25 September 1993.

23. Iraqi News Agency, 1 July 1990.

24. Saddam Husayn, *Ad-Dimuqratiya: Masdar Quwwa li'l-Fard wa'l-Mujtama'* (Baghdad: Dar ath-Thawra, 1977), p. 20. The same passage also includes a call for children to report on their parents.

25. This generalization applies to legal misdeeds as well as political ones: for example, to believe in O. J. Simpson's innocence logically requires a conspiracy theory about the Los Angeles police.

26. Islamic Revolution News Agency, 10 December 1991.

27. Efraim Karsh and Inari Rautsi, *Saddam Hussein: A Political Biography* (London: Brassey's [UK], 1991), p. 41. Karsh and Rautsi cite examples (on p. 208) from 1968, 1969, 1979, 1982, and 1990.

28. Radio Baghdad, 18 July 1990.

29. For a sampling of evidence, see *Middle East Record* 2 (1961): 117-39.

30. Aburish, *Beirut Spy,* pp. 47-48. Aburish has so shakey a grasp of the facts, he has this event off by two years, placing it in 1959.

31. Sawt Filastin (Sanaa), 27 December 1989.

32. Richard W. Cottam, *Iran and the United States: A Cold War Case Study* (Pittsburgh: University of Pittsburgh Press, 1988), p. 223.

33. Khalil, *Republic of Fear,* p. 38.

34. Saïd K. Aburish, *Cry Palestine: Inside the West Bank* (Boulder, Col.: Westview, 1993), p. 87.

35. Sattareh Farman Farmaian, with Dona Munker, *Daughter of Persia: A Woman's Journey from Her Father's Harem Through the Islamic Revolution* (New York: Crown, 1992), pp. 269-70.

36. Michael Field, *Inside the Arab World* (Cambridge, Mass.: Harvard University Press, 1994), p. 169.

37. William Powell, *Saudi Arabia amd Its Royal Family* (Secaucus, N.J.: Lyle Stuart, 1982), pp. 10-11.

38. *Kayhan,* 30 March 1995.

39. Saad El-Shazly, *The Crossing of the Suez* (San Francisco: American Mideast Research, 1980), p. 293. The same author observes in another book, *The Arab Military Option* (San Francisco: American Mideast Research, 1986), p. 173: "Word-of-mouth is the true medium of the Arab people and rumours are its daily headlines."

40. Hisham Sharabi, *Nationalism and Revolution in the Arab World* (Princeton, N.J.: Van Nostrand, 1966), p. 101.

41. Ze'ev Schiff and Ehud Ya'ari, *Intifada: The Palestinian Uprising—Israel's Third Front,* trans. Ina Friedman (New York: Simon & Schuster, 1990), p. 18.

42. Samir al-Khalil [pseud. of Kanan Makiya], *Republic of Fear: The Politics of Modern Iraq* (Berkeley: University of California Press, 1989), p. 117.

43. Elie A. Salem, *Violence and Diplomacy in Lebanon: The Troubled Years, 1982-1988* (London: I. B. Tauris, 1995), p. 88.

44. Fawaz Turki, *Exile's Return: The Making of a Palestinian American* (New York: Free Press, 1994), pp. 124-25.

45. Jean Said Makdisi, *Beirut Fragments: A War Memoir* (New York: Persea Books, 1990), pp. 189-90.

# Conclusion

# Hope For the Future?

If you believe you can avoid the plot it will be all right.
—*Ahmad Jibril, leader of the Popular Front for the Liberation of
Palestine—General Command*[1]

The conspiracy theory is at this time what paralyzes
Muslim political thought.
—*Olivier Roy*[2]

One might think that Khomeini's phenomenal success in overturning
the shah, plus the fact that he and his heirs have ruled Iran for nearly
two decades, would disincline Iranians to conspiracy theories. That, however, has not been the case. In fact, the regime has maintained a thick veil
of conspiracism.

But how long can this last? Conspiracy theories appear less to be a
permanent feature of the Middle East than one of the West's unintended
influences on a laggard people. In theory, anyway, conspiracy theories
should have an end. Will they?

This matter has great importance, for only by going beyond conspiracism can the Middle East escape its current political morass. Only by
taking responsibility for themselves can Arabs and Iranians overcome the
current turmoil and negative trends. "The most dangerous enemies of the
Muslim peoples at this time," Bernard Lewis argues, "are those who assure
them that in all their troubles the fault is not in themselves but in open or
occult hostile forces."[3]

## REASONS FOR OPTIMISM

What chance that Arabs and Iranians will leave grand conspiracy theories behind? We begin with evidence to support an optimistic assessment, then conclude with thoughts about the changes required for the Middle East truly to free itself of conspiracism.

### Taking Responsibility

Despite the many examples in this study of evasion and blame, some Middle Easterners analysts and politicians do think clearly and honestly about their problems. They demand accountability; they even declare conspiracy theories to be false.

Taking responsibility for one's actions seems to becoming more widespread; Kevin Dwyer gives highlights of his long conversations on the human rights predicament in Arabic-speaking countries with Egyptian, Tunisian, and Moroccan intellectuals; hardly one blamed current problems on Israel or imperialism.[4] Along these lines, an Iranian newspaper sensibly pointed out that the West's cultural encroachment in Iran is less "a cultural aggression planned by statesmen" than "the undesirable overflow" of Western ways.[5] Some politically involved individuals actively fight the impulse to impute conspiracies. Sattareh Farman Farmaian tells how she wanted no part of the "suspicion, mistrust, and sense of impotence that crippled us [Iranians]."[6] She also quotes an anonymous Iranian poem of 1989:

> Do not denounce the foreigner, or lament anyone but us.
> This is the heart of the matter — our affliction came from us.[7]

After the Arab military defeats of 1948-49 and 1967, intellectuals such as Qunstantin Zurayk and Sadiq al-'Azm openly critiqued Arab political life, dissecting and prodding it to discover key flaws. Along similar lines, the Kuwait war prompted a number of writers to take a long, hard look at their politics. For example, Zuhair al-Jaza'iri comments that "Whenever the pressure of reality on the [Iraqi] Ba'th increases from outside, it turns into an enemy or worse still a conspiracy. There can be no question of comprehending reality or responding to it."[8]

In one noteworthy analysis, an Egyptian writer found the Iraqi people highly culpable for their ruler:

How can we absolve the Iraqi people of responsibility [for Saddam]? Their position is astonishing and is due to one of two things: either they are satisfied and happy with what is going on in their country, and they support the man; or they reject these comedies leading to Iraq's ruin. If the latter is the case, they must rid themselves of this stigma, impose their own will, and establish a regime that can achieve freedom and democracy for them. The entire matter is still in the hands of the Iraqi people, and they must rise up to safeguard their dignity.[9]

Interestingly, this robust ascription of responsibility to the Iraqi citizenry went far beyond that of the U.S. government, which portrayed Iraqis as victims. Sobered by the Saddam catastrophe, some Iraqi intellectuals reached similar conclusions. Ayad Rahim, a scholar of Iraqi origin, finds that

most Iraqis—and I've witnessed this particularly among those living abroad—are not facing up to their historic responsibility for their country's current condition. They would rather treat the ruling regime (and thereby the catastrophe it has brought upon the country) as a foreign creation imposed from outside. They do this, of course, because it is simply much easier and more comforting to deal with an external cause for one's problems than to look within for faults and causes. Saddam Hussein is seen as a monster, alien to the society and culture, inflicted upon Iraqis by non-Iraqis.[10]

Kanan Makiya takes this same issue squarely on:

Instead of recognizing their own fallibility and frailty, Arabs have, on the contrary, been perfecting in the last quarter of a century a different kind of language, one that is constantly preoccupied with blaming others, in particular blaming the West and Israel for problems that are largely—although not completely—of their own making.[11]

Makiya makes responsibility for oneself a central goal of his political program:

If the cycles of violence, bloodshed, hopelessness, and despair are to be brought to an end, then Arabs must look inward—not outward to the West—and begin to realize that they are overwhelmingly responsible for the deplorable state of their world. . . . The first step out of the morass is the ruthless and radical one of uprooting, from deep within our own sensibilities, the intellectual and moral authority that blaming someone else still carries today among us Arabs.[12]

Behind closed doors, politicians sometimes take responsibility for their actions. In a statement worth quoting at length, Gamal Abdel Nasser privately berated himself and his closest associates for their failings.

> Just imagine —we are the members of the Supreme Executive Committee which is the highest political authority in the country, and there were only seven of us, and yet we did not speak out and tell the truth at the proper time. . . . This means that the system deteriorated and gradually collapsed to the point where we were afraid to speak out and to tell the truth. . . .
>
> [I]t is we, the high-ranking officials in the system, who have caused the system to crack. Each one of us is destroying what another one is doing whereas all of us, at every level, should be aware of our united destiny. . . .
>
> Our enemies have been unable to dismantle a single brick in our internal structure in spite of all the efforts they have exerted whereas we, the ones who were responsible for building that structure, have gradually destroyed it. This is why it is impossible to continue as we were before 1967. If it becomes evident to us that our new rivals are better and firmer that we are, then let us declare with the utmost courage and honesty that we are leaving so that we can be replaced by others who are more eager than ourselves to serve the people and to serve the interests of the country. Our selection of an open system will also require a lot of change, otherwise it will be nothing more than words and the people will have no confidence in it.[13]

Unfortunately, these wise words did not have any practical or public consequences; but at least they indicate that Abdel Nasser realized how far he had strayed from the correct path.

## Speaking Out against Conspiracy Theories

Middle Eastern opinion leaders occasionally go further and specifically condemn conspiracism. An Iranian newspaper ridiculed those who implied about their enemies "that every night the CIA or Mossad call that person up and tell him that he is doing a good job."[14] Ibrahim Sa'ada, the editor-in-chief of a Cairene daily, caustically commented on the actions of Yasir 'Arafat (also known as Abu 'Ammar) after the Palestinian insulted a deceased Egyptian prime minister:

> Certainly, Abu 'Ammar will back down on this slander, if he has not already done so — and swear that he did not say what he said, or that, at least, U.S. imperialism and world Zionism distorted his words with a view to harming Palestinian-Egyptian ties. This has been 'Arafat's habit. . . . He slanders us publicly and hastens to apologize in private.[15]

Mahmud an-Naqu'a, a Libyan intellectual, denounced conspiracy theories, arguing that they hold Arabs back from development. Even before he fled Iraq, Sa'd al-Bazzaz, editor-in-chief of the Iraqi daily *Al-Jumhuriya,* criticized Saddam Husayn and the Iraqi leadership for being "overly influenced by conspiracy theories."[16]

Religious leaders also lend their voices to this effort. Egypt's leading Islamic authority, the grand imam of Al-Azhar, told his audience that "What is happening to the Muslims now is their own doing."[17] A top Iranian ayatollah, Musavi-Ardebili, made the same point at length in this remarkable statement:

> We have problems in the country, economic problems, political problems, non-economic problems. We have problems. America is the mother of corruption. It creates these problems, carves them out, and imposes them on us. . . .
>
> But to say that all our problems stem from America is not true. That is forgetting ourselves. Some of our problems — be it more or less, I am not concerned whether it is 50, 40, 60, 70 percent — 30 percent of our problems are of our own doing. We are not using our active work force. Is that America's doing? We love luxuries. Is that America's fault? We take advantage of the chaotic market situation. Is that American's fault? We are opportunists. Is that America's doing? We lack proper management in the country. Is that America's fault? We have thousands of problems of our own. Why should they be attributed to America? . . .
>
> [N]ot all our problems have to do with America; only some of them are brought about by that regime. These problems, however, cannot be resolved through cooperation and compromise with

America. However, if we become aware, independent, and self-confident, and if we try to solve our problems independently and have confidence in ourselves, all our problems will doubtless be resolved, be they those which have to do with us only, or the ones brought about by America. . . .

Let us turn toward ourselves. Let us solve our problems ourselves, God willing and through God's grace. We possess many capabilities. We have oil, we have mines, we have forests, we have fields, we have agricultural potential. If we make use of these capabilities through hard work, through endeavor, with high motivation; if we rise up and work hard and work well, all these difficulties which I referred to—I do not wish to elaborate on them—all these difficulties will be solved.[18]

Intellectuals also weigh in. Here are three examples from Egypt. Muhammad Sid Ahmed, a leftist, noted that Islamic groups "imagine that everything is conspiratorial. There is nothing more damaging for human rights than a conspiratorial attitude, an attitude that reached its *summum* in the terror of the French Revolution. You look upon everything that is not in line with your own thinking as a conspiracy against you and you end up attributing social phenomena to a subjective conspiracy."[19] A columnist pointed out that "Israel is neither an American satellite, nor is it one of the states of the United States. It is also neither a lackey nor a protégé, but a party with a long reach."[20] Saddam talked about a plot against Islam, but Ahmad Bahjat, a writer, held that "his suspect role and his dominion over Iraq constitute the real plot against Muslims."[21]

Scholars confront conspiracism by bringing to bear the tools of their craft. Thus, Jahangir Amuzegar looked carefully at the conspiracy-theory explanations of the fall of the shah and dismissed every one of them as without merit.[22]

Artists occasionally chide their audiences about the hidden hand mentality. 'Aziz 'Ali, a satiric Iraqi singer of the 1940s and 1950s, sang how "The disease that is in us, is from us and inside us."[23] Lenin ar-Ramli's *In Plain Arabic* attempted to shake up Egyptians by making them aware of their assumptions. "We look for causes to our problems far from us," he explained, "when these causes are within ourselves. We do not confront reality. We believe in our fantasies."[24]

Politicians also publicly denounce the hidden hand mentality.[25] Sa'd Jum'a, the Jordanian prime minister during the 1967 war, broke with the conspiratorial analyses of the Arab military defeat in the Six-Day War. For him, Israeli victory "was not a matter of an unheard-of miracle or extraordinary capabilities, but the logical result of sweat, fatigue, faith, and effort over nineteen years, during which time the Arabs were drowning in swamps of vituperation and conspiracy."[26] Other politicians make sensible comments on the subject of Israel. Foreign Minister Tahir al-Masri of Jordan berated his own people: "We Arabs live as if the ghost of conspiracy controlled our every brain cell. . . . Any issue, regardless of how clear, immediately evokes doubts and interpretations on the motives behind it."[27]

Shahpour Bakhtiar, the shah's last prime minister, often noted that "We Iranians are not willing to face reality. We have to recognize that whenever we have failed, the worm is in our own tree."[28] Hasan at-Turabi, the effective leader of the Sudan, observed that, "Unfortunately, most people think in terms of conspiracy and people who pull the strings behind the scenes."[29] The Egyptian interior minister, Muhammad 'Abd al-Halim Musa, calmly and firmly refused to blame foreigners for the sectarian strife taking place in Egypt in early 1990. He even offered specifics:

> Had there been any financing from the outside, Shawki ash-Shaykh, leader of the New Jihad Organization killed during the Fayyum incidents, would not have resorted to imposing fines and fees on farmers and residents of Fayyum. . . . I cannot say that Israel is taking part in the sectarian sedition in Egypt.[30]

The Iraqi invasion of Kuwait in 1990 stimulated unusual soul-searching in the Middle East. Abdulla Y. Bishara, secretary general of the Gulf Cooperation Council, accused Saddam's regime of living "in a soap opera world in which everything it does or says is unreal."[31] President Husni Mubarak commented: "The Arab nation has become afflicted by a disease. When I do not agree with you, you call me a traitor and an agent. . . . In Europe there are endless differences but Europeans do not indulge in insults as is the case in the Arab nation."[32]

The situation, in short, is not entirely bleak; voices of sanity and responsibility in the Middle East raise the hope that this way of thinking may eventually be superseded. Not only do some Arabs and Iranians appear willing to recognize their own responsibility, calling for their peoples to take matters into their own hands, but some public figures explicitly denounce conspiracism.

## THE NEED FOR MODERNIZATION

### Is Optimism Justified?

Some Middle Eastern observers see in these and similar statements the basis for a basic shift in outlook. Ayad Rahim is optimistic about Iraqis, deeming them "far less conspiratorial in their thinking than they used to be, say ten or fifteen years ago." He notes that "many Iraqis have been looking inward, exploring themselves and Iraqi society for clues as to how and why Iraq got into such a mess."[33] In like fashion, Mehrdad Izady finds that Kurds tend to take responsibility for their own problems. "In the aftermath of the 1991 Persian Gulf War, it was not a surprise to those familiar with the Kurdish character to see Kurdish refugees first and foremost blaming their own leaders and not their non-Kurdish enemies for their predicament."[34]

Western specialists tend also to find improvement. Richard Cottam believes that the notion of a hidden American hand dictating developments inside Iran "is gradually losing credibility."[35] Bernard Lewis perceives "a growing readiness among Arabs, in discussing the ills of their society, to seek the fault not in their stars—or in their enemies—but in themselves."[36] John Entelis writes that Arab intellectuals appear for once more inclined to blame chaotic conditions in their countries "on the Arabs themselves instead of searching for conspiracies among Western imperialists or other outsiders."[37] Journalists concur with this assessment. *The Economist* holds that "growing numbers of Arabs are at last willing to say . . . that the main problems of the Arab world are self-inflicted; and that solving them must begin with political reform at home."[38] Michael Field finds conspiracism "a more popular explanation for events among the older generation than it is among the young."[39]

But this optimism may be premature. Statements denying conspiracy theories are rare, while conspiracy theories themselves remain near ubiquitous. The whispers of common sense get lost in the thunder of accusations and fears.

There is another, far more profound reason for doubting that the Middle East's era of conspiracy theories will end any time soon. Leaving them behind requires more than a few declarations; it requires deep-rooted structural changes in thinking. The conspiracy mentality flourishes not because of a people's emotionalism or flightiness, but because it meets a real need. Preposterous notions circulate only so long as they have a use and will fade only when no longer functional. In this instance, events drive thinking; what takes place on the ground has great impact on what happens in the head.

## What Must Change

What fundamental changes must Middle Eastern political culture pass through before conspiracism loses its grip? Four deep and perhaps inter-related problems appear to cause Middle Easterners to rely on conspiracy theories: the Muslim fall from grace, the influence of European conspiracism, the legacy of real conspiracies, and the near ubiquity of autocracy.

The latter three explanations ultimately connect back to the first one—the trauma of lagging behind the West in all important ways. This leads to the Middle East's having come under European influence and having failed to establish an independent and stable state system. Muslims will probably move beyond conspiracism only when they come to terms with a lowered position or achieve mundane success commensurate with their self-expectations. How do the prospects look?

Accepting a permanently inferior position seems out of the question. Nothing in the Muslims' long history points to such resignation. Nor should they. The wheel of fortune always turns; the civilization least fortunate today will some day find its liabilities neutralized or perhaps turned into assets.

What, then, is the prospect for success? This depends on the Middle Eastern ability to modernize. One comparative study of the region's modernization concludes it has achieved "disjunctive development." The people are more skilled than most around the world but the political structures more tyrannical; the wealth greater but also more dependent on outsiders; in all, the region's potential is great but its path to success very far from assured.[40]

Modernization requires a thoroughgoing commitment from a population to learn from the outside world, to set up strong structures, and to implement policies conducive to economic advancement. All these steps imply a confidence in self not presently found in the Muslim world. Only when such a self-assurance exists will modernization occur, and only then will Muslims be able to deal with the West as an equal. At that point, the conspiracy theory era should come to a close.

None of this, however, is in the cards for the foreseeable future. At this time, the region appears not to be catching up but falling further behind. And so, one must reluctantly conclude that the Middle East will not soon be relieved of the conspiracist burden.

## Can Westerners Help?

While in the end Arabs and Iranians must solve their own problems, Westerners must recognize that the Muslim predicament results in large part from the bruising encounter with their own civilization. This insight should encourage an approach to Middle Eastern conspiracism based on a constructive spirit of understanding. *The Encyclopedia of Human Behavior* advises those treating clinically paranoid patients "to steer a midline between directly challenging the patient's delusions and reinforcing them by implying agreement";[41] by analogy, Westerners attempting to discourage conspiracism must also tread a fine line. They might start with five steps:

*Teach.*    Westerners can help Middle Easterners learn some critical points about modern life.

First, while Arabs and Iranians first encountered such concepts as democracy, freedom of speech, freedom of religion, civil rights, and the rule of law almost two centuries ago, these principles remain alien to all but a small minority of them. Not comprehending these doctrines, Middle Easterners cannot make out the motives of Western governments. Cultural distance thus encourages credence in conspiracy theories about Europe and America. Only when they "develop a greater sense of openness and awareness of the workings of other states"[42] will Middle Easterners realize that not all governments — and especially not democracies — engage in perpetual conspiracies; only then will they abandon the belief that plots drive international politics.

Second, conspiracies usually fail. Take the big three of Middle East plots — the Sykes-Picot Agreement, the Lavon affair, and the Iran/*contra* affair: all three misfired dismally. And that, indeed, is how schemes usually end.

Third, conspiracy theories entail dangers. Promulgating conspiracy theories sometimes does real harm to the one who spreads such accusations. "The Shah," Marvin Zonis observes, "despite his attacks on the West and his efforts and those of his officials to foist the failings of their rule onto foreigners, never managed to convince the Iranian people that they were not part of some foreign conspiracy to crush Iranian culture."[43] Quite the contrary; in the end, the shah managed only to convince Iranians that his government served as agents to a foreign power. Saddam Husayn's conspiracism has contributed directly to the ruin of his country. Conspiracy theories prolonged and worsened the Lebanese civil war.

Fourth, the paranoid mentality traps its own practitioners. Accuse others of conspiring and you get accused in turn. The Saudis often accused Zionists of fronting for Communism; so it was particularly fitting when Isa Muhammad, leader of the Ansaaru Allah Community in Brooklyn, New York, condemned the Saudi-sponsored Muslim World League as a Communist front. The more emphatically an Arab proclaims Israeli conspiracies, the more likely to be tarred with the brush of Zionist conspiracy. After 40 years of anti-Zionism Yasir 'Arafat still found himself hounded with gibes about his being an Israeli agent.

Throw dirt and it gets thrown right back. Gamal Abdel Nasser, the great conspiracy theorist, ended up accused of agentry for both Washington and Moscow. He delivered so little on what he promised, those he disappointed made the first charge; his announcing a crackdown of the Muslim Brethren while visiting the Soviet Union prompted fundamentalist Muslims to understand him in league with the Communists against themselves. As for the Muslim Brethren, they accused the great Arab belle-lettrist Taha Husayn of working for French intelligence (which, thoughtfully, even provided him with a French wife). It was poetic justice when Hasan al-Banna, founder of the Muslim Brethren, found himself accused of agentry for the Freemasons. And just as the Muslim Brethren portray every opponent as a Zionist agent, it in turn is suspected of working for the Central Intelligence Agency.

Western diplomats should counsel that the best way to diminish such accusations is not to make them oneself. Husni Mubarak of Egypt offers a happy example. Moderate in style, he engages in few conspiracies, rarely accuses others of them, and in turn is little accused by others.

**Deny.**    The high road — not dignifying the outrageous with a response — does not work. Left alone, conspiracy theories fester. Europeans and Americans should do as Middle Easterners: respond promptly. Without being rude, they can signal their disdain of Middle Eastern fancies and rationales.

When talk of Syrian complicity in Lebanon with the Maronites and Americans gathered force, Syria's President Asad responded directly, denying in an April 1976 speech as "groundless" all charges that he was siding with Christians against Muslims.[44] Three months later he explicitly raised and denied the charges of an "American-Syrian plot" in Lebanon. Asad eventually tried to put this issue to rest by reasserting the "firm and principled" Syrian position.[45] "Sick voices" was the Saudi characterization of Iranian efforts to blame the July 1990 deaths of pilgrims in Mecca on the police.[46] One day after Baghdad accused the Saudis of participating in a scheme to undermine Iraqi currency, Riyadh mocked the report. Egypt's Communications Ministry responded to conspiracy theories about a U.S. firm building the country's telephone system and so being able to tap it at will, even when Mubarak or 'Arafat were on the phone, by insisting there was "absolutely no truth" to this report.[47]

The Kuwaiti foreign minister-in-exile did not hesitate to call Iraqi accusations against his government "fabrications and unfounded lies."[48] When the PLO spread rumors about Israelis making up part of the American expeditionary force in Saudi Arabia, both the Israelis and Saudis immediately denounced the report. In one of the more colorful and direct efforts to cope with the accusation of conspiracy, President Husni Mubarak of Egypt confronted Mu'ammar al-Qadhdhafi of Libya at an emergency Arab summit meeting just after the Iraqi invasion of Kuwait. After a morning session, Qadhdhafi regaled PLO officials with accusations that calling the summit meeting showed Mubarak part of an "imperialist conspiracy against the Arab nation." Hearing this comment, Mubarak confronted the Libyan: "Mu'ammar, if you think I would be party to such a conspiracy, as you say, then I would long ago have sent a couple of armoured divisions to occupy Libya; I had a hundred and one pretexts for doing so, as you know." This apparently left Qadhdhafi speechless, so Mubarak put a hand on his shoulder and added, "Come, I will buy you lunch."[49]

The Russians know what to do. When alarm spread during 1990 about the decline in tensions between Americans and Soviets, and what this would mean for the Middle East, the Soviet ambassador to the United Arab Emirates, Feliks Nikalayevich Fedotov, explicitly denied the existence of a "U.S.-Soviet conspiracy."[50] This sort of denial may not be heeded, but it needs to be made, repeated, and amplified.

The Israeli government usually hastens to deny a conspiracy theory. After Yasir 'Arafat presented X-rays of the Hamas fatalities in November 1994 and noted that the type of bullet was found only in the Israeli arsenal, the reply came quickly: "The IDF today rejected 'Arafat's hints that Israel was involved in some way in the death of demonstrators in Gaza last Friday."[51] Faced with rumors about Israel seeking economic hegemony over the Middle East, Shimon Peres replied, "[W]e are not giving up control over Arab territory in order to win control of the Arab economy."[52]

Americans should emulate this practice. Sometimes they do. Postwar suspicion of Jewish power was so strong, recalls Miles Copeland, a CIA operative at the time, that American diplomacy in the Arab world from 1947 to 1952 consisted largely of trying "to convince the various Foreign Offices that our Government was not under the control of the Zionists."[53] In October 1989, Secretary of State James Baker directly responded to Iraqi accusations about Washington attempting to bring down Saddam Husayn: "the United States is not involved in any effort to weaken or destabilize Iraq."[54] During his now-notorious meeting with five U.S. senators in April 1990, Saddam Husayn repeatedly alluded to "a large-scale campaign" in the West against Iraq. Senator Alan Simpson (Republican of Wyoming) replied to this barrage: "There is no conspiracy by the U.S. government, or in England or Israel, to attack this country."[55]

Those denials did not work, but others may eventually pay off. Anwar as-Sadat credited his own enlightenment to just such persuasion. "My talks with Dr. Kissinger convinced me," he explained, "that he rejects the simplistic notion of some of your strategists who see — or saw — Israel as the American gendarme in this part of the world."[56] Sadat is not likely soon to become a model for other Middle East leaders, but to the extent they realize the excessive quality of their fears, the more likely it will be that they live in peace with their neighbors. Western rejection of conspiracism, along with hints that Middle Easterners will win international respect only by dropping this mentality, can go a long way, for Arabs and Iranians take Western opinion very seriously.

*Refute.*     An inquiry, medical, legal, or otherwise, can puncture the conspiracist balloon. Schoolgirls in the town of Jenin on the West Bank fell victim to spells of fainting, dizziness, and body pains in March 1983. The mayor of Jenin accused nearby Jewish residents of spreading a poison specifically aimed at the girls. The symptoms then spread so that by April girls in many West Bank towns were overcome by the same symptoms. Finding nothing in the blood or urine of the afflicted girls, the Israeli authorities called on the U.S. Centers for Disease Control to investigate. The Americans found the cause to be hysteria, not poison. Gary Sick's "October Surprise" allegations prompted two congressional probes into the issue, both of which forcefully denied the truth of his allegations about the 1980 Reagan campaign making a deal to delay the release of American hostages in Tehran.[57] Such inquiries can put conspiracy theories to rest, although not always; the *Protocols* and the assassination of John Kennedy have survived more than one in-depth investigation.

*Do not conspire.*     Were Westerners to act more scrupulously, they could begin to shed their long-established (and partially deserved) reputation for deviousness; Middle Eastern suspicions might then diminish. This means acting with special propriety: make no back-door deals, permit no major discrepancies between stated policy and actual behavior, and avoid even the appearance of deviousness.

On occasion, Westerners do take care not to raise suspicions. This appears to have been the motive of George Allen, the U.S. ambassador in Iran, when he refused to coordinate actions with the British embassy in 1946. Similarly, Lyndon Johnson hesitated to meet with Foreign Minister Abba Eban of Israel on the eve of the Six-Day War to avoid the appearance of collusion.

But there is no assurance of success, as the case of Anthony Parsons, the last British ambassador to the shah's court, shows. When suspected of supporting Khomeini against the shah, Parsons denied the charge, but to no avail. As one Iranian told him: "But of course you have to say that. I know. I was educated in your country and am married to an English lady. You cannot deceive me."[58] During his final meeting with Shah Mohammad Reza Pahlavi, the monarch pressed Parsons to recommend a course of action. Parsons avoided an answer, protesting that the shah would construe whatever he said as a British plot. Only when the latter gave his word of honor that Parson's advice would not be misrepresented did the ambassador volunteer his own thinking.[59] Even so, he could not escape suspicion; what one Iranian called Parson's "inordinately defensive stand" had the perverse effect of confirming Iranian assumptions that he supported Khomeini.[60] In some instances, any response will be as proof of malign intentions; conspiracy if you do, conspiracy if you don't.

While outsiders can help at the margins, Middle Easterners alone can take the steps that will enable them to transcend conspiracism. Only when the utility of conspiracy theories ends will their reliance on this crutch come to an end. Each people has to realize the mistake of conspiracy theories on its own and cannot be taught this from the outside. The burden ultimately has less to do with the actions of outsiders than with the circumstances and psychology of Middle Easterners.

### NOTES TO CONCLUSION

1. *Ash-Shuruq* (U.A.E.), 3-9 December 1992.

2. Olivier Roy, *L'Echec de l'Islam politique* (Paris: Seuil, 1992), p. 34.

3. Bernard Lewis, "The Middle East Crisis in Historical Perspective," *The American Scholar*, Winter 1992, p. 46.

4. Kevin Dwyer, *Arab Voices: The Human Rights Debate in the Middle East* (Berkeley: University of California Press, 1991).

5. *Tehran Times,* 10 December 1992.

6. Sattareh Farman Farmaian, with Dona Munker, *Daughter of Persia: A Woman's Journey from Her Father's Harem Through the Islamic Revolution* (New York: Crown, 1992), p. 202.

7. Quoted in ibid., p. 329.

8. Zuhair al-Jaza'iri, "Ba'thist Ideology and Practice," in Fran Hazelton, ed., *Iraq Since the Gulf War: Prospects for Democracy* (London: Zed, 1994), p. 49.

9. *Al-Wafd,* 1 May 1992.

10. Ayad Rahim, "Attitudes to the West, Arabs and Fellow Iraqis," in Hazelton, ed., *Iraq Since the Gulf War,* p. 189.

11. Kanan Makiya, "Intolerance and Identity," in Hazelton, ed., *Iraq Since the Gulf War,* p. 197.

12. Kanan Makiya, *Cruelty and Silence: War, Tyranny, Uprising, and the Arab World* (New York: W. W. Norton, 1993), pp. 283, 326.

13. Quoted in Abdel Magid Farid, *Nasser: The Final Years* (Reading, Eng.: Ithaca Press, 1994), pp. 78-79, 87, 88.

14. *Ettala'at,* 24 October 1989.

15. *Akhbar al-Yawm,* 21 July 1990.

16. Report on a book by Bazzaz titled *Harb Tulid Ukhra,* in *The Christian Science Monitor,* 3 August 1992. Bazzaz defected from Iraq in October 1992. Bazzaz further elaborated on this theme after leaving Iraq. See Saad al-Bazzaz, "An Insider's View of Iraq," *Middle East Quarterly,* December 1995, p. 71.

17. Jadd al-Haqq 'Ali Jadd al-Haqq, quoted in *'Aqidati* (Cairo), 14 February 1995.

18. Voice of the Islamic Republic of Iran, 19 November 1993.

19. Dwyer, *Arab Voices,* p. 63.

20. Mahmud 'Abd al-Mun'im Murad, "Kalimat," *Al-Akhbar,* 25 June 1990.

21. *Al-Ahram,* 20 August 1990.

22. Jahangir Amuzegar, *The Dynamics of the Iranian Revolution: The Pahlavis' Triumph and Tragedy* (Albany, N.Y.: State University of New York Press, 1991), pp. 79-96.

23. Quoted in Makiya, *Cruelty and Silence,* p. 320.

24. *The New York Times,* 31 January 1992. Muhammad Subhi, the play's director, adds to this: "We have to understand that we [Arabs] have a problem, and the problem is that we do not recognize that we have a problem" (ibid.).

25. In addition to the cases cited here, see also the statements of five politicians—Salah Khalaf, Hafiz al-Asad, Zulfikar Ali Bhutto, 'Abdolkarim Musavi-Ardebili, and Shah Mohammad Reza Pahlavi—in chapter 11, "Assessment."

26. Sa'd Jum'a, *Al-Mu'amara wa-Ma'rakat al-Masir* ([Beirut]: Dar al-Katib al-'Arabi, 1968), p. 194. Even though Jum'a argues against conspiracies, he titled his book "The Conspiracy and the Battle of Destiny."

27. *Al-Majalla,* 31 December 1986.

28. Quoted on "It's All a Plot," BBC World Service, 15 March 1993.

29. *Le Nouvel Observateur*, 25-31 August 1994.

30. *Al-Jumhuriya* (Cairo), 8 May 1990.

31. Letter to *The Washington Post*, 4 February 1991.

32. Middle East News Agency, 27 September 1990.

33. Ayad Rahim, "Attitudes," pp. 180, 189. Rahim goes on, however, to note that "the conspiratorial proclivities of other Arabs are becoming more pronounced."

34. Mehrdad R. Izady, *The Kurds: A Concise Handbook* (Washington, D.C.: Crane Russak, 1992), p. 187.

35. Richard W. Cottam, *Iran and the United States: A Cold War Case Study* (Pittsburgh: University of Pittsburgh Press, 1988), p. 17.

36. Bernard Lewis, "What Saddam Wrought," *The Wall Street Journal*, 2 August 1991. See also Lewis's "The Middle East Crisis in Historical Perspective," *The American Scholar*, Winter 1992, p. 44.

37. John P. Entelis, "Introduction: State and Society in Transition," in John P. Entelis and Phillip C. Naylor, eds., *State and Society in Algeria* (Boulder, Col.: Westview, 1992), p. 3.

38. "Survey: The Arab World," *The Economist*, 12-18 May 1990, p. 26.

39. Michael Field, *Inside the Arab World* (Cambridge, Mass.: Harvard University Press, 1994), p. 168.

40. Cyril E. Black and L. Carl Brown, eds., *Modernization in the Middle East: The Ottoman Empire and Its Afro-Asian Successors* (Princeton, N.J.: Darwin Press, 1993), p. 311.

41. Robert M. Goldenson, *The Encyclopedia of Human Behavior: Psychology, Psychiatry, and Mental Health* (Garden City, N.Y.: Doubleday, 1970), vol. 2. p. 921.

42. Graham E. Fuller, *The "Center of the Universe": The Geopolitics of Iran* (Boulder, Col.: Westview, 1991), pp. 22-23.

43. Marvin Zonis, *Majestic Failure: The Fall of the Shah* (Chicago: University of Chicago Press, 1991), p. 206.

44. Radio Damascus, 12 April 1976.

45. Radio Damascus, 20 July 1976.

46. Saudi Press Agency, 9 July 1990.

47. Middle East News Agency. 26 March 1994.

48. Kuwaiti News Agency, 31 October 1990.

49. Quoted in Adel Darwish and Gregory Alexander, *Unholy Babylon: The Secret History of Saddam's War* (New York: St. Martin's, 1991), pp. 287-88

50. WAKH, 1 March 1990.

51. Israeli Television Channel One, 21 November 1994.

52. *The Jerusalem Post*, 5 January 1995.

53. Miles Copeland, *The Game of Nations: The Amorality of Power Politics* (New York: Simon and Schuster, 1969), p. 48.

54. *The New York Times*, 19 July 1992.

55. Radio Baghdad, 16 April 1990.

56. *Newsweek*, 25 March 1974.

57. On which, see chapter 15, note 60.

58. Anthony Parsons, *The Pride and the Fall: Iran 1974-1979* (London: Jonathan Cape, 1984), p. xi.

59. Ibid., pp. 124-25.

60. Amuzegar, *Dynamics of the Iranian Revolution*, pp. 87-88. This raises the opposite tact: exploiting the vulnerabilities created by conspiracy theories. For thoughts on this approach, see Daniel Pipes, "Dealing with Middle East Conspiracy Theories," *Orbis* 36 (1992): 51-56.

# Appendix

# Conspiracy Theories in Turkey and Israel

Turkey and Israel stand out as the only two Middle Eastern countries where leaders are fully accountable to electorates, where the West is viewed more as an ally than as an enemy, and where conspiracy theories have a relatively minor role in public life.[1] At the same time, the rise in Turkey of fundamentalist Islam (and Pan-Turkic nationalism, too, brought out by the Soviet bloc's collapse) and the tearing of Israel's civil society through the peace process have led to a growth in conspiracism in both countries. With an eye to the future, then, here are some conspiratorial themes found in Turkey and Israel.

## Turkey

Few mainstream politician, intellectual, or religious leaders engage in conspiratorial thinking, which exists mostly at the fringes of polite society. As ever, the United Kingdom and United States feature prominently in the role of villain; but instead of Israel, the other culprit is often Germany.

Despite the decline of Britain, some Turks continue to see it as the source of the world's problems. "For the last three centuries," writes M. Sıddık Gümüş, "any sort of treason committed against the Turkish and Islamic worlds has had the British plotters at its root."[2] The leader of the Anatolian People's Front likewise blames the British for the world's ills:

The British Secret Service is the mother of terrorism. If you cast a glance at history, you will see the intrigues, plots, and treachery committed by the British in the Middle East. Today there is no USSR, but terrorism continues. Why? Because it is the British Secret Service which makes the plans on terrorism, and executes them. Some of the planning is also done by the American CIA.[3]

As this quotation suggests, many Turkish conspiracy theories concern a malevolent United States. According to one Istanbul newspaper, a Turkish general lost his life in late 1993 when he discovered the extent of U.S. assistance to the PKK, a Syrian- and Iranian-backed terrorist group rampaging through Turkey's southeast. Why would Washington help the enemy of its ostensible ally? To destabilize the region and keep it poor.[4] Along similar lines, a newspaper commentator calls all three principal Kurdish leaders—Talabani, Barzani, and Öcalan—"just puppets" of the Western powers that use them to get access to northern Iraq's oil reserves.[5]

The murderous Istanbul rampage in early 1995 by Sunnis against Alevis left some thirty persons dead and prompted the city's fundamentalist governor, Hayri Kozakcioğlu, to speculate about American culpability. He spun a complex theory connecting the murders to a Turkish military operation in northern Iraq a few days later, then concluded with this vision of a Turkey surrounded:

For many years the United States used religion, nationalism, and every regional problem, and conducted intensive activity with considerable forces in the region in order to bring about the collapse of the Soviet Union. Following the dissolution of the Soviet Union, it has moved its forces to the Balkans, the Middle East, and Turkey.[6]

Conspiratorial suspicions lead, as ever, to contradictions. Necmeddin Erbakan, Turkey's leading fundamentalist, holds that "The West is trying to use Turkey to control the resources of the [ex-Soviet] Turkic republics."[7] Yılmaz Ozkan, a descendant of the nineteenth-century hero Sheikh Shamil, a University of Colorado graduate, and a member of the pan-Turkic party MHP, agrees on the U.S. goal but finds precisely the opposite tactics: "Following the collapse of the Soviet Union, the United States does not want to see a strong united Turkic community. The Turks are seen as a threat to the United States. That is why it has been covertly helping Russia for the last three years to keep it on its feet."[8]

Mustafa Necati Özfatura, a Pan-Turkic nationalist, is a one-man conspiracy theory factory. He claims that CIA agents tried to convince Central Asian Turks that they are not Turks at all, but "Japanese who emigrated from Japan 6,000 years ago."[9] He finds the "new world order" fancy talk for the "annihilation" of Muslims in all Europe (even Istanbul) and the Caucasus, and the suppression of Muslims elsewhere.[10] He sees Turkey as the victim of the "fifteenth crusade," jointly launched by Russia and the United States to "destroy the Muslims."[11] Turkey, in fact, he sees caught in a terrible pincer movement:

> The clashes in the Balkans, Caucasus, and southeastern Turkey all target Turkey. A crusade has been launched against Turkey, which is under fire in these three quarters. The "Council of Europe" . . . is the headquarters of this crusade. . . . The Armenians are the Council of Europe's pawns in the Caucasus, and the Serbs and the Greeks are its pawns in the Balkans. . . . If we do not intervene in Nakhichevan [a part of Azerbaijan bordering on Turkey] today, it will be too late tomorrow. After Nakhichevan, the Armenians will turn their attention to Kars, Ardahan, and particularly to Ararat and Van [locations in eastern Turkey].[12]

As in other parts of the Middle East, Zionists and imperialists dominate the Turkish conspiratorial mentality. Özfatura captures this twin concern in a piece of exceptionally detailed and imaginative writing.

> Zionism is the source of former U.S. President Bush's "New World Order" declaration after the Gulf war. The Jews formed the "New World Order" organization in 1772 to establish their hegemony in the world and in 1782 they incorporated the secret "Freemasons" association. With its economic system based on interest and usury, the "New World Order" gained control of the financial resources by acquiring the world gold markets. This organization destroyed national and spiritual values, traditions, and religious beliefs and morals of world nations by using the media. They succeeded in creating an artificial cadre of Jewish leaders, intellectuals, and bureaucrats by means of organizations such as the Freemasons, the Lions, the Rotary, and numerous other waqfs and establishments. All these for the sake of a Greater Israel.[13]

As the Middle Eastern country with the thickest ties to Germany (in World War I, almost every Ottoman army had a German officer in command or serving as chief of staff; 1.5 million Turkish guest workers and their families now live in Germany), Turkey retains a certain suspicion of that country, especially after Germany's unification in 1991. The Kurdish insurgency prompted the most worries. Abdullah Gul of the Welfare Party (despite its name, a fundamentalist party) called it "an artificial problem" created by Germany and America. During the Ottoman period, he noted, "there was no such thing as Turks and Kurds." The European states came up with an ideology and incited rebellions to weaken the Turkish state.[14] Mahir Kaynak, a former intelligence official in the Turkish government, accused Bonn of supporting PKK plans to establish hegemony over the Arab countries.[15] Even President Turgut Özal noted that Kurds collected funds in Germany "and then come and kill our people," implying German connivance and ulterior purposes.[16]

Pan-Turkic nationalists go beyond the Kurdish issue to portray Germany as Turkey's "main rival" in the Balkans and the Caucasus regions,[17] a fear shared by Balkan Muslims. Muhamed Cengic, deputy prime minister of Bosnia-Herzegovina, has claimed, for example, that "the war between the Serbs and the Croats broke out under Germany's influence," in an attempt to undermine the Muslims of Yugoslavia.[18]

## Israel

The great political issue in Israel concerns Arab intentions: Do they accept the Jewish state as a permanent fact, or do they yet seek to destroy it? Optimists push forward with the peace process—meaning, they withdraw from territories won in 1967; the pessimists insist on keeping those same lands. Tensions between the two have caused conspiracy theories to blossom.

On the left, Shulamit Aloni, a minister in the Rabin government, suggested in mid-1995 that associates of her own prime minister were "agitating Golan Heights settlers against the withdrawal under the assumption that their opposition will help the prime minister in the negotiations with Syria."[19]

On the right, a member of Kach claimed that Baruch Goldstein actually did not massacre Arabs at the Tomb of the Patriarch in Hebron in early 1994. In fact, Arabs began shooting at each other that morning, so the army called on Goldstein to help with the wounded. On entering the Tomb, Arabs shot at him and he shot back in self-defense.[20] The

Judean Voice on the Internet explained that three forces seek to weaken Israel: "hidden powerhouses in America" want U.S. soldiers on the Golan Heights to dominate the region militarily; the "men behind Peres in the Vatican" want control of Jerusalem; and the United Nations wants Israel to be absorbed as part of "a world central government" it would run.[21]

The Rabin assassination inspired many speculations about police connivance in the murder; it is too early, at this writing, to decide whether these are conspiracies or conspiracy theories.

### NOTES TO APPENDIX

1. Vamık D. Volkan and Norman Itzkowitz, *Turks and Greeks: Neighbours in Conflict* (Huntington, Eng.: Eothen, 1994), p. 193, see Turkey's lack of conspiracy theories resulting from its people's earnet efforts to catch up with the West.

2. M. Sıddık Gümüş, *British Enmity Against Islam*, 3d ed. (Istanbul: Hakikat Kitabevi, 1993), p. 90.

3. *Tercuman*, 9 March 1993.

4. *Aydınlık*, 19 September 1993.

5. Ertuğ Karakullukçu, *Hürriyet*, 2 April 1995.

6. *Aydınlık*, 1 April 1995.

7. TRT Television, 29 April 1992.

8. *Tercuman*, 12 January 1995.

9. *Türkiye*, 29 September 1991.

10. *Türkiye*, 16 March 1995.

11. *Türkiye*, 3 October 1994.

12. *Türkiye*, 13 May 1992.

13. *Türkiye*, 7 August 1994. The Jewish "New World Order" organization founded in 1772 suggests the Order of the Illuminati, founded in May 1776 in Bavaria by Adam Weishaupt, completely suppressed by 1787, and completely unrelated to Jews. For details, see Richard von Dülmen, *Der Geheimbund der Illuminaten*, (Stuttgart: Frommann-Holzboog, 1977).

14. Dilip Hiro, "Koran as Well as Credit," *The Middle East*, August 1992.

15. *Milliyet*, 6 November 1991.

16. *Der Spiegel*, 23 December 1991; *Milliyet*, 16 November 1991.

17. *Türkiye*, 13 December 1991.

18. *Der Spiegel*, 23 December 1991.

19. Qol Yisra'el, 9 June 1995.

20. *The Jerusalem Report*, 15 June 1995.

21. *Judean Voice*, 11 August 1995.

# INDEX